Praise for
The Death of Innocence

"PART MEMOIR,
PART MURDER MYSTERY ...
a more than plausible picture of a family
victimized. . . . As we read [the Ramseys']
account of the hellishness of their lives
since their daughter's murder,
we realize that nothing has been fair."
—*Publishers Weekly*

THE DEATH
OF INNOCENCE

JonBenét's Parents Tell Their Story

———

JOHN AND PATSY RAMSEY

AN ONYX BOOK

ONYX
Published by New American Library, a division of
Penguin Putnam Inc., 375 Hudson Street,
New York, New York 10014, U.S.A.
Penguin Books Ltd, 27 Wrights Lane,
London W8 5TZ, England
Penguin Books Australia Ltd, Ringwood,
Victoria, Australia
Penguin Books Canada Ltd, 10 Alcorn Avenue,
Toronto, Ontario, Canada M4V 3B2
Penguin Books (N.Z.) Ltd, 182–190 Wairau Road,
Auckland 10, New Zealand

Penguin Books Ltd, Registered Offices:
Harmondsworth, Middlesex, England

Published by Onyx, an imprint of New American Library,
a division of Penguin Putnam Inc.
This is an authorized reprint of a Janet Thoma book, Thomas Nelson Publishers.

First Onyx Printing, January 2001
10 9 8 7 6 5 4

Unless otherwise noted, Scripture quotations are from THE NEW KING JAMES
VERSION. Copyright © 1979, 1989, 1982, Thomas Nelson, Inc., Publishers
Scriptures marked NIV are from the HOLY BIBLE, NEW INTERNATIONAL
VERSION®. Copyright © 1973, 1978, 1984 by International Bible Society. Used by
permission of Zondervan Publishing House. All rights reserved.

Printed in the United States of America

For JonBenét

Wherever we go . . .
Whatever we do . . .

CONTENTS

ACKNOWLEDGMENTS

Throughout the past three years, countless old friends and many, many new ones have come to our aid. They have comforted us, they have encouraged us to rejoin life when our minds and bodies said no, and they have protected us. The outpouring of compassion and caring shown to our family has been overwhelming. It is said that you know God loves you by the people He puts into your life when you need them the most. We have found this to be true.

At first, we had included these friends' names here as a way to acknowledge each in at least a small way. There is no way we can repay any of them properly. After reflection, we decided not to put their names here to protect their privacy. That is such a vanishing commodity in America today. We were afraid the list of friends who helped us, which would be lengthy, would also be a shopping list for the bad side of the media. We have been exposed to this side and don't want our friends to be. It would be akin to advertising in the want ads for a lawyer: you wouldn't hear from the good ones, only the bad ones.

But they know who they are. We hope we have shown them our appreciation in the only way that really counts—with our love.

We want to acknowledge our family members who have stood with us. We thank God for you.

Melinda & Stewart
John Andrew
Burke Hamilton
Don & Nedra Paugh
Dick & Irene Ramsey Wills
Pamela Paugh

Grant & Paulette Paugh Davis & family
Jeff & Peggy Ramsey & family
Lucinda Ramsey Johnson

To the professionals who devoted themselves well beyond the call of duty to the cause of right and justice. We salute you. You are people of the highest principle and integrity, and you give hope to the system of American justice.

Mr. Michael Bynum
Mr. Patrick J. Burke
Mr. G. Bryan Morgan
Mr. Harold A. Haddon
Mr. H. Patrick Furman
Mr. Lee D. Foreman
Ms. Saskia A. Jordan
Mr. James K. Jenkins
Mr. William Gray
Mr. Linwood

To the team of investigators who remain committed to justice for JonBenét.

H. Ellis Armistead
Jennifer Gedde
David & Ella Mae Williams
R. Jon Foster
Gene Matthews
Lou Smit
Ollie Gray

To the members of the press who have refrained from passing judgment and have refused to compromise the integrity of truth in journalism; you know who you are . . . and who you aren't.

To the compassionate physicians who have walked us through the valley of the shadow. God bless you.

Special tribute to those who have helped us prove that the pen is mightier than the sword.
Janet Hoover Thoma
Robert L. Wise

To our new friends at Thomas Nelson Publishers and their associates, without whom none of this could have been transformed from memory to the printed page.

Rolf Zettersten
Connie Reece
Kathie Johnson
The staff & friends at Thomas Nelson

And finally, with special thanks and love,
To Glen & Susan Stine & Doug

You have given of your time and your hearts in so many countless ways. We shall never be able to thank you enough. Your reward will be in heaven.

FOREWORD

Our lives and our hopes for the future both suffered a near-fatal arrow when our daughter, JonBenét, was murdered in our home during the night of December 25, 1996. The overwhelming grief stressed our basic will to live. The suspicions cast on us by an inexperienced police force and the world media almost crushed our ability to live.

What happened to us after JonBenét's death should not happen to anyone, but based on what we have seen and experienced through our ordeal, we are certain that the same thing has happened to other people in our society. Innocent people are unjustly suspected, publicly accused, arrested, prosecuted, jailed, and in some cases, executed. Our criminal justice system now operates on the presumption of guilt, and then challenges the defendant to prove his or her innocence. Some police officers are all too eager to have their work on the evening news. We lost our daughter to the worst imaginable monster in our society and then were persecuted by the police and the media because they knew "the parents are always guilty."

We believe the time has come for us to tell the world what really happened following JonBenét's murder. If by telling our story the balance of liberty is brought back to the constitutional premise of "innocent until proven guilty," then something worthwhile will have come out of this tragedy.

It seemed the story could best be told through our eyes by sharing our feelings and memories. We have not tried to construct a moment-by-moment account of what occurred but have shared our hearts, emotions, and reflections. At this date, more than three years after that Christmas, our memories are not completely trustworthy on some details; we simply do not have total recall. Some of the events you will recognize from your own recollection of media coverage. Other events will be new to you because they went unreported or were reported completely wrong.

The following account is based on our recollections; it represents the way things looked from our perspective—what we thought, how we felt, and how we coped as we struggled to keep from jumping off the edge of the world.

This is what happened to us, as parents, when our daughter, JonBenét, died.

1

CHRISTMAS DAY, 1996

A few flakes of snow drifted over the mountains towering above Boulder, Colorado, as multicolored lights sparkled in houses up and down the streets, well before the first rays of sunlight broke on December 25. A thin curtain of darkness still hung over Fifteenth Street when our nine-year-old son, Burke, and six-year-old daughter, JonBenét, bounded up the back stairs to our third-floor bedroom at about 6:30, jumping on our bed and bouncing up and down. Childhood innocence and excitement in its purest form.

"C'mon, wake up! It's Christmas!" shouted JonBenét.

"Yeah. We gotta see what Santa brought for us!" Burke chimed in. "Hurry up."

The previous year on Christmas Eve, Burke had gone to bed at the normal time and then gotten up at 12:30 A.M., ready to open presents. We tried to explain that Santa was still working his way across the country. "He's probably just now in Georgia. You must be sound asleep until morning, to make sure he stops by."

We were doing much better this year since the kids waited until 6:30 A.M. to rouse us.

"Be careful, guys!" Patsy said, forcing her eyes open. "You'll fall off the bed."

"Get up, Mom," they cried in unison. "It's Christmas!"

Patsy got up and moved toward her bathroom at the other end of the master suite. I slipped out of bed and went down the two flights of stairs to the living room, where Santa had left his surprises. When I was a child, my dad would keep my brother, Jeff, and me waiting in great anxiety while he plugged in the tree, put Christmas records on the hi-fi, and set up the 16 mm movie camera and flood lights to record the events of the morning. I couldn't stand all that waiting then. Now, here

I was doing *exactly* the same things to my kids, in *exactly* the same way—making them wait when they were so excited. Funny how we become so much like our parents as we grow older.

The kids still believed in Santa. Why shouldn't they? They always had presents from Mom and Dad—and then got special gifts from Santa. Stop believing in Santa, and you lose out on a set of gifts. Burke and JonBenét knew how to work the system. Patsy and I savored the night before Christmas, helping Santa Claus put everything in place.

Last night had been no different. We had made several trips to the basement, where Patsy kept the wrapped gifts stashed away. Then she had arranged them under the fat Fraser fir, which reached to the ceiling of our living room. Joe Barnhill, our neighbor, had met me in front of our home with the new bicycle for JonBenét, which he had been hiding in his basement for us. JonBenét had outgrown her training bike. A bigger bicycle had been on her wish list, and we could now look forward to some family bike trips together.

All Burke really wanted this year was a Nintendo 64 video game system, and Patsy felt she had scored a real coup by locating one just a few days prior to Christmas, even though this was the hot item, sold out everywhere. Several other unwrapped gifts from Santa were arranged next to the bicycle and the Nintendo so each child would know whose pile was whose. Santa's unwrapped presents were a tradition from Patsy's side of the family. It was always a challenge to merge these family traditions; but after sixteen years, we had our routine down pat.

That Christmas Eve, with all the gifts arranged, Patsy and I had taken in the beauty of the evening. The tree, the lights, the gifts. *It doesn't get more magical than this,* I thought as the timeless melody of "Silent Night" from the Mannheim Steamroller CD played softly in the kitchen. No other night of the year held the anticipation of Christmas Eve. Looking up at the magnificently decorated tree, I thought that it really seemed as if there were peace on earth. We had no idea how fragile this moment was.

Now, with Christmas morning here, Santa had just one more thing to do before the little ones waiting on the third floor were allowed to rip into the picturesque setting. I slipped out to the garage and quickly wheeled in a new bike for Patsy.

"Okay, everyone," I called up the stairs. "Looks like Santa has been here!"

Down they came, giggling and shouting, and running immediately to their respective treasures.

Patsy was right behind them; she stopped at the threshold of the living room and looked at me with wide eyes.

"Would you look at that!" I teased. "Santa even brought Mommy a new bicycle!"

We exchanged quick glances. "Boy, that Santa. He's really full of surprises this year!" Patsy said with a grin, mostly for the kids' benefit.

The kids screamed and cheered as they realized that Santa had brought just about everything on their lists. JonBenét wanted to take her new bike outside for a spin, but Burke suggested, "Let's get all the other gifts opened first." Ah, the wise and experienced big brother. JonBenét agreed. They quickly busied themselves playing Santa's elves and distributing the beautifully wrapped gifts. JonBenét asked for Burke's assistance with the name tags, since he could read and she couldn't. It was the most fun in the world, doling out the gifts and seeing whose pile would become the biggest.

I always insisted that everyone take turns unwrapping a gift, starting with the kids, since their piles far outweighed ours. Patsy had spent a lot of time wrapping all those gifts, and we wanted the moment to last as long as possible. We had inherited this tradition from the Ramsey side of the family; Patsy's family had always just ripped everything open at once.

"Wow! A remote-control car!" Burke shouted as he raised the prize overhead for everyone to see.

"That's nice—who is it from?" Patsy asked.

"I dunno," he replied, shrugging his shoulders.

"Let's keep track, so we can write thank-you notes," she urged.

Patsy rearranged the gifts in JonBenét's stack so that a very special box would be opened last. Inside was a My Twinn doll, fashioned to look like JonBenét from pictures Patsy had furnished the dollmaker, with a couple of matching outfits so JonBenét and the doll could dress alike.

JonBenét opened the box and examined the doll with a look of curiosity.

"Well, now, doesn't she look like you?" Patsy asked.

JonBenét held the doll at arm's length and tilted her head slightly. "I really don't think she looks that much like me," she concluded and laid the doll to one side. She quickly returned to a jewelry craft set, which she had previously opened.

Patsy looked at me, raised her eyebrows, and gave a disappointed shrug. Sometimes the big gift you had in mind for your kids really wasn't the hit you had expected.

Soon JonBenét slipped under the tree and removed a brightly wrapped gift from its hiding place near the back. She had found exactly the right present for me at FAO Schwarz during a trip to New York City with her mom in November. Patsy later told me that when JonBenét had seen the shiny red gumball machine that dispensed jelly beans, she insisted I had to have it because I love jelly beans. She marched across the room and proudly presented the gift to me, with a big hug and kiss.

"Betcha can't guess what this is!" she teased.

"Give me a little hint," I pried. The suspense was too much for her, so she quickly helped me unwrap the package.

"Oh, wow. Would you look at that!" I exclaimed.

"Do you really like it, Daddy?"

"I sure do, honey. I love it and I love you!" I gave her a big hug.

A moment later she looked up at me. "Daddy, what about . . . ?" She did the standard charade symbol for a movie camera with one hand to her face and the other cranking the film reel. She was excited and wanted me to take home videos.

"Well . . ." I said rubbing my chin. "I forgot to charge the batteries of the video camera last night. They're all run down. But here is our regular camera. I can take a few pictures. You get over there next to Mommy."

Since the death of my oldest daughter, Beth, I hadn't wanted to take away from the moment at hand by stepping out of the scene to videotape or photograph it. I felt that life was too precious and went past too quickly to interrupt it by fussing with a camera. Now I wanted to live in the moment, rather than preserving it for later enjoyment. We had learned the hard way that sometimes later can be too sad. I still was not up to looking at the home videos we had made of all those earlier Christmases when Beth was still with us.

I thought about just how special this Christmas morning was as I snapped a few pictures of the children with their opened gifts lying around the room. I had no way of knowing these would be the last photographs I would take of my youngest and most defenseless daughter.

While the kids played with their gifts, Patsy and I went to the kitchen to prepare our traditional Christmas morning breakfast of pancakes, bacon, corn beef hash, and hash browns. I usually made the pancakes, so I got all the ingredients together while Patsy set the table and cooked the rest of the breakfast. JonBenét always loved to get into the act and was right under my elbows, standing on a stool by the stove, to help pour the pancake batter. She normally liked to make a Mickey Mouse shape with the batter and decorate it at the table with fruit and raisins to make the face come to life, but there wasn't time for that on this Christmas Day. Too many new things to play with. Burke came to the table just long enough to eat a bite. As far as he was concerned, eating got in the way of playing.

Once breakfast was over, the day unfolded with the usual chaos of the neighborhood children coming and going, reporting on the loot that had been left for them. The boys from across the alley drifted in with their remote-control toys, and they all went outside to race their battery-powered cars up and down the street in front of our house.

I watched the scene with a mild sense of amusement. Once the gifts are opened, dads tend to fade into the wallpaper while the rest of the family rushes through the day. Patsy got busy preparing for our early morning departure the next day to Charlevoix, Michigan. She had some last-minute gift wrapping to finish for John Andrew and Melinda, our older children from my first marriage. There were a few things for the Charlevoix neighbor kids as well as a few special gifts for Stewart, Melinda's fiancé, who would join us for this first-ever family Christmas get-together at our summer cottage in Charlevoix.

In addition to those tasks, Patsy was packing summer clothes and bathing suits in suitcases laid out on the bed in John Andrew's bedroom. We had booked tickets on Disney's Big Red Boat in Florida upon our return from Charlevoix. The trip would last from December 29 through New Year's, a great way to celebrate Patsy's fortieth birthday and the New Year. Burke and JonBenét were very excited about the trip. We had never been on a cruise and thought that being with Mickey Mouse and Company should be great family fun.

Patsy was always juggling several balls at once. That day she was even preparing ahead for a pageant that she and Jon-Benét were to attend the first week of January. Most of Jon-Benét's pageant clothes hung in the big closet in Melinda's room. Patsy laid out a yellow swimsuit and cover-up on the dresser in anticipation of the event.

With everyone so busy, I decided to take the opportunity to scoot out to Jefferson County Airport (Jeffco, as local pilots had nicknamed it) to check out the airplane for our departure the next day. Patsy reminded me to be back in time to get ready to go to Fleet and Priscilla White's house for an early dinner.

On the way to the airport, I scanned the skies. Looked like the weather would be fine for travel tomorrow. I always started watching the weather days before we were to travel. Since weather moves from west to east, it was easy to anticipate the weather to the east, based on the weather that had moved through Colorado earlier. We had talked about going to Charlevoix before Christmas, but it would have been a logistical nightmare to arrange for Santa to find us there; we would have to get all of the goodies to Charlevoix ahead of time and then haul them back to Colorado afterward. Too hard. Best just to have Christmas in Boulder and join up with the big kids the day after.

John Andrew, Melinda, and her fiancé, Stewart, would fly Delta Air Lines from Atlanta to Minneapolis, and since our flight path would take us right over this city on our way to Charlevoix, it would be easy to stop and pick up the big kids. (Minneapolis worked because the kids could get cheap tickets from Atlanta to that city, since no one seemed to want to go to Minneapolis in the winter.) Patsy, Burke, JonBenét, and I planned to meet Mike Archuleta, our pilot, at Jeffco in the morning for a 7:00 departure. That would put us in Minneapolis in time to rendezvous with Melinda, John Andrew, and Stewart when their plane arrived at eleven. Then we would all travel together in the family plane to Charlevoix.

Though I was qualified to pilot the Beechcraft King Air C-90 alone, it always made things easier when Mike came along. With plans for landing in a busy terminal like Minneapolis during the holidays, his copiloting would add an extra safety factor. Besides, Mike was like part of the family; he and his wife, Pam, had no children of their own, so he really took up with Jon-Benét and Burke when he was with us. He was comfortable at the cottage and always helped out around the place; it just seemed natural for him to come along on this trip.

Of course, everyone enjoyed Charlevoix, a great place to spend the summers. We had bought our little house, almost sight unseen, in 1992. For years before that we had visited Charlevoix and spent hours with real estate agents—and by ourselves—scouting out property in the area. Patsy named the house Summer Hill because we usually visited in the summer and it was perched on a hill.

I always loved hanging around airports, and Christmas Day was no different. I loaded some of the gifts that were going to Michigan in the baggage area of the plane and made sure the plane was ready to go. I inherited the flying bug from my father, Jay Ramsey, who had been a decorated World War II pilot. His many missions across the treacherous Himalayas between India and China had earned him a Distinguished Flying Cross. Flying the "Hump" was risky business, and these pilots suffered a much higher fatality rate than fighter pilots in the European theater; I was lucky to have a dad who survived World War II. Dad had taught both my brother and me how to fly when we were in our early twenties.

When I returned home in the afternoon, JonBenét and Burke were playing outside with the neighborhood gang. Soon Patsy called for the kids to come in to clean up a little before the party. She wanted JonBenét to wear a red turtleneck with her black velvet pants so that mother and daughter would be dressed alike, but JonBenét wanted to wear the complete outfit she'd chosen. Finally Mom gave in. JonBenét put on her outfit with her black boots, which zipped up the front and had a bit of animal print trim along the top. JonBenét loved to dress up. Burke could care less.

As we were leaving for the Whites' house, JonBenét begged

me to help her ride her new bike, which she had managed to bring outside. She was a tad wobbly because this bike was quite a bit bigger than her other one, but she soon steadied herself.

"Daddy, please help me ride my bike around the block, just once."

We didn't have much time before we were due at the Whites', so I promised that we'd go around the block some other time. She looked disappointed, but agreed. Later I wished I had taken those extra few minutes. I wish I had remembered the oft-quoted axiom that children spell love T-I-M-E. I would never again be able to watch her ride a bike. The new bike was later donated to a church without her ever having enjoyed it.

With a gift basket of different coffees in hand, we arrived at the Whites', where the festivities were well underway. Several family members and friends were visiting from out of town, including Priscilla's sisters, their companions, and her parents. Missing from the gathering were the senior Whites, because Nyla White, Fleet's mother, was spending the holidays in a hospital bed in Aspen. Most of us helped ourselves to the snacks and hors d'oeuvres that Priscilla had prepared, including leftover cracked crab, which they enjoyed as a family tradition on Christmas Eve. Priscilla made a small plate especially for JonBenét to make sure there would be some left for her to try.

Dinner was served in the living and dining rooms, next to the beautifully decorated Christmas tree, glistening with silver ornaments and ribbons that reflected Priscilla's passion for all things silver. We had eaten together last Christmas, so it was beginning to feel like a new tradition for us to join their family. The fire was ablaze in the fireplace. It was Christmas Day, and life was good.

After supper, Fleet and I eventually ended up on the living room floor making paper jewelry with JonBenét and Daphne, the Whites' six-year-old daughter. Although it was a child's toy, quite a bit of dexterity was required to make the little paper beads from scratch. Everyone poked fun at the sight of these two grown men (Fleet is a big guy, over six feet tall and upwards of two hundred fifty pounds) sitting on the floor with the girls, trying to wind little strips of colored paper into beads to be strung into a necklace. Later, some carolers arrived, and we all gathered at the front door to listen. Fleet and Fleet Jr. went out with the carolers for a round of stops in the neighborhood.

Sometime around 8:30 or so, we decided to head for home; we had a big trip ahead of us in the morning and needed to leave on time so we could arrive in Minneapolis by 11:00. Besides, Patsy wanted to drop off a couple of gifts on our way home from the Whites'. We pulled up the driveway at the Walkers' and Patsy took a small package to the door, talked for a few minutes, and returned to the car. Then we drove over a few blocks to the Stines' house. Patsy had bid on three gift baskets at a recent silent auction benefit, and she and Burke took one of the baskets to their door. We had another basket in the trunk of the car intended for our friends the Fernies, but decided it was too late now to make any more visits. We would deliver their gift when we returned from Michigan.

After leaving the Stines', we returned to our house and drove down the narrow alley to our garage at the back of the house. I pushed the automatic garage door opener and we rolled in. On the way home, JonBenét had fallen fast asleep in the back seat. I got her out of the car and carried her upstairs to her room, laid her on the bed, and took off her coat and shoes. I was amazed at how sound asleep she was. It had been a long day for her. Patsy came in to finish getting JonBenét ready for bed.

Meanwhile, I went downstairs to try to get Burke to come up to bed, but he was deeply involved in assembling the miniature parking garage he had received that morning. I could tell he wasn't going to go to bed until the project was finished, so I settled down on the floor beside him. Helping him complete what his mind was focused on was the best way to get us both in bed quickly.

At about 9:30 I led Burke upstairs and got him ready for bed, then tucked him in and turned out the light. I went on up to our room on the third floor, which we had converted from an attic space to a master suite in 1993. Patsy was already in bed. I got ready, took a melatonin tablet to insure a good night's sleep, set the alarm clock for 5:30 A.M., and read in bed for a short while before turning out the light.

Unfortunately, I slept soundly.

2
___

DECEMBER 26, MORNING

I hear John turning on the water in his bathroom and realize that it is still dark. As we always do before departing for an early morning trip, John and I will get dressed before waking up the children. Just before we're ready to leave, we'll get the kids up. Sometimes we even load them in the car in their pj's so they can resume sleeping in the airplane. Slowly the normal routine for an early morning flight comes into focus. *Take a shower, get dressed, get going.* I swing out of bed and abruptly remember that my shower is still broken.

Don't need one this morning, I think to myself. *Just put my clothes on. And: of course, my makeup.* I remember my mother's words. "Never leave the house without your makeup." Plus we are going to be with Melinda's fiancé, Stewart, so I want to make a good impression.

Got to be at the airport by 6:30 or so. Going to push us to get everyone going because time is so short. I reach for my clothes and start dressing.

Minutes later I hurry down the back stairs from our bedroom to the second floor, where the children's bedrooms are located. I stop at the top of the spiral stairs that lead down to the first floor, and I turn to the laundry area.

Need to get a few things together for the trip, I think to myself. *Not much, since we've already got clothes and most necessary items at the house in Charlevoix.* I quickly shove some of the laundry into a plastic garbage sack that will go on the airplane as-is. John likes us to pack in soft-sided bags because it makes loading the plane easier. I hurry down the spiral staircase to the bottom floor and stop.

What's this? I wonder. I turn around to look at three pieces of paper on a step near the bottom. I bend over. *Must be a note from the cleaning lady, Linda,* I think. *Probably reminding me that she needs to borrow twenty-five hundred dollars. I must leave a check on the kitchen counter before we leave.*

"Mr. Ramsey," the note is addressed across the top. I look again more closely. "Listen carefully!" My eyes fly across the top lines. "At this time we have your daughter in our possession. She is safe and unharmed and if you want her to see 1997, you must follow our instructions to the letter." I quickly scan the page. "$118,000," the writer demands.

I gasp for air. For a moment my heart pounds so hard I can barely move. I race back up the stairs and stumble toward JonBenét's bedroom, pushing the door wide open. The bed is empty!

"J-o-h-nnn! John-n-n-n! Help!" I scream. "JonBenét's gone!" He meets me wearing only his underwear.

"There's a note downstairs." I can barely speak. "Someone has taken JonBenét!" I feel the blood rushing from my head. For a moment I feel like fainting. "She's gone!" I cry. "Jon-Benét is gone!" My stomach wrenches.

John tears down the stairs; he seems to be shouting, but nothing makes any sense.

"Burke!" John yells. "What about Burke?"

Both of us race to Burke's room at the far end of the second floor and find him apparently still asleep. *Best not to arouse him until we figure out what's happening here*, I think. *He's better off asleep for now.* I step into the hall.

John runs down the main stairs and into the back hallway. I grasp my stomach and run after him. By the time I get to him, he is down on his hands and knees, staring at the sheets of paper spread out on the floor in front of him. He is examining the ransom note, under the ceiling lights of the back hall. The note reads:

Mr. Ramsey,
 Listen carefully! We are a group of individuals that repre-sent a small foreign faction. We respect your bussiness but not the country that it serves. At this time we have your daughter in our possession. She is safe and unharmed and if you want her to see 1997, you must follow our instructions to the letter.
 You will withdraw $118,000.00 from your account. $100,000 will be in $100 bills and the remaining $18,000 in

$20 bills. Make sure that you bring an adequate size attache to the bank. When you get home you will put the money in a brown paper bag. I will call you between 8 and 10 A.M. tomorrow to instruct you on delivery. The delivery will be exhausting so I advise you to be rested. If we monitor you getting the money early, we might call you early to arrange an earlier delivery of the money and hence a earlier pick-up of your daughter.

Any deviation of my instructions will result in the immediate execution of your daughter. You will also be denied her remains for proper burial. The two gentlemen watching over your daughter do not particularly like you so I advise you not to provoke them. Speaking to anyone about your situation, such as Police, F.B.I, etc., will result in your daughter being beheaded. If we catch you talking to a stray dog, she dies. If you alert bank authorities, she dies. If the money is in any way marked or tampered with, she dies. You will be scanned for electronic devices and if any are found, she dies. You can try to deceive us but be warned that we are familiar with Law enforcement countermeasures and tactics. You stand a 99% chance of killing your daughter if you try to out smart us. Follow our instructions and you stand a 100% chance of getting her back. You and your family are under constant scrutiny as well as the authorities. Don't try to grow a brain John. You are not the only fat cat around so don't think that killing will be difficult. Don't underestimate us John. Use that good southern common sense of yours. It is up to you now John!

Victory!

S.B.T.C

"What do we do?" I stammer.
He shouts, "Call the police!"
"Are you sure?"
"Yes. Call them!"
Standing next to the wall phone, I instantly dial 911, and try to make the voice on the other end of the line understand. It is as if she doesn't believe what I am saying. I slam the phone back into its cradle on the wall. *Got to have someone here*, I think. I dial the Fernies' number. "We need help!" I scream.

"Please come over here!" I take another deep breath and grab the phone again from its cradle, dialing the Whites this time. "JonBenét's missing!" I yell into the phone. "Please get over here. We need you!" I hang up immediately and slump against the wall.

Got to get the money, I think to myself. *We've got to get the money.* I start through the kitchen toward the front door entry. *Money will get her back.* "Just get the money," I mumble, trying to calm down but feeling everything slipping away from me.

After a while I see the headlights of a squad car, which slowly comes to a stop across the street in front of our house.

For the first time I am aware that I have been racing around the house in my underwear. I hurry back to the third-floor bedroom to grab my clothes. I stop in JonBenét's room and look under the bed to make sure she isn't there.

Standing alone in the bedroom, feeling as if I had been kicked in the stomach by a Clydesdale horse, I wring my hands in anguish and stare at the wall. I force myself to get my wits about me. This was different from the loss of my daughter Beth, who was killed in an automobile accident. That day, January 8, 1992, I had assumed that my brother, Jeff, was calling with news about my father, who was lying in ICU in a Tampa, Florida, hospital, near death. I was wrestling with the possibility that he might not make it when my brother called, saying he had bad news. I asked if it was Dad.

"No," he said. "Beth's been killed in Illinois in a car accident."

There was nothing I could do. It was over. Done. I couldn't comfort my daughter; I couldn't do anything to bring her back. But this time it wasn't over and I could do something.

I can get JonBenét back, I think resolutely. *I've got to get my wits about me. This isn't like it was with Beth! I* can *do something this time.* I put on pants and a shirt, and hurry back downstairs.

I meet Patsy and Officer Rick French in the hallway, near the front door. I tell him my daughter has been kidnapped.

The uniformed officer walks in and asks us to repeat our problem again. He keeps asking questions, and seems to grasp the situation quickly. He insists we move to the corner sunroom. I feel my head spinning, and my anguish seems to be crushing the life out of me. Any parent who has lost track of a child in a shopping mall, even for a moment, knows an intense pang of fear. For me that pang is now constant. I keep wondering, *Is JonBenét alive? Will we see her in an hour? Will we see her in ten years?* I keep remembering the total helplessness I felt when I found out about Beth. This time I can do something—must do everything possible to get JonBenét back.

Another officer, Officer Veitch, I believe, comes in after he moves the squad car to the next block. He is shown the ransom note.

Soon friends arrive. The Whites and the Fernies. Father Rol Hoverstock, our priest from St. John's Episcopal Church and a close friend and confidant. The cold, empty vacancy in our house fills with these friends.

Father Rol immediately leads us in a prayer, asking God to bless and protect JonBenét as well as keep his hand on us. "Change the heart of the kidnapper," he prays, "so JonBenét will be returned to us." After he finishes, he stays with Patsy, trying to comfort her.

I remember Burke, asleep in his bedroom. I don't want him to get up in the midst of this madness and wonder what is going on. I ask Fleet White if Burke can go to his house and be with Fleet Jr. He agrees.

I wake Burke up and as gently as possible tell him that JonBenét is missing and that he is going to his friend Fleet's house for a while.

Burke looks distressed and begins to cry, so I know he understands the gravity of our predicament.

I help him get dressed, and momentarily he and Fleet are leaving the house, Burke carrying his new Nintendo 64 game under his arm.

Somewhere in here, Detectives Linda Arndt and Fred Patterson come in. By this time I think the officers have looked around the house a little. I don't realize it at the time, but the first action police should take in a missing-child situation is to thoroughly search the entire house, in case the child has fallen asleep—or is playing or hiding—in some unusual place. Unfortunately, the police do not conduct an extensive search of our home.

Now confusion is starting to set in. Everyone wants to run and do something or the other.

Officer French takes Detective Arndt in to meet Patsy. "Mrs. Ramsey," he says, "if my child were missing, this is the detective I would want working on the case. You can rest assured, you're in good hands now."

Linda Arndt reassures Patsy too. She tells her that often-times kidnappers will get scared and drop the child off at a supermarket parking lot—and then we'll find her. Patsy desperately hangs on to that hope. She stares out the window and prays to see JonBenét come running down the street at any moment.

I look at the doors. *How did someone get in?* I wonder. I suddenly remember our large walk-in refrigerator. *Could Jon-Benét have been put inside, trapped there?* I open the door to check. She isn't there.

The house starts to feel like a zoo.

I call my banker friend Rod Westmoreland in Atlanta to arrange for the ransom money and discover that he has left for his parents' home in Tupelo, Mississippi. I get through to his assistant at Atlanta's Merrill Lynch office; I'm thankful today is a work day. I quickly explain what has happened, and she says she'll get in touch with Rod right away.

Now police begin to arrive with phone monitoring equipment. Two women from the Boulder Police Department Victim's Advocate Unit show up. More squad cars are moved away from the front of the house to locations down the block. We don't want the kidnapper to think we have called the police, since he said he was watching the house. Yet the police officers do not seem to be using much discretion: the cars are marked, the police are wearing uniforms.

Suddenly I remember that Mike Archuleta is to meet us at the Jeffco Airport. I need to call him and explain what has happened.

"JonBenét's been kidnapped!" I tell him, then ask him to get a message to the big kids to call me immediately when they arrive in Minneapolis. At this point I'm not sure whether they should come to Denver or go on back to Atlanta.

When I hang up the telephone, feelings of panic start churning up again, and I realize that I must maintain my senses. JonBenét needs me to be strong, now more than ever.

The note says the kidnappers will be watching. Maybe I can catch them looking at us. I race upstairs and find a pair of binoculars. I start looking up and down the street.

There's a strange vehicle in the alley behind the Barnhills', I note.

After several minutes of watching the vehicle, nothing happens so I finally go back downstairs. The phone rings. Everyone freezes as I slowly pick up the receiver.

"Hello," I answer tentatively.

"John. This is Rod. We've arranged for you to have a credit line of 118,000 dollars on your Visa card. You can go to a local bank and get the money as a cash advance."

"Thanks, Rod!" I say quickly. I do not want to keep the phone line busy any longer than necessary.

As I hang up the phone, I want to cry. Maybe this thing is going to work out okay after all.

3

DECEMBER 26, MIDDAY

Sometime during the morning, events start to blur together in an unending string of police appearing, disappearing, doors opening and closing. Things come into my awareness and disappear at random. In and out. Confusion. Noise. People talking. People preparing food in our kitchen. The sweep of the day seems to be occurring in a swirling muddle of chaos.

Patsy spends most of the morning in the sunroom, praying and clutching a cross that was part of our Christmas decorations. I can tell she is going in and out of sensibility; most of the time she seems to be completely distraught and lost. I would not be any better, but I keep remembering the difference between this situation and Beth's, and know my decisions and actions could make the difference in getting JonBenét back or not. *She is strong and she is smart,* I remind myself. *She will be working to get to us as well.* As the morning unfolds, I feel as if I am walking through a waking nightmare, trying to run but not able to keep my legs moving fast enough.

John Fernie has been in contact with the president of a local bank, a personal friend of his, and is working to get the ransom money ready. John goes to the bank with my credit card to get the cash. The bank has already been instructed to copy each bill before giving it to him, but it's hard for them to come up with that many hundred-dollar bills.

I assume the FBI has been called and I wonder why they haven't shown up yet. I believe that Linda Arndt tells me they are on the way. In the meantime, things have to be done. Something, but I don't know what for sure. It's such a helpless feeling.

Detective Arndt takes me to the back of the house and begins to brief me on what to do when the kidnapper calls. I sit slumped in a chair, listening.

"When he calls, it's important to buy as much time as we can," Arndt says. "Keep him on the phone."

I nod my head.

"Insist that you speak to JonBenét. This is the most critical thing . . . You must hear her voice."

"Yes, that makes sense." I keep nodding my head.

"In order to stall, tell this person that it's not easy to raise over a hundred thousand dollars. Say you will need until five P.M."

"Why? I don't want to wait that long."

"We need that much time. There's lots of things we've got to get set up," she answers.

This is going to be the ultimate torture for me, I think. *I want her back now.*

Arndt also asks me questions about where we were yesterday, when we came home, and about any phone calls.

Thoughts run through my mind like a runaway computer typing out continuous messages and directives. Everything seems scrambled and chaotic. I slowly begin to realize there is not much I can do except hope, pray, and wait. I am captive in my own home while this monster is out there somewhere with my daughter. I am angry, afraid, upset, but ultimately helpless.

We get several calls throughout the morning from a wide range of people. Every time the phone rings, we all jump. I answer each time, but only after the police start the tape recorder they have attached to our line. Even our old nanny, Shirley Brady, picks that morning to call from Columbus, Georgia, to say hello. I am probably rude to her as I tell her I can't talk, but I want to keep the phone line open. Rod Westmoreland calls a couple of times to confirm the details of the cash transfer. We get one hang-up, and instantly I wonder if that might have been the kidnapper.

When the phone rings, Patsy drops to her knees, clutching the cross and praying this is the call we are waiting for. At one point she becomes physically sick, and a friend quickly brings a bowl for her in case she needs it. Patsy covers her face, as if she can block out the hysteria of the bizarre scene.

I see some new mail lying on the foyer floor, beneath the mail slot in our front door. I think, *If the kidnapper is going to communicate with me, maybe there is a note from him in this pile of mail.* I sort carefully through the letters. Nothing.

The police want to know if I know of anyone who would do this. Linda Arndt asks if there is anybody who might be upset with me—personally or workwise? Anybody who has threatened me?

I think for a while and then tell them about Jeff Merrick, who had been released recently by our company and left very angry. Jeff had been a friend since he was just out of college, when we both worked for AT&T, and I had arranged for his job with Access a few years earlier. I had tried to make sure that Jeff landed on his feet now and had time to find a new position. Still, Jeff's reaction went way beyond distress. He told people he would bring me and the company down to our knees. He filed a long ethics violation complaint with our corporate headquarters at Lockheed Martin, alleging all sorts of misdeeds. Jeff clearly was one person who was extremely agitated with me. Sadly, he was someone the police would need to check out thoroughly because of how outspoken he had been.

I call Gary Merriman, our human resources director at Access Graphics, trying to get the names, addresses, and phone numbers of recently released employees for the police. Now Gary is aware of what is going on in our home.

The police ask Patsy these same questions about who might have been angry or acting strangely, and she begins to think about our cleaning lady. Linda Hoffmann-Pugh had called Patsy a couple of days before Christmas, very distraught and in tears. Linda said her sister, who was also her landlord, was going to evict her if she didn't come up with the past-due rent. She asked Patsy if she could borrow twenty-five hundred dollars to cover it. Patsy had consoled Linda and agreed to lend her the money. In fact, Patsy had intended to leave the check for Linda on the kitchen counter before leaving for Michigan; Linda would let herself in the house and pick it up while we were gone for the holidays.

Patsy remembers that her mother, Nedra Paugh, had said that Linda had remarked to her at one time, "JonBenét is so pretty; aren't you afraid that someone might kidnap her?" Now those comments seem strangely menacing.

Finding the phone number in her digital Rolodex, Patsy

tells a police officer where Linda lives in Ft. Lupton, Colorado. Patsy later tells me she was thinking, *If it's Linda, it's okay, because she is a good, sweet person. She is just upset. She may need the money, but she won't hurt JonBenét.*

The police tell us they will arrange for the Ft. Lupton police to drive by Linda's house to see if they notice anything unusual, but they don't want to alert anyone there that they are being watched.

I pace back and forth in front of the telephone, desperately wanting it to ring. But it doesn't. Ten o'clock comes and goes. Nothing. The note says the kidnapper will call "tomorrow." I suddenly realize I don't know when the note was written, so I don't know for sure whether "tomorrow" means the twenty-sixth or the twenty-seventh.

By this time several officers are dusting with black fingerprint powder. There is a lot of movement around the house, with officers carrying out various assignments, although it is hard to know who's issuing the orders. It doesn't occur to me that we should be contained in one area to keep us from contaminating any potential evidence. The chief of police, Tom Koby, will later say they didn't treat the house as a "crime scene" because they thought it was "only a kidnapping."

I look at my watch again and worry because the FBI hasn't shown up yet. *No matter where their offices are, they should be here by now. Where are they? What are they doing? We need more help.* A new sense of desperation wells up inside of me because I am sure the FBI could help get JonBenét back. I urgently want more resources but don't know how to make it happen.

Got to do something, I think. *Anything. Whatever will get JonBenét back.*

Sometime that morning, I remember a day back in the summer when I had left my keys inside and was locked out of the house. To get in, I broke one of the panes in a basement window; then I reached in and released the latch, so I could climb inside. I think about the basement now. I jump up and hurry down there.

That entry place needs to be looked at, I tell myself. I move down the basement hall and find the window. The pane is still broken, and the window is open, with a large old Samsonite suitcase sitting right under it. *Odd,* I think. *This doesn't look right. This suitcase is not normally kept here.*

Maybe this is how the kidnapper got in and out of our house. The window ledge is about five feet off the floor, so a person would need something to stand on in order to get up and out.

I don't look further after finding the open window, but I carefully close it before going back upstairs. I constantly think about JonBenét. *Wherever you are, stay strong.* I try to keep my thoughts straight and keep my feelings of panic from clouding my judgment. *Stay strong, JonBenét,* I keep saying to myself. *Stay strong. I will too. We can make it. I will get you back.*

Walking up the stairs, I feel confused and disoriented. I can't understand why this has happened to JonBenét. *When was she kidnapped? Had to be while we were sleeping soundly.* My heart starts to beat harder again.

At the top of the steps, my thoughts disintegrate for a moment and abruptly I think about Boulder. How could this terrible event have happened in this sleepy little university town? I know Boulder is full of some pretty weird people. Lots of transients and misfits wandering around every day. I certainly know that many of the people in Boulder resent wealth and big business, but I never considered myself wealthy or a big businessman.

My computer distribution business had started in my basement. Patsy worked in the company back in the beginning, and we simply went from day to day, trying to make sales happen. By the standards of the industry, we are still considered a small company. Sure, we have a few problems with some employees, but I can't imagine anyone wanting to take JonBenét or harm her.

Morning drifts into afternoon, and still no phone call. The frustration of waiting for the kidnapper to contact us becomes unbearable. Finally, Detective Linda Arndt asks me to take one person, go through the entire house, and look for anything unusual or out of place.

I want to do anything I can to help, so I agree. I don't stop to think that we should not be allowed to roam around the house without a police officer present—much less search the entire house by ourselves. After all, it's my home. I live here. And I assume a police detective knows how to professionally handle this kind of situation.

Fleet White is standing next to me, so I ask him to go with me. Fleet is my friend and a father himself. Fleet can help.

I decide we should start at the basement and work our way to the top floor. It is highly unlikely that we will find anything amiss in our bedroom on the third floor, and we will need some kind of a system to make sure we don't miss anything. A bottom-to-top search will do that. Fleet doesn't mention to me that he had been down to the basement earlier that morning.

We head downstairs, and I take Fleet over to the broken windowpane and explain my breaking in there last summer. I tell him that I had found this window open earlier. We look for glass splinters and find some small ones.

We continue our search, and a few minutes later I'm at the door by the furnace. I open it and see JonBenét lying on the floor, with a white blanket around her. Black tape covers her mouth. *That's my baby, lying there like that.* Her hands are above her head, tied together with a shoestring-like cord.

My heart leaps and a rush runs through my body. *I've found her! Thank God, I've found her!*

I fall down over her body. Instantly I rip the tape off her mouth, begging her to talk to me. I pull the blanket off of her. Her delicate eyelids are closed and her skin is cool to the touch.

I can't stand the sight of her hands tied and have to do something to get them loose. I start untying her, but I can't get the tight knot undone. Everything begins to blur and I'm slipping out of my mind and losing control. I grab JonBenét under her arms and pick her up. Stumbling out of the room, I run to the stairs, carrying my still child. From somewhere far inside of me, a scream erupts. That's all I can do. I scream like I'm in a nightmare but my body is still asleep; I'm deathly afraid.

I run to the living room, where Linda Arndt is standing, and lay JonBenét on the floor in front of the Christmas tree. I still believe we can do something. *We've got to get her awake and out of this unconscious state. Breathing. Moving. Talking. Anything.*

All I can do is comfort JonBenét. Hug her and kiss her. I've found my baby. Abruptly Officer Arndt is down beside me, checking JonBenét's vital signs. The policewoman straightens up, looks me in the eye, and tells me JonBenét is dead.

The shock is overwhelming. I can't cry. The pain is too deep for that. I'm not sure what is going on around me, except that I'm drowning in the excruciating pain.

Patsy will be coming into the room, I think. Her friends have kept her in the TV room at the back of the house. *She must not see JonBenét like this.* I push myself off the floor and get a blanket to cover JonBenét. I lay the blanket over her as I have done many times when she falls asleep.

Then Patsy is fighting to get into the room to see her baby. She rushes past me and falls onto JonBenét's body. I can hear Patsy crying and screaming in agony, but she sounds a million miles away. Somewhere in the fog, Father Rol is in the living room. He says something I struggle to grasp.

"God the Father," Father Rol speaks, and then his voice fades away.

"Jesus, redeemer of the world . . ." The priest's voice floats back in and then disappears once more.

I can't seem to hear or see what is happening. Faintly, Father Rol's voice is speaking at what seems to be an enormous distance from me. He becomes clearer again.

"Into your hands, O merciful Savior, we commend your servant, JonBenét. Acknowledge, we humbly beseech you, a sheep of your own fold . . ."

The words are too painful and I blank out momentarily. Father Rol tells me he has performed the last rites of the Episcopal Church for JonBenét.

Patsy is wailing. "Jesus raised Lazarus from the dead. Ask him to raise our daughter. Pray for JonBenét!"

Father Rol puts his arm around Patsy and seems to be shaking his head. My body is numb. Like a stick. I can't respond. Can't do anything. I want to be with her. I'd rather die.

I found JonBenét. Oh, my God! She is dead.

I realize that more police have arrived. I don't care now what is happening. Seems like we are herded into the sunroom. Everything is a strange mosaic of noise and sound. Most of the time I'm not sure where I am or what is happening.

I watch Patsy kneel down and curl up in a corner behind the china cabinet like a terrified child. She seems to be praying or muttering to herself.

A person comes up and says he's Detective Mason. I assume he is with the FBI. *Finally, the police will get help,* I think. Later I will learn that Mason is another Boulder PD detective and that the police, in fact, have kept the FBI at bay, not letting them inside the house. We are told we must leave the house now.

I try to focus on what we are going to do next. *Boulder isn't really our home. Atlanta is. We need to go home now. To our parents, to our family, to my brother, Jeff. That's what we should do.*

Detective Mason asks me what our plans are, and I tell him we will go to Atlanta. He says something about staying around for a few days, and I agree.

But where will we stay? I wonder. This house is now a house of horrors.

The police come back into the room, and I hear them asking everyone to leave the house. Slowly the rationale sinks in. The police are taking over our home. We must leave. We have to go somewhere. I try to get my mind going again.

Someone suggests that we go to the Fernies'. One of our group notifies the police that we will be at the Fernies' if they need us. We stumble out of the house.

Now, as I get into the car, I see a taxi pull up to the curb. John Andrew, Melinda, and Stewart get out. They have arrived from Minneapolis after frantically arranging to take the first flight they could get. Mobilizing everything I have left in me, I go over to the kids and tell them JonBenét is gone.

The older kids begin crying, and I see Patsy running across the street toward us. The scene is so distorted, I later don't remember much of what was said or done. I sign a paper—about an autopsy, I believe.

As we leave, I suddenly realize that a police officer is coming with us. For a moment his presence doesn't seem to compute. Then I think, *We're under police protection.* That reassures me. After all, whoever killed our daughter is at large; we might still be in danger.

Later, I will reflect on that twenty-four-hour police guard on duty at the Fernies'. Even then, we were probably the prime suspects, and we didn't even have a clue.

4

DECEMBER 26 AND BEYOND

Patsy, the older children, and I arrived at the Fernies' like refugees staggering in from a storm. We didn't know what had happened, what to do, where to go. The Fernies graciously took us in, and we crumpled on their living room floor

A while later, when Fleet White brought Burke to the house, Patsy tearfully put her arm around him. "Honey," she said, "JonBenét has gone to heaven."

He hugged Patsy and acknowledged her words by a nod of his head, and then went to the downstairs playroom with the Fernies' son. Burke seemed unable to face JonBenét's death; it was just too difficult for him to process at the time.

Most of the time I faded in and out of shock. Neither Patsy nor I were able to take care of ourselves, much less Burke. We were completely and utterly helpless. Months later, when Patsy looked at photographs of Burke at the grave site, she noticed that his shirt tail was hanging out and he had on a pair of pants that were too short. She said, "I feel so bad. Why couldn't I have been there for Burke to make sure he was dressed properly for the funeral?"

That night I tried to sleep, but I didn't want to sleep. Terrible feelings of sadness devoured me. I had several drinks. I had done the same thing the night of Beth's death. Not social drinking, but drinking to achieve numbness of mind and body.

The Fernies' home became a cocoon in which I could seal myself away and feel safe from the terrible world outside. My mind needed to retreat as far away as I could go. I had now lost two children.

Two beautiful daughters. One's death, an accident. The other's, a murder. And I didn't protect her.

Later, reporters, television personalities, and various talking heads speculated about how I should be responding to

JonBenét's death. Some thought me too emotional. Others said I was too composed. Newspapers ran opinion columns on my behavior and why it made me look guilty. Contradictory, confusing, and bewildering comments circulated everywhere. What should I have acted like? Had any of these people ever lost two children? There are no guide books about how to act after such a loss. Who were they to judge?

At twenty-two, my daughter Beth died in an automobile crash. She and the young man who had become dear to her were on their way to one of Chicago's art museums in the middle of the day on Friday, January 8, 1992. They pulled onto the freeway and a truck sideswiped them. As horrible as Beth's death was, it was an accident.

But JonBenét was murdered. Someone had entered our home while we were asleep. And in the security of our home, our personal sanctuary, this vile creature murdered our child. When a criminal breaks into your home, your sense of security is violated, devastated, destroyed. People who have been robbed have some feeling of how we felt: nothing seemed secure anymore. There was no safe haven.

For a long time afterward I couldn't exist without people around me to guarantee my family's security. I wanted Burke to sleep on the couch close to our makeshift bed. I couldn't deal with what people normally face every day. The horrible feeling wouldn't go away. It would have been much easier to have died myself. I have learned that, with time, this feeling mellows; but it doesn't leave.

It's difficult to recall much of what happened during the next twenty-four hours at the Fernies'. I do remember that Detectives Arndt and Mason came back and forth a number of times to talk to us. Uniformed police officers were there around the clock, listening, watching, and taking notes about our behavior, I suppose. Only vaguely can I recall them talking to me. The police kept asking questions, and we answered the best we could.

I also had questions for them, wanting to know how many police were working on our case. Where was the FBI? The police officers' answers seemed vague and undefined, but I was so distraught, I could barely communicate and found it hard to focus. I found my short-term memory was impaired.

Rod Westmoreland, my good friend who had helped raise

the ransom money, arrived from Atlanta. I was grateful to see him. Over the twenty years I had known Rod, he had always come to my aid when I needed him. For him to leave Atlanta during the Christmas season, and during a busy time of the year for him professionally, was no small sacrifice. He started questioning the police, hammering away on what I wanted to know.

"How many of you are on the case right now?" Rod pressed.

"Well, there's eight of us."

Rod pressed further. "Well, where are the rest of them?"

"Actually a couple are on vacation . . . and a few are sick," the detective answered.

"Let me put it another way," Rod bore down. "*Exactly* how many are working on solving this problem *right now*?"

"Detective Arndt and I are here." The detective sounded as if he were backpedaling. "We have another person working at the house."

"You're telling me that you only have two or three at most working on the case?" Rod glared at the man.

"Something like that," the detective admitted.

"The FBI?" Rod asked again.

"We only have to call them . . ." the detective explained.

"They're not *really* on the case yet?" Rod concluded.

"They're available whenever we call."

I looked at Rod. We both realized the meaning of what we had heard. Our kidnapping-murder case was not being given the earth-shattering importance we wanted and expected. The morning of the twenty-sixth, I had been told the FBI was "on the way." Now I learned they weren't even on the case.

Later, Rod spoke privately, telling me that what he had heard made him suspicious of the ability of these police officials and what they were doing. He didn't like how they were handling our case.

I agreed, recognizing that the detectives had not been telling me the truth. Something was wrong.

Detective Linda Arndt returned and wanted to see me again. She said they needed to ask Patsy and me more questions, and asked us to come to the police station.

I blinked my eyes several times. Wasn't this woman able to recognize the state Patsy was in? She could barely walk. I told

Arndt we couldn't leave the house, but we would answer their questions here.

I could tell that Arndt didn't like my answer and she intended to persist. Mike Bynum, a good friend who had arrived earlier with food in hand, overheard Arndt insisting that we go down to the police station. He immediately talked with our family pediatrician, who had also come to support us. Dr. Francesco Beuf told Mike that, in his professional opinion, Patsy was in no condition to leave the house. When Mike related the message to the detectives, they continued to insist that we go downtown.

I felt distraught. Sure, Patsy and I desperately wanted to help solve this crime, but why couldn't they talk to us here in the privacy of this living room?

Mike had been a prosecutor for the district attorney's office in Boulder before becoming part of the largest law firm in town. Like Rod, he was suspicious of what the police were trying to do.

"Look, John. I have to level with you," Mike said.

"Of course."

"I know this is going to sound strange, but right now you and Patsy are in no condition to make any decisions. Would you give me permission to make some choices for you and do what needs to be done?"

"Mike, I'd be grateful. Please do whatever you think should be done."

Mike marched out of the room and confronted the two detectives, telling them there would be no interviews at the police station. Under medical advice, John and Patsy Ramsey were in no condition to do anything more than they were doing right now. That was the end of the discussion and probably the beginning of the infamous "Ramseys not cooperating with police" headlines.

Later in the afternoon of the twenty-seventh, I got a call at the Fernies' from Gary Merriman, our human resources director at Access Graphics. He said he had received a call from someone inside the justice system who told me that I should get the best criminal defense attorney I could, as soon as possible.

"Why?" I asked incredulously. "Do they consider me a suspect?"

"I don't know," he answered. "That's the message I was told to give you."

I hung up slowly. Everything seemed scrambled again. Why in the world would the police in any fashion suspect *me*? The idea was so preposterous, I decided not to tell anyone about Gary's warning.

As the day wore on, I was grateful for the police security guards. They stood in the living room or by the dining room table twenty-four hours a day. They were polite and professional but always remained there, watching everyone come and go. People were bringing in so much food that I think I encouraged the police to eat with us. Only later would I learn that the many notes they were constantly taking were observations of our behavior. At this early stage I was squarely under the umbrella of suspicion.

During much of this time I was overwhelmed with grief, but it was still contained within me. The pain I was feeling was so great, I found it nearly impossible to think about anyone else. Patsy was in the house, but I couldn't seem to bring myself to talk to her or anyone for very long. The weight of JonBenét's death bore down like a gigantic rock, crushing the life out of me. Most of the afternoon and evening of December 27 I did little more than struggle to keep from losing my mind. My body seemed to be running on automatic, even though barely.

The press and media were all over the place. Cameras were pointed at the windows, and I could see reporters walking around outside, talking to each other. The horde seemed like vultures, waiting to find tidbits of flesh to pounce on.

Patsy and I were terrified for our safety. We had no idea why this horrendous crime had been committed. While we were safely inside the Fernies' home with police protection, outside in the streets there was a killer who must be apprehended before he or she could strike us again.

When Mike Bynum returned the next day, I had a private conversation with him. He told me that it would be prudent for me to retain an attorney. Gary Merriman's call earlier was still working in my mind, so I told Mike to do whatever he thought was right. But I still wasn't making sense of it all. Couldn't the police see what a loving family we were? How could they think otherwise? Except for a few speeding tickets and a host of parking tickets (I often thought of Boulder as the parking ticket capital of the world), neither Patsy nor I had ever had trouble with the law. Any suspicion of us simply didn't make sense. I constantly wondered how these detectives could think we could possibly have done this. I would have given my life for JonBenét in an instant.

Mike later learned a distressing bit of information that he chose to keep from me. Pete Hofstrom of the district attorney's office had informed Mike that the police were refusing to release JonBenét's body for burial in Atlanta unless we submitted to a police interrogation, under their terms.

Mike was outraged and told Peter, "Look, I don't know what happened here for sure, and neither do the police. What I do know is that these people are parents of a murdered child, and they need to be treated with respect and compassion. If the police persist, tell them, 'We'll see you in court.'"

While Mike did not inform us of this act of police stupidity and brutality at the time, he started to take the actions necessary to protect us from the mounting police assault. Bynum quickly arranged for Bryan Morgan of Haddon, Morgan, and Foreman in Denver to represent me and for Patrick Burke to represent Patsy. By Saturday night, we had been introduced to both of these men. I did not understand why two attorneys were necessary, but I was in no condition to discuss the matter.

If the police had been suspicious before, now that we had retained counsel they became totally convinced we were guilty. We later learned that their rationale was that innocent people don't need attorneys; only guilty people hire them.

Yet our friends realized what was happening.

Two years later, on a British documentary about Jon-Benét's murder and the resulting media lynching, Bryan Morgan told why it was so necessary for us to have legal representation. "It is foolish to blindly throw oneself into the maw of the justice system," he said. "One simply must be thoughtful about the way one acts, especially in a case where the media attention reaches the point of near hysteria, and especially in a case of media attention which from the outset portrays certain people as clearly guilty. This is the way towards the conviction of innocent people in this country."

On the same program Mike Bynum offered this observation from his years working as a lawyer in the criminal system. "If you're guilty, you should have a lawyer. And I want to tell you that if you're innocent, you'd better have a great lawyer. There is no difference."

Although we were unaware of it at the time, the police had interrogated Burke quite extensively on the morning of December 26 while he had been at the Whites'. Police cannot legally question a child without a parent or guardian's permission. They claimed in their written report that they had received permission from his grandmother to do the interview. (At the time his maternal grandmother, Nedra Paugh, was in Atlanta, and his paternal grandmother had died before Burke was born.) The police tape-recorded the session. However, we didn't learn about this improper improper interrogation until Burke was subpoenaed to appear before the grand jury in 1999.

Soon we learned that the police supervisor in charge of the investigation and head of the detective division was Commander John Eller. He never once talked to us or sat across the table from us, yet apparently he was the one who concluded from the beginning that I killed JonBenét. Eller set the theory in motion, and his minions dutifully followed.

Eller had kept the FBI out of the case and refused help from those more experienced with murder cases, such as the Denver Police Homicide Unit, who had offered their help and expertise. Apparently easily threatened, Eller took an extremely defensive attitude toward anyone outside the local police department. His refusing expert help is the most critical mistake for which I hold the Boulder police accountable.

Only after our attorneys confronted Peter Hofstrom in a face-off did the police release JonBenét so we could bury her. Mike Bynum had contacted Howe Mortuary in Boulder to handle taking JonBenét back to Atlanta for burial. My brother Jeff and I went to the funeral home to finalize the arrangements and learned that Howe's did not charge for their services when a child died. I protested but was told that the tradition started when their father began the family business years earlier, and they intended to continue the practice. I had discovered one of the first of many compassionate strangers whom we were to meet during our long ordeal.

When Beth died, I had been fortunate enough to find a peaceful old cemetery in Marietta, Georgia, dating back to the mid-1800s, with only six contiguous grave sites still left. While making arrangements for Beth, I had purchased all six plots. At least this was one decision that did not have to be made when we brought JonBenét back to Atlanta. We knew where we were going to lay her to rest—next to her half sister Beth.

Members of Patsy's family—her sisters Pam and Polly, Polly's husband, Grant—and John Andrew, Melinda, and Stewart, and my brother, Jeff—gathered with us at the Fernies'. Other good friends, like Penni and Chek Beuf, Roxy and Stuart Walker, and Glen and Susan Stine arrived. Many people came and went. Some I remember talking with, others I don't. Most of the conversations didn't stay with me. We were still numb.

We talked some about the services and our trip back to Atlanta. During the discussion, it became obvious that someone should go back to our home and gather up a number of items that we needed before we left for Atlanta. The task would not be easy emotionally. The police had taken possession of the house, so detectives were not going to let anybody simply walk in and out of the crime scene. No one really wanted to go back into that horrible house.

Eventually, arrangements were made for Pam Paugh, Patsy's younger sister, to go back to the house under police supervision and get a few things we needed. She would be allowed to stand at the door of a room and point at the items. Then the police would carefully catalog these possessions and deliver them to her.

Most of the items Patsy wanted were in a curio cabinet of keepsakes in our bedroom. Treasures from over the years filled the cabinet: our children's first shoes, a christening gown Patsy had made for both of the children, baby teeth, Jon-Benét's baby locks, Patsy's baby shoes, and my baby rattle. Patsy particularly wanted Pam to get the My Twinn doll from under the Christmas tree and the pictures of the kids she kept on the sink in her bathroom.

After gathering up what we had asked for, Pam was getting ready to leave when she had a feeling that something important had been missed. She asked to go back to JonBenét's room, and as she stood in the doorway, her attention was drawn to a seemingly insignificant gold medallion that Jon-Benét had won in the recent All-Stars Christmas Pageant, her last competition. The round medallion had been placed around her neck as the overall winner of the talent competition. Even though neither Patsy nor I had said anything about the medal, Pam felt a personal urgency to retrieve it, and the detective didn't object.

Over the past two years JonBenét had won a number of medals and trophies in her little pageants. She was always so proud to show them to Daddy. I had told her many times that the most important part of these contests was not beauty or costumes but talent. "Your talent is the most important thing," I said. "And it doesn't matter if you win or not, just that you do your best." She would sing and dance her heart out. Sometimes she might be slightly off-key, but JonBenét always gave her best.

"Dad, I really worked hard on my talent this time," she would say to me, knowing that's what I thought important.

"Good. That's what counts," I always replied.

Her last contest had been in early December and was called the Little Miss Christmas Pageant. I had planned to be there for the talent show, but the program ran ahead of schedule and I missed both the performance and the award. When I sat down beside Patsy, JonBenét lit up like a Christmas tree. She took the little medallion from around her neck and placed it around mine.

No one knew that during those chaotic days that followed December 26 the medal Pam now held had been on my mind. That was the one item of JonBenét's I wanted for myself as a keepsake, because of the way she had given it to me. No one had known of the significance of that medal except JonBenét. Only God could have seen into my mind.

When Pam pressed the medallion in my hand, I was overwhelmed. I could not possibly tell her what it meant for her to bring this one object back to me. I placed the medallion around my neck and have worn it continually every day since.

I felt as if JonBenét had somehow spoken to me through Pam's bringing me this medal. My daughter reached across eternity and gave me this gift that touched my heart as nothing else in the world could. I knew from then on she was all right. Now, when I get down, I simply touch the metal that lies against my chest and suddenly I feel better. It is my touchstone. When I look at it, I am reminded not only that JonBenét is with God but also that she will someday welcome her mom and me to our heavenly home.

5

SAYING GOOD-BYE

John and I spent three days at the Fernies', but I remember little of what happened. I returned to some semblance of awareness in the shower. I was in the master bathroom and Patty Novack, a friend from church who was a nurse, was helping me. Out of the surrealistic dream, the chasm of grief, I had begun to return slightly. It felt like I was coming up for air after being submerged in a bottomless pool for a long time.

The days after December 26 merged together in a blur of pain without distinction between them. At one point I became so disabled that someone had to feed me, literally holding a spoon to my mouth. In the midst of the turmoil, my sister Pam came in with three of JonBenét's dresses for me to choose what she would wear. I reached for the white chiffon because it looked so angelic, and I hugged the dress before I gave it back to Pam.

The loss of my child was like a phantom arm that people retain in their memory after an amputation. My world had two children and I couldn't grasp the idea that one of them was gone, so my body slid into a protective mode in which I functioned superficially but without genuine connection to much of anything else.

On December 28, a department store in Denver sent some clothing to the Fernies' so I could pick something to wear to the funeral, since all our clothes were still in the house. Roxy and my sisters were there to help me sort through the dresses and hopefully come up with something I could wear to my daughter's funeral. I chose a black knit, two-piece dress.

At that moment a picture of Jackie Kennedy abruptly flashed across my mind. I remembered seeing her wearing a black veil, walking hand in hand with her two children to

JFK's grave site. Now I could see why people wore veils at such times: the filmy material surrounds you like a cocoon, overshadowing your face and closing out the world. With the covering and protection, I could cry, be private in my grief. I decided I wanted to wear a veil to JonBenét's funeral, so I asked one of my friends to help. She found a sheer black scarf and attached it to a black felt hat, then packed it for the trip to Atlanta.

On Sunday, December 29, when I came down the Fernies' stairs in the black dress to go to the hastily arranged memorial service at St. John's Church, John glanced up and said, "You look beautiful." How I appreciated his compliment and his love. I took a deep breath and was finally ready to face the service for my daughter.

JonBenét's memorial service was held on Sunday, December 29, at St. John's Episcopal Church, a small stone church in downtown Boulder, just a block off the Pearl Street Mall. After Beth's death, the church had been John's foundation, offering him a place of spiritual comfort so he could grow and rebuild.

That Sunday afternoon St. John's was packed to overflowing. The service started very simply as Father Rol came down the center aisle, right into the congregation, and spoke from the heart. "Welcome to JonBenét's church," he began.

I thought that St. John's was, indeed, JonBenét's church. She had been a spiritual person and understood God. Once she had asked me, "How much do you love me, Mommy?" And I had answered, "I love you and Burke and Daddy more than anything else in this world." JonBenét shook her head and said, "You're not supposed to love anyone more than Jesus." I remembered another time when we were sitting in a pew of this church listening to a beautiful hymn, and when it was over, JonBenét announced in a very loud voice, "That was a nice song," and the whole church chuckled.

Even though my mother had dutifully made sure I was in worship services each week, I don't think I would have had such insights when I was a six-year-old child at Stout Memorial United Methodist Church in Parkersburg, West Virginia.

Father Rol asked, "Does anyone in the congregation have

personal thoughts or comments about JonBenét they would like to share?" Silence settled over the crowd as people reflected.

John Fernie and my sister Polly stood to say a few words. Then from the middle of the church a man in a dark suit stood, and I recognized Bill McReynolds, a retired Colorado University professor. With his long white beard and hair, McReynolds was a natural to play the town Santa Claus, and we had met him several years ago in a cafe on the Pearl Street Mall. We'd been having breakfast when this Santa Claus came in, greeting and encouraging people. He asked our children if they had been good that year. "What do you want for Christmas?" he had inquired. Burke and JonBenét laughed, giggled, and enjoyed him immensely. As McReynolds left, I ran out to get his name and address to invite him to come to a Christmas party I was planning.

Now, in the church, for a few seconds I didn't understand what McReynolds was doing. He walked to the front of the sanctuary and turned around and began telling the congregation how much he had adored JonBenét. He spoke for over four minutes, during which he walked over to me and gave me a bottle of gold Tinker Bell fairy dust, which JonBenét had given to him.

Then John stood up and began his tribute by telling the story of JonBenét's medal, which he was wearing. He thanked people for coming and then slowly sank to the pew.

I don't recall many of the other comments made that Sunday. Suddenly it hit me. December 29. My fortieth birthday— and I was burying my baby. My fortieth birthday. A landmark in anyone's life, a tombstone in mine. The pain overwhelmed me. Why had I lived to be forty? Why would God do this to me? I had survived what should have been terminal cancer. Could I survive the murder of my child?

I heard the organist begin a familiar melody, "I Am the Bread of Life," a praise song that had given John such strength after Beth's death and a favorite we had often sung as we took communion as a family. John had already told me, "I want this song to be sung at my funeral." Little did we realize we would be alive to sing this worship song at our daughter's service. Now the song seemed unusually meaningful to me.

I am the resurrection,
I am the life.
They who believe in me, even if they die
They shall live forever.

And I will ra-aise them up.
I will ra-aise them up,
I will ra-aise them up on the last day.

Those words blessed me. I knew I would see my daughter again someday, sometime in the future.

For some reason (I do know not why; maybe it was the medication), I began walking up the aisle toward the altar, with Burke dutifully following me and John holding me up. The music seemed to lead me forward, just as we did at communion, just as we had done that Christmas Eve. John gently guided me back to my seat in the pew, aware that my overwhelming grief was making me delirious.

Afterward we walked into the fellowship hall for more greetings and expressions of condolence. As we were leaving the church, I glanced up and noticed Burke's close friend, Anthony, standing beside him. Roxy Walker was at my side, helping me walk, and she heard me say, "Wouldn't it be wonderful if Anthony could go to Atlanta with us to be a support for Burke?" She said, "Of course. I'll see what I can do."

Roxy spoke with Anthony's parents, and they readily agreed that he could go with us to Atlanta later that afternoon. I was so grateful that Burke would have a friend his own age close by during the service there. He would be lost without his sister.

The first time I observed the media harassing Patsy and me was at the memorial service in Boulder. Some creepy looking guy sauntered up to me and whipped out a camera. He brazenly pointed it at me and snapped a picture. Somebody chased the man away, but I was offended by the aggressive and inappropriate intrusion into my family's private grief. Patsy and I were only beginning to be aware of the degree to which the media would affront us.

Later that day we left the Jefferson County Airport, south of Boulder, where Lockheed Martin had made a corporate jet available to us for our trip to Atlanta. This was the first of many acts of kindness from this company that had purchased Access Graphics. Arranging airline tickets and going through a public departure would have been extraordinarily difficult under the circumstances.

Our good friend Mike Archuleta volunteered to fly his airplane to take the overflow of our friends to Atlanta. We arrived at the DeKalb Peachtree Airport in North Atlanta late that night. Approximately fifty of our Atlanta friends were there to meet us. I looked at the crowd and saw people I hadn't seen in five years. I wanted to hug every one of them and say thanks for so graciously coming out to meet us. But I mostly just cried.

The humidity in the cool night air felt wonderful to my soul. It was so good to be back home. I tried to drink in the atmosphere as a healing balm for my broken heart.

Our family left the airport and drove to Roswell, a northern suburb of Atlanta, where Patsy's parents, Don and Nedra Paugh, live. I knew it would be trying for me to stay there because that's where we had come immediately after Beth's accident. The bedroom where we slept was filled with desperate memories of weeping for Beth. Now I was to weep for my daughter JonBenét in the same room. To this day I cannot go into that room without flashing back to those nights.

Later I discovered that Charlie Brennan of the *Rocky Mountain News* reported that I had personally piloted my own jet back to Atlanta. This unfortunate, and untrue, report launched a hundred questions—and was one of the flash points of suspicion directed at me. "Shouldn't the FAA know about this? How could a grieving father possibly have piloted his airplane to Atlanta unless he wasn't grieving at all?" On and on the accusations went.

I struggled to focus on the questions as John and our friends talked about the funeral service. Most of the time I was too anesthetized to contribute much. I knew that Dr. Frank Harrington, the senior minister of Peachtree Presbyterian Church, who had married John and me and baptized both Burke and JonBenét, would do the services.

My sister Polly asked me what special hymns and readings I wanted for the services in Atlanta. Suddenly I remembered an especially inspiring song. Over the Thanksgiving holidays, Polly and I had attended a musical production at the East Side Baptist Church in Marietta, Georgia. Burke, JonBenét, Polly, and her children sat in the front row of the church's gymnasium, which was transformed into the setting for a Broadway-scale production. I watched JonBenét as she enjoyed the music and the costumes and the lights. During the show, the church's choir director, Mickey Henderson, sang a profoundly moving solo, "In Christ Alone." Polly suggested we ask him to come to JonBenét's service and sing it once more. I loved the idea.

Hundreds and hundreds of people attended the visitation at the Mayes-Ward-Dobbins Funeral Home in Marietta the night before the funeral. The *Atlanta Constitution* reported the story under a headline banner, "Georgia Says Good-bye to JonBenét." Although we didn't know it at the time, people stood in line for hours outside the funeral home, waiting to get in to express their condolences. John and I tried to shake hands with each person and say thank you for such an overflowing expression of love and concern. One couple told us they had lost two daughters. We were very touched; parents who have lost children bond immediately.

The last time we saw JonBenét was in that funeral home. My mother and dad, Nedra and Don Paugh; my sisters, Pam and Polly; John and I; John Andrew; and Melinda stood around the coffin saying our good-byes. Mother had a special gold bracelet she had saved to give to JonBenét when she was older. Mother reached down and slipped it over her wrist.

Polly put a large gold cross in JonBenét's hands. During the time I had cancer, Father Rol had performed a healing service for me and had given me a cross that had been blessed by Native Americans in South Dakota, where he had formerly pastored a church. Later I had found gold crosses similar to that one at a jewelry store in Boulder and bought those crosses for my mother and sisters. Polly had worn the cross through some difficult times; JonBenét would wear it forever.

Pam had brought JonBenét's Little Miss Christmas tiara, which she had won during December's pageant competition in Denver. Now Pam bent over and lovingly placed the crown on JonBenét's head.

Then it was John's turn. He had recently purchased a beautiful silk scarf, and he tucked it around JonBenét as if surrounding her with a final blanket of love.

Suddenly my friend Priscilla White rushed in. She and Fleet had found Sister Socks, a stuffed kitten that was so dear to JonBenét. I couldn't believe that Priscilla had the gray-and-white cat. I had asked to have the toy brought from the house in Boulder, but the stuffed animal that was given to us earlier was the wrong one. Priscilla knew that, and somehow, even though she was now in Atlanta, she had gotten hold of the right Sister Socks, the one with the red ribbon around its neck. I tucked Sister Socks under JonBenét's right arm.

"Don't you think you should keep Sister Socks?" Priscilla asked. "You'll need it more than JonBenét."

"No. Sister Socks belongs with her," I whispered.

Ever since that time I have tried and tried to find another gray-and-white kitten just like that one, because the story of Sister Socks was so special to us.

The story began the first summer we stayed in Charlevoix, when a gray-and-white stray cat turned up at our house. Her paws looked like they had white athletic socks on them, so the kids named her Sister Socks. We set out a bowl of milk in the mornings, and the forlorn cat became a family friend. Burke and JonBenét would look forward to the cat's visit each day and play with her.

Then Sister Socks disappeared for several days. The children were really disappointed, but we all assumed she'd found a new home. One morning John was working in the garage when he saw Sister Socks gingerly walking toward him with a tiny kitten in her mouth. She laid the kitten down at his feet and stood back, as if to say, "Here's my baby. Could you help me take care of it?"

John made a box, lined with a blanket, to put the little kitten in. Soon Sister Socks came back with another kitten—and another one. John is not particularly a cat person, but he and Sister Socks were now bonded. I know he would have taken her and her three kittens back to Boulder at the end of the summer, but I was afraid to ask him—and he wasn't about to volunteer. Eventually Sister Socks and her kittens moved in with our neighbors, the Witthoefts, for the winter. Sister Socks was a wonderful part of our first summer in Charlevoix.

Months later JonBenét and I were shopping at the Pearl

Street Mall when we looked into the window of the Printed Page Bookstore. Sitting there on the shelf was a stuffed cat.

"Mommy, that kitty looks like Sister Socks!" JonBenét cried out.

"Maybe a little," I replied. "But Sister Socks was gray, not brown like this cat. Wasn't she? That one is the wrong color."

"I know, but she had stripes like that cat. Please, Mommy!" JonBenét begged. "I want a Sister Socks cat. I bet they have the right color one somewhere in there."

"Okay," I acquiesced. "I'll check and see."

I could tell that the stuffed animal was important to Jon-Benét. It was on the top of her list to Santa that year.

Later I called the bookstore and asked if they could find a gray cat. Eventually they did, so my father arranged to pick up the stuffed animal, just in time for our Christmas party. The highlight of the evening was when Santa Claus pulled a gray-and-white Sister Socks out of his sack. JonBenét loved her kitty—and the real Sister Socks who still roams the narrow streets of Charlevoix.

6

FACING THE CAMERAS

Christmas garlands and poinsettias still decorated the Peachtree Presbyterian Church when the Rev. Dr. Frank Harrington conducted JonBenét's final services on December 31. He had baptized JonBenét six years earlier; now the minister eulogized her.

I sat next to Patsy on the front row and listened as he spoke of our child, her life, her joys, and what she had given to others. Rev. Harrington described the song from *Gypsy*, which JonBenét had enjoyed singing with her mother. The words say, "Wherever we go, whatever we do, we're gonna go through it together." During the service I rubbed Patsy's back and thought of how our lives had been such a "together" experience during our time with JonBenét.

Many in the congregation wept when they sang the familiar child's song "Jesus Loves Me." Later a soloist offered "The Lord's Prayer," and Patsy raised her hands in prayer. We were both deeply moved and worshiped God for the gift that JonBenét had been to us.

Suddenly Patsy got up and went down by JonBenét's coffin and knelt to pray. I don't know why she did that. We were both still in shock and medicated so we could function without breaking into tears. Later, when Patsy saw parts of the service on television, she said she didn't remember kneeling by the coffin.

After the service, as we prepared to leave the church, I realized the sanctuary had been packed with hundreds of people.

Outside the church, the media swarmed. Reporters were everywhere. John Andrew had to put himself between one obnoxious photographer and Burke. When we reached the cemetery, people forced the photographers and cameramen to leave the grave site and stay out of the cemetery. We were starting to learn what a vicious crowd the media could be.

After the burial, we began making plans to return to Boulder. As distasteful as this trip would be for both Patsy and me, we wanted to help find the killer.

During our planning, we learned the extent of the media frenzy for the first time. They had already reported the false story that I piloted my personal jet to Atlanta. Then a Denver radio program reported that our son John Andrew was a suspect—and that he may have sexually abused JonBenét. Fleet White had heard talk show host Peter Boyles before leaving Boulder and called the police and news media, attempting to stop such horrible and false accusations. Fleet also called Rod Westmoreland and told him to find John Andrew and to tell his mother, Cindy, to get out of her house in case the media arrived. Rod eventually tracked down John Andrew and warned him.

After Fleet arrived in Atlanta, he kept arguing that we didn't need lawyers to defend us. His solution was for Patsy and me to go on national television and tell our story, since he was convinced that the media were rapidly painting us in guilty colors. If people could see us, he argued, they would be able to get the story into perspective.

As I listened to our friends debate what we should do, I felt like a Ping-Pong ball. As a father, I carried the horrible guilt of not having protected my precious daughter as she lay sleeping in bed. Most abhorrent to me was the accusation that Patsy or I could be considered guilty of causing her death.

For several reasons, Patsy and I finally agreed to do an interview with CNN reporter Brian Cabell. We were in Atlanta and CNN wasn't far away. Moreover, Fleet had convinced me that a public appearance was necessary. Although the idea was slow in settling, I came to see the need to protect our family's reputation. My worst thought was that we would be portrayed as the kind of people the media frenzy appeared to be creating. We weren't perfect, but we had tried to live good lives; maybe people would see this as they watched CNN. And the television broadcast would also give us the opportunity to say thank you to the people who had waited outside the funeral home for hours, many of whom we didn't get to meet during the visitation.

We decided to do the interview.

*   *   *

I finally agreed with John to do the CNN interview, although I was still overwhelmed by grief and heavily medicated. Even the smallest task seemed impossible. My concentration was gone. That day, January 1, 1997, I decided to wear the same black dress I had worn to the funeral.

Soon a dilapidated taxi station wagon pulled up in front of my mother's house. John and his brother, Jeff, who was accompanying us for moral support, and I got in the backseat. I thought, *Boy, this is a rickety car for CNN to be running around the country in. No seat belts.* I kept sliding all over the backseat of the car.

As the car pulled away, the man in the front seat turned around and immediately started asking questions. I looked at the driver and then back at the interviewer without any idea who the man was. He simply kept drilling us with questions as we headed south to the CNN headquarters building in downtown Atlanta. Jeff answered some of them for us; we were still so enveloped in grief, it was difficult to focus on the questions.

The forty-minute ride in that rickety cab proved to be very uncomfortable. At CNN John and I followed the interviewer inside like wooden soldiers, marching along behind him through the maze. Eventually we came to a brightly lit room with two chairs in the center and went inside.

"Have a seat," he said.

My first thought was that we were in a reception area. More spotlights blasted in our faces. Men began bringing in electronic equipment and adjusting the lighting. John and I watched the parade go back and forth in silent amazement.

"Now take a breath, and I'll tell you what we're going to do," the interviewer who had been in the front seat of the taxi said, sitting down in front of us. "We're ready to begin."

"You're going to interview us?" I asked incredulously.

He nodded his head. "Of course. My name is Brian Cabell."

Abruptly, the show started. I couldn't believe this procedure: come in, sit down, and boom, you're on the air. Cabell began by asking us an obvious question. "Why did you decide to talk now?"

"We have been pretty isolated—totally isolated—for the last five days but we want to thank those people that care about us," John said. "The other reason is that for our grief to resolve itself, we now have to find out why this happened."

Cabell broached the topic on everyone's mind. "There has been some question as to why you hired a defense attorney."

"I know," John said. "We were fortunate from almost the moment that we found the note to be surrounded by friends—our minister, our family doctor, a personal friend of mine who is also an attorney—and we relied on their guidance . . . My friend suggested that it would be foolish not to have knowledgeable counsel."

Cabell then went back to December 26, and he asked me to talk about finding the ransom note. I answered first, describing what had happened, then John added his perspective. And we went back and forth, describing that morning.

At one point in the interview, Cabell seemed rather surprised to learn that we were indeed trying to cooperate with the police. "You were asked," he said, "for a hair sample and writing sample, blood sample. Who else was asked for this?"

John replied that our entire family had been asked to give DNA evidence.

"Including your two elder children?" Cabell asked.

John answered in the affirmative.

"Did you give the samples?"

"Uh-huh," John said again.

"Oh, really? Because the word was that they thought you were too grief stricken. So both of you, you gave samples?"

"Yes." John confirmed it for the interviewer yet again.

"Were you offended by that?" Cabell asked.

"No," John said.

"It was difficult," I added. "But, you know, they need to know—I mean our handprints are all over our home, so they need to know." I was too distraught to express myself clearly, but at least we made the point that we had already complied with the investigation by voluntarily giving DNA and handwriting samples.

The interview then turned to the fact that the murderer had not been apprehended. Cabell said, "The police said a couple of days ago, to assure other residents of Boulder, 'There is no killer on the loose here'. . . . You believe it's someone outside your home?"

I answered immediately. "There is a killer on the loose."

John agreed. "Absolutely," he said.

At the moment Cabell asked that question, I thought of

Kady Hasley and Theresa Beck, friends in Boulder whose children had played with JonBenét. I could see their faces, as well as their children's. I didn't want our tragedy to happen to them.

"I don't know who it is," I added. "I don't know if it's a he or a she. But if I were a resident of Boulder, I would tell my friends to keep—"

I broke down, thinking of the violence that had attacked our home. John put his hand on mine and reassured me. "It's okay."

His support helped me regain my composure. I looked straight into the camera at my friends at home. "Keep your babies close to you. There's someone out there."

Cabell finally referred to the suspicion of our involvement in our daughter's murder. "Inevitably, speculation on talk shows will focus on you. It's got to be a sickening—"

"It's nauseating beyond belief," John interrupted.

Indeed, my stomach churned just thinking that people could possibly believe we could have had a part in murdering our daughter. It was inconceivable. "America has just been hurt so deeply with the tragic things that have happened," I said. "The young woman who drove her children into the water, and we don't know what happened with O.J. Simpson. I mean, America is suffering because we have lost faith in the American family.

"We are a Christian, God-fearing family," I emphasized. "We love our children. We would do *anything* for our children."

Cabell concluded the interview by asking, "Do you take some comfort in believing that JonBenét is in a better place?"

"Yes," John answered. "That's the one thing we want people dealing with us to know, to believe that. We know that in our heart."

"She'll never have to know the loss of a child," I said. "She will never have to know cancer or the death of a child."

"We learned when we lost our first child that people would come forward to us," John added. "That sooner or later, everyone carries a very heavy burden in this life. And JonBenét didn't carry any burdens."

As the interview ended, I sighed in relief. The time at the station had proven to be emotionally difficult to endure.

* * *

CNN taped the interview and edited it after Patsy and I left. The broadcast aired that evening. I was surprised when Brian Cabell abruptly ended the interview with the caveat that "Ramsey has been removed from his job at Access Graphics."

Cabell took a cheap shot. The truth was that I wasn't capable or interested in being in charge of my company. Gary Mann, my boss and president of Lockheed Commercial Systems Group, had put out a simple internal statement to the staff at Access, saying that he would act in my capacity for the time being. Gary had talked with me about this action beforehand, and I fully agreed with the move; I knew I could not contribute to the leadership of the organization—but I certainly had not been removed from my job.

When the interview aired on television, I realized that CNN had cut out the parts where I had been overcome with tears and emotion. They presented us in the light they chose.

During the CNN interview, Patsy and I stated that now that JonBenét was properly laid to rest, we wanted to return to Boulder and help with the investigation. The police had leaked false information that we were not cooperating and had refused to be interviewed. Our comments would have helped refute those leaks; but, for whatever reason, Cabell eliminated that portion of the interview.

The talking heads of the media criticized our CNN interview. Some commentators thought Patsy too emotional; others saw me as not being emotional enough. I wondered what they would have thought if they had seen the entire interview as it actually occurred.

In the days afterward other comments were voiced. Patsy had said, JonBenét "loved her daddy, she was Daddy's girl." Some people wondered if she were speaking out of jealousy.

We had said we believed JonBenét was in a better place. Instead of realizing that this was a statement of our faith and our only source of comfort, some viewers took offense at these words, as if they provided us with a motive to kill JonBenét.

Others focused on my words ". . . for our grief to resolve itself, we now have to find out why this happened." Some critics said, "He didn't say *who*, he said *why*, because he knew who did this."

We began to realize that no matter what we said, it could be twisted and turned and taken in a different light. We became more and more afraid of the press and their ruthlessness.

On January 3, two days after our CNN interview initially aired, we were at my mother's. After dinner, John and I found Mom sitting in front of the television with a glum look on her face.

"Well, your friend Leslie Durgin sure did a dirty trick on you," she said.

"What?" I answered. "Leslie, the mayor of Boulder?"

Mother nodded her head. "On the news tonight they replayed the piece of your CNN interview where you said a killer was on the loose, and then they cut to Boulder. Boom! And there's this Mayor Durgin talking."

I moved closer, staring at the television set.

"What did she say?" I asked.

Mother shook her head. "She said *no! No!* There's no killer out there ... Your friend just called you a liar on national television."

I looked hard at my mother.

"Isn't Leslie Durgin the one you talked with about her cancer and your cancer?" she asked me.

"Yes," I said slowly.

"I'm telling you that your friend called you a liar on national television in response to your comments."

Later we heard the mayor's statement replayed over and over on the news. She said, "People in Boulder have no need to fear that there is someone wandering the streets of Boulder, as has been portrayed by some people, looking for young children to attack. Boulder is safe, it's always been a safe community. It continues to be a safe community."

Some people later told us they believed Durgin's comment started the ball of public opinion rolling against us. We suddenly had the mayor of the little town of Boulder responding to our warnings, saying that there was no killer on the loose.

In an A&E documentary in 1998, Leslie Durgin backpedaled, trying to explain her statements away. "What I said was done in large part to allay the fears of the children in our community and to let people know that the information that

I had at the time was that we did not have some crazed person wandering the streets of University Hill." Whatever her intentions were, those statements were made at our expense and set in motion a media feeding frenzy of unprecedented proportions and viciousness.

7

LIKE MOTHER, LIKE DAUGHTER

One of the most hurtful occurrences since JonBenét's death is the way she has been portrayed in the media. In early January the first pictures of her participation in children's pageants hit national television. Patsy and I were stunned because we had no idea that videos of these events could be obtained by the media or anyone else. Videos that were never meant to go beyond the family living room ended up on national television in the entirely wrong context. Sponsors of the pageants taped these events for distribution to the parents, or so we thought. These tapes of JonBenét as she participated in children's pageants have been shown over and over again during the last three years.

We finally discovered that a Californian named Scott McKiernan of Zuma Press in Laguna Beach, California, had purchased all rights to the videos shortly after JonBenét's death and started renting them to everybody standing in line with a big checkbook. We also learned that part of the deal struck between the buyer and the seller was that no other child could ever be shown in these films. As the pictures proliferated, we quickly saw that some of the tapes had been slowed down to portray a flirting expression or to accentuate JonBenét's movements and make them look seductive. Suggestive music— not the music played at the pageant—had also been added, and presto, something innocent became something ugly. Many of the still photos had been doctored with eye shadow, heavy lipstick, and rouge. Our daughter's innocence had been lost.

We were horrified! How could people exploit a child, much less a murdered child? Could it be to keep the story exciting enough to sell tabloids and increase television ratings? That is what made us so angry. No thought for our feelings or for the truth—only ratings, money, and greed.

One instance in particular stands out in my mind. Jon-Benét's Grandma Nedra happened to be watching CNN when Mary Tillotson, the news anchor, made an off-the-cuff remark about JonBenét. Tillotson said she looked like a hooker.

Nedra was so hurt. Can you imagine how this grief-stricken grandmother felt? She was so angry, she called CNN in Atlanta and spoke directly to the president, Tom Johnson. He later wrote her a note of apology and claimed that Ms. Tillotson had deviated from the prepared script and was not supposed to say things like that on her own. But the damage to a child's innocence had already been done.

Soon other personal pictures of our family appeared in print—without our authorization. We had a family Christmas picture taken at A Better Light Photography in Boulder for our 1992 Christmas cards. The photographer was still in possession of the negatives, and four years later, when the Ramsey family became newsworthy, he went back through his archives and sold the pictures. A professional photographer from Aartvard K. Studios in Charlevoix who had taken family pictures for us one summer also sold those photos. After the police released our home back to us, our private investigators took a number of photographs of the interior of the house, and someone in the developer's shop sold those pictures to the tabloids. As a result, since JonBenét's death we have taken very few personal photos.

When I started pursuing how such personal pictures could possibly be distributed all across America without our permission, I discovered a startling and frightening truth. The photographer who takes the picture and charges you for the sitting and the finished portraits owns the copyright on the photos. Professional photographers can take pictures of you and your children and sell them without your permission, and you can do nothing about it! Your personal rights are nonexistent when it comes to photography! Frightening? You bet it is! If this could happen to us, it could happen to you.

And there is no law whatsoever to restrict a freelance photographer from taking your picture anywhere and selling it for profit. Remember Princess Diana and the paparazzi?

Some celebrities are trying to rectify this situation. Actors Michael J. Fox and Paul Reiser testified before the House Judiciary Committee on May 21, 1998. Both men had stories that sounded all too familiar to us. Fox said, "They intruded upon my father's funeral under false pretenses, carrying cameras with which, presumably, to take pictures of his body and my family in mourning." Reiser told how photographers besieged him when his son was born prematurely.

At the time, the House and Senate were considering bills making personal intrusion for commercial purposes a federal crime. The Privacy Protection Act of 1998, introduced by Representative Elton Gallegly (R-Calif.), would make it punishable for a journalist to harass an individual in order to obtain a visual image. Similar bills were sponsored by the late Representative Sonny Bono (R-Calif.) and Representative John Conyers Jr. (D-Mich.). Although the House Judiciary Committee held hearings on the proposed legislation, none of the bills was enacted. In the Senate, Dianne Feinstein (D-Calif.) offered the Personal Privacy Protection Act. Her bill also died in committee.

In early 1999 Representative Conyers reintroduced his bill, titled the Personal Privacy Protection Act, to the 106th Congress. It was referred to the House Judiciary Committee and then the Judiciary's Subcommittee on Crime. As of this writing, H.R. 97 still has not come up for a floor vote. We certainly hope that Congress will act soon to change this dreadful invasion of personal privacy.

Patsy and I want to make this very clear: JonBenét's participation in pageants was one of her many hobbies. She also loved in-line skating, arts and crafts, and gymnastics. She took violin and piano lessons. She could hula hoop and stand on her head. Her next challenge was rock climbing. Patsy had already signed her up for rock climbing lessons at the East Boulder Recreation Center. She had taken JonBenét there one afternoon, and she immediately started climbing up the wall like a little spider. At the time she was murdered, JonBenét hadn't lost any of her baby teeth, but one of her front teeth was loose, and she was looking forward to using her tooth fairy pillow.

Just as young boys may like Little League or go-cart racing and little girls may choose to enter gymnastics tournaments or dance recitals, participating in pageants was an activity Jon-Benét enjoyed. She loved to perform. She was a natural entertainer and had no fear of getting up in front of a crowd, unlike her dad. Anyone who has a daughter knows that little girls like to play dress-up and enjoy putting on lipstick. That's part of being a little girl. JonBenét just had an extra level of ham in her.

John and I first discovered JonBenét's penchant for performing when she was three years old and participated in her first dance recital, held at the Boulder High School theater. Five little munchkins tap-danced as they sang "I Want to Hold Your Hand" by the Beatles. They were all so cute and knew the routine fairly well (and if they didn't, so what?). But JonBenét just beamed. I was sitting on the front row, and afterward several moms came up to me and said, "Where did JonBenét learn to do that?"

The truth is, she didn't learn that gusto and infectious smile anywhere. It just came from within. I knew how much she enjoyed performing, which reminded me so much of dance recitals I had been in as a child growing up in Parkersburg, West Virginia. It was a lovely place to grow up, as small towns usually are, the sort of place where most residents turned out for the junior varsity and the varsity cheerleading tryouts at the Field House. The city took pride in its children and seemed to care about them. The newspapers always included uplifting stories about local kids' activities. Whenever we had a championship competitor—be it a football team or a touring choir or a pageant contestant—the whole town supported the effort.

When Dianne Barnett, one of Parkersburg's own, was a candidate for Miss West Virginia on our hometown stage, we all felt a part of the excitement. Her younger sister, Jan, and I were junior high school friends. That year Dianne became Miss West Virginia and went on to Atlantic City to compete in the Miss America Pageant. On Labor Day weekend my group of girl friends sat up the night of the telecast, eating popcorn and crossing our fingers that Dianne would win. Phyllis George, Miss Texas, won that year, and we all giggled when her crown fell off her head as she walked down that famous runway. I was smitten.

Seven years later, I found myself walking down the same runway, listening to the refrain of "There she is, Miss America . . ."

sung off-key by the same Bert Parks. I didn't place in the finalists, but I did win a talent award to bring home to my family and friends. I was just happy and proud to be there representing my home state.

In 1993 I was invited back to the Forty-Ninth Annual Miss West Virginia Pageant in Clarksburg to help select the representative to attend the Miss America Pageant that year. Two weeks after that I was diagnosed with Stage IV ovarian cancer, and I was in for the fight of my life. At the time I didn't think it would be possible, but in June of 1994, I returned to the pageant's Fiftieth Anniversary Celebration and a reunion of former Miss West Virginias. I was bald from the chemo treatments, so I wore a wig. I was emaciated from losing so much weight, but I found a bright red beaded gown that only someone really skinny could wear, one side benefit to the chemo therapy. My sister Pam, who had been the 1980 Miss West Virginia, and I sang "A Gershwin Melody" under the spotlight. I had the time of my life and just thanked God that I was alive!

My little girl, who was only three-and-a-half at the time, was in the audience that night, and watched me just as I had watched Dianne Barnett years ago. JonBenét loved every moment of the performance and instantly wanted to be part of the fun. As a part of the show that evening, the president of the Miss America Pageant, Albert Marks, presented my parents with a special plaque of commendation for having sent two daughters to the national Miss America Pageant. Pam and I were only the third pair of sisters to have participated in the national event. In his remarks Mr. Marks said that he had met a little blonde angel in a pretty pink dress who looked to him like a future Miss America. He was talking about Jon-Benét.

Like her mom and Aunt Pam before her, JonBenét became star-struck. When we returned home to Colorado, she began begging to be in a pageant. I would hear JonBenét playing a new game she called "Presenting" with her friends. As the announcer had introduced each girl in the Miss West Virginia Pageant, he had told about her hometown, her background, and her interests, and he would finish by saying, "Presenting Miss So-and-So." Now, JonBenét wanted me to play the emcee. She would stand beside the door to the living room and give me the okay. Then I would say, "Preeeesenting Miss

JonBenét Ramsey." And she would jump out into the doorway. "Presenting" became JonBenét's favorite game.

In the summer of 1994 the Paughs held their family reunion in Charlevoix, a part of which was our annual family talent show. Good, bad, or indifferent—everyone had to perform on the makeshift stage on our back porch, overlooking Round Lake harbor. Little Jacob, my two-and-a-half-year-old nephew, performed his animal imitations—including the best pig oink you've ever heard. I sang my rendition of "Crazy" by Patsy Cline, and thought I was great until I realized that everyone was applauding and cheering because I was so bad. My sister Pam is really a singer, and she kept us all mesmerized with her gospel music. This time the applause was authentic. My cousin Debbie recited "Itsy, Bitsy Spider." Finally JonBenét and her cousin Jenny sang a duet, "I Was Raised on Country Sunshine." They looked so cute in their Daisy Mae cutoffs and pigtails.

Then JonBenét went upstairs and changed into another outfit so she could sing another song for everyone. And then another one. Nobody wanted to squelch her enthusiasm, but soon it was long past bedtime. Of course, she persisted. "Wait," she said, "I still have one other." This time she came down in the pretty pink dress she'd worn to the Miss West Virginia celebration and sang "Somewhere over the Rainbow."

That summer we bought her a karaoke machine at the Charlevoix K-Mart. She could sing along with the prerecorded music forever. You could make yourself appear to be a stage-ready performer, and that was just what JonBenét loved.

I noticed an ad in the Charlevoix newspaper promoting an upcoming Miss Charlevoix contest for girls of all ages. The two-day event was to be held at the East Jordan High School over the Fourth of July weekend. Pageants were still taking place on high school stages in small towns, just like the contest I'd been in nearly twenty years earlier in West Virginia. The event sounded tailor-made for JonBenét.

The pageant had a patriotic theme since it was held over the Fourth. When we arrived, we learned there were only two other little girls in JonBenét's age group. I remember her marching around the stage waving a little flag amidst twinkling red, white, and blue lights while the emcee sang "Proud to Be an American." She was proud to be part of the show with all the bigger girls. And I was proud of her. She was just beaming. JonBenét won the title of Little Miss Charlevoix, and now she was all fired up to do it again.

I decided if this was what she liked to do, then I would see if I could make it possible. I always worried that my cancer would return someday, so I was glad to have found an activity that we could have fun with together. Mother-daughter experiences were to be treasures for me, now more than ever before. If God did take me before she grew up, I reasoned, I could leave her these memories.

Children's pageants occur everywhere in the South; they are a regular part of many girls' upbringing. However, I had no idea of where to find such an event in Colorado, so I put the thought in the back of my mind.

In the spring of 1995 I was asked to be on the cover of a Boulder women's magazine that spotlighted local women who had been involved in the community in various ways. They wanted to run a story about my struggle with cancer, and I went to a photographer in Denver for the photo shoot. As the makeup artist was fixing my hair and makeup, she began telling me about her daughter's participation in pageants.

"I'd love to get some more information on that," I told her.

The woman stepped back and said, "Let me see what I can find out right now." Within minutes she had made a phone call and discovered that the Colorado All-Star Kids Pageant was coming up in a few weeks. "Here is the director's name and telephone number if you're interested."

I entered JonBenét at the last possible moment, and we were soon on our way to a contest. JonBenét was one excited little girl.

I called my mother in Atlanta because I didn't have any idea where to look for pageant dresses in Denver, and I didn't have much time to find out. The event became a family project. My youngest sister, Polly, had bought her wedding gown at a bridal shop in Marietta, which also had flower girl dresses and other dressy apparel for little girls. She knew they would find a party dress there. My mother and my other sister, Pam, were visiting Biloxi, Mississippi, and found a Mardi Gras costume shop. They brought back a white satin cape and collar that could be made into a Ziegfeld Follies costume, reminiscent of the one I had worn in the Miss West Virginia Pageant some twenty years earlier. Like mother, like daughter.

Finally the big day arrived. We were surprised to see JonBenét's picture on the cover of the program of the day's activities. I had mailed the photograph to the pageant as part of JonBenét's entry, but we never expected her to be featured on the program cover. Even though it was just a ten-page photocopied and spiral-bound pamphlet, you'd have thought that program was *Vogue* magazine, based on how excited we were! After all, we were the newcomers on the block; most of these girls had already been involved in these pageants throughout the year.

The event was held in a small ballroom of a Denver hotel where a stage had been erected in one end of the room. There were about sixty or so folding chairs set up theater style. At the back was a sound system, manned by an older gray-haired gentleman, most likely the grandfather of one of the participants.

The competition at the Colorado All-Star Kids State Pageant was divided into four age groups—four to six, seven to ten, eleven to thirteen, and fourteen and older—and the girls competed in four different categories: talent, party dress (the equivalent of the Miss America evening gown competition), sportswear, and costume.

JonBenét was the last one in the lineup because she was a late entry. There were four little girls in her group. I sat in a row near the front and watched the three girls ahead of her doing little turns and spins with the poise and polish that only comes with practice. *What's JonBenét going to do?* I worried. *She's never done this before.*

I underestimated her. Apparently she watched the three preceding contestants, and once she was on stage she was able to mimic them so well, she looked as if she'd been doing this all her life. In the sportswear competition she wore a little black jacket dress with a butterfly on it and a ruffly petticoat underneath. For the party dress category she wore a blue chiffon dress with a white bodice and matching white anklets, which Aunt Polly had sent from Atlanta.

John and Burke arrived just in time to watch her talent

presentation with the rest of us—Grandma and Grandpa, Aunt Pam, and me.

Again, the other little girls went first. One little girl, about three-quarters the size of JonBenét but about a year older, was performing tap dance steps I didn't learn until I was sixteen. I couldn't believe how good she was! JonBenét had resurrected her little patriotic tap dance from the Charlevoix contest, and performed it with her typical gusto.

The older girls were amazing as well. One young lady in an exquisite black velvet evening gown played a beautiful cello arrangement. As I watched her perform, I thought of the hours these contestants' parents had devoted to driving them to music and dancing lessons. It takes the support of good parents for children to perform that well. We read too often about kids and the malicious activities that occupy them. Instead, these girls were spending their afternoons and weekends developing a hobby that built confidence and poise and talent for their future. I knew JonBenét had found an activity that would benefit her throughout her life.

At the end of the pageant, while the judges were tallying the points and getting ready for the crowning event, the granddad operating the sound system played the Macarena. Most of the moms and grandmas, and some of the grandpas and dads and little brothers, joined the girls dancing and laughing on the stage. Then he played "Y-M-C-A," and we all waved our hands to the music. Everyone was enjoying the event with their children as they looked forward to the presentation of the awards.

And all the girls went home with a prize that day—most photogenic or best costume or biggest smile or prettiest eyes, as well as the prizes for placing in the four different categories. That was part of the program. Everybody wins at something, so everyone leaves feeling good about themselves. There were as many prizes as there were contestants. That day JonBenét won the award for cover girl. We should have known that when we saw the program cover, but we were too green at the time to know that was a category. She also received a trophy for the first runner-up in her age group. JonBenét was proud of herself. She came running back to me with her "hardware."

"That was fun, Mom," she said. "I want to do it again." And away she ran with one of her newfound friends.

That day we met Pamela Griffin. She mentioned that her daughter, Kristine, had been a pageant contestant since she was JonBenét's age. Kristine had won many national titles and now at eighteen was looking forward to someday being a contestant in the Miss America Pageant. Pamela said that Kristine coached the younger girls and choreographed their modeling routines. She offered to help JonBenét.

At times JonBenét was so eager to practice that she created her own pageants at home. Our house had a little eating area, just off the kitchen. Often we would be sitting around after dinner with the Whites or other friends, lingering over coffee, and JonBenét and Daphne White would go to JonBenét's bedroom and dress up in the costumes from her barrel-top trunk. Then they would reappear in the hallway by the dining area, which became a makeshift stage.

They demanded the undivided attention of the adults. They would not allow any talking. And we had to announce them, of course. "Now, ladies and gentlemen, preeesenting for your after-dinner entertainment JonBenét Ramsey and Daphne White." Their favorite duet was "Wouldn't It Be Loverly" from *My Fair Lady*.

If we started talking while they were performing, they would stop, put their hands on their hips, and give us a disgusted look. Then they would begin all over again.

In the next year JonBenét participated in a few more pageants, and won Miss Sunburst Colorado in one of them, which enabled her to go to the national three-day Sunburst Pageant in Atlanta during the summer of 1996. She knew that would be extra fun because Grandma and Grandpa and Aunt Pam and Aunt Polly would all be there.

Sunburst was a big national event. There were lots of categories in which to model—sportswear, fancy dress, party dress, active wear, western wear, costume, and beach wear—and about sixty girls in each age group from all over the country. Most of the videos that have appeared on television have come from this pageant because there were so many categories in which she competed.

The talent competition was also a big part of it. I ordered the videotapes from the previous year's event to get an idea of what it was all about. I was amazed at the obvious level of preparation that had gone into it. I decided that if we were going to nationals, we were going to be prepared. Between Pamela Griffin and Anna Zapp we made some great outfits for JonBenét. Anna was a dressmaker in Lafayette, Colorado, who typically made haute couture clothes and bridal gowns. She made a masquerade party dress out of black-and-white harlequin taffeta, and I completed the ensemble with shoes and a party mask. She was also able to fashion the sportswear Coco Chanel-style outfit from a sketch that Aunt Pam had drawn on a napkin. Anna always said she loved sewing for JonBenét because it was like making doll clothes.

Pam Griffin made the pink "cowboy sweetheart" costume out of some polyester fabric I bought in Atlanta for seven dollars a yard. Again, I doctored up the white cowgirl hat and boots. It was precious. Pam Griffin's entire basement was wall-to-wall with costumes, dresses, dance wear, and accessories. She also kept every color of sequins and rhinestones known to man in her sewing room. I will never forget how surprised I was to find all this stuff only a few miles from Boulder, where earth shoes and tie-dye T-shirts were still the norm.

That summer JonBenét went prepared, I could give her that. I couldn't give her the stage presence that God gave her. That was a gift.

For her talent she sang "Cowboy Sweetheart," a song chosen by Aunt Pam and Grandma from Grandpa's large selection of country music CDs. Kit Andre, who was Kristine Griffin's dance instructor, choreographed JonBenét's motions to the song. Where JonBenét excelled was in her expression. Her eyes and the smile on her face so captivated you, you didn't pay attention to what her feet were doing or how well she sang. JonBenét made the top ten, but did not make the cut to the top five.

After the close of the pageant, the director came up to us and said, "I was really surprised that somebody from Colorado was as prepared as you were. JonBenét is a beautiful and talented little girl." We both acknowledged that the southern girls were usually the best prepared since there were more pageants in the South to gather experience; many of these girls did this every weekend. In two years JonBenét participated in nine pageants. Only two of these were national pageants, an earlier Royale Miss and the Sunburst.

Many of these memories are painful now. We were having the time of our lives then. We both enjoyed every minute of it together and would probably be having fun with it today if she were still alive. JonBenét was looking forward to the day she could wear real evening gowns, just like her mother. I find myself smiling as I think back on those wonderful, happy times. I'm glad JonBenét found an activity she so enjoyed. She learned to win gracefully, accepting congratulations. She learned to lose in the same gracious way. John and I and our whole family were very proud to see her wear those crowns—and now she wears the most glorious crown of all, but one we selfishly hadn't wanted her to wear so soon.

8

THE PROMISED LAND?

In the fall of 1990, driving toward the majestic mountains looming in the distance, John and I felt a sense of excitement and anticipation as we made our way west on I-36. You can't help but feel exhilarated as the horizon comes closer and you realize what is really meant by "purple mountain majesties." It is awe-inspiring. And then, almost without warning, you reach the crest of the road, where it feels as if you are coming over the top of a gentle roller coaster. There it is. In the distance . . . the valley below. The promised land. Boulder, Colorado, nestled next to the foothills of the Rocky Mountains, just twenty-five miles northwest of Denver.

As I look back now, I realize that's how it happens really, doesn't it? You seem to be lulled toward the false sense of comfort of the promised land, not knowing what's really in store.

The regional computer products distribution business that John and my dad had started a few years earlier was at risk of being eaten alive by the larger, more financially powerful, national computer product distributors. Classic American capitalism—big guys grow and overtake the little guys. Unfortunately, we were the little guys. It was getting very difficult for little guys like us to compete in the market. Size meant efficiency. Efficiency meant lower costs. Our costs were running too high. *Better grow fast to save the little ship*, we thought. John and I were on our way to meet with our counterpart in the western region to try and figure out if we should put our two businesses together.

And there sat the promised land, just ahead in full sight. It had to be the right decision. How could anything this beautiful, this majestic have anything wrong with it?

We parked in the Walnut Street parking garage and made

our way down to the Pearl Street Mall. On this brisk fall day, the pedestrian parkway was in all its glory. This old western main street had been converted to allow for walkers only. Wandering minstrels, artists, lovers strolling, kids playing— and to top it off, the backdrop of the Flatirons, a massive out-cropping of the Rockies that God must have sculpted when he was experimenting with the Ice Age.

Due to the foresight of some Boulder leaders and citizens in the 1960s, the city had imposed stringent development re-quirements within the city limits, especially near the western boundary, which extended up into the beginning of the Rocky Mountains. The result? An unspoiled view of the face of the Rocky Mountains, as natural as it was a thousand years ago.

The sun was shining on Boulder that day, and the town seemed alive and filled with promise. We made our way past the book shops, coffee houses, and art studios on both sides of the mall until we reached our destination. The enigma among the artistic surroundings: Jim Hudson's computer company, Cad Distributors. It seemed an unlikely place for a computer distribution company, in the midst of such an eclectic group of shops.

The first tip-off that something was amiss in the promised land should have been when our corporate host mentioned that he noticed an "aura" around us as we lunched at the his-toric Hotel Boulderado. I wasn't exactly sure what an aura was, but it sounded good. In fact, everything seemed to be almost too good to be true. As it turned out—it was.

Lurking just south of God's handiwork, the Flatirons, was another giant outcropping of rock, referred to by locals as Devil's Thumb. A glimpse of Satan, just left of center, standing by waiting for the right moment to spring. Only his ugly thumb jutted out to taunt the innocents who barely noticed him be-cause they were gazing at the wondrous cloak of beauty called the Front Range.

John and Jim eventually put the two companies together along with a third, and Access Graphics was born. Then, in February of 1991, when the board of directors of Access Graphics asked John to take over the job of president, we were mentally ready to move our family to Boulder and start finding the right place to live.

Soon I began making numerous house-hunting trips to

Boulder each time John traveled there for his new duties. He had already rented an upstairs apartment at the corner of Nineteenth and Pearl Streets to stay in during the weeks he was in Boulder. The kids and I moved in along with my dad, who now was also working for Access. Every day, while John went to the office at the Pearl Street Mall, I would go out with Joel Ripmaster, our realtor.

The little town of Boulder had its own charm. Many places had a western flavor and most of the town was well preserved with a unique look; however, some parts of town were pretty rundown. Newer, larger houses were generally located a good distance from town. We really wanted to live in the town of Boulder proper; Atlanta suburban life had shown us the problem of having to spend hours and hours driving to go somewhere. By living inside Boulder's city limits, we would be able to take advantage of small town compactness. The problem was that most of the in-town houses were older and had not been taken care of over the years.

We must have looked at a hundred houses in the course of the next six months. Joel showed me everything from old worn-down shacks priced at several hundred thousand to the new big ones miles from town, which seemed to be out on the prairie. During our months of searching, we covered virtually everything that was on the market in Boulder. Joel would show me places that looked like they were ready to fall down. "They just need a little fixing up," he'd assure me, and then quote a selling price of four hundred thousand dollars. There was no yard, no trees, and junk cars parked in the next-door neighbor's side yard. I would come back to the apartment and cry. This was not Atlanta.

Southerners take great pride in their homes, entertain frequently, and go so far as naming them in some cases. I got the feeling that a Colorado home seemed mostly to be a place for a shower, a night's sleep, and then a quick exit to the next outdoor activity. Not a bad way of living, I suppose, just different from the way I'd been used to.

The people also seemed very different from southerners. Many Boulder public officials and citizens seemed to pride themselves in being on the cutting edge of progressive causes, like the environment, the welfare of the poor, China's human relations policies, independence for Tibet, and the rights of homosexuals, bisexuals, and transvestites. These people claimed to be very tolerant, but that tolerance only seemed to extend to those who held similar views.

I soon noticed there were no fur coats in politically correct Boulder. Capitalism was bad, and self-expression was good. People joked that the Boulder city council had a secretary of state for conducting its business, and people from Denver often referred to Boulder as the "Republic of Boulder, twenty square miles surrounded by reality." Almost every car had a bumper sticker with a message of some kind. But what a beautiful spot. We were seduced.

We had looked at 755 Fifteenth Street, located on University Hill, just four blocks from the Student Center of the University of Colorado, a couple of times with Ripmaster. The house was near Chautauqua Park, which had been established in 1898 as part of a then-popular movement to create areas where people could gather for the purposes of education, culture, and recreation. The movement took its name from Chautauqua Lake in New York state, where the concept originated. At the height of the Chautauqua movement, some twelve thousand sites scattered across the nation hosted orators, performers, and educators. Today, the park in Boulder thrives as the only Chautauqua west of the Mississippi River with its original buildings intact.

I could see us coming to the park for summer concerts. After we bought the house, we did, in fact, take Burke and JonBenét in their pajamas—with a bag of freshly popped popcorn—to the park's old auditorium to watch a silent movie or a Disney film.

The English Tudor house on Fifteenth Street was built in the 1920s. (We had seen pictures of the foundation being dug by a mule-drawn shovel.) Though the house was built on three narrow lots, there was not much room for a driveway in the front, so the garage was attached to the back of the house, facing the alley. Even though we weren't used to houses that were so close together, we conceded that this would give us a feeling of in-town living and security.

On one particular Saturday morning in the fall of 1991, we had biked from the apartment on Pearl Street to the University of Colorado football game. CU was losing miserably, as I recall, so we decided to ride up the hill to take another look at the Fifteenth Street place. The sun was shining, the leaves were golden yellow, and it was so neat to be able to bike to all these places! We came to the front door and let ourselves in. (John had seen the place so many times, he knew the lockbox code!)

We took another look at the empty house with stark white walls. For a while I stood in the living room, trying to picture our furniture and belongings in this house. *I can make this place into a home, but it will take a lot of work*, I thought. *It doesn't really matter where we live, just as long as we're all together.*

Suddenly John called out in a loud whisper. "Patsy . . . come quickly. In the dining room."

I hurried into the large room with triple windows spanning the side of the house.

John pointed out the window. "Look!"

My mouth dropped. Under an old fir tree in the backyard lay a huge buck deer with antlers I'm sure would excite the most experienced deer hunter. *Wow! This must be a sign. The buck stops here!* I thought. *I guess this must be the place for us.*

We made our offer, and after several exchanges back and forth, we purchased the house for more than the price we had sold our home in Atlanta for—and it certainly wasn't as nice. *Oh well, that's the price you pay for in-town quaint and charming,* we told ourselves. *It will just take a little fixing up here and there.*

The Boulder paper later published the selling prices of the highest-priced homes in Boulder that month, along with the buyers' names. Ours was the most expensive home sold during the period, and I was embarrassed and a bit upset that it was made public in the local newspaper. My first exposure to "privacy" in America.

The house was long and narrow and had three stories, plus a basement. Doors were everywhere, and old windows, some of which were original and opened inward, were held closed by a simple latch. Once we moved in, we realized that this was a real problem since we would often find the windows open after a typically strong Colorado wind. The original part of the house had steam heat, which I loved, and fine-grained oak floors. That old section had a lot of character, but the new addition was poorly done and needed lots of work.

On Thanksgiving Day 1991, I stood in the driveway of our Atlanta home, watching as all our worldly possessions were loaded into a big moving van headed west. It is a very unsettling feeling to see all your belongings strung out all over the front yard, as if someone has pulled the tablecloth out from under everything and sent it flying. Things that were arranged so lovingly inside now just sat in the driveway looking forlorn. My home was being uprooted and stuffed into a truck. Something made me feel uneasy about that. *Silly, isn't it,* I thought. *It's just for a little while,* I assured myself. *We'll be back to Atlanta soon enough. Besides, look at it as an adventure. We are going to explore the Wild West.*

The little "fixer-upper" on Fifteenth Street turned out to be a very costly, 6,500-square-foot sinkhole. The first thing we had to do was remove an elevator, which had been added in the center of the house, rising through all four stories and ruining each floor. It was fairly new, but it ran so slowly, you could fall asleep waiting for it. Another major problem was that there were no interior walls on the second floor of the original house; the previous owners had removed them. Only a lone wood-burning stove (and the elevator, of course) stood in the center of the open expanse. We quickly hooked up with architect Thomas Hand, who began to help us with the remodeling plans.

Our handyman's dream also turned into a remodeling nightmare. Before long, workmen were in our house from 7:00 A.M. until 5:00 P.M. every day for months on end. Ever try to keep a toddler out of the way of a remodeling project going on in virtually every room of the house? It's not easy, believe me. I was always concerned with keeping Burke and JonBenét safe around all the construction. Nails and saws and sheetrock dust were everywhere. All our belongings were heaped in the center of the living room and covered in plastic.

We spent the first Christmas at 755 Fifteenth Street with all five of our children. Beth, Melinda, and John Andrew flew out to be with us, and we went up to Eldora, the local ski area, because the kids loved to ski. I remember working with my cleaning lady, Regina, for an entire day, trying to make a little area of the living room presentable enough to celebrate Christmas morning there. We mopped up sheetrock dust as we both sneezed our heads off. Finally, I hung a few decorations for the holiday, even though the new carpet still wasn't down and plywood subfloor was everywhere. I placed a small artificial tree on the piano in the living room and positioned gifts around it.

That Christmas Beth and Melinda slept in what later became JonBenét's room. The girls kept catching their socks on the carpet tacks left on the floor from the old carpet, which had been pulled up the week before. The house was a wreck, but we were all together . . . for the last time, it turned out.

That year Beth gave me a birdbath and John some monogrammed towels for his new bathroom; we cherish those gifts to this day. Two weeks later she was killed in an automobile accident in Chicago. The Christmas holidays would never be the same again.

As Beth's father, I have a special place in my heart for her. She was our oldest daughter and my first child, born in the Philippines while I was serving as an officer in the Navy. Beth had a birth certificate from Olongapo City, probably the roughest liberty port in the world. I often wondered if she'd want to keep her birthplace a secret when she grew up. After all, who would brag about being born in Olongapo City? We moved back to the United States when she was about a year old and her life started as an American citizen.

When the other children came along, Beth became the spokesman for Melinda and John Andrew. She was a talker, a planner, and really cared about her dad.

When she was in grade school, Beth frequently invited me to have lunch with her at school. Her class ate lunch at 12:02, and it was always a big effort for me to leave work, rush to school, and get there exactly at the appointed time. One day I walked into the cafeteria a few minutes late. Beth was standing there, holding her tray, tears rolling down her face because she thought her dad had forgotten her. Once she saw me, everything was fine, but I realized then how much you can disappoint kids in little ways.

I always enjoyed going to Lake Lanier, just north of Atlanta, to look at the sailboats. I had wanted a sailboat for a long time, but never felt I could afford it. One particular Christmas, it was below zero in Atlanta, and after breakfast I looked around the table and asked, "Who wants to go to Lake Lanier today—and look at sailboats?"

Everyone but Beth looked at me as if I were crazy. After a short pause, Beth said, "I'll go, Dad," and off we went. That was Beth. She'd go with her dad anywhere, at any time, just to keep me company.

Beth and I used to laugh a lot because she had such a wonderful sense of humor. After college she became a flight attendant with Delta Air Lines and had a thousand funny stories about her flying experiences. She told how some passengers really take seriously the emergency instructions in the seat pocket and the flight attendant's spiel about the oxygen mask dropping down, etc. Sometimes a passenger a tad on the compulsive and fearful side would stop an attendant and ask further questions about emergency procedures.

One of the inside jokes among the flight attendants, though never played on anyone, was to answer, "Don't worry about it. You're in seat 13A, and no one's ever survived a crash sitting in seat 13A."

Beth probably learned her love of flying and traveling from me. She certainly enjoyed flying with me but, then again, most of the time she went with me simply to keep me company.

Beth always did well in school and was the captain of her high school cheerleading squad. I expected she would do well in college and wasn't disappointed. At Miami University of Ohio, Beth majored in finance and spent the summer of her junior year studying in Oxford, England. She was a Kappa Alpha Theta. Listening to her stories of college life always made me both happy and proud. Without reflecting much on the possibility, I simply assumed Beth would always be there, keeping an eye on me as I became an old man.

Beth cared. No surprise there. Beth's affections took a different turn. During her time at the university, I was taken back by the unexpected turn her affection took. Beth began to tell me about Dan Mudler, a fellow student she had fallen in love with. Dan had cystic fibrosis. As I saw their relationship turn into a real romance, Beth confided to me that Dan's prognosis wasn't good. She wanted to do everything she could to help his life be easier. Dan was a fine young man who was excelling in life despite a difficult burden.

If Dan wasn't feeling well, she'd be there to read to him or do whatever she could to help, including pounding on his chest to loosen the phlegm that gathered in his lungs. During Beth's senior year at Miami, Dan's condition worsened. I knew she felt the pressure to comfort and support him while continuing her own studies. Dan was too ill to attend school the next semester, so Beth frequently drove to his home near Cleveland to be with him.

One day I got a long-distance call in my Colorado office from Beth.

"Dad," she said and then started to cry.

"Beth? What's wrong?"

She struggled to talk. "Dad, I'm at Dan's. Would you come and be with me?" Her voice was breaking, and I knew something was very wrong.

"Of course," I answered, "but what's happened?"

"Dan is real bad, Dad."

I caught the next flight to Cleveland. When I got off the plane, Beth hugged me and cried.

"He's gone, Dad." That was all she could say. As we stood there with people brushing past, I remember thinking, *What a horrible burden for this young child to bear*. Such an early age to have to deal with the death of a person she loved so much. But I also knew that Beth had ministered to Dan in a way that made me profoundly proud of her.

That evening I sat with Dan's parents and tried to offer comfort. Cindy, Beth's mom, had arrived from Atlanta. I really didn't know what to say because it was the first time I'd ever been with a parent whose child had died. I felt a sense of the depth of their pain. We simply sat around their kitchen table and cried and prayed together.

Dan was buried on December 24, 1990. That night, Beth, Cindy, and I flew back to Atlanta. I could never have imagined that a year and two weeks later, the Mudlers would come to our side when Beth died.

It took a while, but Beth returned to her classes and finished her senior year. A year after graduation, she met another young man, Matt Darrington, at a Miami homecoming reunion. Before long, Matt was clearly becoming a deeply significant part of Beth's life.

I finally met Matt when he came to Atlanta in December 1991 for Melinda's debutante ball. Patsy and I liked him immediately; he clearly met our hopes and expectations for our old-est daughter. The two of them talked about Beth going with him to meet his parents in January, right after spending Christ-mas with us in Colorado. I could tell Beth was happy again.

Christmas 1991 came and went with the usual wonderful touch Patsy gave the holidays. Beth went to Chicago to meet Matt's parents on January 7, 1992. I was working in my office on January 8 when my brother, Jeff, called and told me about the car wreck.

I was so angry and in such shock that I didn't cry at that mo-ment. How could God let a beautiful, wonderful child die like this? How could there even be a God? My whole body wrenched and twisted in pain. My shock was so deep, the tears simply wouldn't come. I got my father-in-law, Don Paugh, to take me home because I couldn't even drive my car.

We left for Atlanta immediately. I called Skybird Aviation to arrange for transportation, and that's when I first met Mike Archuleta; he flew us back to Atlanta that night.

Jeff didn't have much information about the accident. Ap-parently Matt and Beth were on their way to a Chicago art museum just before lunchtime. The winter temperature was somewhere in the high thirties, and it had been raining. How-ever, the rain seemed to stop about the time that Matt pulled up the ramp to enter one of Chicago's freeways. For some rea-son, his car spun out of control, sliding in front of a truck that broadsided them.

Matt died at the crash scene, but Beth was airlifted to Loy-ola Medical Center, where the emergency room physicians fought to save her life. This beautiful twenty-two-year-old girl lay on the operating table while the doctors did everything possible to restore her vital signs. They could not. Months later, we had the opportunity to speak to these good men and thank them for their efforts to save our daughter. As we talked, they obviously were still upset that they hadn't been able to save her.

When Patsy and I saw Beth at the Mayes-Ward-Dobbins Funeral Home, I cried uncontrollably with grief. As we quietly prayed together, I suddenly felt an overwhelming sense that she was okay. I didn't have to worry about her. I truly believed Beth was in heaven now, still worrying about me . . . as she al-ways had.

At the service, I saw one of Beth's college friends who was obviously grief stricken. I went over and hugged her. "It's okay. Beth is all right," I repeated several times. I think I had come to the turning point where I realized that rather than being angry with God, I knew he was truly taking care of Beth. I could release her into his care.

At the time of Beth's death, our family did not have a burial plot. It's not something you think you'll need for a while. Patsy and I, together with Cindy, visited a few cemeteries in the area, and became quite depressed. You could only use a certain kind of flower pot, you couldn't have a headstone bigger than a certain size, you could only visit on certain days— so many rules governed these places of rest.

When we returned to Cindy's home that afternoon, exhausted, a friend from her church suggested we look at St. James Episcopal Cemetery in Marietta. We called and learned that one little area was still available in this old cemetery, a plot right under an old dogwood tree. When we saw it, we knew it was perfect for Beth.

Patsy knew that the cemetery would look desolate in the winter, so before the funeral she called a landscaper we had used when we lived in Atlanta. She asked him to plant azaleas and put flats of pansies and fresh pine straw around the area. We buried Beth there, and after months of consideration Cindy and I decided on this epitaph:

ELIZABETH PASCH RAMSEY
BETH
JULY 15, 1969
JANUARY 8, 1992
Beloved Daughter, Beautiful Sister, Loyal Friend
Gone before us in life's journey, now guide us
To our eternal reunion.

In the months after Beth's death, the very foundations of my faith were tested to the core. I couldn't have imagined the pain I felt over losing Beth. As the shock subsided, I allowed the tears to flow. In the end, I desperately wanted the hand of God to soothe the pain and ease the loss. As the days went by, my anger turned into pure grief, and with it, frequent crying.

Patsy remembers waking up in the middle of the night and

realizing I wasn't in bed beside her. Then she would hear a moaning, an agonizing wailing like I was in physical pain. I had thought I wouldn't bother her from my study, beside our bedroom. She would lie there silently and pray, *Dear God, what should I do? Should I go to him?* Yet she realized that I had to work through this grief myself. She could only provide a quiet, safe place.

I read voraciously everything I could find on Christianity and life after death, not only to try to make sense out of Beth's death but also to understand the broader spectrum of what life means. Some books gave me instant hope; others had a more long-term message, deepening my faith and broadening my insight into the Christian faith. In such an evolution, I believe there's a point where one steps over a line and all doubts are left behind. You know and understand the truth of what God has done through human history and you grasp his plan for the future through his son, Jesus Christ. I think I finally crossed that line forever, but only after JonBenét's death almost five years later.

One thing I learned after Beth died is that many people carry heavy burdens that the rest of us may not know anything about. I was amazed at the number of people who would come up to us and say, "I know your pain. I've lost a child." Employees, people in our church, neighbors, ministers, and business associates had experienced similar tragedy.

Now, when I look back across these past several years, I know that Beth's death strengthened my faith and softened my character. The very foundations of what I believed in were tested as never before. As my mind cleared and became more focused, I knew that I wasn't personally capable of helping myself get through this loss and that I needed help from somewhere else. I needed help from God.

So many times Patsy and I have thought about the poem titled "Footprints," where a man dreams he is walking in the sand, and scenes from his life flash by. In each scene he notices two sets of footprints in the sand, one belonging to him, the other to the Lord.

Finally, at the end of his dream, he looks back at the footprints and notices that many times, during the very lowest and saddest times of his life, there was only one set of prints in the sand. His question was my question after Beth's death: "Lord,

I don't understand why, when I needed you most, you would leave me."

The Lord's answer to this man was equally relevant to me: "During those times, when you see only one set of footprints, it was then that I carried you."

By the end of 1992, I realized that the Lord had been with me too—from the moment my brother first called with the news. Now the tears only come when I am sitting alone in an airline seat, looking ahead with nothing else on my mind except my loved ones. I see the flight attendants and remember Beth. I carry her Delta flight attendant wings with me at all times.

Beth's death was an accident, but JonBenét was purposely killed by another human being, and that made everything much worse. I had thought losing Beth was the burden God expected me to carry. Even though that load was almost impossible to bear, my faith had become stronger and I could stand with greater strength. Now I was given the loss of Jon-Benét to carry as well.

As I struggled to understand how an all-powerful God could allow the murder of a child, I pondered a statement that someone made to me. I've forgotten where it came from, but the person said, "When we weep, God weeps with us." I began to understand that although good and evil exist in this world, God is not the author of evil. One of the heavenly Father's children died when JonBenét was killed, and that hurt his heart as deeply as it did mine. Slowly a powerful thought took shape, and I started to know that in the deaths of both Jon-Benét and Beth, God grieved with me. And they were safe in his loving arms.

One of the most comforting thoughts I had after losing two children was that each one knew how much we loved her. At the time of their deaths, there was no question about that. Nothing was left undone or unsaid between us. Not a day went by that I didn't tell my children, "I love you." We shared the deepest parental-child affection possible.

Beth's death helped me get "today" in the proper relationship to "tomorrow." I'd always been a careful planner with my five-year and ten-year master plans tucked away in my hip pocket. But after Beth's death, I could see how foolish it was to live in the future. All I really have is this moment, now.

I know that death and tragedy often destroy marriages, but the two deaths in my life have only increased my love for Patsy. She often tells me that she doesn't know what she'd do if she didn't have me to lean on. Our moods do seem to compensate so that when I'm down, she's up, and vice versa. I know exactly what Patsy's gone through in the loss of these two children and how much she grieves. Our mutual grief has bonded us at the most vulnerable point that human beings share. We are stronger together than we could ever be separately. Walking hand in hand through these terrible crises has bonded our souls in a unique way.

Today when Patsy and I think of Boulder, we can still see the beautiful majesty of the purple mountains and feel the crispness of the fall air, but we also see that outcropping of Devil's Thumb more clearly. The beauty of the Rockies remains, but we must forever remember this as the place where we learned the hardest lessons of life and the true meaning of evil.

9

THE SHADOW OF DEATH

The tragedy of JonBenét's death was foreshadowed not only by Beth's death but also by my own struggle with ovarian cancer. In June 1993 I served as one of the judges for the Forty-Ninth Miss West Virginia Scholarship Pageant. As I was getting dressed for the final night's events, I noticed that my evening gown wouldn't zip up quite as easily as it had when I tried it on before packing. I could hardly suck in my tummy enough to get the zipper to meet.

Hmm, I thought to myself. *Must have eaten a little too much this week.* I managed to squeeze into my dress that night, but just barely.

After the conclusion of the week-long pageant, we left Clarksburg, West Virginia, and flew to Hyannis Port, Massachusetts, to visit with some Boulder friends who were vacationing nearby. We had a great time exploring Cape Cod, but privately my stomach was still worrying me.

By the following Wednesday, the distension of my abdomen became even more apparent. At the end of our stay in Massachusetts, we flew on to Charlevoix to spend a few days at our summer cottage, which we had just started renovating. There I made a hasty trip to the local K-Mart to buy a pair of maternity pants. My stomach had grown that big in seven days' time.

Something had to be wrong! I called my mom in Atlanta. "I don't know what's going on," I said. "But I look like I'm pregnant." I found out later that she had immediately called my sister Polly, who is the medical guru in our family. She always reads medical information in magazines and encyclopedias. Both she and my mom began wondering if my symptoms signaled some kind of cancer.

The next day my stomach seemed even larger, so I went to the emergency room of Charlevoix Community Hospital.

I told the doctor about the distension and he examined me. Then he asked, "Could you be pregnant, Mrs. Ramsey?"

"No . . . impossible. My husband has had a vasectomy," I replied.

"Is it possible that your stomach has actually been getting larger for quite a while, and you just haven't noticed it?"

"No," I said again. "That's not the case. This is something unusual."

After this initial examination, the doctor performed a couple of tests, which included drawing blood. I spent four hours at Charlevoix Community that night, while several ER doctors tried to figure out what was wrong with me. Finally the original doctor came into the examining room, with a perplexed look on his face. "We can't be sure what is wrong with you, Mrs. Ramsey," he said. "This could be a bowel blockage, but we're just not sure."

He told me I could go home, but said to return if my symptoms persisted or became worse.

And they did. Prior to all this, I had been seeing an internist in Boulder for the terrific pain I'd been having in my neck and shoulders. She had recommended Advil for the pain and sent me first to an orthopedist, then to a chiropractor, and eventually to a physical therapist. I'd been through all the usual procedures, such as the therapist putting a weight on my neck to stretch it and release the pressure, but nothing had helped my pain. Finally I had insisted that this doctor do an MRI.

"That's awfully expensive," she had cautioned me.

"At this point, I don't care about the expense," I said. "I can't leave for the summer without knowing the source of this pain."

So the doctor ordered an MRI to be taken from my breastbone down to just below my lungs. Nothing was found. I left Boulder without an answer for my severe pain. Later I learned that if the MRI had only extended a few inches lower, it would have picked up the large tumor developing on my ovary. The tumor was pressing on a nerve and sending "referred" pain to my neck and shoulders.

Now, about a month after that MRI, the distension in my stomach could not be ignored. On Friday, July 2, I went back to the Charlevoix Community Hospital emergency room. This time the hospital called in a retired surgeon to examine me.

He still couldn't figure out what was wrong, so I said, "I am leaving to go to Boulder tomorrow. Please type up everything you have done to me during the last two days so if I go to a hospital there, they will not have to repeat the same tests." It was 1:30 in the morning before I left the hospital.

The next morning, at the last minute, we decided to fly to Atlanta for the Fourth of July holiday, instead of going back to Boulder. When we walked into the kitchen of my parents' home that Saturday afternoon, my mother took one look at me and said, "Oh my, what's happened to you, Patsy!" She muttered something to herself and then said, "Which hospital shall we go to?"

Her response shook me, and I knew that my problem must be serious. We told John to go ahead and take Burke and Jon-Benét to the fireworks display at the Capital City Country Club; we would meet him there after Mom and Dad and I stopped by the hospital. My sister Polly, who was seven months pregnant at the time, also came with us.

I hadn't been alone in the emergency room at Northside Hospital very long when the doctor returned.

"Mrs. Ramsey," he began professionally, "I know that my diagnosis will not be a comfort to you, but I think an exploratory procedure is demanded immediately."

I frowned. "What are you suggesting?"

"With the swelling I've observed, I believe a vaginal sonogram is needed at once."

"You're sure?" My voice rose as I spoke.

"Absolutely," he answered. He was not smiling.

"Okay, but my husband and children are waiting for me at the fireworks show," I muttered. "Will it take very long?"

During the humiliating process, in which they insert a wand into the vagina, I tried to keep calm, but it was almost impossible. Two technicians kept watching a screen and talking to each other. I squirmed uncomfortably.

"We're going to transfer you to a larger observation room," one of the technicians finally told me. "Do you have a local doctor?" he asked.

I nodded my head yes. "My obstetrician is part of the OBGYN of Atlanta."

I know God puts you in the places you need to be at the right time, and I could see that he had done so now. I had been complaining about my pain for five months in Boulder, been to the hospital in Charlevoix twice, and none of the doctors had been able to successfully diagnose my problem. We had almost returned to Boulder, but instead had come to Atlanta. We were much better off here, where my parents could help with the children, where the doctors were familiar to us (I had delivered both Burke and JonBenét in this same hospital), and where we had friends who were medical people. I believe this was the first divine intervention in my cancer experience. God knew I had a problem and that I needed to be in Atlanta to take care of it. But at this moment I was not really ready for what was waiting on the horizon.

Not long after the sonogram, Dr. Tom Modi, who was from OBGYN of Atlanta and was on call at the hospital that night, came into my room. Although Dr. Modi had not delivered my children, I had seen him several times during my obstetrical visits. I was so glad to see a familiar face.

Dr. Modi sat down and tried to prepare me for the worst. "There is a large mass on your left ovary," he said. "We're calling in an oncologist."

"Oncologist?" I gasped. "Doesn't that mean cancer?" I started to panic.

"We don't take any chances. It could be nonmalignant, but we won't know until we operate," he said soberly.

My parents and Polly looked at each other as if to say, "That's what we were afraid of." I asked my dad to call Dr. Gil Kloster, a plastic surgeon in Atlanta who was a close family friend. Another intervention of the hand of God—Gil was at home and only moments from the hospital. Once Dad had him on the phone, I asked to speak to him myself. I begged him to come over right away to help decipher my situation.

Gil came immediately and was there when Dr. Burrell, the oncologist, began to explain what he wanted to do. "We don't know if the tumor on your ovary is malignant or not, but we're going to go to surgery on Monday. If it's not malignant, we will remove the mass and leave everything else intact. If it is malignant, we will do a complete hysterectomy, which will take six or seven hours.

"I'd also like to do a colonoscopy. If it is cancer, I want to be sure it hasn't metastasized into your colon. We'll do that tomorrow."

"Oh great!" I blurted. "What's going to happen to me? Will I be dead in a year, or what?" Silence. There are no promises in medicine, I've learned.

The doctors tried to reassure me, but I was shaken to my foundations, and my mind started racing through a thousand alternatives. Most of all, I was horrified to confront John with this condition. He certainly didn't need me being sick; he was still reeling from Beth's death.

"My poor husband," I kept crying. "My poor husband doesn't need *this*!"

That Saturday night I was admitted into the hospital. On Sunday morning, when I was supposed to be watching my stepdaughter Melinda run the Peachtree Road Race, I was instead getting ready for the colonoscopy. Like a saint, my dear friend Carole Simpson was at my bedside coaxing me to drink this horrible white creamy barium liquid, which was necessary to light up my insides so the doctors could take a look around. The examination was no picnic, but it had to be done.

By the time I went into surgery on Monday morning, the doctors knew that the colon was not affected. *That's one down*, I thought. *Now if the tumor is not malignant, I'm home free.* I would know the outcome when I woke up; the doctor had told us that if the mass was benign, the surgery wouldn't last very long—just in and out.

The operation began early Monday morning, July 5, 1993, and took most of the day. I remember waking up in the recovery room that afternoon, trying to focus on the hands of the clock mounted on the wall. Nearly 3:00 in the afternoon. *Guess it was malignant*, I thought to myself. Obviously they had removed my ovaries and performed a radical hysterectomy.

Here I was, a thirty-six-year-old woman with two small children to raise—and I had ovarian cancer. A chill ran up my spine. Now what would I do? I tried to find something positive about my plight. The only up side I could figure was that I would now go through menopause with its incredible hot flashes almost instantaneously, instead of the six months or so it usually takes. John was wonderful. He brought in an oscillating fan to help cool me down during the hot flashes; my mother worried that the fan would give me pneumonia.

By the time I returned to my mother's house, I had received

many gifts and cards. Linda McLean, my high school teacher, sent the dearest remembrance of all—a brown stuffed teddy bear, with a lovely card. "Bears," she wrote, "are so important they even made it into the Bible: 'Love bears all things, believes all things, hopes all things.'" I later sent this cuddly bear back to Linda when her husband was diagnosed with cancer in 1995. And then Linda returned the bear to me in 1997 after JonBenét died. The bear now sits in JonBenét's child-size antique Victorian chair in our living room; she had picked out the chair for herself at an antique shop in Boulder.

John and Gil Kloster researched where I might go to get the best chemotherapy treatments following the surgery. Gil knew of experimental trials being conducted at the National Institutes of Health (NIH) in Bethesda, Maryland, because his son's mother-in-law, Peggy Fairchild, was undergoing chemo there at the time. She had been diagnosed with the same kind of cancer in this same hospital, only six months earlier.

Sadly, Gil's first wife had died of breast cancer while they were living in Boulder, Colorado, many years before. His recommendation, based on first-hand experience, was that the best chance to overcome cancer is to hit it hard during the first attack. Gil made some calls to see about the possibilities of my going to NIH, where I would be taking the most potent drugs available; he was concerned that we might not get a second chance.

At the same time John thoroughly researched other ovarian protocols at other medical facilities around the country. He waded through databases of information, assisted by a lot of the folks at Lockheed. Ultimately, we made the decision to try NIH because they were experimenting with three of the best drugs in combination and at very high dosage levels. Exactly two weeks after my hysterectomy, we were sitting in the waiting room of the Twelfth Floor Clinic in Building 10 of the National Cancer Institute in Bethesda, Maryland, a division of the National Institute of Health.

NIH is a massive facility, and after trying to work our way into the system, John had finally realized that the National Cancer Institute worked just like the navy. The clerks and secretaries, just like the enlisted men and chiefs, know how the place runs, not the doctors. As soon as he figured that out, he went to work and we were quickly put on the appointment schedule for the ovarian cancer experimental treatment program.

I remember feeling so weak, I was slumping in my seat when a concerned nurse came over and asked if I'd like to lie down in one of the examining rooms. I gratefully accepted and began to cry as she helped me onto the hospital bed.

"I'm so frightened," I told her. "What will it be like?"

She looked at me with compassionate eyes and said, "Well, it's not going to be easy. But this is the best place in the world for you to be right now."

"But I have two small children at home who need me," I cried.

"Well," she said, "they are going to need you for a long time, so you'll have to do everything you can to get well."

The nurse calmly told John and me that if I were accepted into the experimental program, I would come to the clinic every three weeks to undergo chemotherapy treatments. The protocol for this experimental program called for a combination of Taxol, Cytoxan, and Cisplatin—all drugs that had been used previously in ovarian treatment, but not in this combination, and not in such heavy doses.

Shortly after she left, another nurse called me into another examination room. Soon the doctor appeared and began to give me a physical examination. At one point he was feeling for the lymph glands along my collarbone. He paused momentarily with a quizzical look on his face. Then he touched that area again. "I think I'll call for the lab to come aspirate this node," he said.

"What for?" I wanted to know.

"Oh, just checking," he replied. The doctor left the room.

In a few minutes a technician ran the test, leaving with the samples to be examined in the laboratory. Then, after the inspection was made, the doctor returned to the exam room.

"The cancer has spread to your lymph nodes," he said. "This means that you are at Stage IV, rather than Stage III, as they told you in Atlanta."

My heart pounded and my breathing became shallow. I panicked. All I could think of was that Grandma Janie had always said, 'If it's in the lymphs, you're a goner!' Later I learned that Stage IV ovarian cancer has a 95 percent fatality rate within five years.

The doctor paused before he went further; he could see the tears running down my cheeks, but he knew I'd want to know everything, so he finally continued. "There's also a tumor about the size of a golf ball behind your pelvic bone," he said. "It may have developed since your surgery."

I wiped the tears from my eyes and tried to sound somewhat normal. "Then let's get it out of there."

"Don't worry," the doctor said. "We'll use it as a tumor marker. We'll measure that mass on the CT scan and then we'll watch how it's affected by the chemotherapy. Each time we do a new scan we will measure it. If the chemo is working, the tumor will shrink."

I had been crying throughout the doctor's diagnosis, but now I broke down completely. John tried to calm me, but I knew he was afraid too. The attending physicians, Drs. Eddie Reed and Elise Kohn, came in, along with Pat Davis, the head RN for the program. They also tried to help me deal with what I'd heard. They said I would be a good candidate for the program and asked us to sign a lot of papers. I knew of nothing else to do but follow their instructions. They tried to allay my fears by saying that the chemotherapy would attack the cancer wherever it was in my body, even the lymph nodes, by traveling throughout the entire bloodstream.

"It doesn't matter whether you're Stage III or IV," Dr. Eddie Reed reassured me. "We will give you the very same drugs."

"If it's going to work for you, it will work everywhere the cancer exists," Dr. Kohn added.

They handed John a file, full of paperwork, and me a brown plastic container that I was supposed to urinate in for the next twenty-four hours. We were free to go to a hotel until the next day, but I felt drained and terrified.

Free to go? Go where? What in the world were we supposed to do now? Here we were in a strange town, and I had just been told I might die. I was coming unglued, but John, always the voice of reason and calm, had a plan. He put me in the rental car, and we headed toward Annapolis, Maryland. Since we had a free evening, we might as well stay someplace nice, he thought. We checked into a lovely historic hotel and I plopped down on the bed, exhausted. John quickly turned to the phone to call the office and return some messages. Always the CEO. Always worrying about his responsibilities. He was going to carefully manage every aspect of my disease in the same way he directed Access Graphics.

I stared at the ceiling, missing Burke and JonBenét so much. They didn't deserve to have a mother with cancer! Before I started to cry again, I reached for the Gideon Bible on the nightstand. (I had never looked at one of those motel Bibles before.) I opened it and pointed randomly to the first verse I came to. I looked down and read Psalm 57. "In the shadow of Your wings I will make my refuge, / Until these calamities have passed by."

I reread the passage. *"Calamities" is right!* I thought. I read the passage a third time. Now I realized that the words were telling me that the calamities would someday pass by, be over with, gone. I couldn't believe my eyes. These lines had to be a message from God. A sense of strength and the presence of the divine settled around me. I went to sleep, knowing my problem was in the right hands after all, the hands of my heavenly Father.

I took my first chemo treatment at National Institutes of Health on July 27, 1993. I had just gotten plugged in to everything in the intensive care unit when the phone rang in my small room. Suzanne Savage, our baby-sitter from Colorado, who was taking care of Burke and JonBenét at my parents', was calling to say that my sister Polly had gone into premature labor that morning and delivered a baby boy. He was in intensive care at Kennestone Hospital in Marietta, Georgia, but would soon be transferred to the Scottish Rite Children's Hospital for observation.

I thanked her for calling and asked about the kids. She said, "They keep asking when Mommy is coming home." *That's a question I'd sure like an answer to myself,* I thought.

I hung up the phone and tried to untangle the maze of wires and tubes around me so I could look up the telephone number for a florist. I wanted to send Polly some flowers and a balloon. I just knew she had gone into labor because she was so upset about my cancer. I closed my eyes and repeated, "In the shadow of your wings I shall seek my refuge, until these calamities have passed by."

*   *   *

The first chemotherapy treatment took thirty-six hours. Afterward, I was transferred to the oncology unit in 6 East. A vase with a single red rosebud was waiting on my bedside tray. I was surprised and puzzled.

"I thought you might need a little cheering up," a sweet voice from the bed next to mine said. "I'm Peggy Fairchild. Gil Kloster's son is married to my daughter. I guess I'm part of the reason you're here . . . We're going to be roomies for a couple of days."

"Oh, Peggy! You're so sweet—you sent the rose!"

She beamed. "I'm glad you like it. Don't worry. The first chemo is a real doozy, but have faith. It gets a little easier. This is my last one. I've been coming here every three weeks for nine months. You're going to make it."

I smiled. I was so sick, though, I could scarcely talk. I managed to whisper a puny "thank you" and fell asleep. When I awoke, John was by my bed, patting my hand, trying to make everything all right. "You get to leave as soon as you feel like it," he encouraged me.

The mere thought of lifting my head from the pillow made me nauseous. I couldn't bear the idea of getting on an airplane. I rolled over, moaned, and felt as if I were dying. But by Saturday, I was able to get on an airplane and fly back to Boulder. The first step in my ordeal had passed.

Each step in the nine-month process was arduous and painful. The trauma was so staggering that I prayed continually for the hand of God to touch me and return me to wholeness. I immediately lost all my hair, and my body deteriorated. During this ordeal I was to meet other wonderful people who were also struggling to survive the identical agony. One very special person was Howard Early from Kentucky. He and I talked and wrote letters, and I tried to give him the hope I had found.

Vicki Chabol was my regular roommate for most of my treatments. My mother and I accompanied Vicki to the NIH hospital chapel where Rev. Fitzgerald baptized her and she received Jesus as her Lord and Savior. She often spoke of her son, Justin, and how much she loved him.

My impromptu ministry proved to be meaningful, I think, to these new friends and certainly to me.

Every three weeks I traveled from Boulder to Bethesda to

continue the chemotherapy treatments. On Monday the NIH doctors would examine me to check on how I was progressing, then on Tuesday morning the chemotherapy treatment began and continued through Thursday afternoon. The treatments consisted of all these chemicals being fed into a Porta-cath tube that had been surgically implanted in my chest. As soon as the treatment was over, I would get on an airplane and return to Boulder, usually on Friday, where the struggle for life *really* began.

I stayed in John Andrew's bedroom, because the bathroom was only about six steps from the bed. The bathroom in our master bedroom on the third floor was the entire length of the house away from our bed, and too far for comfort.

By Monday following the week of chemotherapy, I would have to check my temperature every thirty minutes; if it started to rise, that signaled an infection in my system. Everyone who came into my room wore a surgical mask—and I wore one myself. JonBenét and Burke could stand at the doorway of my room, but I couldn't hug them as I desperately wanted to do. Since most of my white blood cells had been killed by the chemotherapy, I had virtually no defense against even minor infections. The steadily rising temperature meant that I had to be rushed to Boulder Community Hospital to battle the infection. The doctors would immediately pack me in ice to force the temperature down, and begin intravenous antibiotics. Then we waited. The painful battle was on full tilt for at least the next eight days while my white blood cells multiplied.

John would bring JonBenét, who was three at the time, to the hospital and she'd sit on my bed. One day I remember her coming while I was having a blood transfusion to raise my white blood cell count. JonBenét squeezed the little crimson bag and followed the tube that ran up my arm and disappeared under my hospital gown to the Porta-cath in my chest.

"Where's that going, Mommy?" she asked.

"Into my body," I answered.

"That's going to your heart!" JonBenét sounded exuberant. "It's going to make you feel much better!"

That gave me the extra charge of energy I needed to keep going. The love flowing into my heart from my children was more important than the transfusion to the success of my treatment. Burke and JonBenét came to visit as much as possible and didn't seem to mind coming to the hospital to see their mom all wired up.

Often my dad would help them make cookies in the small oven in the visitors' waiting room. The hospital kept cookie dough in the refrigerator for just that purpose. It's amazing how a freshly baked cookie can lift your spirits.

One morning I was feeling extremely depressed. I knew I was staring death in the face. I wanted to be mad at somebody for doing this to me, and the only one I could think of was God. I saw my children, my babies who were only three and six at the time, as a gift from God. What an ugly trick to give me this wonderful gift, only to let me die a few years later and leave them without a mother. I felt betrayed and I told God so.

That night Burke and JonBenét came to see me in the cancer ward, and we had pizza in the little family waiting room. Afterward the kids made cookies with their grandpa as usual. At the end of their visit, I walked them down the hall toward the elevator. It was cold outside, and JonBenét was bundled up in a puffy pink coat and little white snow boots. They were giggling as they raced down the hall to see who could get to the elevator first to push the button.

We called JonBenét the "up girl." That nickname came from the times we'd get on an elevator; JonBenét always rushed to push the up button. She would run ahead, jump on the elevator, and say, "I want to push the up button. I'm the up girl." Boy, was she ever the "up" girl.

We ended up splitting the button-pushing job fifty-fifty between Burke and JonBenét. By default, Burke became the person starting us in the opposite direction. Sometimes we'd go up when we wanted to go down because JonBenét always went first.

I stood there in my robe and bedroom slippers, my terry cloth turban on my bald head, and thought, *Thank heaven they have no idea how serious this is. I dearly wish I could go home with them tonight.*

I went back to my room and lay in my bed crying. Soon I felt as if the Lord were saying, *Those babies are your reason to live. Get up and get with it.* Just as he had told Job, "Gird up your loins," he told me to get up and live.

I thought, *You're right . . . We're going to beat this together. God and me and the chemo.*

During the three weeks at home between each chemotherapy treatment, my local oncologist, Dr. Pat Moran, was struggling to keep me alive until my white blood cell count got back to normal and I could return to NIH for the next phase of my treatment. I would take chemo for a week, I would usually be in Boulder Community Hospital for a week, and then the third week I would manage to get well enough to be at home. Usually I would lose about fifteen pounds. I gave myself two shots of GCSF, a bone marrow stimulant, every day for fourteen days after the chemo. Slowly my ability to taste returned and my appetite increased. Just about the time I felt better again, the next cycle of my chemotherapy started!

My mother or John usually made the trips to Maryland with me, while Suzanne Savage helped with the children. Each time, the journey was arduous and tough. On Thursday afternoon, after the chemotherapy treatment, Mom would wheel me out of the hospital, white skinned, bald headed, and sick. I was in bad shape for traveling back to Denver—a four-and-a-half-hour airplane ride; I really needed to be lying down.

Mom would start praying for an empty seat next to me on the airplane so I could lie down for the trip back. We'd reach the ticket agent and be told, "We're sorry, but all the seats are full." Yet, as I boarded the airplane someone would move, or something would happen to cause a seat next to me to open up. On every trip I was able to fly lying down!

After the first two chemo treatments, I felt very weak, and my hope for recovery was pretty dim. Then a remarkable event changed my life.

After we had come back to Colorado following Beth's death in 1992, John had found the liturgy at St. John's Episcopal Church very comforting. We began attending there regularly. The services reminded him of going to worship with his mother when he was a child, and I was glad to be in a place that meant so much to him. I came to love the worship at St. John's and found the quiet, prayerful atmosphere touching my deepest needs. Here was a place I expected to feel the Holy Spirit at work.

One of my dearest friends at St. John's was always praying with me during my physical struggles and encouraging me to endure. One night after my second cycle of treatment, she called with a special purpose.

"Father Rol and I want to have a healing service for you," she announced. "We think something good can happen."

"What's a healing service?" I asked.

"Trust me on this one," my friend answered. "I talked it over with Father Rol, and he wants to have the service in your home, preferably in your bedroom with just a few close friends."

I hesitated a moment but knew this must be something good. When you have cancer, you embrace any chance for a cure. If there was a possibility I was missing, then I was ready to buy in. "Okay," I agreed, "come over whenever you can."

As best I can remember, Father Rol and a few of my friends came to visit on September 14, 1993. My mother and John were there, as well as Patty Novack, Roxy Walker, Lori Smith, and my friend and her husband. We gathered in a little sitting area in our master bedroom. Father Rol and Roxy sat on the sofa. Two people pulled up an ottoman and a desk chair. Others knelt on the floor or stood behind me. I settled back anxiously.

Father Rol began reading from Isaiah 53. He explained to me that as Jesus Christ walked to Calvary, he was lashed and beaten; those stripes on his back were for our sickness and healing. Then, as Christ hung on the cross dying for our sins, the agony that he endured there was also for the health of the entire human race. For the first time in my life, someone told me that both physical and emotional healing are extended to us through the pain and agony that Christ absorbed during his last hours on Earth.

A light bulb went on in my head and I realized what was happening in this little service in my bedroom. The Bible said there will be "laying on of hands," and I was about to receive this ministry. As I sat in a little black cane-bottomed chair, with my head covered by a turban to conceal my baldness, Father Rol, John, my family, and friends gathered around me. They laid their hands on me and began to pray, and the warmth of the Holy Spirit's presence settled over me. I felt the healing touch of Jesus Christ working in my body.

Two days after that, before I returned to NIH for my third treatment, I had a CT scan. I asked the doctors to check the size of the golf-ball tumor that remained in my pelvic area. Had it shrunk as we hoped?

The doctor shook his head in amazement. "The tumor is gone," he told me.

I was so overwhelmed, I called the doctor at the National Institutes of Health and asked if it was necessary for me to come back for chemo. "It's gone," I told him. "I don't need the treatments. God has healed me!"

After a long pause of silence, the doctor on the other end of the telephone finally answered. "Even if it's gone, we need you to go through the full treatment process. There's always a chance that some minute cancer cells are still there, which haven't shown up on the CT scan. You signed up to be a participant in this experimental protocol, and it calls for eight treatments."

I agreed to continue, even though I felt I had been cured. A couple of months later, after the fourth treatment, I again had a CT scan in Boulder before returning to NIH. Even though I was only supposed to pick up the tests that Friday afternoon, I couldn't help looking inside the envelope. I noticed that the radiologist had attached a note that said succinctly, "The disease has metastasized." In other words, the cancer had spread.

Almost stumbling off the curb to the pavement, I was overwhelmed. A good friend was watching Burke and JonBenét and her kids in the park across the street from the hospital, so I ran over to her and told her what I'd seen. "What am I going to do? The cancer has spread. I'm going to die and leave Burke and JonBenét alone."

She put her arm around me and said, "Let's pray."

We stood there in the middle of the park praying, with kids running all around us. Then I asked her to watch the children a little longer while I went and talked to Dr. Moran. Had all of this effort been in vain? Was it only going to result in my death? The doctor tried to console me, but my hope was shattered. That weekend I was a wreck; I spent most of the time in tears.

On Sunday night I got ready for the return trip to Bethesda by taking a huge bubble bath. I had talked to my mother about the X rays. She said, "Let's don't take the doctor's report. Just take the film. We'll let the doctors there read the film for themselves." I had agreed. Sinking beneath the foamy layer of suds,

I started praying again, begging God to spare me from this horrible killer.

God, I said, *I don't know how you are going to do this, but I know you are going to change what that film says. I have faith that you can do this. I don't know how you are going to take a physical piece of plastic film with a picture of my diseased body on it and erase the cancer. But I have total faith this can happen if you choose it to be.* With that prayer, the matter was sealed and concluded. Once again I put my complete faith in God.

The next morning Mom and I flew off to Maryland. I kept praying over and over, "God, whatever it takes, I know you can make this turn out all right." After we arrived and went to the examination room, one of the nurses came to talk to me.

"The attending physician feels that the film you brought is too fuzzy," the nurse said. "Would you mind letting us do the scan again?"

"Absolutely not," I announced. "I'm ready when you are." I knew that something divine was happening, and I only wanted to go with the flow.

"Let's do that right now," she suggested.

The CT scan was taken, and shortly the nurse returned. "Everything is fine," she announced. "We don't see any trace of cancer."

No matter what the NIH doctors might tell me, I knew that God had healed my body. I had survived ovarian cancer and everything looked normal. The journey through my valley of the shadow of death was over.

Finally, after six treatments of chemotherapy and several CT scans, the doctors wanted to do a laparoscopy, a procedure where they go directly in through the abdominal wall with a microscope and look around the interior above your organs. This procedure on December 10, 1993, went well, and no signs of cancer were noted.

I was now ready for the final step, which unfortunately was a big one: a laparotomy, a "stem to stern" opening up of my abdomen to take tissue samples and make sure that no malignant cells were hiding inside me. I knew the surgery was horrendous and that the doctors would make about a twelve-inch incision, which would run from my breastbone to my pelvis, and then take over forty tissue samples from my abdominal cavity.

Obviously there would be a fairly extensive recuperation process, so I begged to have the operation postponed. "I want to be home with my children for the holidays. I'll come back the day after Christmas," I promised.

The doctors knew I'd been through a difficult year, so they allowed me to be with the children for Christmas. Then, on December 26, I returned to NIH for this final surgery. At the end of the four-hour operation, the doctors would literally "wash down" the inside of my pelvic area to make sure they could not detect even microscopic traces of cancerous cells; this procedure was a final check on the success of the chemotherapy.

Once the surgery was completed, the medical staff wheeled me back to the ICU, where I agonized in extreme pain and needed frequent doses of morphine. At that point I still didn't know the result of this inspection. I spent my birthday and New Year's in the ICU.

As I slowly regained some strength, I just felt so strongly that the report had to be positive, but there was no way to know for sure. The agony of "no report" ate away at me. One morning, thirteen days after I went into surgery, as I was getting ready to leave the hospital, head nurse Pat Davis came bouncing into my room. "I'm not authorized to tell you anything, you understand, because I'm not a doctor." A huge smile flashed across her face. "*But you're clear!*"

Peace settled over me like a warm blanket on a cold night, and joy surged through my veins. *Thank God! I was alive!* The cancer was gone. Completely gone.

However, I still had to undergo two more chemotherapy treatments; they call it "two for good measure."

In March of 1997, three months after JonBenét died, I went back to the National Institutes of Health for one of my regularly scheduled six-month checkups. While the rest of the world was convicting me of killing our daughter, I knew these people would know the truth; they were my "blood brothers," and despite what the media and the Boulder police were saying, they would know that neither John nor I could have killed JonBenét. Anyone who has faced the possibility of death and been given back life, as I had, cherishes every moment of that new life.

When I walked in the waiting room on the twelfth floor, the

receptionist and several nurses came up to me, offering their sympathy. Then Pat Davis, the head nurse who had been with me through the cancer treatments, took me into an examining room. She looked at me very seriously and said, "I know Jon-Benét is in heaven, and I know how beautiful it is there." She paused and then said, "Do you want to know how I know that?"

"Yes, desperately. Please tell me," I said, on the verge of tears.

"When I was a child, I had an illness and died for a few minutes. I saw a glimpse of heaven, so I know heaven's real, and I know she's there . . . All I can tell you is that I never felt more perfectly loved. I've been there, and it is wonderful. That's where JonBenét is."

For Pat, a seasoned nurse who walked among terminally ill patients year after year, to tell me this—and not toss the experience out as an hallucination—was a priceless moment that brought comfort in the middle of the painful reality of a murder.

And so was the moment in the late spring of 1999 when I received a letter from Howard Early's wife, whom I had met when I was struggling against cancer. The letter said:

> Patsy, Howard passed away November 2nd. He was in the hospital one week, hospice unit one week, and home one week. He was such a wonderful person, a wonderful Christian. He never complained about his pain.
>
> Howard often said, "I wish I could talk to Patsy and tell her I am praying for her and her family every day." It hurt Howard and myself that you had to be hurt by the tabloids and media.
>
> The first time we met you, Patsy, we both felt like we had been touched by an angel. When we first saw you in the cat scan waiting area, you took off your coat and wrapped a lady up in it while you had your cat scan. When you came out from having your scan we met you. You made us feel so good. You were so comforting. Howard said to me when we left the area, "Marlene, I feel like I have been touched by an angel." I felt the same way . . .

When I read the letter for the first time, I started crying. *How can I help people as the Lord challenges me to do when I don't know who the needy are? Nobody knows me?* Eventually I prayed, *God, I will do whatever you want me to do . . . but nobody knows who I am.*

I looked at Marlene's letter again. Suddenly a thought raced through my mind. People all over the world know who I am because they know JonBenét. Can it be that our personal tragedy can be used as a tool for Jesus Christ to reach hurting people with his love and care?

Months earlier those few lines from Psalm 57 had meant so much. In my darkest hour they had turned on a light. "Until these calamities have passed by," the Bible had promised. The calamity of cancer had passed. I am a living example that God keeps his word.

10

CHRISTMAS PAST

One of the perspectives that changed for us after my cancer was that John wanted our family to live more for the moment and not worry about the future so much. In the past, he had always worried about tomorrow, about whether we would be able to keep our bills paid. Now we both realized how important it was to enjoy what we had each day. John had found the saying that went, "Don't regret yesterday, it's over and can't be changed; don't worry about tomorrow because when it gets here, it usually isn't as bad as you think it will be; but rather enjoy the day that God gave you today." Those thoughts were running through my mind as I planned for our Christmas in 1994.

Christmas and its meaning had been celebrated by the Ramsey and Paugh families in the same manner that I imagine most American families celebrate the holiday. We were not only deeply devoted to the meaning of the Nativity, we also loved the color, the pageantry, and the festivities that surrounded this wonderful and important day. Each year the Paugh family looked forward to the traditions with joy and expectation. Grandparents and uncles and aunts came to our house on Christmas morning to exchange gifts. Santa Claus was always important because he came secretly in the night with special presents for each child, and we always had big dinners and lots of laughs. With time, the special significance of Christmas had made it my favorite day of the year.

In 1994, shortly after we had remodeled our Boulder home, the Boulder Historical Society asked if John and I would be willing to open our house at Christmas for the public tours they put on to raise money. Each year the nonprofit society alternated between houses on Mapleton Hill and University

Hill for their fund-raising tour. Usually a dozen or so homes would be open for display during the days of Advent. Because I always went to such great lengths decorating for the holidays, I felt that being part of the Christmas tour would be great fun. I had just recovered from cancer and was ready to get back into the pageantry of Christmas.

Our home was large, with a lot of rooms, so there were many different places to display Christmas items. We always had a huge live tree in the living room, which would this year be the focal point of the house when people came through the front door.

In anticipation of the tour, I decorated each of our bedrooms with a small tree that reflected the personality of its occupant. Burke's tree had an airplane theme, with Santa flying through the air, as well as lots of other little airplanes diving down through the branches. John Andrew's tree reflected a western theme with cowboy hats, saddles, bandanna bows, and ornaments to mirror his life as a "cowboy" student at the University of Colorado. In Melinda's bedroom, I put up a three-foot tree festooned with paper dolls and pink-and-white Victorian lace. JonBenét helped me decorate the full-size angel tree in her room with items we had picked up in our travels and ornaments from her baby years, like her little pink tennis shoes. She had one special glass angel that she hung on her tree because it reminded her of Beth.

Down in the kitchen, I had about a dozen birdhouses displayed year-round as decorations atop our cabinets. So on a corner of the kitchen counter, I placed a three-foot tree filled with bird nests and ornaments made out of birdseed. Upstairs in the children's play room, I decorated a whimsical eight-foot tree with nursery rhyme characters, teddy bears, and Donald Duck and Mickey Mouse ornaments. Finally, our master bedroom had a full-size artificial tree glistening with gold, silver, and crystal ornaments. In addition to the garlands of pearls and white pearl lights, I hung handblown glass I'd brought with me from West Virginia.

With all these Christmas trees, no one could miss that Santa would be coming to the Ramsey house!

All the extra decorations made our house look like something out of Disney World. Patsy's theory was that if people were going to pay to go through our home, it should be a memorable experience. We were decked out well beyond what was normal for us.

I knew the historical society would send over tour guides to show people through the house and explain its historical significance, which wasn't very noteworthy, except that it was one of the older houses in Boulder. My assignment as the man of the house was simply to stay out of the way. In fact, it was really to stay out of the house.

Most of the homes on the tour had been built in the early 1900s. The art deco mantel in our living room had been added much later, and we had replaced it with a limestone mantel that better suited the character of the house. Above the mantel hung a European painting from the late 1800s, but that's about all the history there was to talk about. I couldn't imagine what the tour guides would find to say about our home; it was mostly just decked out for Christmas.

As the tour got underway, I stood in the corner of the living room, listening as one of the guides started explaining the history of our home. With every group that came through, the tour guide added years to the age of everything he described. The limestone mantel became part of the original home in 1927. As he kept on winging it, the late nineteenth-century painting over the fireplace eventually reached back to the Renaissance period. What a story he spun.

A bit embarrassed by this expanding history, I went outside for a breath of fresh air.

As I was standing on the front walk watching people file in and out, I noticed a woman come out of our front door and speak to one of the tour guides who had also come outside.

"Who lives in there?" the woman pressed.

"I think he's the president of Access Graphics," the man explained.

"Hmmph!" she snorted. "Access? This place is *excess*, if you ask me." She stomped off to her car. She didn't know I was standing there, and I wasn't about to tell her I was the one she had just insulted.

That's Boulder, I thought. *We've probably broken all the rules of political correctness. Too many trees and too much electricity used to light them. Oh, well, Atlanta came to Boulder. South met West.*

The weekend of the tour provided beautiful sunny weather and, consequently, about two thousand people bought tickets. Could one of those people who went through our home have been the murderer? Experts have told us that the killer was familiar with our house. We may never know. Looking back, I only remember the joy and wonder of the Christmas holiday we had that year.

John and I usually had a family Christmas party a few days before December 25. One year I'd gotten one of the Rich's Department Store Santas to come and entertain our guests when we lived in Atlanta. That became a tradition. We would invite our close friends and their families. Santa would show up and knock on the door. We always made sure one of the kids opened the door.

The first year we did it in Boulder, Burke answered the door and was mystified to see Santa standing there. After the commotion of Santa's arrival died down, we couldn't find Burke. Lo and behold, he had rushed upstairs, put on his pj's and jumped into bed. I guess he thought he had almost blown it by being up when Santa arrived.

I had not planned to have a family Christmas party in 1996, but Bill McReynolds called me on the twentieth. He told me that Charles Kurault and his *On the Road* television program were going to be in Boulder and would be filming him as Santa. Bill wanted to include our party in the filming, if possible, and he strongly encouraged me to have the event. I agreed. After all, the children would love the excitement of the TV cameras, and we had a number of friends we could invite. Why not?

On December 23 thirty-one people arrived for the party: the Whites, the Barnhills, the Fernies, the Stines, and the Barbers, and all their children, plus their assorted house guests. Later that evening, Glenn Meyer, a single man who rented a room in Joe and Betty Barnhill's basement, showed up looking for them. I invited him in because the Barnhills were good neighbors—our family dog, Jacques, lived part-time at their house.

This bichon frise had become part of our household shortly after I recovered from cancer. During my illness, JonBenét had repeatedly asked, "Mommy, can we have a dog?"

I would always answer, "Yes, when Mommy gets better."

Well, Mommy did get better, thank heaven, and JonBenét did not forget my promise. One afternoon she was very persistent. "Please, can we go to the pet store?"

"Okay," I said. "But just to look."

We went to a small pet store at Crossroads Mall, and Jon-Benét found this bichon frise that looked more like a tiny stuffed animal than a dog. She looked up at me, with this pleading look on her face and this little white puppy in her arms, and what was I to do? We bought the dog on the spot.

About two or three weeks later, we noticed that Jacques didn't seem to be acting right, so I took him to the vet. After examining the dog, the vet shook his head and said, "You have a problem. Jacques is a very sick dog and probably won't survive." I was devastated. Now my kids, who had fallen in love with the little puppy, would have to deal with its impending death. That just seemed like too much to put on these little ones who had already lost a sister and seen their mother ill with cancer.

I asked the doctor to write down the dog's ailment, and then went back to the pet shop and explained the dilemma. There was another bichon frise puppy available, and the pet shop manager suggested that we trade. They would do what they could for Jacques, and I would take a healthy puppy home to my kids.

The new dog was a month younger, so he was smaller. But I hoped we could pull off the transfer without JonBenét and Burke knowing.

First I took Jacques II to the vet and had the doctor run all kinds of tests to make sure we wouldn't be in the same situation a few weeks later. He was given a clean bill of health. I told the kids, "Jacques hasn't been feeling well, so he's at the vet. He'll be home in a couple of days."

If Jacques II passed the JonBenét test (she was down on the floor all the time, playing with him), we'd be home free.

As soon as I brought Jacques II in the house, JonBenét looked at him quizzically and then said, "He looks skinny." I explained that he might have lost weight because he had been sick.

Soon she noticed that he didn't seem to recognize his name, he didn't know where the door was to go outside, he didn't remember the little games they always played, and, most important, he didn't light up when he saw her.

"I think maybe Jacques has a little amnesia from being so sick," I said with my fingers crossed. Thankfully, JonBenét seemed to accept that. Jacques II became as much a part of our family as Jacques I. And after the Barnhills' dogs died, they really grew attached to Jacques. He probably spent as much time at their house as he did at ours. They had agreed to baby-sit him while we were in Charlevoix that Christmas. Now Glenn Meyer was at our house, looking for the Barnhills.

Soon the friends at our Christmas party gathered in the living room for Santa and his show. I had already prepared a script for Bill to use in handing out the gifts to the children, with appropriate comments about each child. This year "Mrs. Claus" came with him for the first time, since he was recuperating from open-heart surgery. Bill McReynolds had been a Christmas fixture around Boulder for a number of years, but Doris "Janet" McReynolds was new to the act, as far as we knew. During the party, Janet mainly clung to Santa's arm, saying little as he walked around and talked to the children. Smaller in size than Bill, Janet looked like someone's older aunt, with auburn rather than white hair.

During the party Fleet White used our phone to make a series of calls, trying to get some medicine to his mother in a hospital in Aspen, Colorado. Apparently he dialed wrong and got 911. The police called back, but after checking with Fleet and the rest of the people in the house, Susan Stine informed them that the call was a mistake. The 911 call still remains somewhat of a mystery.

By 8:00 P.M. the party was over, and the children were on their way home to bed. Our cleaning lady, Linda Hoffmann-Pugh, and her daughter had stayed for the party, and she checked to see if I needed her help in cleaning up; I told her no.

Another part of our Christmas tradition in Boulder was the children's parade that Boulder held each year. For several years both JonBenét and Burke had been two of the many children joining the event.

Our first involvement occurred in 1993 when Patsy was still struggling with chemotherapy. Burke's Boy Scout troop wanted to participate, so Patsy came up with a design for a float. Her father, Don Paugh, and Adam Schneider went out to our airplane hangar and went about building the float; a parent had donated a flatbed truck, and Patsy ordered streamers and crepe paper to decorate it. Don wired the float so that music played as the kids marched down the street. Jon-Benét begged to ride with them on the float but wasn't old enough yet. With taped music blaring in the background, the Boy Scouts walked down the street with red foam rubber noses while singing "Rudolph the Red-Nosed Reindeer." As they sang "Feliz Navidad," the boys played maracas. When they went into "Jingle Bells," they donned Santa stocking caps. Patsy was still bald from chemotherapy and had to wear her wig, but we went through the motions as if we didn't have a care in the world.

For 1995 Patsy came up with a float made from a sailboat decorated to look like "The Good Ship Lollipop." Dressed like Christmas packages, the scouts walked beside the float, handing out candy. We even had life-size gingerbread men. Jon-Benét got to sit on a red seat in the back of the boat, singing the Good Ship Lollipop song. What a sight!

When 1996 rolled around, our friends Mike and Pam Archuleta drove a Christmas-red BMW convertible with Jon-Benét and some of her little friends riding on the top of the backseat and waving at people. Pam was director of the Boulder United Way, and the parade gave her a way to promote the organization. As always, almost as many people walked in the parade as watched it from the sidewalk. Nevertheless, Boy Scouts and Girl Scouts from everywhere marched down the street. It was a neat small-town family activity . . . or so we thought.

Could one of the people watching the parade have been the killer, perhaps a pedophile who was attracted to the little girl riding on the red convertible? Pam did report that a strange man approached the car during the parade. My instincts later told me it was a terrible idea to put your kids on display like that; but that thought never occurred to me at the time.

When I think back to these events, I know they were conceived in innocence and intended to be nothing but fun. Yet, now that I look back across the fabric of the 1996 Christmas season, I am disturbed by the bumps under the cloth. Strange and unexpected people appear. Events and details that Patsy and I had never noticed emerged in frightening ways that now terrify us.

A killer was standing somewhere in the shadows. And we had no idea.

11

BACK TO BOULDER

On Friday, January 3, 1997, Patsy, her family, Burke, and I came back to Colorado from Atlanta. Just after dark our car crested the hill leading down into the Boulder valley, and Patsy broke down. She was suddenly afraid to return; someone in that town had killed her daughter, and she was frightened for the rest of the family. For a few moments we thought about turning around and staying in Denver, where we could rent hotel rooms. Finally, Patsy pulled together and we went on.

We had returned to Colorado for one reason—and one reason alone—to help the police find the killer of our precious little girl. Later we also realized that the familiar surroundings of High Peaks Elementary School and Burke's classmates would probably help return some normalcy and stability to his life.

We soon learned that Patsy had reason to be apprehensive about returning. In the next days we felt as if we were walking through an endless field of land mines, and each day set off new bombs from the media and the police. I was glad I had been able to protect Patsy from some of the land mines when we were still in Atlanta, and somewhat removed. Right after the New Year, I had discovered another dimension of media intrusion as the press desperately searched for publishable pictures of JonBenét in her pageant attire. One of the central figures in this disruption turned out to be a Denver photographer named Randy Simons.

Simons had been recommended to us by Pam Griffin as a man with a talent for photographing children. In 1970 Simons had been a professional news photographer and had at one time worked for the Associated Press. Following some close calls shooting forest fires, he left newspaper photography and shifted to advertising and fashion work. Opening a studio in Denver, Simons developed a relationship with Joslins, AP&S, Miller Stockman, and Fashion Bar, allowing him to continue in his new business. In time, Simons also began photographing children as models and contestants in pageants.

In the spring of 1996, JonBenét had participated in the Royale Miss State Pageant in Denver, and had won her division title. To be prepared for the national competition, we needed additional photos to develop a portfolio for JonBenét. We contacted Simons to set up a mutually convenient time. On June 5, 1996, Randy Simons devoted an entire day to Jon-Benét, photographing her with cowboy hats, flowers in her hair, and many costume changes. JonBenét loved every moment of the experience, and she later won the national division title of America's Royale Miss.

Now I had discovered that Simons had sold those photos of JonBenét to the Sygma Photo Agency in New York City for seventy-five hundred dollars. I was shocked that such a transaction could occur without our permission and at these high prices. I was beginning to see the degree to which we were becoming cuisine for public consumption.

On January 3 Detectives Jane Harmer and Ron Gosage descended on our summer home in Charlevoix and systematically took the house apart. Patsy remained so disconnected, I don't think she fully realized that the police wanted to search the house in Michigan. I offered them the key to the front door, but they refused. Instead, they got a warrant. Even though I was aware that the house was being investigated, I felt no apprehension. Charlevoix had given us nothing but good and happy times. The police could look at whatever they chose to explore.

That January every aspect of our life at Summer Hill was investigated. The police gave us a receipt for everything they took. From the list, which included Patsy's daily planner and our address books, it was obvious they were searching for handwriting samples.

This became even more clear when on Saturday, January 4, right after we returned to Boulder, we were asked to submit more handwriting samples. We had already given the police handwriting, blood, hair, and fingerprints. On the morning of December 26, I had given Detective Arndt handwriting samples. She told me this was just routine. In addition, I provided her with a pad of 8 x 11 paper that also contained samples of Patsy's handwriting. Pads of paper like this one were always lying around the house for the children to use for everything from making airplanes to their latest art projects. It was reported that during their investigation, the police had discovered part of a "practice" ransom note on one of the pads I had given them. (It reportedly only said "Mr. and Mrs. Ramsey.") The police immediately saw this evidence as supporting the theory of our guilt. Yet, why would I have given them the note pad if either of us had actually written the note?

Before we had left Boulder for JonBenét's funeral, the police had asked Patsy, Burke, and me to give formal handwriting samples. At this point, the police seemed to have elevated me to the role of the writer of the ransom note. Giving additional samples of our handwriting proved to be an arduous process.

I wasn't sure that Patsy was physically able to go to the police station, where we would be hounded by the press, and our pictures would inevitably end up on the news that evening. She was still so emotionally fragile. The police compromised: we could undergo this ordeal at Peter Hofstrom's home. When we got there, it was decided that Patsy would go first, so Linda Arndt took her into the kitchen, where they could work on the dining table.

Peter, who was a member of the district attorney's staff, could tell I was concerned about Patsy's ability to handle this grueling experience. He tried to relieve some of my tension and make me feel comfortable in his home by showing me some pictures on the wall of his living room. Then we sat down, and he told me a story from the days when he attended law school at the same time that he worked as a prison guard. In one law class the professor had explained how the prison system worked to rehabilitate inmates, these poor offenders of justice.

"I went up to the professor after class," he said, "and told him he was out in left field. Totally wrong."

"But he wouldn't believe me. Finally, I invited him to a weekly rehabilitation class I conducted for inmates at San Quentin." He paused, then went on to explain. "Teaching this class got me ahead in the system, and the inmates attended because their interest helped them get early parole.

"While my professor was observing the class, one of the inmates arrived late. Instead of coming in through the door, he climbed in the window.

"I asked him, 'What are you doing?'

"He replied, 'Staying in practice.'

"Guess that helped my professor get my point," Peter said.

I couldn't help but laugh at his story, and I really appreciated his attempt to help me relax.

Suddenly I heard profuse sobbing in the kitchen. I rushed in to see what had happened and learned that when Detective Arndt read the words, "Speaking to anyone about your situation, such as police, F.B.I., etc., will result in your daughter being beheaded," Patsy had become hysterical. Having to write and rewrite those words in that horrible ransom note was brutal for Patsy. As she looked at that scrawled note, it brought back the initial terror of finding the note on the back staircase. I tried to comfort her, but I knew nothing would relieve the pain she was feeling. The evil intentions of that phrase—and much of the ransom note—made her realize again the terror that night must have held for our daughter. We both struggled as we wrote the note several times then and later. We were asked to write it with both our left and right hands. Patsy and I are both right-handed. To have to go through that note many times, word by word, was simply gruesome for both of us.

Strangely enough, someone leaked to the local media that we had not gone to the police station. Naturally, this touched off a flurry of suppositions. Some started to surmise that we had received special treatment because of our supposed wealth and position in the community. I wonder how these people would have felt if they were walking in our shoes, with their lives crushed and the police suspecting them of this horrible atrocity? The media pressure just didn't let up. In fact, it gained momentum. Little did we know that this hysteria would continue for the next two and one-half years.

On January 9 Police Chief Thomas Koby called a press conference, which he said would be a weekly event until the killer was arrested. I'm sure the BPD expected to wrap the case up quickly. After all, the police knew it was one of the parents. They just weren't sure which one. As soon as they could get one of us to confess, this would all be over. Chief Koby assured the public, "Over the last five years, 1990–95, we have had fifteen homicides in Boulder. We have solved thirteen of them. That means we have an 85 percent rate of success with these investigations."

District Attorney Hunter also announced that he had retained a former Miss America, Marilyn VanDerbur Atler, as his expert on child abuse and incest. Then Hunter spoke as if directly to the killer, asking him to come in before it's too late. Patsy was watching the live press conference in an office at Chrisman, Bynum, and Johnson. Immediately following the broadcast, she insisted on making a direct phone call to Alex Hunter. Patsy wanted to thank him for his promise to find JonBenét's killer.

Many in the media, however, inferred that Hunter was addressing his comments directly to me. The announcement of a child abuse specialist was interpreted by the media as meaning the cops had hard evidence that JonBenét had been abused or sexually molested by her father. The media saw the finger pointed squarely at me and ran with the story, lock, stock, and barrel.

Meanwhile our attorneys had informed the police that the Ramseys would submit to interrogations with one condition: that a representative of the DA's office be present in the room to observe them. Our attorneys felt this was very important, because at this point they did not trust the police and wanted the DA's representative present to make sure that someone other than the police heard our interrogations. We also told the police that in the meantime we would thoughtfully answer any questions they would put to us in writing.

We responded fully to all their written questions. However, the media misinformation campaign had already begun with the headline in the *Boulder Daily Camera* that read, "The Ramseys are not cooperating with the police." These false accusations were the beginning of a slam that would follow us throughout the next three years. The media would not listen or try to understand the real facts or the truth. Networks, newspapers, tabloids, and all forms of electronic media were becoming saturated with a rash of allegations that no one was checking for accuracy or reliability of sources.

Patsy and I could not have survived all of this without the extremely important contributions made by Mike Bynum.

He had graciously invited us to stay with his family when we returned to Boulder in January, even though he had a houseful of kids home for the holidays. A few days later we moved to Jay Elowsky's place. Jay, a good friend, owned Pasta Jay's on Pearl Street, a small Italian restaurant that Mike and I had invested in.

When John and I awoke on Sunday morning, January 5, I felt like I couldn't possibly get out of bed. My entire body felt like lead. I didn't want to move, but John encouraged me with a cup of hot, black coffee. "We really ought to go to church this morning," he said. Even though we knew the media would be waiting with their cameras, John felt we shouldn't let that keep us away. I slowly got up and started trying to get dressed for the worship service at St. John's Episcopal Church.

As we always did, John and I entered the sanctuary and tried to focus on worship. I didn't really want to talk with anyone. I could see that the Rt. Rev. Jerry Underwood, the bishop of our diocese, was visiting St. John's that day. Even now I can't remember much of what occurred in the service, but somewhere in the worship I looked down at the liturgy of the morning and realized that a memorial was going to be prayed for JonBenét. My eyes filled with tears. I certainly wouldn't have wanted to miss this moment and was glad John had encouraged me to come.

When the congregation began praying the liturgy for the Ramsey family and for St. John's, John and I were truly blessed to have the congregation remembering JonBenét and supporting us in this way.

Near the end of the service, Father Rol spoke extemporaneously to the congregation. "As we leave today," he explained carefully, "there will be a good number of media people outside taking pictures. They will be watching us. If you want to show your support for this family, I would like you to line each side of the sidewalk leading to the parish hall and show our friends in the media what we think of the Ramsey family. Let's show the world that we stand with them."

Unknown to the parishioners, Pat Korten, a media relations guy, had let the media know that we would attend church that day. He had been hired by our attorneys to answer the hundreds of media requests for information, which had started to clog their switchboard from day one. Pat had made a deal with the media. "The Ramseys will walk out the front door of the church and give you plenty of time to video them. In return, you need to agree to leave them alone in the future." All was agreed to, but we later realized it was impossible to get a consensus agreement from a mob like that. Pat later told us, "The media were going to be there anyway, scrambling for photos, so we might as well try to make it nonconfrontational."

Following the recessional hymn, John and I started toward the front door to go down the walk that would lead to the parish hall, where most of the congregation traditionally stopped for a cup of coffee and a few words of fellowship. Bishop Underwood led the way in front of us. We stopped at the top of the stairway leading from the church, knowing that we were going to get caught on camera, but also knowing we had agreed to get caught. A woman crouched down in front of us with a monster camera. To this day I'm not sure how she managed to walk backwards with her knees bent and that big camera on her shoulder. Slowly we made our way down the walk over to the parish hall. There were several verbal altercations as photographers tried to break through the wall of parishioners who lined the walks.

Later a member of St. John's who was also a writer for the *Boulder Daily Camera* wrote a column in which she characterized the entire exit from the church with the congregation surrounding us as "another well-staged Ramsey publicity stunt." Father Rol would later tell this parishioner that her article was all wrong, and it was he who asked the other parishioners to surround us on our way out. Of course, the correct story never made the papers, and the media had driven one more nail in our reputation and further convinced the public of the certainty of our guilt.

I can still see John shaking his head. "Can you believe that Father Rol's spontaneous request for an outpouring of support for us could be interpreted in such a cynical manner?" He ran his hand nervously through his hair. "Unbelievable!"

At 9:00 in the morning of Wednesday, January 8, I faced another difficult process when I took Burke to the Child Advocacy Center in Niwot to be interviewed about his knowledge of JonBenét's death on Christmas night. Burke was only nine years old, and both John and I were very concerned for his well-being. We had agreed to allow the interview but insisted it must be conducted by a professional who was specifically trained in dealing with children. We didn't want some inexperienced detective interrogating our son. When we arrived, I was told to wait in the center's coffee break room, and Burke was sent alone into a room with a large two-way mirror on the wall. On the other side detectives Linda Arndt, Jane Harmer, and Ron Gosage stood listening while Dr. Suzanne Bernhard, a child psychologist, talked with our son.

Burke was still in shock from the events of the last thirteen days. Talking under forced circumstances was frightening enough without the highly sensitive subject matter the psychologist presented. In many respects, Burke is much like John, introspective and quiet, and often seemingly indifferent or distant when under intense pressure. JonBenét and I were born with the extrovert gene; we were the more outgoing, talkative side of the family. Dr. Bernhard's examination wasn't an easy experience for Burke; I hated that he had to go through this. But anything that could help find JonBenét's killer had to be done.

For two hours, the psychologist probed Burke's mind while the detectives sent in questions. Every so often Linda Arndt would come into the break room to reassure me. I just couldn't believe that I was sitting in a child advocacy center, where my son was being interrogated about the death of his little sister. At times I would begin to cry and shake uncontrollably.

Linda Arndt could see my pain, and she tried to comfort me. She promised me that she was going to stay with the case until the killer was found. I appreciated her concern and felt that I could count on her for support. I now realize that she believed that John was an abusive, domineering male and that I was also his victim, and that he had killed JonBenét.

As we left the Child Advocacy Center, I was in more distress and turmoil than Burke was. Kids are so resilient.

We had agreed to this interview because we thought it would help with the investigation. Later we learned that if violence has occurred in the home, the standard police procedure is to examine the remaining children—and remove them from the home if there is an indication of an abusive situation. We understand that Burke didn't want to talk about his sister's death, but he also didn't answer questions about neglect, abuse, or sexual assault the way a victimized child might. The thought that the Department of Social Services might have considered removing Burke from our custody still horrifies me.

Toward the end of that first week back in Boulder, two new bombs in this gigantic minefield exploded. A tabloid headline screamed, "Daddy Abused JonBenét's Sister" and related some of the details of my oldest daughter's death in that automobile accident. Patsy and I were dismayed that innuendoes had now turned into "fact" in the tabloids. The police subpoenaed Beth's medical records from the hospital in Chicago where she had been airlifted as they made a desperate attempt to save her life. The national media obtained footage of the accident scene and began playing it on the evening news and talking about how I might have abused Beth. This was the first time I had seen video footage of Beth's accident, and it was extremely distressing to all of us. Later Chief Koby would announce that the investigation into Beth's death was of no significance. We wanted to scream at him, "Then why on earth did you bring all this up and serve it to the media?"

On January 9, suddenly out of nowhere, a Boulder radio station broadcast the wild rumor that I had confessed to killing JonBenét. I was both horrified and furious. How could they broadcast such lies? The report was quickly discredited but left me shaken and angry. Someone had totally fabricated a libelous story implying my guilt; this is the kind of irresponsible journalism that plagued this case from the very beginning.

After hearing the fabrications about my sexually abusing Beth and my confessing to JonBenét's murder, a full-scale meeting with our attorneys seemed even more essential. We met at Mike Bynum's office in the third-floor conference room. Bryan Morgan and Pat Burke and private investigators Ellis Armistead and David Williams all gathered around the large glass-topped conference table. Our attorneys had brought in Armistead and Williams to help us pursue the killer. Ellis Armistead had eighteen years' experience as a veteran police officer working homicides, prior to starting his own agency. David Williams, also a former cop with years of experience, had worked previously with the Haddon, Morgan, and Foreman law firm. Our legal advisors knew both of these men were top investigators. As time would later prove, these two men and their staffs would be very valuable in following up on the many tips and leads we would receive in the ensuing months.

The police were losing valuable time finding the killer because of their preoccupation with us. Everywhere we looked, we saw nothing but the results of their failure. Video satellite trucks filled the streets of Boulder. Reporters booked rooms at the Hotel Boulderado for six months in advance. JonBenét's investigation was quickly becoming a media firestorm fueled by police leaks of misleading information. The issue was not our innocence but what would sell newspapers and magazines and boost television ratings.

The war was on, with the Ramseys served up as both the prize and the victims in the battle.

With our life blown into a million pieces and no home to live in, Patsy and I floated like lost driftwood in the ocean. Although our basic objective was to find the killer or killers, our private lives had been shattered so badly it was impossible even to concentrate. We were both on medication and in a state of semi-shock. Exhaustion plagued me and thinking remained difficult. We just weren't prepared for the ongoing personal assault caused by the media and police. Periodic explosions created by leaks of false or misleading information ripped deeper into our private world and hurled us even further into a state of despair. Life continued to be a blur in which we seemed to rise and sink a hundred times each day.

Trying to set these problems aside, I was anxious to continue assembling a team of experts as I had vowed I would do in the CNN interview. Our attorneys contacted John Douglas, the world's leading crime profiler and former FBI agent. He agreed to meet with us and our investigators.

Soon Patsy and I started hearing that Boulder County didn't have the funds to pay for some of the investigative work. Apparently DNA testing is expensive. We offered to pay for the DNA testing. *Just get it done,* was our feeling. We would also cover Douglas's cost if the police would use him to help. The police seemed to be quite baffled when their prime suspects were offering to pay for serious parts of the investigation. They must have concluded that our overtures were just another well-orchestrated scheme by the Ramseys to throw them off track.

John Douglas did eventually receive a two-hour audience with two of the detectives who had been assigned to the case, Steve Thomas and Tom Trujillo. Douglas later described the meeting as what he would have expected to encounter in a small town in southern Mississippi in the 1960s. He characterized the Boulder police as cold, arrogant cops, challenging the credentials of the big-city outsider.

Our investigators tried to sift out what was going on inside the Boulder police department. We were giving our leads and follow-up information to the police. We had hoped this would begin an exchange of information to try and solve the case. They weren't interested. We soon learned that Steve Thomas, who was heading the investigation, had only been a detective for six months. I was shocked. Thomas was a former narcotics officer with no significant homicide background. We began to realize that this police force had no experience or training in what they were trying to undertake.

This was a direct result of the Boulder police union's contract, which requires that police officers regularly and frequently rotate through the various units—traffic, patrol, and investigations—rather than developing extensive experience in a particular area. Thus, Boulder police rotate in and out of detective duty, which is highly desirable for the officers because they don't have to work weekends or wear uniforms, but also means that relatively untrained detectives have to handle criminal cases. This is a major difference from contracts in other Colorado cities.

Imagine how we felt when we learned that an officer who had only been a detective for several months was the major police investigator on the case.

Our friends began telling us that the Boulder police detectives were contacting them and saying things like, "The Ramseys think you may have something to do with the death of their daughter. Would you like to tell us anything about the Ramseys?" A dishonest investigation technique. Bias the witnesses against a suspect and let them spill their guts out. We

also heard the police made comments like, "The Ramseys refuse to talk with us. Will you help us?"

Simultaneously, John Douglas was also looking more
deeply into the facts. He was convinced that JonBenét's murderer was someone we knew, perhaps a person who had been
in our house and had a personal grudge against me or was
jealous of me.

Patsy and I racked our brains, trying to think of who the attacker might be. In order to help us in our scrutiny of possibilities, Douglas encouraged us to publish the ransom note in
its original form. He said that by showing what the lettering
and the script looked like, as well as the content, someone
might recognize something familiar about the note and come
forward. When our attorneys broached the subject with the
district attorney's office, they received an absolute no.

As Patsy and I reeled from the constant barrage from the police
and the media, yet another blast exploded in our faces. The *Globe*
tabloid hit the streets with a story that they were in possession of
six autopsy photos of JonBenét. Their announced intention was
to print the pictures in an upcoming edition. My total revulsion at
the possibility of our beloved daughter being exposed in such a
gruesome and nauseating manner turned me inside out.

Boulder County Coroner John Meyer quickly responded,
telling the *Globe* that he had not authorized the public release
of any photos, but his statements didn't make a dent in the
newspaper's position. The public had a right to know; the
Globe would print the pictures. Mike Bynum's law firm even
sent a copyright attorney over to the DA's office to help them
copyright the pictures in an effort to prevent publication.

On January 14 *Globe* editor Tony Frost stated the position of
the newspaper. Without emotion or remorse, Frost said, "The
Globe is a supermarket tabloid. We deal in checkbook journalism. We buy sensational photographs and stories, and we publish them." Frost had given the world his conditions as well as
defining the role of the newspaper. If we didn't like it, tough! It
wasn't his daughter.

The fact that the dignity of our daughter was violated, our
family's well-being assaulted, and an innocent child turned into
a spectacle did not make any difference to Frost. Selling tabloid
newspapers was all that counted.

Now the spectacle of the threatened publication of the pictures put the county sheriff's office into action. Once the sheriff was convinced the pictures were actual autopsy photos, the sheriff's staff began pressuring the people related to the autopsy to take polygraph tests to determine who had sold the pictures. Three of Sheriff George Epps's top investigators were called in to discover the truth. Sgt. George Dunphy, Lt. Steve Prentup, and Detective Steve Ainsworth were charged with the task of polygraphing the coroner and everyone on his staff. Then they followed the same procedure with Photo Craft, the lab that developed the film.

Around 9:00 that evening the owner of Photo Craft called the sheriff's office with information about one of his employees, Shawn Smith, who had personally developed the film. When the police showed up at his house, Smith indicated no knowledge of what had occurred and was asked to take a polygraph test at the police station the next day. He agreed.

The next morning Smith was wired up and the questions began. Slowly and carefully, the examiner, Jeff Jenks, took him over the issues involved in the release of the film. By the time the test was over, Jenks was convinced that Smith was involved in some way. Jenks pressed hard, but Smith wouldn't budge or admit any involvement.

Later in the day, Lt. Steve Prentup received a call from Peter Schild, a local defense attorney. Schild knew who had released the pictures and wanted to bargain on behalf of his client. Prentup forwarded the call to Pete Hofstrom in the DA's office.

The *Globe* appeared on the newsstands featuring the shocking story at the same time Hofstrom was meeting Peter Schild for breakfast to bring the matter of the theft to a conclusion. A plea agreement was worked out, and an hour later Schild called the DA's office back, ready to produce the thief—Brett Sawyer, who had been a deputy sheriff before becoming a private investigator.

Hofstrom learned that Brian Williams, an editor at the *Globe*, had offered Sawyer a paltry fifty dollars an hour to obtain any kind of material that no one else had. Sawyer claimed he hadn't known the *Globe* was part of the tabloid press. Sawyer then contacted Shawn Smith at Photo Craft, suspecting they did processing work for Coroner Meyer. Smith made the pictures and gave them to Sawyer, who in turn received five hundred dollars plus a five-thousand-dollar bonus. Sawyer later confided that he had turned himself in because "his conscience" got to him.

Once the name Brett Sawyer ended up in front of Shawn Smith, the charade was over. Smith folded and the story of the release of the photos was finished. At least the police had somebody. I have heard that Shawn Smith got a few hundred dollars for his part in the scheme, but later felt so guilty that he flushed the money down the toilet, not unlike Judas throwing away the thirty pieces of silver after he betrayed Christ.

I suppose the *Globe* autopsy story epitomized the strangeness of the world in which we now lived. Alex Goulder, a private citizen in Boulder whose child attended High Peaks Elementary School, asked the supermarkets to boycott the *Globe* and not sell any of the tabloids with the photos of JonBenét. A number of stores complied, including Safeway, 7-Eleven, Wal-Mart, Conoco, Albertson's, and King Soopers. They refused to carry that issue of the publication on their shelves. However, another Boulder merchant who managed a small convenience store claimed that people ought to be able to read what they chose and literally gave away his twenty copies to interested patrons. What a contradiction!

Patsy and I could not, would not, and will not ever look at these autopsy photographs.

12

BACK TO SCHOOL

I vaguely knew we had been in Boulder for more than a week, but I wasn't aware of much that was going on and wasn't much help with anything. John was taking care of the details and demands confronting us on a daily basis. I slept most of the time and was out of it the rest of the day. My body felt like a thousand-pound weight dragging behind me. I constantly struggled to keep going at all.

Jay Elowsky's home was a bachelor's pad, and since Jay wasn't there during the day, the house maintained a sparse quality. Located out on the prairie in North Boulder, the home's interior was close to bare bones with little silverware, no coffee pot, few chairs, and one sofa. I didn't really pay much attention because most of the time I slept to avoid facing the ugly pictures my mind kept showing me of what had happened to our daughter. Dropping into a medicated sleep shut everything out, but when I woke up the reality of my loss hit me all over. I cried constantly and felt beyond awful. John and I were so thankful that the women of St. John's and other churches in Boulder began providing a hot meal for us each evening.

We both knew that Burke needed to be back in school, but I was absolutely scared to death to let him out of my sight. A murderer was walking the streets. Still, Burke was seeing a counselor, and the doctors and everyone else felt that a return to a school routine would be best for him. I knew they were right.

School had started again on January 6 with a school assembly that tastefully and sensitively explained JonBenét's death. After the assembly the fourth-grade students in Burke's class had gone back to their room. A counselor, sent by the school district, was there to help the teacher put the students at ease.

The counselor immediately asked members of the class to

discuss their feelings about JonBenét's death. Obviously, they were reluctant to do this. The counselor then asked Doug and Anthony, who had spent considerable time with Burke since his sister's death, to tell the class how Burke felt. Again the two boys were hesitant to discuss their feelings.

The counselor then tried a different approach. "How should the class welcome Burke back to school?" she had asked.

One of the nineteen girls in the class raised her hand. "I know," she said, "why don't we each bring Burke a present?"

"What a nice plan," the counselor replied.

Burke's good friend Doug raised an immediate objection, since he knew Burke didn't want any special attention. "Burke doesn't want any presents," he told his classmates. "He doesn't want it to be different . . . If you were nice to him before, just go on being nice now."

Doug paused and shot a look at one of the seven boys in the class. "If you were mean to him before, you can still be mean to him."

"Okay, that's good advice," the counselor interjected. But she still wasn't ready to move on. "Does anybody have any other ideas?"

A little girl raised her hand. "Let's all give Burke a hug when he comes back."

Again Doug objected. "I would like to remind everyone in this room that there are *girls* in this class." He glared at the girl who had made that suggestion. "*You* can't hug Burke."

Immediately the class realized its terrible mistake. "Just treat Burke like you've always treated him," Doug advised. "He doesn't want you to make a big deal out of all this stuff."

Eventually the entire school planted a tree in JonBenét's memory in front of the school, and John and I attended the ceremony. High Peaks Elementary School Principal Charles Elbot said, "This past autumn I entered Mrs. Haun's music class. There I saw JonBenét sing and dance and smile her happiness to everyone present. Although her life was brief, it was full of life and promise. I miss that lively kindergartner, yet I am glad that the time she had was lived fully. May we all do the same!"

In talking with our friends, John and I expressed our concern about Burke returning to school. Even though a sign was posted on the wall near the entranceway, saying that visitors were to report to the principal's office, anyone could walk down the halls and never answer a question about who they were and what they were doing in the school building. Actually, anyone could walk into the school at virtually any time. This gap had to be closed for John and me to know that Burke would be safe and not vulnerable to attack from the killer or intrusion by the media.

As a result of our conversations, Roxy Walker went to Charles Elbot, the principal of High Peaks Elementary School, and requested a conference. Susan Stine set up a meeting for Thursday, January 16, at Mike Bynum's office. The participants included the principal; a representative from the school district; Ellis Armistead, our investigator; Roxy; Susan; and Tracy Temple of Temple Security. John and I listened to the exchanges but said little.

The school district representative kept saying, "We have security people."

"Great," Susan said. "Are you going to assign one to our school?"

"No," he replied. "Our security people are all too busy . . ."

Counselors seemed to be acceptable to the school's supervisors (quite a few had been available to children and their parents in the days and weeks following JonBenét's death), but physical protection did not seem to be included in their scheme of things.

Then Ellis Armistead spoke up. "We've talked to Tracy about protecting Burke at school. Could the Ramseys hire her to watch Burke during the day?"

Tracy Temple, a private security officer, looked just like another mom, so we knew she wouldn't be a disruption to the students or the school routine.

No, the principal and the school district representative weren't comfortable with a bodyguard in the classroom, but the representative had another suggestion. "Maybe we could give you more parapro time." He was referring to the paraprofessional teacher aides who were in the school on a regular basis to take care of children with special needs.

"No," Roxy said, "these can't be parapros. We're talking about the security of our children! This cannot be left to the teacher's aides who are in and out and are not trained in security.

"Some parents have volunteered to be there to protect Burke," Roxy said. "Could they sit in the classroom? After all, parents are often there volunteering, so the students and the teacher are used to having them in class."

Both the principal and the district representative thought this would be fine. And they agreed that Tracy Temple could provide security around the exterior of the building.

In addition, John offered to put a security system in the school to meet the additional needs that we could foresee. Soon afterward, Foothill Security System employees installed units that included an alarm system which sounded in the principal's office. Volunteers would wear a little necklace with a security device; when pushed, the device set off an alarm in the principal's office and dialed 911 and the security company.

Now there didn't seem to be any reason why Burke couldn't go back to school from 8:00 to 2:30 each day and step back into some semblance of normal life. I didn't want Burke's childhood completely destroyed on the day his sister died. When Susan drove him to the school on that first day, I prayed desperately that God's protective hand would cover our son.

Once the word got out, a number of parents signed up to help provide surveillance at our school. We nicknamed the volunteers the Burke Watch. The parents could sign up for two, three, or four-hour sessions to provide security during the school day. Eventually, Margaret Harrington took over the job of scheduling volunteers. Margaret's quiet, loving nature added the sensitive touch to make the operation run like clockwork.

Every time the children were outside, Tracy Temple watched. She was there first thing in the morning to meet Susan Stine when she brought Burke and Doug to school, and she was there during recesses and after school. Once we had security inside and outside, I began feeling better.

Parents started coming into the classroom, sitting quietly and observing. When the children walked to gym, art, or music classes, a parent filed along with them. Burke was well covered by loving, caring parents until the end of the school year on June 6.

But nothing was easy. Two incidents in particular unnerved us. One morning Burke and the children were on a field trip.

But the necklace security device was left back on the teacher's desk, since it only operated within a six-hundred-foot radius of the school. Apparently someone set it off. The principal came charging down the hall but found only an empty room. Elbot wasn't sure what had occurred but thought to himself, *Okay, let's see how long it takes the Boulder police to arrive.*

They never came.

On another occasion a Japanese film crew abruptly showed up at the school, attempting to video students and hoping to corner Burke. The principal dialed 911, but once again the police didn't come. The school principal worked hard to help, but the lack of police response left us worried and insecure. Other parents proved to be our salvation and hope.

After Burke started back to school, I tried to get up in the morning and shuffle around in the kitchen until he was on his way. Before he got home at 3:00, I took a shower and tried to look presentable, but from 8:30 to 3:00, I slept most of the time.

Sometimes the pain hurt so badly I walked hunched over like an old woman. It was difficult to breathe, and my chest ached constantly. During my chemotherapy treatments, I had gone to Barbara Mahler, an acupuncture practitioner, because of similar pain. Each time I had visited Barbara, I had found relief, and I thought she might be of help now. As I sat humped over on her couch, Barbara listened while I described the extreme pain in my chest.

"It feels almost worse than a heart attack," I told her. "I can't do anything to get free of this continual hurting."

Barbara nodded her head slowly. "I understand," she said softly. "In Chinese medicine they call your condition a broken heart." Shaking her head, Barbara added, "a *badly* broken heart."

I closed my eyes and felt a tear run down my cheek. "Yes," I agreed. "That's what's wrong with me."

One day about the third week in January, a friend came to Jay's house to check how I was doing. I wasn't feeling well, emotionally or physically; a cold had set in and I was coughing. My friend listened to me hacking away and said she was getting me to the doctor right away. She feared the cold would develop into something more serious if left untreated.

Sitting in her car on the way to the doctor's office, frightening thoughts started racing through my mind. Almost as if Jon-Benét's death were occurring for the first time, the terror and horror of what had happened settled over me. My heart pounded like a bass drum booming away inside my chest. The "thump—thump—" kept increasing and I fought to breathe. As if someone were strangling me, I desperately gasped for air. I kept thinking, *I've lost my daughter. Who killed my child?* The fierce reality of it all came crashing down, and a panic attack swallowed me.

By the time I got to the doctor, I was shaking and trembling uncontrollably. The nurse quickly showed me into an examination room, but the anxiety didn't subside. Out of the corner of my eye, I noticed a *National Geographic* magazine with a picture of Genghis Khan on the cover. The ugly, terrifying face shocked me and hurled me further into the panic attack. I kept thinking that another face like this monster had assaulted and killed my child. I couldn't help myself. Everything inside me erupted like an exploding volcano. I couldn't stop my hysteria.

The doctor rushed in and slipped an Ativan tablet under my tongue. As the pill dissolved in my mouth, I breathed more deeply and slowly. Fear was being forced back into a remote corner of my mind, but I was far from back to normal. She referred me to a psychiatrist on an emergency basis.

As the anxiety attack subsided, I realized that I did need professional help. I couldn't ride in a car without looking to the left and the right, wondering, *Is that person the one who killed my daughter?* And I couldn't sleep at night, I was so frightened that my home would be invaded again.

Later I learned that my symptoms were typical of post-traumatic stress disorder. My reactions were not unusual for someone who was grieving the murder of her child. Gradually my panic attacks diminished, although it sometimes felt as if the nerve endings of my mind and soul were dangling out of my body. Horrible, raw feelings returned day after day, even flash-backs of the gruesome mental pictures of my child lying dead in front of that Christmas tree.

Throughout this time I kept dealing with photographers and reporters, who leaped out from behind parked cars as flashbulbs exploded in my eyes. Each of these experiences set off a fireworks display of emotion inside me that nearly burned me to the ground. Weeks of counseling helped ease me out of a whirlpool of my own fear and back into the world of reality. In many respects, it saved my life.

Everywhere Patsy and I turned, strange, unexpected intrusions in our life became new sources of difficulty and embarrassment. Most of the time, we did what grieving parents do, crying and retreating, trying to regain personal stability; but our most common actions produced havoc. We appeared to be marked for untold problems.

For example, the issue of our purchases at McGuckin Hardware store blew up on January 20. McGuckin's had for years been the village store where you could find a thousand and one things.

The story became public knowledge that Patsy had charged goods at McGuckin Hardware in early December. On December 2 she had spent $46.31 there and again on December 9 made another $99.88 purchase. One item she bought for $2.29 was from the "Builder's Hardware" department, which carries rope, among many other things. Another purchase of $1.99 was from the "Paint" department, which carries tape, among other things. Because the receipts weren't itemized, the police wanted to know what Patsy bought. Was it possible she had purchased the rope that tied JonBenét's hands and the duct tape placed over her mouth? Of course, the media marched these questions into headline stories.

The truth is that Patsy had no idea what she had purchased on those days because she bought tons of stuff from this store. The unidentified dollar amounts meant nothing to us. We later learned that McGuckin's stocks over two hundred thousand different items. A group of journalists discovered that some 1,100 items could be purchased from McGuckin Hardware for the dollar amounts in question. Light bulbs, sandpaper—the possibilities were endless. Yet once again the story surged through the papers, pointing innuendoes at us when there was absolutely nothing of substance to the report. We were learning that once something had been repeated so many times on CBS, NBC, ABC, and newspapers and magazines hither and yon, the urban legend became fact.

On January 22 both the *Denver Post* and the *Denver Rocky Mountain News* announced that the 118,000-dollar ransom note demand was close to the amount of my bonus at Access Graphics for the calendar year 1995. We had given this information to the police in confidence. Once again the papers raised the suspicion that only Patsy and I could have known about this figure. More evidence that we were guilty, they implied.

To this day, more than three years later, we still don't know why the killer chose this odd figure. It is one of the strangest components in this mystery. Patsy knew nothing about the amount of the bonus because I took care of the finances and we rarely talked about money. The 118,117.50 dollars I earned that year was deferred compensation, so there was no point discussing the matter with her.

Actually, a number of people had access to this figure. Since I was awarded the bonus in January 1996, the amount was printed on every pay stub I had received during 1996. Someone nosing through our house could have found a pay stub. Numerous workers at Access Graphics could have accessed the information as well. And I might have discussed the figure with anyone working with our taxes or investments.

Another strange component in the crime was the signature of S.B.T.C at the end of the ransom note. What could this strange series of letters actually mean? Speculation grew as the note and the signature spread across the country. We had leads on suspects with SBTC baseball caps and SBTC T-shirts that could fit into some arrangement of these letters.

The police saw a hand-carved, Philippine mahogany plaque in my closet, which had been given to me by my employees at the U.S. Naval Subic Bay Public Works Center when I was stationed there in the '60s. They theorized that the initials on the ransom note stood for Subic Bay Training Center, and again saw the evidence as pointing to me. But there is no Subic Bay Training Center at Subic Bay, and the plaque did not contain those words.

Like the strange ransom amount of 118,000 dollars, the meaning of S.B.T.C remains with the killer and has not been solved. Possibly only when the killer is brought to justice will we know why that signature was used. Beyond that point, anyone's conjecture is pure speculation.

On January 23 the Boulder police issued an ominous warning to the citizens of the area to lock their windows and doors at night because of a rash of nighttime burglaries around the town. The break-ins apparently dated back to December 12, 1996, with the most recent entries on December 25, 1996. Common information appeared to link the crimes to the northwest part of the city, although they affected other areas of Boulder as well. Our home was located north of Baseline Road and west of Twenty-Eighth Street, which could be considered the northwest portion. Following our experience with JonBenét's death, the reports were unnerving and unsettling.

Detective Sgt. Doyle Thomas said, "Suspects enter homes through open doors between the hours of 10 P.M. and 8 A.M., usually while residents are home sleeping. The suspect or suspects take small, easy to transport items such as cash, jewelry, compact disks, and credit cards. The suspect does not have any contact with anyone in the house and essentially sneaks in and out through open doors."

Could this person (or persons) have entered our house? Surely the killer might have been running throughout the city, looting and attacking in other homes. Maybe ours was the most unfortunate of the lot. This rash of nighttime burglaries stopped on December 25, 1996.

13

BACK TO WORK

Going back to work at Access Graphics was like seeing old friends you haven't seen in a while after there's been a big change in your life. A monumental change.

As it is with a lot of baby boomers, work was a big part of my life; I enjoyed the fast pace and the challenges. Before becoming president of Access, I had never been the chief executive officer of a billion-dollar company. I had never been an elected officer of a Fortune 500 company. I had enjoyed rising to the demands all of this presented to me—a guy who used to work out of his basement because he couldn't afford to rent an office. Money was always secondary to the thrill of the ride, and I had ridden the wave of the explosive computer revolution of the late '80s and early '90s to heights I could never have imagined. After Lockheed Martin bought us out in 1991, I had stayed on as CEO because I had really enjoyed building this company and had high expectations for its future. I knew that my returning to work now was more important than ever to my mental and physical well-being, but it wouldn't be easy.

I had tried to return to work on January 24, but when word got out that I might be coming back to work that day, the company received an alarming phone threat: if John Ramsey returns, the caller warned, Access Graphics employees will die.

My return was postponed, and security measures were tightened at our offices. *No rush,* I thought.

When I finally did return to work in February, our problem was, once again, the media. Photographers were everywhere, harassing, questioning, probing, prying, inappropriately popping up out of nowhere for surprise pictures. Cameramen were either hiding, hanging around the front and rear doors, or set up with a zoom lens to obtain the "unexpected" insider shot. The experience weighed on me because I wasn't emotionally up to these potential surprise attacks every minute of the day.

It was obvious that I couldn't work at my desk in our building without bringing the chaos inside with me. Mike Bynum again became the source of a solution. Mike's law offices were across the street from our building, and he had a small, unoccupied space that I could turn into a makeshift office and begin the rehabilitative process of getting back to business. Work didn't need me; I needed work.

With the help of Mike's secretary, Barbara, I set up a clandestine work area where the people from across the street at our real office could slip in and out unobserved. My assistant relayed selected phone calls, and a new work pattern slowly emerged.

The experience of having cameras pulled out and aimed at me so often made me realize that I'd much rather have a gun pointed at me than a camera. As strange as it sounds, the intrusion of one's privacy is a very personal violation. As we were to learn, a camera can cause long-lasting and unimaginable injury. A photo attached to a made-up story in a supermarket tabloid can be horribly damaging. At least with a bullet I know the worst it can do.

I was still suffering from severe trauma, and I found that I didn't have the emotional reserves to deal with the constant tension and demands of a full workday. And I still thought about JonBenét most of the time. Why hadn't I heard any struggle and been able to protect her? The thought of what she had faced during that time of violation was often more than I could bear. My little girl, whom I so wanted to protect and would gladly have given my life for, had been brutally murdered. Why hadn't the killer killed me instead, if he was angry with me?

Unless someone has gone through what happened to me with the death of two of my children, he or she could not really say, "I know how you feel." Even friends couldn't really understand. My short-term memory had been affected, and I had a very difficult time remembering what day it was, let alone more important matters. I fought unbearable depression every day of the week. Having a murderer break into our home had destroyed my hope for the future. I was nervous and often fearful. The horrible, ongoing trauma had damaged my sense of business acumen and dulled my edge. "Going on" was tough. At first I was only able to work three or four hours a day. Fatigue simply overwhelmed me, and I had to go back home.

I was proud of how well the company had functioned in my absence. As president of the company, one of my duties was to keep everybody pointed in the same direction. I was the author and keeper of the long-term strategy. As the leader of the team of executives, I was always trying to get us to really function as a team. With a core group of people, who by themselves were leaders in their own right, it was always a battle to make this happen. I was expected to mitigate differences of opinion among top management and make sure the whole team knew what play we were going to run next. A company president is like the coach of a sports team. If I couldn't get a consensus, I had to either work to bring the parties together or make a decision myself and move forward. Without my presence there was no mitigator, but the company executives had kept the business on course, resolving their differences and making decisions as a group. They played very much as a team.

A month of media hullabaloo passed before I could go back inside the Access building and work out of my own office in a modified but normal manner. I knew this would not be easy. It's awkward being around people who have experienced a tragedy. Friends often don't know what to do or say when someone has lost a child; they may even try to avoid you because they're just not sure how to let you know they care.

I put out a memo to the entire staff. "You don't have to say anything. You don't have to say 'I'm sorry' or 'You have my sympathies.' That's understood. Don't worry about that. Hugs and handshakes are just fine. That's all that's necessary."

When I walked in the door that day, people had tears in their eyes. Friends hugged me. Some said, "God bless you." Others shook my hand and smiled. The love was real and deep. That was more than enough to let me know where their hearts were.

Most everyone in the Access offices wore ribbons to say "we're with you," and those little pink bows really touched my heart. These people were not only my colleagues but also my friends, and they had done a great job to keep things going even though they, too, had been shocked by this tragedy. In the past weeks they had had to face the normal daily problems, in addition to those that were dumped in their laps by the police and the media. Hour after hour, the distraction caused by these interventions were tough, and I was grateful that they had graciously borne up under the hard struggle.

"We care!" was everywhere and it made reentry enormously easier for me.

That first day back in my own office on the third floor, I was haunted by the many times JonBenét would ride into work with me in the morning and sit on my lap for a few minutes behind my desk. She would play with all the objects on my desk or draw a picture while I got organized for the day. I would then walk her over to her school at the First Presbyterian Church, which was diagonally across the street. I could see the church from my office now, and it hurt to remember JonBenét playing on the small playground area or to remember the hand-in-hand walks to school I so much enjoyed as a proud dad. She was always so eager to get to class, and as soon as she walked in, she became absorbed with her little chums, sometimes forgetting to say good-bye to me.

The path to Boulder had almost been accidental. There were many twists and turns, and Patsy and I had worked our way through the hard times and the good times alike. Now I sadly thought about all the "what ifs." What if I had not moved my family to Boulder in the first place? We would still be living in our house on Northridge Road in Atlanta, Georgia, and JonBenét would still be alive. You can't let your mind wander to such thoughts, or it will drive you insane.

Getting back into my office in a normal fashion proved to be impossible. I had an appointment with a psychiatrist twice a week to try to work through my pain, so I had to leave the office during the day and get through the wall of "photojournalists," as the tabloid scavengers call themselves. My employees tried to help me solve the problem in a number of rather ingenious ways.

Our inside sales force, which consisted of a hundred or so hotshot young kids who were on the phones all day, cutting deals and making orders happen, was located on the second floor in a wide-open room that just pulsated with energy. They came up with one of the more memorable approaches of dealing with the paparazzi. One afternoon a number of the young men rushed up to the roof of our building and began making snowball "bombs" to throw at the cluster of photographers three stories below. We'd had a good snow and the roof was covered; however, because of the high rim around the top, they couldn't really see over the edge to accurately hit their intended targets. Soon their compatriots solved the problem by manning the windows on the second floor and talking to the roof crew via telephones, advising them which direction would prove to be the most effective for hurling huge snowballs over the side of our building.

"More to the left," one salesman-turned-spotter on the second floor shouted on his phone to the gunnery located on the roof, pointing to a photographer retreating as the snow sailed down from above.

"Try two feet to the right," another ordered into his cell phone. "You almost got him that time."

"Down the center," someone else yelled. "Direct hit!"

The instructions sounded like military officers advising their artillery where to shoot their cannons at the enemy. I came down from my third-floor office because I could see these snowballs coming off the roof and dropping past my window onto the scattering paparazzi. I also wanted to see what all the cheering and laughing was about. I found my entire sales force lined up along the windows, looking down on the street below as snowballs arched from the roof. I peered over a secretary's shoulder in time to see a photographer run backwards to avoid the ball of snow coming at him. However, when the office crew realized I was standing behind them, there was a moment of awkwardness as I'm sure they wondered what I would say. I cheered them on and told them it was a great relief to watch the media run from us for a change!

Getting into the building in the morning and out at night was always a challenge. I had turned to a few disguises to help get me past the waiting cameras. We had a crew of construction workers working on an office expansion that was underway, so several times I borrowed one of their hard hats, some old jeans, and a worn down vest. Looking like a hard-working laborer with a set of plans under my arms, I walked by the cameras without my adversaries having any idea whom they'd just missed. If they had looked down at my polished loafers, they would have seen through my disguise; but they were never that observant. Evading the media had become a game we refined to a sport as time went by.

Often, I reflected on where this thriving business had come from and how I came to the office I now occupied. After spending three years as a junior officer in the Navy, I returned to Michigan State to finish a master's degree in business administration. For a sixties-era baby boomer, that degree, coupled with my electrical engineering undergraduate degree, was supposed to be my automatic ticket into a good job. By the time I got out of the Navy and finished my MBA, a lot of Vietnam vets were hitting the job market, and I really struggled to get my first position. I was hired by AT&T into their management development program, but was fired after a year when they concluded I didn't have the potential for middle management. (I've always wanted to go back and talk to the boss who fired me and compare resumés. I was proud of what I had achieved, even if a lot of it had been through luck.) Several jobs later, I ended up working for a California electronics company named Acurex and began selling data acquisition systems in the Southeast, living in Atlanta. In 1977, after several repeated attempts, Acurex finally gave me an ultimatum: "Move from Atlanta to Mountain View, California, or else." In order to grow with the company, I needed to be at headquarters.

I needed little reflection to recognize that moving to California would be a heavier financial load than we could possibly carry. I couldn't imagine how anyone could afford to pay eighty or ninety thousand dollars for a house in what was to become Silicon Valley. I had paid forty thousand for my house in the Atlanta suburb of Lilburn, and even that was a stretch for me. Though the job offered opportunity and security, it just wasn't feasible for me to make the move. I eventually gave Acurex a counteroffer: let me stay in Georgia and become the company's manufacturer's representative in the Southeast. Acurex management bought the idea, and so I started down the tenuous road of being in business for myself.

By 1980 my new company, which consisted of myself and

one employee, had moved into a three-hundred-dollar-a-month space at the DeKalb Peachtree Airport. I struggled to keep my bills paid and money in my pocket. There were times when I simply did not have any money. During this time, I met Patsy and knew that she was someone special. She not only became my wife but my business partner as well. Eventually, to save the three hundred dollars, I turned our basement into my business office and started working out of our house. Patsy proved to be a real savior, bringing a new level of energy and a positive outlook to our struggling business, which gave me the encouragement I needed.

The late seventies and early eighties proved to be a revolutionary time in the computer world, as home computers started to evolve and IBM legitimized the personal computer with their introduction of the PC. New computer products accompanied this surge and were beginning to get widespread usage. I was at the right place at the right moment in the right business.

Since we were still a very small company, I never mentioned that we were headquartered in the basement of our home, because I wanted our customers to think I was a "big" business. As it turned out, working from my home had both advantages and disadvantages. An advantage: One winter day when the heavy snowfall shut down all business in Atlanta, I was sitting at my desk in my pajamas when a customer called. "Wow, I'm surprised you are there," he said. "How did you get to work this morning?"

"Oh, it really wasn't that bad," I answered.

The tone of his voice told me how impressed he was with my dedication as he imagined my struggling through the snow to get to the office.

Yet there were disadvantages. One lady wanted to see a demonstration of one of our software products, and I gave her directions to our house. We told her to go around to the back of the house, because the basement "office" was entered from the ground level. Once she saw what a ma-and-pa business we were, she was probably wondering, *What in the world am I doing here?*

But that was just the beginning of her disillusionment. As she walked around the corner of the garage and into the backyard, our golden retriever, Liberty, took out after her, pinning her against the garage wall. Shaken, she politely watched a brief five-minute demonstration and then left. We never heard from her again.

Even with setbacks like that, boxes of computer products began going through my garage-turned-warehouse like bread in a grocery store. We were selling more and more, sending printers, plotters, and digitizers, first to business users, and then to resellers who were beginning to come on the scene as demand for computers was growing.

One Saturday morning I woke up to the sound of air brakes locking in place, looked out my window, and discovered an eighteen-wheeler parked in front of my driveway with men unloading boxes. Neighbors were watching in amazement. My basement business had been a well-kept secret, but now the word was clearly going up and down the street of our until-now quiet residential area. A neighbor must have complained to the authorities; early the next week a Fulton County zoning inspector showed up at my front door with his badge and clipboard in hand. I had thirty days to move the business to a properly zoned location. He was polite, but I knew I had no choice in the matter.

Patsy helped me slide through many of these narrow places in the road. Since our marriage she was also doubling as my secretary. She had special insight into what happened in the business, and would be aware when a particularly important customer presented a special challenge. Often she'd suggest that we go out to dinner with the individual for a more personal approach. Her warmth and positive outlook usually broke the ice and often helped us win the deal. She typed letters, made deposits at the bank, ran errands, talked to people who were important to us, and helped keep us on the right track. Her dad, Don Paugh, eventually joined our company, since we were growing faster than we could find good people to work it.

In 1982 one of our customers called us with news of a young startup company. "You know, I saw this new software program called AutoCad. You guys ought to look at it, because it ties into what you are doing."

Armed with that tip, I went to Comdex, the big computer show in Las Vegas, and found the AutoCad booth—a little nothing stall at this huge trade show. The booth, however, was packed with people. *A good sign,* I thought. Usually small booths packed with lookers are an indication of the next hot product. (I remember several years later going to Comdex and wondering what all the people were doing around the small Mosaic–Netscape booth. Netscape, of course, later became one of the biggest IPOs ever as it ushered in the Internet revolution.)

AutoCad certainly was the kind of product I was looking for. I had a gut feeling that this new little company could be good for our business. We eventually became their first distributor, and AutoCad provided the "horse" that we were able to ride for the next ten years.

Operating on the new IBM PC computers, AutoCad proved to be a winner with architects and engineers who could now do their design work on a personal computer. AutoCad software became the driver of our business, a "killer application," as we say in the computer business. Quite by luck again, we'd found the key to our future and literally had grabbed a tiger by the tail.

Our new business thrived and did quite well for two or three years. We moved into cheap office space (if a small business is in a glitzy building, I believe the entrepreneur is thinking too far ahead of the curve), and our revenues that year increased to two and a half million—from the efforts of what were now seven employees. We knew we needed to hire more help, but we didn't have the space, so I asked the landlord to rent us the vacant area beside ours. We literally cut a hole in the wall and made a passageway.

Yet, despite our robust success, I always feared we would fail. I tended to look at each month and think, *Whew, we got through that month and came out all right, but we have another big month ahead. Will we make it?* I never thought, *We've got it made.* (Even later, when our revenues topped two hundred million dollars per month, I still worried if the bubble would burst.)

I also recognized that larger, better-financed companies were growing around us. Even though we were doing fine, I was afraid that unless we expanded, our company would soon be swallowed by the competition. My father-in-law, Don Paugh, recommended that Patsy and I go to Boulder, Colorado, to talk with Jim Hudson, whose company, CAD Distributors, carried a lot of the same product lines and was strong in the AutoCad market in the western United States.

We met Jim in the ground floor cafe of the Hotel Boulderado, and as we ate lunch together we realized that our concerns were the same: How could we avoid being swallowed by the big guys? How could we keep growing? An alliance or merger seemed a likely answer.

Yet we still wouldn't have operations in the Northeast, so Jim suggested we talk to Eric Korb, who had a small company called Cad Source, based in Piscattaway, New Jersey. After many conversations, our company, Advanced Products Group from the Southeast; CAD Distributors, Jim Hudson's company from the West; and Cad Source, Eric Korb's company from the Northeast; merged, and Access Graphics, a new nationwide distribution company, was born. Jim's operation was the biggest, so we decided to make Boulder the national headquarters.

I became vice president of operations and later vice president of sales and marketing. I stayed in Atlanta, as I had no interest in moving to Boulder. I guess I naively thought Jim's staff could run the company, and I would watch from Atlanta. Our new combined company had annual sales of thirty million dollars. While this sounds significant, by the standards of the industry, we were still small and struggling. Combining cultures, personal differences, and trying to keep employees' egos in line proved to be a monumental job. The company that merged from the Northeast wasn't sure anyone existed west of the Hudson River. The Boulder people thought all southerners were Bible-pounding segregationists, and we southerners thought the Boulder mall contained the most bizarre collection of people we'd ever seen.

It's difficult enough to get three people to decide where to eat lunch; getting three business partners to agree on a common strategy was almost impossible. We soon discovered that we had put three small profitable companies together to form one larger unprofitable company. We were short on cash. We had people who didn't trust each other. We had three different agendas. We had a southern culture, a western culture, and a New Jersey culture.

In order to keep our company going, I began traveling to Boulder on a regular basis. My father-in-law, who became our operations vice president, and I first took up residence in the Hotel Boulderado and then ended up living in an apartment a few blocks from the company. With two beds and some cheap furniture in our apartment, we made the run back and forth from Georgia to Colorado on a weekly basis, usually leaving Sunday night and returning on Friday afternoon.

Because our company was struggling for cash, we jumped at the chance to sell 25 percent of our stock to Lockheed. And we started to court some of the emerging Unix workstation manufacturers: Sun, Hewlett Packard, and Apollo. Auto-Cad was starting to run out of gas for us, and we needed a new "horse" to ride. Sun Microsystems was making a big shift into the distribution channel, which we represented, so perhaps we could get the Sun contract, even though we were still a very small distributor.

Over the course of six months in 1990, our company did a hard press to become a Sun distribution partner. After numerous presentations, one issue came down to the wire: did we have adequate finances to cover a contract with them? Sun told us they liked us, but they were afraid we were too small. No Sun contract, no more Access Graphics, we were beginning to realize.

I just couldn't let this deal go by without a last-ditch effort, so I thought of every possible solution—and some not so possible. Lockheed was a minority partner, but they were not convinced we were going to survive, so they weren't sure they wanted to provide the fifteen million dollars in operating capital we needed, even though we told them this Sun opportunity could be huge. Finally they agreed to finance us, with a lot of conditions.

One of the conditions was that we bring in a new CEO. Jim Hudson had served as CEO during the "war years," the time we were trying to get the three cultures integrated and trying to learn how to operate with big-business Lockheed as a minority shareholder. Jim took the hit for many of these problems, and Lockheed wanted a fresh face, even though, in retrospect, Jim had done many of the things that positioned the company for its rapid growth, not the least of which was the Sun contract.

Jim agreed to the concept of bringing in a new CEO, and we went back to Sun with the news that we had the money we needed to support their business. Their reply was, that's great, but how do we know you are going to use that money to pay us? You guys are losing money. If we ship you five-hundred-thousand-dollars' worth of product, we have to know that we are going to get paid.

We'd gotten the money but still couldn't convince Sun we could handle their business. We were running out of time. Sun finally gave us the word that they were going to make their selection by 5:00 P.M. If we had any other proposals, they would listen to them up until then. Late that afternoon we were all sitting in Jim Hudson's office straining to salvage this situation.

Jim finally said, "Well, that's it, boys. Let's throw in the towel. I don't see that there is anything else we can do."

Most of us agreed; we were out of cards to play. There seemed no way to salvage the company.

Then an unusual arrangement occurred to me. "Why don't we set up a joint bank account, with both Access and Sun having signature authority? We'll pay our bills through that account, and we'll always keep it funded at an agreed-to level. They will know we can't get checks out of the bank unless they sign them, and they won't ship us product unless we have the cash in the bank account."

"Sun will never accept that. No way," our chief financial officer (CFO), Tom Carson, said. Everybody agreed with him. Yet I insisted it was worth a try. After a lot of bantering, I bet Carson a steak dinner that if he would present the idea to Sun, they would accept my unconventional idea.

We contacted Sun's chief operations officer, who returned our call from a pay phone at a restaurant. Tom Carson presented the idea. "Look, would you consider this arrangement?" he said in his most official-sounding voice. And then he went on to explain my proposal.

After a short pause to think through our offer, the Sun executive who was the final decision maker said, "Sure, that would work fine."

Tom hung up the phone, and we all slumped back in our chairs. We were too exhausted to celebrate, and had too much to do now. It was months before I collected on my steak dinner.

*   *   *

On February 10, 1991, the board of directors and I met all morning in a conference room of the Hotel Boulderado to interview candidates for the new president/CEO. At two that afternoon I called Patsy at our home in Dunwoody, Georgia.

"Well, how'd it go?" she asked. "Did anyone take the job?"

I knew Patsy had been praying that God would intervene and help the board find the best man or woman for the job. She felt I was already spending far too much time in Colorado, and she wanted the board to find the right person so I could quit going to Boulder every week.

In fact, one day several months before, Burke's teacher at Dunwoody Baptist Preschool had asked where his parents lived. The teacher told Patsy that Burke had responded, "My father lives in Boulder, my mom in Atlanta." The teacher had assumed we were divorced.

I knew Patsy was not prepared for my news, so I asked her a question to prepare her. "How would you like to move to Colorado?"

"Why do you ask?" she replied. "What do you have in mind?"

"The Board couldn't agree on any of the applicants, and they asked me if I'd take the job. I told them I'd give it my best shot."

"You took the job?" Patsy asked. I could tell by the tone of her voice that she was hesitant to leave the South. We had talked many times of raising our children in a southern lifestyle with lasting roots, a sense of family values, and a culture that runs deep. Patsy was unsure of my decision, but later she agreed. Initially, we only intended to be in Colorado a couple of years, but that time line ultimately expanded into five years.

At that time no one knew how really well Sun would do. They were a Unix-based system, which was competing with Microsoft and their Windows operating system. The industry pundits always knew Microsoft would win the PC business hands down, and felt Unix, and therefore Sun, had only a few years to survive. Since we were pinning our hopes on Sun, our competitors also felt we only had a few more years. We even believed that ourselves, although we were growing nicely in the meantime.

Then along came the Internet, and all of a sudden Windows wasn't the clear answer to operate the complex networking applications required by the Internet. Unix now had a future beyond just the scientific and university community. And we now had a new niche in the market place.

Growth of 30 to 40 percent a year quickly turned our small company into a medium-size business.

In 1991 Lockheed bought the remaining 75 percent of our business in their attempt to diversify into the commercial markets. We gave them a growing level of commercial business to add to their seven-billion-dollar portfolio of government-related business. They asked and I agreed to stay on as the head of the organization, even though I was no longer a stockholder.

One of my philosophies always was "you've got to be in the game to see the next opportunity." Now the next play seemed to be an international presence. I realized that I had always thought too small. When I had started my own business, we were going to focus on the Southeast, and I really should have been thinking the entire United States. I didn't want that to happen again.

So I forced Access Graphics to expand into Canada because the language was the same, we had easy access to this country from the United States, and we could leverage some of our resources there. Yet I quickly found out how unprepared we were to deal in the international scene.

On our first exploratory trip to Toronto, I took three of my staff to meet with potential customers. When we showed up at the airport in Denver to board our flight to Toronto, only one of them had a passport. One had forgotten his passport; the other thought he could use a U.S. driver's license to get through customs. That day we got into Canada through the grace of some rather disgruntled customs officers. Two years later we opened offices in Europe, and our annual sales reached five hundred million dollars. Yet we never felt we had made it. Our competitors were growing too, and they were probably doing two billion.

Early in December 1996, Tom Carson came into my office. "John, I want you to look at these figures."

I looked up at him, standing at the door with a handful of papers.

"As best I can tell we're going to hit the billion-dollar sales mark in a couple of days. That's a big milestone."

"A billion dollars?" My mouth dropped. "I knew we were close, but I didn't think we were there yet."

"It's on top of us." He smiled. "Probably in a couple of days. I think we should do something to celebrate."

I agreed, if for no other reason than to congratulate our employees. A billion dollars in sales and six hundred employees worldwide was a big milestone for Access Graphics. One of our public relations people thought we should also contact the newspaper to announce our success. I had a gut reaction that the press release wasn't a good idea; I didn't want that kind of visibility outside of the business. Still I agreed, since our employees deserved the recognition. Now I wonder if this publicity might have attracted the attention of the killer—or further irritated the person if he or she had a grudge against big business, Access Graphics, or me.

So on December 16 we threw a celebration at the Hotel Boulderado with a buffet lunch for our employees. We set up a display that morning to announce our achievement at the front entrance to our office, and I stood beside the door to congratulate everyone as they came in for work. We were now a billion-dollar company, and that put us among the top four or five companies in our industry.

I remember thinking, *Where's our next big milestone? Ten billion in sales?* What a thought! Patsy and I seemed to be positioned perfectly. She had been healed of cancer, and my job was going great. Our daughter Melinda had graduated from the University of Georgia and was now a registered nurse, John Andrew was attending the University of Colorado, and we had two wonderful children at home.

Yet Patsy's illness had left a profound impression on my plans. I had been forced to live for the day at hand. We had done okay in business, but I still worried about having enough money for retirement. Now my feeling was that if we spent all our money, I'd make it back again. We couldn't let the joy of the present moment slip away.

Patsy and I had been discussing my leaving the business sometime around May of 1997. I could take a year off. Spend time with the family. Enjoy life. See the world. Go to Australia. In the back of my mind, I still secretly feared losing Patsy to cancer, and I wanted every minute of our time together as a family to count.

Years have now passed since those hours of initial reflection. Instead of a peaceful retirement, the times became tragic and overwhelming. When JonBenét's death became front-page news, one of the misconceptions that swept across the nation was that I was the owner of a billion-dollar company. The truth was that John Ramsey was an employee of Lockheed Martin. While the media tried to paint me as a billionaire, I was merely an employee working for a large corporation. And that, too, would end sooner than I anticipated.

14

EVIDENCE AND EXPERTS

As the month of January ended, Patsy and I found it no easier to get up in the morning and make it through the day than when we first returned to Boulder after JonBenét's murder. Some days were better than others, but each day continued to be a struggle. We were barely surviving. When we weren't sleeping, we were trying to keep occupied with anything other than watching television. It seemed as if every channel carried something about JonBenét or her "evil parents."

However, Susan Stine learned that NBC would feature criminologist John Douglas on a *Dateline* program scheduled to air on January 28. This piqued our interest, since we had met Douglas only weeks before in Mike Bynum's office.

Jane Pauley spoke from Studio 3-B in Rockefeller Center, announcing that John Douglas, the man who pioneered the technique of criminal profiling with the FBI, would share his impressions of what was happening in the investigation of JonBenét's murder. Douglas's credentials were impressive, to say the least. To develop his insights into how the criminal mind works, he had worked on over five thousand homicide cases, including some of the most heinous murders the planet has ever known. Douglas has a doctorate in psychology to back up his real-life experiences. He had accurately profiled the Unabomber years before he was caught, and had accurately predicted who Atlanta's serial child murderer would be before Wayne Williams was eventually caught and convicted. John Douglas had been the inspiration for the creation of agent Jack Crawford in the book and the film *The Silence of the Lambs*.

NBC's Chris Hansen conducted the interview for *Dateline*. He presented Douglas as the man bringing the listening world an "insider's view" of JonBenét's murder.

Douglas started by explaining that his involvement in the case began with suspicions about our guilt, strictly based on the overwhelming tide against us in the media. Only after interviewing Patsy and me for more than four hours did he conclude that we could not possibly have been involved. Douglas said on the air:

> *What struck me as really unusual is that—is that the—bedrooms—the family's, mother and father's bedrooms were so far away on that third floor that even if you weren't a sound sleeper, you would have difficulty hearing any noise on the second floor, because it is so far removed.*

Hansen questioned why the police hadn't searched the house thoroughly that morning. The commentator further noted that our home had become contaminated by all the people in and around the house. Douglas went on to say that the crime scene was very damaged, but the nature of what was found at the scene was significant. He concluded:

> *Generally, if a parent kills the child, they don't want to be the one to find the child. If they do search, say, in a—in a residence, they'll get someone else to say, 'OK Frank, you check this room, I'll be over here checking the other room.' The other thing you look at is how the child is left. When—when parents kill, they usually place the child in a very, very peaceful type of look to it. They—they stage the crime scene.*

Hansen observed that JonBenét's situation didn't fit the pattern Douglas described because of the tape on her mouth and the severe head wounds as well as the other physical bruises. Douglas noted that, in his entire experience of evaluating crime scenes, he had never seen a ligature [garrote] around a child's neck or duct tape placed by a murderous parent.

In Douglas's expressed opinion the three-page ransom note remained the key piece of evidence. He contended that the note was perhaps written as an afterthought, but the precise demand of 118,000 dollars was an extremely important clue. He didn't see that number as selected by chance or accident. Douglas described the killer as someone with extreme anger toward John Ramsey, trying to hurt him in the most devastating manner possible. The murderer, Douglas said, remains a "certain breed of cat, a high-risk type of offender."

When asked if the parents were perpetrators of the crime, Douglas answered decisively, "What I've seen and experienced, I—I say they were not involved."

We were thankful that the public was finally hearing a man of world-class stature who was willing to look at the facts of the case objectively. Patsy and I both hoped that Douglas's wisdom could open the closed minds at the police department and finally give us a breakthrough to finding JonBenét's killer. Apparently, though, Douglas's views had no effect on the Boulder police. They had made up their minds and wouldn't be confused with facts.

A week and a half after the first of February, the *Denver Post* ran an interesting observation on the handwritten ransom note that Douglas had spoken about on *Dateline*. The paper said:

> *Leaving a handwritten document at the scene of the crime, in most cases, is tantamount to leaving one's calling card. Bradley and other forensic document examiners say that it's nearly impossible for a person to disguise handwriting so that an expert can't link a suspect to a document, such as the note found in the Ramsey home. The older a person is, the more automatic and difficult it becomes to conceal the clues. And the longer a document is, the harder it becomes to disguise one's writing.*

The *Denver Post* made some important points. The ransom note left by the killer was one of the longest in the history of kidnapping cases, and the experts the *Post* interviewed said that the longer a document is, the harder it becomes to disguise one's writing. They also noted that the older someone is, the harder it is to disguise handwriting. Patsy was thirty-nine at the time, forty only days later. I was fifty-three. And Bradley and the other examiners said that it is nearly impossible for a person to completely disguise his or her handwriting, and that, given enough samples, it was usually possible to come up with a certain match.

The original police theory seemed to be that I was the killer and had written the note. All the police had to do was match my handwriting, and they would have enough proof for their theory to make an arrest. No wonder they refused help from the outside—they already knew the answer.

Patsy and I had given all the handwriting samples the police wanted back in December. It was extremely painful to sit there and write and rewrite that horrid note, word by word, over and over. It was especially hard on Patsy.

But between January and April of 1997, Patsy voluntarily participated in four other handwriting sessions, during which the police exhausted many different approaches, ranging from taking individual letters, numerals, and digits, to reading a story and then asking her to write. They also had Patsy write what is known as the London Letter, a standard handwriting analysis, because it covers so many of the commonly analyzed points.

The police investigators would dictate material quickly so we wouldn't have time to reflect or adjust our handwriting in any way. Most of the time, we wrote with a felt-tip pen, similar to the implement used to write the ransom note, although other types of pens were also used in the analysis. They even asked Patsy to pretend she'd made a mistake and cross out a word. I knew that this was a complete waste of time, but the police had to try to prove their theory that one of us had written the note. We were beginning to sense that the police were getting more interested in Patsy.

Later Patsy told me that one single agonizing strand of thought ran through her mind during all this: *Why would they possibly think that I've killed my daughter? What have I ever done that would make anybody think I was capable of doing something like this?* The implication that either she or I wrote this crass, cynical note assaulted every value in her personal sense of dignity.

Our attorneys hired two of the top handwriting experts in the country to analyze the note as well. The experts we retained had worked with the examiners used by the Colorado Bureau of Investigation (CBI) to analyze our handwriting samples. Our experts had impeccable law enforcement reputations. They went through the same materials the police did. In the end, they totally eliminated me as a potential writer of the ransom note, and Patsy came out with a low similarity score, indicating little likelihood of having written it. On a scale of one to five (with one being a definite match and five being a virtual impossibility), the experts assessed the possibilities of my being the author at 5 and Patsy writing the note at 4.5, a very low probability.

Consequently, the police had to modify their theory. They came up with a new one: the father was the killer, but the mother wrote the note because she was frightened to death of the cruel father. Patsy gave handwriting samples five different times, plus the many existing examples of her handwriting, which were obtained from her daily scheduling calendar, the family scrapbook, and other letters and notes that had been taken from our Colorado and Michigan homes. If Patsy had written the note, the police had far more than enough samples of her handwriting to prove conclusively that she did. But they couldn't prove this because she did not write the note, pure and simple.

Yet the police persisted with their new theory that Patsy had written the note. I've often wondered what the police would have done if Patsy had scored a five, which would have totally destroyed any possibility of our involvement with the ransom note. Where would they have gone with their theory then? Probably they would have decided that we had hired someone to write the note! At the outset the idea that we wrote the note was a very weak position for the police to hold, since their own psychologist told them that this ransom note wasn't the kind of note a parent would write.

If the note was as critical a piece of evidence as John Douglas and the article in the *Denver Post* indicated, then once again the Ramseys should have been clearly on the outside of the circle of possible suspects. But the police held onto their revised but flawed theory. Eventually this theory was further updated to conclude that Patsy killed JonBenét *and* wrote the note. Why they made that leap is beyond me.

The media siege seemed to increase during the early part of February, and John was afraid for me and for Burke because photographers were lurking everywhere. They frightened us, because we didn't even know for sure that they were photographers. They could also be the killer, as far as we knew. My nerves remained on edge, and the constant pressure of being stalked by the media did not allow us any rest.

When the press discovered that we were staying at Jay Elowsky's house, which was located on the outskirts of Boulder, it became the new center of their attention. I felt as the early settlers must have felt when hostile Indians circled their sod houses. Jay didn't usually have many people cruising in and out of his neighborhood, much less a continuous assault of reporters and photographers. The media put a lot of pressure on Jay as well as us, since he was our friend and cared about our welfare.

On the morning of February 9, I looked out the window and noticed someone who seemed to be a telephone repairman kneeling down by the connection box in front of Jay's house. The man's truck looked like a U.S. West repair truck with similar markings, except it didn't actually say U.S. West on the side. Jay went outside to talk with the repairman.

"What are you doing?" Jay asked.

"Putting in another line," the repairman explained.

"Who ordered it?" Jay demanded.

"It says right here that you did, if you're the occupant of this house." The repairman showed Jay an official-looking repair order form.

"Really?" Jay looked perplexed. "I didn't order a new line to be installed in my house."

"Just doing my job." The man smiled as he kept working.

Later that day, when Jay called the regional offices of U.S. West, the phone company had no idea what he was talking about. Their records didn't indicate *any* request from *anyone* for a new line on that box. Only one conclusion was possible: Jay's telephone had been tapped by the so-called telephone repairman! Was the man working for the tabloids? Who knows, but probably. Police? Not likely. U. S. West came out within a few hours and untapped the phone line.

We couldn't even look out the windows without being seen. Reporters and photographers stood poised, ready to shoot whatever appeared in their camera sights. Later we were to learn that all they needed was a picture, then they could make up a story to fit the picture. "Tabloid magic," someone called it.

Jay finally became so frustrated that he drove over to the

vacant lot where a group of photographers were hanging out and tried to run them off. He carried a baseball bat in his hand, for added effect. In turn, the photographers picked up large lengths of metal pipe and held them in the air as if to strike. For a few moments I thought we were going to have a gang war!

Jay gave them a few harsh words, telling them to leave us alone, and then returned to his car. He was leaving when the police pulled up. He hit the brakes and turned around, glad to see that the police had come to run the paparazzi off. To our total dismay, the police arrested Jay! He became the culprit, not the photographers who had been stalking us twenty-four hours a day. I couldn't believe what I was seeing, but the police hauled him away in a squad car and towed his car away.

Trying to help our friend, I followed Jay down to the police station a few minutes later with Pat Burke, my attorney, to clarify what had actually happened. I broke into tears as I told the police about the media intrusion on our lives. "Someone broke into our home and killed our little girl," I reminded the police officers. "A killer is out there, and we are being hounded to death by the media!"

After I gave my brief testimony, I knew it would now be impossible to return to Jay's house without the struggle starting up again. The media would have multiplied like ants coming out of the ground, hungrily awaiting photos of our return. Instead, I went to Susan Stine's house because I had to pick up Burke after school. He and Doug Stine were working on a China project there because we didn't have any poster board or other project-making materials at Jay's house.

When John heard about the incident later that afternoon, he called me at the Stines'. "Are you okay?" he asked. "How about Jay?"

"I'm okay, just feeling a bit abused by the system. That's all," I answered. "But Jay's in some hot water." I told him the story of Jay's arrest.

"I don't think any of us should go back to Jay's house then," John advised. "Ask Susan if you can stay there."

"Okay," I said slowly. "I'll talk to her."

When I asked Susan if we could stay, she immediately agreed. Weeks later she joked that when I had asked if we could stay, she thought I meant for dinner. In the end the

Ramseys proved to be the family that came for supper and stayed for five months. The Stines graciously took us into their home and became our protectors. Their house felt like a safe haven to us, even when the media staked it out a few days later.

John and I later learned that the police had found a loaded 9 mm pistol under the seat of Jay's car—as well as the baseball bat. Jay was charged with a felony, but the case was eventually plea bargained to misdemeanor menacing, since it is legal to carry a gun in your car in Colorado. Our friend had only tried to protect us from the invasive paparazzi, and now he had a police record. The gangrene from the killer's evil act was beginning to destroy everyone around us.

Near Valentine's Day I was pressed into one of the most embarrassing and humiliating aspects of the police investigation of our family. The police requested that I donate pubic hair for DNA testing purposes. On December 26, when the blanket on which JonBenét had been lying in the basement was examined, a single pubic hair was discovered on the fabric. The police naturally pursued the source of that hair. I went to the Boulder Community Hospital *voluntarily* to have pubic hair taken from me for comparison with that single strand found on the blanket. Pat Burke drove me to the hospital. I dreaded the trip. It brought back bad memories of my cancer treatments and the battles I fought there to stay alive.

Detectives Linda Arndt and Jane Harmer were there to observe the testing and verify that everything was conducted legally and in accordance with acceptable procedures. I went back into a private examination room, where I removed my clothes below the waist to prepare for this humiliating examination of my pelvic area.

Once I was on the table, a nurse entered the examination room and prepared to take the sample of my pubic hair. The two detectives stood to one side, watching closely. The nurse began combing my pubic hair and transferring the sample to an envelope. As she worked over me, I suddenly noticed that the pink sweatshirt she was wearing had puffy red hearts painted across the front. Valentine's Day had been especially fun for JonBenét. The love celebrated on this occasion always touched me, and I had tried to make the day special for our family. My mother says it was her favorite holiday as a child, as well. Just a year earlier, JonBenét and I had gone to Michael's to buy puffy paint and two sweatshirt dresses to fashion into Valentine outfits. Together we had hand-painted the dresses. JonBenét had written, "I love you," on hers, and I had made little felt hearts with lace on the other one.

Until I saw the puffy red hearts on the nurse's sweatshirt, I hadn't even realized that we were on the eve of another Valentine's Day. The longer I looked, the more the sight of her shirt made me miss JonBenét, and I started crying. The nurse stopped. "I don't mean to hurt you," she said.

"No," I said. "You're doing okay. That isn't what's bothering me."

"Oh? . . . What's wrong?" the nurse asked. Over her shoulder I could see Detectives Arndt and Harmer, watching and listening.

"It's the pink shirt you're wearing," I explained.

"My sweatshirt?"

"Yes. JonBenét had a dress similar to that. We made it together last Valentine's Day." I swallowed hard. My throat had a big lump in it. "Your sweatshirt reminds me so much of JonBenét."

"Oh!" The nurse caught her breath. "I see," she said slowly. "I'm so sorry."

The nurse quickly snipped off more samples, which she placed in the small envelope to give to the two female police officers. The two cops had stood at the side, observing every detail, saying nothing. Totally humiliated by the procedure, I was grateful when the job was finished. I was told to put my clothes on, as I could now go home.

Taking a long, deep breath, I hurried out of the hospital, trying to be inconspicuous so no one would see me.

I don't know how anyone could have thought that we weren't cooperating with the police. Though the pubic hair sampling was a difficult and embarrassing task, I gladly complied to try to help the investigation. John was also put through the same embarrassing procedure. Detective Tom Trujillo supervised his sampling. We had already given our fingerprints, palmprints, and hand prints, as well as blood, hair, and handwriting samples. John Andrew and his roommate were also asked to give similar DNA evidence. This didn't seem to satisfy the cops; they continued to say we were being uncooperative.

A good example of our struggle to get evidence properly pursued was the announcement on February 15 that an unidentified palmprint had been discovered on the basement door—and still remains unidentified. To this day, we are not confident that the police actually did a thorough comparison of palmprint samples.

John and I instinctively felt that our civil rights were under assault, but we were anxious to talk or cooperate if it would get us closer to finding the killer. Even though we knew we were being pursued hard, we had always offered to meet with them as long as a representative of the district attorney's office was present. The truth is, the police simply didn't take us up on our offers. Instead, they seemed to leak stories to the media that portrayed us as uncooperative parents.

Like a hailstorm continuously pelting our house, another blow hit Patsy and me when a University of Colorado art student created a collage of blown-up pictures of JonBenét under the heading "Daddy's Little Hooker."

In the entry hall of the Sibell Wolle Fine Arts Building is a display area used for student work. Usually senior projects or personal art exhibits are posted there. This art student took JonBenét's picture from a national magazine cover, as well as other reproductions of her that appeared in a multitude of tabloids, enlarged them, and assembled the pictures in a collage that included lots of scribbled epitaphs. It created a grotesque portrayal of JonBenét.

The very large display ran the length of the hall in the Fine Arts Building. The newspapers rushed to photograph the distasteful display, and the story about the collage made national television news. It hurt us so deeply to see our daughter portrayed in this horrible manner. With John Andrew as a student at CU, the damage seemed even more horrendous.

A number of students had the same offended reaction and tore much of the display down, but the University of Colorado would not act. A university spokesman responded publicly with the explanation that the student was expressing free speech and "artistic integrity," and that the university could not ask him to remove his work. Because he was an art student, the whole sickening display could go back up again in the name of free speech. We were distraught that such an offensive portrayal of our child had been erected in the first place, and on top of that, the faculty seemed to find the work acceptable. I later heard that the exhibit finally came down only because university officials feared that the use of previously copyrighted photographs could end up in a legal confrontation. I received a particularly hard letter from a man in Denver during all this which said, "If you're any kind of a father, you'll tear that down." I had wanted desperately to destroy the grotesque exhibit myself, but knew that would be the media spectacle of the decade.

I decided that maybe the best thing I might do was to write the young man a letter and try to let him know how his cruel and heartless exhibit had affected Patsy and me. In my letter, I told him that he was young now but one day he would probably be a parent. Only when he was a parent himself would he realize how deeply people love their children. Then he might understand how much he had hurt us. I sent the letter but never received a response from the "artist."

Throughout the month of February, stories appeared that either intimated or claimed outright that I had in some way sexually abused my daughter. The art student smearing Jon-Benét's pictures on the wall of the art building played right into this escalating rumor. There is no way to describe the nausea and pain these accounts caused me as well as Patsy. I simply couldn't believe that the press could publish these horrible accusations. Nevertheless, the stories started mounting that JonBenét's death followed my attempts to sexually molest her.

Our pediatrician, Dr. Francesco Beuf, gave a rare public interview on Valentine's Day 1997, responding to these ugly stories and attempting to correct the impression that our family was abusive or abnormal. Earlier, the story had begun to circulate that we had taken JonBenét to see Dr. Beuf more than thirty times over the last year or so, and that must certainly indicate a history of problems, which in turn supported the theory that I had physically abused her. In fact, one University of Colorado psychology professor said publicly that she only took her children to the doctor once or twice a year, and our pattern was very strange. I desperately wanted to respond that we took our dog to the vet more than once or twice a year. But I did not. The fact is that JonBenét had a mild case of asthma, which required frequent visits to the doctor. We had good health insurance and used it freely whenever any of us got sick. That's the reason you have health insurance!

Patsy and I found Dr. Francesco Beuf to be a truly remarkable person. A brilliant man, Francesco's first career had been with the emerging U.S. space program. Our son Burke was fascinated with Dr. Beuf and the pictures in his home from his early days designing and testing rockets. After successfully following this line of work, Dr. Beuf realized how much he loved children and humanity in general, and that desire took him to medical school and then a specialty in pediatrics. He did his residency at Children's Hospital in Philadelphia.

Dr. Beuf knew our family well and believed that the talk of sexual abuse was so slanderous that he consented to an interview with KUSA in Denver. Beuf described his medical experience with our family in this way:

> *I can tell you as far as her medical history is concerned there was never any hint whatsoever of sexual abuse. I didn't see any hint of emotional abuse or physical abuse. She was a very much loved child, just as her brother . . . just a wonderful, happy kid who had the strength to deal with some very tough situations with regard to her mother's illness.*

As a security precaution after JonBenét's murder, Dr. Beuf had put all her medical records in a safety deposit box at the bank. Later he discovered that the box had been opened, even though *the bank had absolutely guaranteed it could only be opened with the client's personal key.* Dr. Beuf was livid.

Obviously, the bank had improperly opened the box and was responsible, so Dr. Beuf contacted the bank, demanding an explanation of what had occurred. To my knowledge, the bank never completely explained how or why the locked box had been opened. I don't know what happened, but I have a hunch that the police thought he might have been lying about JonBenét's records. Either the police or the media helped themselves to her confidential medical information. I still find it difficult to believe that a bank could have allowed something like this to occur. Has privacy died in this country? How secure are your medical records? Or your bank records? Not very, I'm afraid.

During this period, I was not too aware of what was going on in the media. John and Susan seemed to pay more attention to that stuff. It was hard for me to keep from sleeping most of the time. The short time that I was awake, I would get hit with such crazy events as the CU student's "art" exhibit portraying JonBenét in a disturbing manner. It killed my soul to see things like that. My baby, my innocent child, portrayed as a whore! It sent me right back to bed.

As I struggled with my pain from this outrageous verbal and visual assault, my thoughts drifted back to her birth almost seven years before, on August 6, 1990. I suppose it's hard for someone who has never had children to realize how precious these little miracles are to parents. On the joyful end of a scale of memorable experiences, JonBenét's birth holds a special place unto itself.

For three weeks in late July and early August, I had been dilated to three or four centimeters, so I knew the big day was fast approaching. Then on Sunday evening, August 5, Beth, Melinda, and John Andrew came over for a take-out Chinese dinner. I was feeling so tired and uncomfortable that I went to bed right after dinner, and left the dishes to Beth and Melinda. John and Burke took the three big kids back home to Marietta and returned an hour or so later. Then John put Burke to bed and came to bed, as well.

About 12:30 A.M., I woke up and had to go to the bathroom. John didn't stir. Even though I didn't feel any pain, I noticed a spot of blood. I immediately called my mother on the portable phone I had taken into our bathroom. If I was starting into labor, she and Dad would have to come and take care of Burke, who at the moment was sound asleep.

"Mom, sorry to wake you but . . ."

"Patsy!" Mom sounded groggy. "What's going on?"

"Well, you see," I said carefully choosing my words. "I noticed this spot of blood." Sitting on the edge of the bathtub, with the portable phone in my hand, I tried to extend my legs. "I was wondering if I could possibly . . . be . . . going . . ." My voice raised an octave as the first real contraction hit.

"Is John awake?" Mom asked with authority.

"No," I replied.

"Wake him up *now*—and call the doctor . . . We're on our way."

I called the doctor first, waiting patiently while the recording said to press one for this or press two for that. Finally I was able to leave a message, and shortly after that another contraction hit me. I knew I was in full-blown labor. This baby wasn't going to wait, and we had to get to the hospital immediately. I leaned over John to wake him and noticed that the digital clock said 1:00. He jumped straight up and quickly dressed in a plaid shirt and pink-colored Bermuda shorts. Did he realize he was appropriately dressed in pink for our new baby girl? I doubt it. He grabbed the suitcase I had prepacked and pulled the car out of the garage and around to the front of the house.

We left home, knowing Mom and Dad were on their way so we didn't have to worry about Burke. My sister Pam was only two miles away, and she would be coming too, so the only issue was getting to Northside Hospital as quickly as we could. John had a big Mercedes 500 SEL sedan at the time, which he accelerated down the now empty street. He turned south on Highway 400, just as I let out a scream.

John floored the gas pedal and told me later that when he saw the speedometer move through 120 mph, he knew he'd better slow down. The baby was coming fast, and we were still too far from the hospital for me to give in. I had to do anything I could to keep the baby from being born in the front seat of that big old Mercedes Benz. John is kind of squeamish about blood and stuff anyway, so that clearly wasn't going to be an option. Taking a deep breath, I put my feet up on the dashboard and hung on for dear life.

John slowed down to around 100 miles an hour after he calmed down a bit. Fortunately there was virtually no one on the highway at that time of the early morning. The dashboard clock read 1:12 A.M. as we pulled off the highway at the hospital exit and sped toward the main entrance. Once there, John swerved into the entryway. "No," I cried, "we need to go to the emergency entrance!"

When we pulled up in front of the emergency room, John

jumped out and opened the door for me. As I turned to step out of the car, my water broke! I grabbed my stomach and knew that the baby could come any second. As best I could, I started hobbling for the door, and just like Cinderella, I lost one of my slippers on the way in. When we got to the receptionist, John was trying to be very cordial. *Not now, John*! I thought. *Not now!*

"We're here to have a baby," he politely told the receptionist.

"Please take a seat," she urged.

"No!" I screamed back. "The baby is coming *right now*. Someone do something!"

"Oh, my." The receptionist sounded somewhere between frightened and dismayed. She signaled to two nearby women who came rushing over to me, pushing a wheelchair.

"I can't sit in that wheelchair," I cried, holding my stomach as the contractions increased.

Suddenly two women in scrubs materialized in front of me with a gurney. "Let's get you on here," one of them said. "We'll get you to delivery."

"Hurry!" My voice seemed to rise by itself. "Please! Can I please have an epidural!"

The two women raced me down the hall as fast as they could run, almost without looking where they were going. I saw a man ahead of us. His eyes widened to the size of quarters as he saw us coming at him. He quickly flattened himself against the wall so we could whiz past.

Once we were in the delivery room, a woman in green scrubs examined me. Her eyes became larger and larger.

"I've got to have an epidural!" I shouted.

"Honey, we're way past the epidural stage," the nurse answered. "We're on the phone with Doctor Floyd right now. We're doing everything we can to slow you down until she gets here."

I fell back on the gurney and knew the baby would be there any second. I was screaming and writhing in pain. I kept trying to pull my nightgown off, I was so hot.

"It will be okay," John said gently. "Just hold on. The doctor is on the way."

"Dr. Floyd's at the stop light," a nurse said from somewhere in the delivery room. "She's on her way into the parking lot."

She sounded as if she were giving the play-by-play commentary for the Kentucky Derby!

"Get this baby out of me!" I screamed, thinking my body was going to explode.

"Breathe!" one of the nurses demanded, looking directly in my face.

"The doctor's at the door. She's running down the hallway." The nurse with the phone shouted, "Get ready. Here she comes."

I couldn't delay another second. The baby was coming, and I couldn't have stopped her if my life depended on it. Dr. Floyd raced up to the end of the table, jammed on the rubber gloves a nurse handed her, and stepped into place just as Jon-Benét was born.

Suddenly . . . I felt absolutely wonderful . . . great . . . fine! I glanced at the clock and realized that JonBenét had come into this world at 1:36 A.M., about thirty minutes after we had started down the highway! I felt so good, I decided if I were ever pregnant again and had a choice, I'd go for natural childbirth all over again. Doctor Floyd told us later that morning, "If you two plan to have another baby, you'd better live really near the hospital or learn how to deliver it yourself."

My parents arrived just moments after the birth. Mom was carrying my lost slipper, which she had found lying on the driveway as she came in the emergency room door. I looked down at this beautiful baby girl cradled in my arms. This warm, wonderful bundle had arrived with a big bang and seemed to be saying, "Hello, world! Here I am!"

I had come up with JonBenét's name by putting John's first and middle names together into one name. John Bennett became JonBenét. Bennett was John's mother's maiden name. When we wavered back and forth between a couple of other options, I had asked Burke, who was three years old at the time, "What do you think about Caroline or Sarah?" He liked JonBenét the best, he said. After she was born, the discussion turned to her middle name. We had tentatively decided upon Collette, but as I sat in my hospital bed, filling out the birth certificate forms, I thought, *Who is Collette, and what in the world did she have to do with any of this? Her middle name will be Patricia, after moi.* And that was that.

Above all, I will always hold JonBenét in my heart with a sense of thankfulness and wonder. She blessed us for six and one-half years with the same exuberance and excitement with which she entered the world that night.

15

LAUGHTER IS THE BEST MEDICINE

When John and I descended on the Stines' home in mid-February, we inadvertently began a period that probably saved our sanity. Our lives had become so chaotic and shrouded in grief, we couldn't help feeling that the whole world had turned against us. Why that happened, we will never be sure. Our child was murdered and now the world hated us.

The Stines helped us move on.

Nathan, a young CU college student, already lived with the Stines and helped take care of their son, Doug, after school since both Susan and Glen worked at the university. By the time we moved in, though, Susan had retired from her position as director of planning to do some consulting work and have more free time. Her free time soon turned into a full-time job as housemother, nursemaid, and in general, Florence Nightingale.

The Ramsey clan, which included my mom and dad as well as the two of us and Burke, basically slipped into this arrangement and were welcomed as part of the household. Nine people now lived in a house that had formerly held four. To most people, this situation would seem impossible, but somehow Susan made it all work.

She quickly recognized how fragmented and lost we felt, and knew that we must recover some form of normalcy. She also understood how empty I felt, since much of my day had formerly been spent at the elementary school, volunteering in JonBenét or Burke's classrooms. A new routine, she felt, was necessary.

Susan began the morning by checking the Internet to see what might have occurred the day before that could set off some calamity we would have to face that day. The Internet seemed to be taking on a life of its own where the murder was concerned. Then came breakfast, and I tried to get up in time to offer John and Glen some help. Nothing fancy. Just cereal or bagels, usually. Susan would then drive Doug and Burke to school. Usually the boys would have to lie down in the back-seat to avoid the photographers who waited outside.

According to Susan's schedule, the first item of our after-school routine was to get the boys started on their homework. It was my job to help them do this, and I enjoyed the task. Only after the homework was finished could the boys play video games or watch television. (Only Nickelodeon or The Discovery Channel were allowed.) Susan quickly put into place a system of activity that kept John and me occupied and sheltered Burke from realizing how close we were living to the edge of an emotional cliff.

Believing that humor was healing, Susan tried to get every-one to laugh at least once a day. Telling jokes became a din-nertime ritual. The more stupid the joke, the better. One of our favorites was, "What has four legs and barks?" If someone answered, "I don't know," we'd say, "a dog." If someone said, "A dog," we would answer, "Oh, you've heard this joke be-fore." That joke, which showed how desperate we were for anything to laugh at, quickly became old. So Susan got joke books, and the boys would search for the good ones to read at dinner. Other friends joined in her quest, sending over en-velopes with a variety of new material, or bringing the jokes with them when they joined us for dinner.

Weekends were more difficult since everyone was at home for most of the day, and we didn't have the boys' school sched-ule to keep us occupied. The media were often lurking around outside because rumors that we might be arrested frequently occurred at the end of the week. We figured the police regu-larly spread these rumors in order to increase our tension and try to break us.

Susan initiated a "comedy filmfest." She began with a bunch of Mel Brooks movies like *The Producers, Young Frankenstein,* and *Blazing Saddles. The Blues Brothers, 1941,* and other John Belushi movies were also high on the list. After making sure the boys were told "we don't use words like this," she would put on a Belushi movie. Often she would say to the boys, "Count every single car that crashes and tell me at the end of the movie how many police cars and how many other cars you saw get destroyed." Watching these outrageous and funny films shifted our minds for the moment away from our grief and our mounting troubles with the police and the media.

After dinner I would usually excuse myself and retreat to our bedroom. Then I would choose one of the books on grief or faith that people had sent us, and read a few pages before crying myself to sleep. I knew Susan was trying to lighten the mood, but most of the time I just couldn't stand to make small talk or watch a movie when my heart was so broken. John responded in an opposite way. He tended to stay with the family throughout the evening, which helped distract his mind. He didn't like being alone and quiet. When he could stay awake no longer, he finally collapsed in bed. Although we could find no visible indication of it, we worried that our bedroom at the Stines' might be bugged. If so, all the police or media could possibly have overheard was the sound of crying and the dull drone of the white-noise machine Susan had put there to help lull us to sleep.

We were afraid that the Stines' phone line was tapped. Cell phone conversations could also be monitored. To make things more difficult for the media eavesdroppers, we developed a list of code names. We also turned our confrontation with the media into a sport of sorts. For example, one Sunday morning there was a loud knock on the front door. Susan raised the blind on the window next to the door and saw a man in a suit who looked rather unkempt.

He saw her looking out and said loudly, so she could hear him through the door, "I have information that will solve JonBenét's murder. I must see the Ramseys."

Susan muttered, "Oh, great, Sunday morning, and it's already ruined by some idiot." John was sitting on the couch in the living room, just to Susan's left. She was immediately suspicious that this visitor was in reality a media person. She told him to leave immediately. When he persisted, Susan called 911.

"There's a man here stalking us," she said, exaggerating a bit so she could get some help.

"Is he armed?" the operator asked.

"I don't know," Susan replied.

"You're not sure?"

Susan said, "Hold on. I'll go check." When she returned to the phone, she said, "He has something in his hand—a box or something—but I don't know what's in it."

The woman began to ask other questions, like "Do you know who he is?" "What does he look like?" "What is he saying?" Susan realized that the 911 operator was probably stalling to keep her on the line. "Look, I've got to go," she said.

"If you don't talk to me, I won't send anyone . . . Let me repeat. Do you know who he is? Is he armed?" the operator persisted.

"I don't know who he is or if he's armed," Susan repeated, "but I'll go check."

Susan went back to the door and raised the blind. "Let's see some ID," she called out to the visitor.

The man took out a very thin wallet and held it up so Susan could see it.

Susan opened the door and held out her hand. "Let me see it."

This dimwitted soul promptly gave Susan his wallet. She took it, shut and locked the door, and went back to the telephone. Once there, she began looking through the man's wallet to find out who he was, or at least whom he was impersonating. First she noticed several library cards for libraries in south Florida. Finally, a driver's license. But no money and no credit cards. Obviously the man carried this wallet for a specific purpose: to present an identity when asked by people like Susan.

"Okay," she said to the 911 operator, "this is who he is." She read the man's name and social security number to the operator.

Later Susan realized that when she was putting the ID back into the wallet, a small laminated card had fallen out on her kitchen floor. She discovered that it had all the home telephone numbers and cell phone numbers of the *Globe* tabloid big shots.

Meanwhile the man was still standing on the porch, yelling through the closed door, "Hey, lady, give me back my wallet!"

Shortly afterward the police arrived and found the man standing outside the front door, waiting to get his billfold back. The police talked to him and to Susan and finally handcuffed the guy and led him away. As he walked to the squad car, he kept trying to convince the cops that Susan had stolen his wallet.

With the scoundrel in custody, we concluded that the only thing to do was to take very good care of the phone card to make sure it didn't fall into the wrong hands. Somehow the contents of the laminated card were placed on the Internet. The *Globe's* attempt to harass us had backfired on them.

Later one of our friends, who shall remain nameless, decided to give the *Globe* a taste of its own medicine. She had *Globe* editor Tony Frost's home number, which had come from that man's laminated card. Why not give him a call? After all, the editor of such a publication ought to want to talk with one of his fans, shouldn't he?

That evening the friend called his home and in a sweet feminine voice asked, "Is Tony there?"

"No, he's not . . . He's at the office," replied the woman who answered the phone.

"At the office? He's supposed to be here at my apartment."

"What?!"

"He told me he was going to be here by now," our friend said. "Is this Tony's mother?"

"No, I'm not his mother. I'm his wife!"

"His wife! He told me he wasn't married. I can't believe that! . . ." With that, she hung up.

Our friend wished she could have been a fly on the wall of the Frost house the next morning. I'll bet it was frosty, indeed.

As we began to push back at the tabloids just a little, John and I began to loosen up slightly. Laughing helped us deal with the pain and regain some of our faculties.

Susan tried to help us slowly work through our grief and begin to manage our lives again. As she checked the Internet for the rumors du jour, she also looked for Web sites that ministered to people whose children had been murdered. The Compassionate Friends Web site offered advice that guided Susan in these months: "The mention of my child's name brings tears to my eyes but music to my soul." Susan willingly talked to us about JonBenét and listened to our memories.

She also carefully read the pamphlet "Helping a Homicide Survivor Heal," written by Dr. Alan D. Wolfelt, Director of the Center for Loss and Life Transition in Fort Collins, Colorado. The two people from the Boulder Police Victim's Advocate Unit had given us this small brochure on December 26. It discussed the way in which murder casts a social stigma around the family of the victim:

> *A sad reality is that members of a community where a tragic murder has occurred sometimes blame the victim or survivors. Out of a need to protect themselves from their own personal feelings of vulnerability, some people reason that what has happened has to be somebody's fault. This need to "place blame" is projected in an effort to fight off any thoughts that such a tragedy would ever happen to them.*

We could begin to see this reaction from people in Boulder. Thankfully, Susan and Glen were able to accept the extreme intensity of our grief, recognizing that we weren't going to "get over it" any time soon and would have to struggle for a long time simply to come to terms with all that had happened. Murder is especially devastating for the family and leaves everyone feeling that they have lost not only a loved one but their security as well. Being alone is frightening because you know that a killer is walking around out there somewhere. The Stines grasped the fact that fear, grief, and anxiety come naturally with this type of tragedy. Emotions sometimes came to the surface without warning. The least little thing might touch off a crying spell. They understood that John and I needed to wrestle over and over with the question of why this terrible tragedy had happened.

Just as a warm greenhouse shields plants from the cold of winter, their home afforded us the shelter we needed to work our way through the overwhelming, desperate feelings. They let us *feel* what we hadn't yet been able to live through. They didn't try to help our situation by saying, "Think of all you still have to be thankful for" or "I know just how you feel." Instead they listened to our desperation and tried to help us weather the healing process. They knew it was going to be a long, long time.

An average person reading the newspaper got more from the police each day than we did. Their silence was deafening. Each day John and I hungered for some insight, some idea, some answer to what was going on downtown at police head-quarters. Ninety days passed without any word.

Around the middle of March, the district attorney hired a very experienced homicide detective to look at the police investigation for the DA's office. After interviewing many candidates, Alex Hunter called Lou Smit out of retirement from the El Paso County Sheriff's Department and pressed him into service on our case. Smit had earned a reputation in Colorado Springs as a methodical, ethical, and very effective detective who had solved 90 percent of some two hundred homicides he investigated during his thirty-year career. He was best known for tracking down the killer of Heather Dawn Church, a little girl who had been murdered near Colorado Springs. That case lay dormant for four years until Lou began investigating it. With meticulous attention to detail, he identified the killer and ultimately arrested him in Florida. As John Douglas would say about Smit after meeting him, "I would hate to have that guy on my tail if I was a bad guy."

In addition to Smit, District Attorney Alex Hunter asked Boulder County Sheriff George Epp to loan Detective Steve Ainsworth to the DA's office so Hunter could make him part of the new investigative team. At least the district attorney was doing something the police had refused to do: accept help from people with proven experience.

It seemed unusual for the DA to hire his own detectives. John and I were convinced that he was beginning to see the problems with the BPD's investigation. The reputation of Smit and Ainsworth gave us hope that some significant progress might happen in the future. At the very least they would bring an objective viewpoint to the investigation. We were delighted that so much experience was being brought to bear on our daughter's behalf.

During the month of March, I became painfully aware of a new angle being played out at John's and my expense for personal profit. I couldn't believe the lengths to which people would go to make a few dollars. The "Judas Syndrome," I've heard it called.

Out of the clear blue, a former acquaintance of mine started trying to visit me at the Stines' for a "little conversation." Because of my past experience with Judith Phillips's attempts to launch a career as a photographer, I was wary of

what might be going on. Now, Judith showed up at the Stines'
doorstep three months after JonBenét's death, obviously
wanting something, but I wasn't sure what.

While Judith chose to bill herself as one of my closest
friends on tabloid television, I had actually been a business
colleague of her husband's when we all lived in Atlanta. Mel
Phillips had written a software program, and I coauthored the
user's manual that went with his product while we both
worked for Hayes Microcomputer Products, Inc. During this
time I had met his wife, Judy. In those days she was known as
Judy, but by the time John and I moved to Boulder, where they
now also lived, she had become Judith. When we arrived in
Colorado, they were one of the few families we knew, and we
went to dinner with them several times. But since our children
were different ages and went to different schools, we actually
didn't have a lot in common with them.

Judith's "thing" was photography, a hobby she intensely
pursued. I had urged her to take a couple of classes when I
first moved to Boulder, and I encouraged her to enter her
work in the 4-H fair in Longmont. She enrolled in the classes,
and the next thing I knew, she was advertising herself as a
professional, always trying to put together a "photography
show."

Judith began traveling all over Colorado, leaving her family
for days at a time "to shoot." On one occasion, when my
mother was in town, Judith begged to photograph us for a
mother-and-daughter series she was putting together. She also
took pictures of JonBenét and me, which gave her two generations of mothers and daughters. She had approached John
about getting Access Graphics to sponsor this show as she sent
it on a self-initiated tour of Colorado; his company declined.
Our pictures didn't make the cut for the traveling mother-
daughter photo show Judith took throughout the state.

During my struggle with cancer and losing my hair, Judith
frequently asked to take my picture. I had tried to tell her that
I was in a fight for my life and having my bald head snapped
by her camera wasn't high on my list of priorities. However,
Judith persisted, so shortly after I finished my chemotherapy,
I acquiesced to doing a few pictures in the spring of 1994. By
this time, I had about a quarter inch of hair and wasn't as sensitive about my baldness. Saying yes to the brief photography

session was easier than constantly fending off her persistent inquiries.

Several years passed and then JonBenét's death became national news. Now Judith came to see me at the Stines' house, asking for permission to publish the mother-daughter pictures that had previously been excluded from her show. Fortunately, Susan Stine had heard earlier that she was trying to sell some of the photographs to *People* magazine. Susan told Judith in no uncertain terms to leave and not come back. Back in January, when Judith told our friends she wanted to sell the photos, our libel attorney had sent a standard letter to her, telling her not to publish, sell, or distribute any photographs of the Ramsey family without our permission.

Yet a few months later Judith apparently sold the pictures to the *National Enquirer*. She always had her subjects sign an agreement, saying that she could do whatever she wanted with the photographs, and I had apparently signed such a document years earlier, never dreaming she would do anything further with the photos, let alone sell them to a supermarket tabloid.

Spring break was at the end of March that year, so the Stines and Patsy and I decided to take the boys on a trip to Sea Island in Georgia. The media still persisted in following us everywhere, so we couldn't imagine the boys spending spring break sequestered in the Stines' house. We could all stand a change of venue.

The morning we were to leave, Saturday, March 29, the media were everywhere. They knew it was spring break and they expected we might be going somewhere—so they were going to catch the big "getaway" on film! Sure enough, when we boarded the Delta flight for Atlanta, where we would visit our family before driving to Sea Island, the plane seemed to be filled with media people: a representative from every television station in Denver, some of the Atlanta stations, and those ever-present tabloid photographers. In fact, one sat next to me on the plane, but only clutched his camera and didn't say a word.

We put the boys in two seats together at about the tenth row back, and told them, "Pretend you don't know us, but rest assured we will be watching you." Glen Stine sat two seats behind them. The rest of us split up: Patsy sat in a right aisle seat with Susan across the aisle on the other side of that row. I sat a couple of seats behind the two of them.

After the plane was airborne, one man popped up in a seat up front and started taking photographs. The flight attendant quickly warned him, "Put that camera away or I'm going to take it from you." He reluctantly complied and sat back down like a shamed puppy. It's amazing the authority a flight attendant can command.

I suspected we were in for a media sideshow once we got off the plane in Atlanta. So as we neared the airport, I sent a note to the pilot, explaining the situation, and asking if Patsy and I could exit through the back of the plane, rather than going out the Jetway. (I still tighten up inside when I have to walk off a Jetway into an airport terminal. I've become conditioned to having cameras pointed at me, and people putting cassette recorders up to my face.)

As the passengers were leaving the plane, Susan and Glen walked up behind the boys, who had waited in their seats until one of the Stines appeared alongside. They led the boys off the plane as camera lights waited for "the Ramseys." A flight attendant had to order a cameraman out of the Jetway. Thankfully, the media rarely recognized Burke, and they didn't this time either because he was not walking with us.

Meanwhile, Patsy and I watched as the other passengers walked to the front of the plane. As they passed us some said very kind things. We waited in our seats until everyone had gotten off, and then the flight attendant led us to the service door at the rear of the jet, where the pilot had arranged for a ramp car to be standing by. We descended the stairway and into the van waiting there to take us to an offsite car rental facility.

Soon after that, the Stines and the boys were waiting to get our many pieces of luggage and our golf bags off the carousel at the baggage claim. Next to them stood the Atlanta Channel 2 Action News team, desperately searching for the elusive Ramseys. Photographers don't travel light, so the visiting media were now stuck there at the baggage claim, waiting for their trunks of equipment.

"Those Ramseys," Susan heard one of them say to the other, "how did they get their luggage out of here so fast?"

The Stines had to laugh as they put our luggage into a big cart and walked out to the passenger pickup area where we were just pulling up in our rented van. I drove around in front of the large Channel 2 truck, opened the back of my van, and helped Glen load our luggage. That evening we watched the eleven o'clock news and there stood the Channel 2 reporter saying, "The Ramseys came into town tonight under cover of darkness and we don't know where they are at this time." As he said this, we could see our van pulling out behind him. We laughed hysterically and gave high fives all around. We were learning to beat them at their own game!

During this time we also learned that the media paparazzi hate to have their own pictures taken or to be followed. Knowing their fear of cameras gave us an added opportunity to evade or provoke them. Just turn the tables and point a camera in their direction and watch them squirm! Turnabout is fair play, it seemed.

Even though we made a sport of the media game, it still was very unnerving to have these people shadow us. There was always the possibility that the person following us was the killer, not a photographer.

16

GEORGIA ON MY MIND

April blew into Boulder with down-sloping winds off the eastern face of the Rockies, creating moist, warmer air. The snow piles left from plowing began to disappear, and you could smell the possibilities of spring in the air. It was still ski season in the mountains, but that would quickly draw to a close. More than three months had passed since JonBenét's murder, and there was no light at the end of this dark, ugly tunnel.

Patsy and I were still staying at the Stines', but our emotional struggles were far from over; the pain hadn't eased much. We simply moved from day to day, trying to take care of what we had to do. The first waking moment in the morning was the hardest part of the day, when you left the peace of sleep and woke to the nightmare of life.

Patsy and I talked about the investigation constantly. We desperately wanted to do something that would encourage the law enforcement process to go in the right direction. We understood that the police had to look at us, but we feared they were looking *only* at us. We knew that would not find the killer.

In the spring we formed the JonBenét Ramsey Children's Foundation. Some donations had been given in her memory at the time of her death, and in addition we added our own private funds. When Beth died, we had established a foundation in her honor and we wanted to do something similar for JonBenét. The foundation's overriding principle is this: children are our society's most valuable and fragile asset. We must nurture and protect our children with the full force of our abilities and be known as a society that values its children above all else.

We struggled for a time with what specifically we wanted

the foundation to support. After much thought and prayer, it seemed right that one objective of the foundation would be to enhance the safety of children by helping focus resources and attention on the most heinous of crimes, child murder. Our experience had shown that local police in smaller jurisdictions don't have the experience and wisdom necessary to effectively track down child killers. Of the eighteen thousand police jurisdictions in the United States, many must be similar to Boulder, with limited experience and knowledge about this kind of horrible crime. We felt a need to make resources available to them, resources that could be called upon when a child was murdered. We also wanted the foundation to support the building of faith in children's lives, because faith is the ultimate armor for the battle of life. A strong foundation would enable them to grow spiritually for the rest of their lives. I had grown to understand how important my mother's early religious training had been to me. Now that I was walking this particularly difficult path, I was even more indebted to my faith, which helped me keep an eternal perspective and therefore my hope.

Patsy and I guaranteed a reward of one hundred thousand dollars for information leading to the arrest and conviction of the person or persons who killed our daughter. Perhaps a role of the foundation could be to offer substantial rewards for unsolved child killings with a staffed resource center to solicit tips. Money has a way of making people talk. The tabloids know this. Maybe we could put their techniques to better use. We continue to refine the course of the foundation as we take it a step at a time to see where we might be most effective in protecting our children, and we need to find funding sources to carry out this work.

As a matter of fact, leads did start to come in on the tip line, and several proved extremely interesting. These leads were followed up by our investigators and then turned over to the police. The problem was that we weren't sure if the police were taking these leads at all seriously. If they weren't, it seemed to suggest that they had their gun sights on Patsy and me, refusing to pay any attention to anyone else who might conflict with their theory about our guilt.

We had heard that the police did do some follow-up on the two people we had mentioned to them on December 26:

Linda Hoffmann-Pugh, our housekeeper, and Jeff Merrick, a former Access employee. Linda, because she had been very agitated a few days before Christmas and wanted to borrow money, and Jeff, because he had made what seemed to be threats against me personally and our business. Linda, her husband, Mervin, and her daughter, Ariana, had been in our house over the Thanksgiving holidays in 1996 while we were visiting our family in Atlanta. Patsy had asked Linda to put up our Christmas decorations, including the artificial Christmas trees that were stored in the room in the basement where Jon-Benét was later found. We were amazed when Linda said in a television interview after the murder that this room was so obscure, she did not even know it existed. Yet the room was not hidden or out of the way. The door could be clearly seen from the base of the stairs, straight down the hall.

We had heard that detectives had interviewed Linda and her husband and had taken hair, blood, and saliva samples. Certainly we appreciated her comments about us during her television and radio appearances. When she was asked if she thought we killed JonBenét, she replied, "No." Pressed further by the question, "What will you do if it turns out that they did kill JonBenét?" Linda replied, "I'll never trust anybody ever again."

We also heard that the authorities had questioned Jeff Merrick, who had threatened to bring me and Access Graphics down when he left the company in 1996. Jeff said he had been friends with me once but certainly wasn't anymore.

Another former Access Graphics employee had been fired because he had physically assaulted one of our female employees while at work. In his departing interview he sarcastically told his boss, who had just adopted a baby from China, "I hope you enjoy your new daughter" and then left the room. The man took this as a threat against his adopted daughter. That released employee had, in fact, been inside our house in the fall of 1996 to do some work on our Apple computer.

A reporter for the *Denver Rocky Mountain News,* Charlie Brennan, uncovered some startling facts about Santa Claus (Bill McReynolds) and his wife. On March 15, 1978, Janet McReynolds's play *Hey, Rube* had opened off Broadway at the New York City Interart Theater and had run for sixteen performances. Based on fact, the play depicted a young girl held captive in an Indiana basement where she was abused, tortured, and finally killed. The account of the murder originally appeared in *The Basement,* a book by Kate Millett, which proved to be an upsetting read, offering little explanation for the crime beyond the fulfillment of someone's frightening and disturbed fantasies.

The review of McReynolds's play *Hey, Rube* in the *New York Times* said, "It is not clear what the author intended to write. The play could be a psychological study of the killer, a sociological study of sexism, a sympathetic profile of the hapless victim, or a courtroom melodrama." The playwright offered an interview to a local paper, explaining, "I've always been interested in the way victims frequently seem to seek their own death, or to deliberately choose their own murderer."

In time, Janet's writings would prove to be a source of concern and alarm as JonBenét's murder seemed to have similarities to this bizarre play. Equally astonishing was the personal situation of two of the McReynolds's children, Jill and Jessie.

When Jill was nine years old, she and a friend were kidnapped. After the friend was molested, both girls were released, but no one was ever charged with the abduction. The kidnapping occurred twenty-two years earlier *to the day* before JonBenét's death.

Son Jessie had a brief moment in the spotlight when he abruptly announced to the world his innocence in our daughter's slaying. An unknown in the case, Jessie McReynolds's statements didn't make much sense because no one knew who he was or what his relationship to the murder was. Jessie insisted that his family was innocent because they had all been at some family event on Christmas night. We still cannot believe that anyone we know committed this terrible crime, and we have told the police that.

Patsy and I decided to again publicize our reward for information that might help lead to a capture of the killer. We placed a quarter-page ad in the *Boulder Daily Camera* on April 27, repeating our offer of a hundred-thousand-dollar reward for information that would result in an arrest. This time we added JonBenét's most recent school picture to the ad. Our hopes and prayers were that this ad would work on the consciences of the person or persons who knew the identity of the killer and that they would come forward with the tip that would lead to an arrest. Each time we ran an ad, the tip line would light up with calls. Yet in the midst of trying to help find our daughter's killer, we still had to deal constantly with the invasive media.

I always tried to protect Patsy from the paparazzi popping up from behind cars and out of open doorways with a camera or notepad. Suddenly they would start asking questions—or worse, shouting obscenities in hopes of inciting a reaction. The reality of an unexpected intruder still scared her to death.

Once the media figured out that we would always be in church on Sunday mornings, a dozen or so photographers waited every week across the street from St. John's. They became so predictable that one of the church warden's weekly jobs was to move the press back from the church grounds. Soon they actually started coming into the church. I thought, *Hey, that's not so bad. Let's get them into church any way we can. Maybe it will do them some good!* If we had been a child in the church's primary department, we probably would have gotten an award from St. John's for bringing the greatest number of "friends" to Sunday school. As the sun rose on Sunday morning, we really brought out the tabloid people! For many I'm sure it was their first experience inside a church.

One morning at the point in the service when Episcopalians "pass the peace," I turned around to find this sort of greasy-looking man standing behind us wearing a raincoat. "Peace be with you," I said and extended my hand.

The man shook my hand but said nothing. I thought later, *If that guy's not a tabloid reporter, I'll be surprised.* I believe it was Craig Lewis, who was later indicted for attempted bribery.

However, one of the most persistent people I encountered was twenty-five-year-old Jeff Shapiro, a reporter for the *Globe* tabloid magazine. Apparently Jeff Shapiro felt that attending our church was a means of gaining some access to Patsy and me. Although we had no idea who Shapiro was, this young man began sitting behind us in church and participating as if he were a regular church member. I'm sure that most of the time he was mystified by what was going on during Holy Communion, but he played right along.

Another time, when we went up to take communion, Shapiro went to the altar rail and knelt beside us to receive the sacraments. Shapiro became a regular at St. John's for a while. Later we were to learn that Jeff Shapiro had told Father Rol that he wanted to convert from Judaism to Christianity. I'd say that's going to some great lengths just to get a story!

We also learned that Shapiro had graduated from Florida State before going to Washington, D.C., as an intern in the White House Office of Media Affairs. From there the *Globe* hired him in early 1997 to move to Boulder, where his assignment was to "infiltrate the Ramseys' inner circle." As part of that assignment, he even spent a month in Okemos, Michigan, where I went to high school, digging into my early life in that community. Apparently there was no length that was too far for Shapiro to go in trying to find some dirt about our family for the *Globe*. None was found, but Shapiro sent me some complimentary quotes from a few of my old high school girl friends. That was actually pretty interesting.

On most Sundays Patsy and I had taken a seat toward the back of the church since we usually came in at the last minute. It was always hard to get two little kids up and dressed on Sunday morning and make it to church much before the service was to start. After JonBenét's death, the cameras would be waiting for us outside, so we started coming in with Father Rol through an entrance at the front of the church near the altar. We could look over the congregation and see those beady-eyed characters sitting around the sanctuary staring at us, notepads in hand. You could certainly tell that they were in the church but *not in church*.

Ultimately, we felt we had to start going to other churches or "church hop," as we liked to say, since these media guys and the barrage of cameras were so much of a nuisance to the rest of the St. John's parishioners. Many Sundays we would attend a different church in Boulder or Denver; sometimes people would recognize us, and they would treat us with such genuine graciousness and compassion.

Jeff Shapiro was not the only media person intruding into our personal lives. One day in April Susan Stine was returning from taking Doug and Burke to school when she noticed the garbage truck a block behind her, headed toward her house. Yet when she pulled up to the back of her house to go into the garage, she realized that someone else had already emptied her garbage. Susan called the police. "Someone has stolen my garbage!" she said, telling them that whoever did this was invading her privacy and obviously looking for confidential information. But the police didn't really seem to care. In fact, the law in Boulder is: if you put something out as trash, anybody can claim it.

Actually there wasn't anything confidential in the garbage anyway. If a letter came with a return address, we would tear that off before we put the envelope in the trash. (We didn't want anyone who wrote to us to be bothered by the media.) Then we would place these items in a separate container and Glen or I took that trash to work and dumped it there.

After this first trash-taking incident, Susan vowed to find something she could put in the garbage to discourage our tabloid friends from taking it again. She went to McGuckin Hardware and spent an hour going through different departments, looking for the worst-smelling liquid she could find. Finally, in the gardening area, she found a bottle of fish fertilizer. She opened the top and was repulsed by the greenish liquid that looked and smelled horrible. Just what she wanted. She purchased a gallon jug.

The next Tuesday was garbage day. Susan went out before the garbage men came and poured the fish fertilizer into all the plastic bags. The stuff smelled so bad, it made her eyes water. Then Susan stood on a step ladder inside the garage with binoculars and a camera to see if she could photograph the people who were "stealing" the trash. After a while she gave up her stakeout, but that day the garbage disappeared again before the real garbage truck arrived.

This happened week after week for a month, despite the fact that there could have been nothing meaningful in the trash—and that it was heavily spiked with fish fertilizer. I'm not sure how anyone could be paid enough money to steal that trash week after week, and go through it completely, especially when they had to know that we knew what they were up to. Who were the culprits? We never knew for sure, but we obviously suspected the tabloid media.

The one-hundred-thousand-dollar reward that Patsy and I offered for information leading to an arrest lit up the tip line, and we continued to occasionally get pearls of information that seemed legitimately interesting. We also had some negative, cruel reactions to our reward that involved a heartless prank. Around May 7, reward fliers appeared up and down the Pearl Street Mall saying, "$100,000 reward for information leading to the arrest and conviction *of murderer John Ramsey*." Patsy and I were stunned that someone had gone to such lengths to harass and embarrass us. It seemed the systematic attempt of the media and the police to convince the Boulder community that we were involved in our daughter's death was working.

Early in May we decided to place yet another ad in the paper, and we let the district attorney know what we were going to do. At his office's request we added a description of a suspicious, well-dressed man who had been seen approaching children in Boulder over the Christmas holidays; we asked the public for help in identifying this man.

The media went crazy with this ad, and Mayor Leslie Durgin speculated in public that the mention of this suspicious, well-dressed man was just another Ramsey gimmick to divert suspicion from themselves. Newspapers began writing stories on the appearance of our Boulder ads, suggesting they were all part of the Ramsey "P.R. machine." Of course, even negative stories helped spread the word about the reward, but this was a clear example of how we had already been convicted by the lynch mob.

On May 13 District Attorney Alex Hunter publicly responded to the flurry of stories, noting that some people believed "the ad was the work solely of the Ramsey family, when, in fact, it was partly the product of our [the DA's] commitment to follow reasonable leads." We had finally succeeded in working together with law enforcement authorities in a united effort, even though the mayor and the media tried to shoot it down.

During that same week it was reported that the Boulder PD received DNA test results from Cellmark Diagnostics; the company had been testing samples since they received this material from the BPD on March 4. However, the Boulder police indicated they would not release information on the content of these test results to the public or anyone else. Patsy and I had no idea what the police had uncovered, if anything, and remained in the dark.

After we considered this for several days, our attorneys put in an official request on May 16, asking that the Colorado Bureau of Investigation send our investigators the test results. We knew it was important for our people to have copies of all of the available material and evidence, since they were trying to find the killer, even if the Boulder police only seemed to continue to investigate us. What we were beginning to see was that as victims and parents of a murdered child, we didn't have the right to examine or know much of anything, including DNA test results. However, if we were arrested and charged, then we would have the right to see any and all of the evidence that was being used against us. Sound contradictory? We certainly thought so!

By spring John and I had started to think about the possibility of moving back to Atlanta. We had returned to Boulder after JonBenét's death to find the killer, to keep Burke in his school, and to facilitate John's business. But the end of the school year was fast approaching, and we realized how badly we wanted to leave Boulder and go home to live closer to our families in the South. Our experiences in Boulder would always haunt us, and they would be even more traumatic if we stayed.

John and I hoped we could find a home in the Buckhead area, as we had always loved that part of Atlanta. In the springtime, when the dogwoods and azaleas bloom, the city has to be one of the most beautiful places on this earth. In the 1800s the wealthier citizens of Atlanta would build summer homes in Buckhead and drive the twelve-mile distance from their city homes in their horse-drawn carriages. The story is that the area was named Buckhead because an old tavern there had a large deer head mounted over the bar.

In the past I'd always enjoyed looking at houses and inspecting every nook and cranny, but my enthusiasm just wasn't there now. Crying still seemed to occur far more than I would have imagined possible. In addition, I found that I tired easily, since I was still spending a good part of the day in bed. Real estate research turned into a grueling exploration.

Too many of the places we looked at touched raw nerve endings that overwhelmed me. I remember walking into one house I particularly liked on Habersham Road, a meandering lane of large, old Atlanta homes. As I walked into the living room, I discovered a large portrait of a little girl, the daughter of the people who owned the house. The beautiful child's countenance hit me like a brick in the face. Precious memories shot through my mind. I quickly left the living room, but as I strolled through the house, everywhere I looked I saw little dolls on shelves, beds, and the floor. Ribbons and bows seemed to be in every room. Even though the house was a warm home, the reminders of the little girl were heartbreaking for me. I couldn't stay. I had to get outside. I could feel my body constricting, and breathing became more difficult.

I tried to find a place to sit down outside because I was beginning to shake. The afternoon was slipping away, and I was tired from all we'd done that day. The trembling abruptly became more violent and I started crying. Without warning, a panic attack engulfed me in fear. John helped me to the car, and our realtor suggested we call it a day.

Later, I tried to understand what had happened to me. I thought about that house on Habersham and what it looked like. Suddenly I saw both the outside and the inside of the house. The exterior architecture was English Tudor, just like our house in Boulder. I had seen other houses with evidence of little girls around, but that had never been combined with the English Tudor exterior. My conscious mind hadn't seen the similarities, but my subconscious intuitively sensed the familiarity. That had started the panic attack.

John and I also had a hard time looking at homes that had a basement. He simply couldn't look in those basements, and I knew that such a house wouldn't work for our family. Because I was sadly aware that we did not need a house with a lot of bedrooms, seeing a house with five or six bedrooms was extremely painful. Our realtor, Beth, had been a friend for years and understood the strain we were under, but all she could do was present the houses available on the market. Unfortunately, most of them had both a little girl's bedroom and a basement. Beth told us that she prayed that God would lead us to the right home during the weekly Bible studies conducted at her realty company. That gave us great comfort.

At the same time we looked at houses, we also started to check out private schools in Atlanta, looking for the right place for Burke to enroll in the fall. Schools and houses. We went back and forth, looking at each repeatedly. In addition to the emotional strain involved in locating a house, I had to fill out tons of paperwork for the school application process. Fortunately, three dear friends—Susan Sperduto, Mary Justice, and Susan Stine—helped immensely with this arduous task.

I discovered that Burke had to do a number of things in the application process that I hadn't expected. He would need to take a series of tests, and some of the schools wanted to know considerably more about him personally. When we visited the schools in person, I would often see a class of kindergartners, sitting in their classrooms working away. The sight of all of the children JonBenét's age playing and enjoying school would tear me apart. *Why was my little girl taken from me? Why, God, why?*

No matter where I went, I found myself thinking of her all the time. I loved JonBenét so much that it was impossible not to think about the "what ifs." Little incidents around a school brought things she had done to mind. Sometimes I'd cry; occasionally I'd smile. During one of these onsite visits, I thought again of one of JonBenét's experiences at High Peaks Elementary in Boulder.

One of her classmates had brought cupcakes to school because it was her birthday. Unfortunately, the mother had miscounted and come up one cupcake short of the number of children in the class. Everyone was in a quandary, and the little girl didn't feel like she should have to give her own cupcake away.

"Why don't we cut my cupcake in half?" JonBenét suggested.

"That's a good idea," the teacher answered. "Then everyone can have one."

"Fine," JonBenét replied. "I'll take one of the halves and someone can eat the other one."

The teacher reported this incident to Charles Elbot, the principal of the school, who awarded JonBenét one of his "I caught you being good" awards for her thoughtfulness. Was she ever proud! And so was I.

As I thought of incidents like this, I would struggle to keep the tears at bay. The lump in my throat was always there. Even though I didn't mentally grasp the fact at the time, everything that my body and soul was going through was part of the process that victims of homicide experience.

Burke was accepted for enrollment in a private school, and that helped narrow the circle of choices of homes. Eventually we discovered a house on Paces Ferry Road right across the street from the school, and only about ten miles from the cemetery where Beth and JonBenét were buried. Unfortunately, in many of the homes that we inspected, the master bedroom was on the first floor and the children's rooms were upstairs. We had lived for many months in one twelve-by-twelve room at the Stines, with Burke just a short distance away from us and many people around to protect us. One thing was for sure! I didn't want Burke far away from us at night. In this house all of the bedrooms were close together on the second floor. As I looked around the place on Paces Ferry Road, I sensed that this house could work for us, even though it did have a basement.

Besides, a house is just a house. It's the love inside that makes it a home.

17

INSIDE THE INVESTIGATION

One of the most tasteless people who popped up during this whole spectacle was an unknown woman named Kim Ballard from Tucson, Arizona, who started calling my office at Access Graphics, asking to speak to me. From the outset, her calls were suspect, but with all that was going on, we didn't pay much attention to her. My assistant always took the calls, and I never spoke to the woman.

"I must speak to John," Ballard would insist, with worry and familiarity in her voice.

"John who?" my secretary responded innocently but with some intention.

"I need to talk to John Ramsey. Tell him the media are closing in on me. I've got to tell them something," Ballard insisted.

"I don't understand?"

"I don't know what to tell them. I need help," Ballard continued.

"I'm afraid I'm missing something," the secretary would reply.

After these phone calls became persistent, we reported them to our investigators. Jennifer Gedde, an investigator with Ellis Armistead and Associates, called this woman back after one of her calls to me and tried to determine who this woman was and what she meant by "needing help." Had she asked for money, we would have immediately filed a complaint with the cops for attempted extortion. Yet Ballard was clever enough not to ask for a payoff over the phone, but she kept saying that she needed help or she would have "to tell the media and the police everything about 'us.'" Ultimately she must have shifted her requests for money to the media, to get them to pay her for her story.

The next thing we knew, this strange woman was on national television, claiming that a few years ago she had been much more petite (she certainly wasn't now) and that she'd been a blonde who looked a lot like JonBenét. This heavy-set woman started making the rounds on the network news and TV talk shows, telling the world that she was my mistress! Ballard had this incredible spiel worked out with the details of our many alleged rendezvous at the Brown Palace Hotel in Denver during the year Patsy had cancer. She said I would buy her pageant costumes to wear during our trysts. Unbelievable! But the media loved it, and I'm sure this woman made some pretty good money out of it.

The woman claimed that I bought her lingerie from Victoria's Secret, but the story didn't stop there. Ballard even had me flying to Tucson, Arizona, where she lived, for illicit relations with her! Sadly my family and friends sat before their television sets, listening to these horrible stories in total disbelief and profound dismay. Ballard hit the usual TV tabloid shows, including Geraldo, who aired her a few times. Geraldo pushed her to submit to a polygraph test, but she refused.

During the talk shows, the host would always get around to asking, "Do you think that John Ramsey could have committed this murder?"

"Yes," Ballard would thoughtfully sigh and seemingly admit so reluctantly. "Knowing him the way that I do, yes, I do think he could have done this."

I had no clue who this woman was! I had never seen her before, never spoken to her before, and never visited her in Tucson. The only time I had been in the Brown Palace in Denver was for Patsy's birthday—with Patsy. With the million and one serious problems Patsy and I were bombarded with, now we had to listen to some screwball make up these unbelievably damaging stories on national television. This woman's accusations were particularly hurtful, since she had attacked my morals to the core.

Policewomen Melissa Hickman and Jane Harmer even bought into her story and flew to Tucson to interview her. However, after keeping the Boulder police officers waiting for four hours, Kim Ballard refused to meet with them, claiming that she'd changed her mind about everything. This happened a second time, with the police flying again to Tucson. Apparently she was smart enough to know that lying on national television for money was one thing, but lying to the police could result in serious trouble.

Finally, head of Boulder detectives John Eller had to admit, "At this point, we would have to consider anything Ms. Ballard may say as suspect. We don't plan to set up other interviews with her." After spending thousands of dollars of taxpayers' money and wasting valuable time, the police concluded Kim Ballard was a dead-end street and finally wrote her off as a crackpot. I could have told them this if only they had asked, but since I was one of their prime suspects, they wouldn't do that.

Whoever this woman was, I would have to say that one of the gravest injuries inflicted by the media was giving her exposure on national television and newspapers, saying that she committed adultery with me at the same time my wife was struggling to survive cancer.

I think it was during that summer that I happened to channel-surf past Charles Grodin's talk show one evening, when he had three or four guests on talking about me and the Ballard allegations. As they chitchatted and repeated as fact what she had said, Grodin made the sarcastic comment, "Boy, she is such a petite woman!"

Eventually even the *National Enquirer* passed on paying Ballard for her story. One of the editors is reported to have said, "I don't know what she looked like two years ago, but I can't believe that John Ramsey ever had an affair with this woman." Could this have been a moment of journalistic integrity at the notorious *Enquirer*? Probably not. Their refusal to go with this woman's story probably had more to do with her reported asking price—one hundred thousand dollars—for the exclusive story.

On May 14 John and I saw a story in the *Boulder Daily Camera* stating that both Linda Ardnt and Melissa Hickman had been dropped from our investigation. I was upset by the report and hoped it wasn't true. Linda had been the first detective on the scene on December 26, and I felt she was a compassionate, concerned police officer who honestly cared about us and finding the killer. Of course, I would later see her on the national television show, *Good Morning America*, saying she knew on December 26 that John was the killer because she had seen it in his eyes. Apparently her talents went way beyond even my imagination.

The rumor John and I heard circulating through Boulder was that Linda had received a great deal of the blame for the mistakes and mismanagement of our case. I knew that she and the other police had made serious errors, but I couldn't help feeling that she was being treated like the fall guy for the entire mess at the Boulder Police Department, when the real problem was in the leadership.

We wondered if this announcement had been the result of recent press articles, which had begun exposing the errors of the police investigation and focusing on mistakes made in the first hours after daybreak on December 26. Soon the *Denver Rocky Mountain News* started a more detailed investigation and discovered that Linda Arndt had not gotten to our house until two hours and eighteen minutes after I first called the 911 number seeking help. Obviously, a considerable amount of time had lapsed. The newspaper also noted that the Boulder police had refused help from the Denver Police Department, which investigates about one hundred murders a year to Boulder's one or two.

Among the other missteps noted were that although the ransom note said the house was being watched, two or three marked Boulder police cruisers pulled up to the front door of our home—in plain sight. Still another error was that a detective (Linda Arndt) had asked John to search our fifteen-room residence for anything unusual. Experts, the paper said, still shake their heads at the Ramseys being permitted to conduct a second search while police remained upstairs. "Everybody should have been put under control, and police should have done a thorough search of the house, not with the family member leading the search," Robert Ressler, a former FBI agent and specialist in criminal profiling, said.

Then the newspaper noted the BPD's lack of homicide knowledge. "Boulder police simply didn't have the experience to handle the case," according to Robert Keppel, the lead criminal investigator for the attorney general's office in the state of Washington. "In cities where there are few homicides, not only are detectives inexperienced, but their supervisors are inexperienced. They don't know how to tell people what to do. They don't know how to structure an investigation."

The *Denver Rocky Mountain News* then went on to list the qualifications of the BPD. Tom Wickman, now the lead investigator, had been a detective for only a year, and this was his first murder case. John Eller, his boss, had never led a homicide investigation. Eller's principal experience was as the liquor license administrator for the city. Even Tom Koby, the department's chief, had no previous homicide experience.

"If you don't have the experiential background, and if you don't request someone who does have it to come in, you are steps behind the killer," Keppel said. "You cannot even expect, from a rational perspective, that they [the BPD] would know some of the proper procedures to utilize."

The inside story of police errors and missteps was starting to leak out. Later we were to learn that Linda Arndt's attorney had asked Police Chief Tom Koby to stand publicly behind her and clarify the falsehoods from the truth, but Koby refused. The truth was that Linda Arndt was involved in a number of serious mistakes that made it harder to solve JonBenét's murder, but from our perspective she did the best she could that morning and simply didn't get any help from her superiors. Each of the officers involved that morning retained attorneys and refused to talk to the District Attorney's office about what went on. When the D.A. asked to interview the cops, they were told to "talk to our attorney."

Patsy and I were much like everyone else, trying to figure out what was going on inside the world of the Boulder Police Department. We knew little about issues and conflicts that affected us and JonBenét's case, but we didn't fully recognize the degree to which the police were divided against themselves.

We discovered that problems had existed between the police and the district attorney's office for years. The police would often come in to the DA's office with some suspect in hand and demand that the district attorney prosecute the person when, in fact, there wasn't sufficient evidence. The DA's office was not a rubber stamp for the police, as some district attorneys' offices are, and this created irritation up and down the police ranks. Chief Koby seemed to be part of the problem, a man who could make a much better speech before the city council than he was able to give daily leadership to the department.

Matters heated up in the spring of '97 when University of Colorado students got a bit too rowdy and the partying turned into what the police described as a full-scale riot. Small college towns always seem to have their spring "riots" and other campus disturbances, but once again Boulder cops demonstrated a lack of training and leadership. The police ended up in hot water because they overreacted and the confrontation with the students turned nasty. Koby made a public statement, saying in his opinion that the police would have been justified if they had shot students. (I guess he hadn't learned anything from Kent State!) That didn't sit well with thoughtful people, since much of the local opinion was that the police had handled the matter much like they had the investigation into JonBenét's death: poorly.

On May 21 police officers attended a union meeting to discuss holding a no-confidence vote against Tom Koby. The *Boulder Daily Camera* noted that "some officials raised grievances related to the Ramsey investigation leadership." However this was not cited in the documentation presented to the union members; instead, the concerns listed were low morale, staffing issues, and Koby's handling of the University Hill riots. By the end of the meeting, the officers had voted thirty-nine to one to hold such a vote.

Of course, the possibility of a no-confidence vote was not good for Koby, but it had no legal effect on his job; City Manager Tim Honey had the sole authority for the city's fire and police chiefs. Although the police union's decision to take a future no-confidence vote spelled public relations trouble for Chief Koby, the general feeling around Boulder was that both Tim Honey and Mayor Leslie Durgin were staunch Koby supporters. Whatever was happening behind the scene, we knew things were not as they ought to be within the BPD.

On June 3 an unexpected public announcement was made that John Eller was looking to the future with new personal plans. Eller's message was that he was applying for the position of chief of police in Cocoa Beach, Florida. His statement was, "I've had twenty-nine years in, and I would like to be a chief somewhere." With the apparent mess inside the Boulder PD, we looked upon the possibility of his departure as a blessing; at the same time we made a mental note to stay away from Cocoa Beach, Florida, in the future.

While staying with the Stines, Patsy and I learned that every morning, Lou Smit drove by our house on Fifteenth Street and sat out in front for a few minutes to gather his thoughts. We discovered that during this time of quiet, Lou prayed for guidance and spent time thinking about JonBenét's case. The thought that a detective asked for God's guidance was reassuring to us and solidified our confidence that a wise man was, in fact, working on the case. We knew that in some way, we had to let Lou know how much we appreciated his dedication to finding the killer of our daughter.

A few days later, Patsy and I drove over to our old house early one morning, and, sure enough, Lou Smit's van was parked out front. We waited a moment and then got out of our car, went over to his van, and asked if we could speak to him. Much to our relief, Lou smiled at us and his big blue eyes sparkled.

"I'm happy to see you," he said.

"Thank you. I'm John Ramsey." I extended my hand. "This is my wife, Patsy."

"Glad to meet you." He shook our hands.

"We'd hoped to talk with you for a few moments," I explained. "Patsy and I wanted you to know we thank God every day that you're here. We're willing to do anything we can to help this investigation and find the killer. You can call on us any time."

"Thank you." Lou nodded his head thoughtfully. "I deeply appreciate your offer. I'm sure we will be calling."

Then he said, "Maybe we could pray together. We want God's blessing on this investigation."

We held hands and Lou said a short prayer. At the end Patsy and I thanked this good man again before we got out of his van and went back to our car. Patsy and I knew we'd met an important man in our lives and wanted to do everything we could to help this investigator complete his job. Patsy said she had prayed many times that God would send someone who would help find the truth. We believe he sent Lou Smit.

As soon as school was out, John, Burke, and I left for Charlevoix and Summer Hill, our second home in Michigan. The Stines had made us feel comfortable in every way throughout the spring, but we longed for a place that was truly ours again. Charlevoix was the answer.

We had found the house in Charlevoix in the summer of 1992. We loved the area and had wanted to buy a summer home there for years, but never could find anything we could afford that had a view of the water. One day that summer, we were sitting on the balcony of our small room at the Edgewater Hotel, taking in the view of Round Lake harbor. My nose was buried in a property guide. Suddenly I looked up from the page, squinted my eyes, and stared out across the water toward the bluff on the other side.

"John, I think that little yellow house up there on the hill is for sale! And it's in our price range! Let's go take a look."

We biked across the drawbridge to Belvedere Avenue and then pedaled around to the back door of the little house, which faced East Hurlbut. To our disappointment we couldn't see a "For Sale" sign anywhere. Our hearts sank, thinking it might already be sold. I jumped off my bike and headed for the door. "It never hurts to ask," I said.

Soon, a lady wearing a red apron, stained from cooking, answered the door. "May I help you?" she asked.

"We saw your ad in the paper and thought your home was for sale. Has it already sold?" I inquired as the woman invited me to step inside.

"Not exactly," she replied. "Actually, we've decided to take it off the market. We've lived here for many years and can't bring ourselves to sell it right now."

I took a quick glance around and noticed the cherry jam underway in the kitchen. Meanwhile, John walked around back to see the view of Round Lake harbor from the bluff. It overlooked some 1970s-looking condos, but they were below the line of sight, and you could see the boats coming in off Lake Michigan into what has to be the most picturesque harbor on the Great Lakes.

"Well, would you take my name and phone number, just in case. If you ever change your mind, we'd appreciate your calling us," I continued.

When the realtor called six months later and said the owners had indeed changed their minds, John agreed to buy the house over the telephone. Originally built in 1887 and remodeled a little along the way, it had three very small bedrooms (two upstairs and one down) and a bath with a shower downstairs. It also had original Victorian gingerbread ornamentation in each peak of the steeply sloped roof. The view from the storm-windowed porch was great, and it was close to town. We decided that if we opened up the front porch and added a bathroom upstairs, it would suit our needs perfectly. As most remodeling projects go, we ended up doing a lot more than adding a bath, but we wanted the house to become the roots of our family, where everyone could come summer after summer to enjoy rest and repose from the demands of life.

Now, five summers and a lifetime later, we were going back to that refuge at 112 Belvedere Avenue. In the last few months John and I had taken comfort in people surrounding us with their love and concern, since the fear of being alone continually haunted us. Returning to our summer home proved to be more difficult than I might have expected. It was hard to go into JonBenét's room for the first time. The constant temptation to sleep all day still nagged at my heels, and I had to struggle to overcome the urge. Working around the clock with the investigators and attorneys, John was gone to Boulder much of the time, and I knew that he was trying tenaciously to find the killer. In addition, John had the enormous load of running what was still a booming company. His plate was full. Fortunately, Susan and her son, Doug, came with us to Charlevoix, and her presence proved to be a godsend during those first weeks.

John put in an alarm system, which we had thought about when we remodeled, but the local builder had looked at us as if to say, "What do you need an alarm system for? This is a small, safe town." The new system would offer me genuine assurance that no one would slip in without buzzers sounding, fireworks going off, and the police being summoned. And the Charlevoix police and the sheriff's department were terrific! They responded immediately whenever we needed help. I was so afraid of someone hiding out in an obscure place in our home that I literally couldn't lie down to sleep at night until I was convinced we were safe. I would look under the beds every night and often have one of our neighbors help me check.

Chip and Vicki Emery lived up the street from us and had always been good neighbors and friends. Periodically I'd ask

Chip to come down and put a ladder up to the attic entry, take a long look inside, and let me know that everything was okay. Then he'd go down to the basement and look behind everything and also check out our clothes closets. As silly as it sounds, he even looked under the beds for me. It suddenly seemed as if our small house had too many hiding places, and I would simply get overwhelmed and devoured by my fear.

Luckily, Susan understood my anxiety. She knew that a homicide survivor often feared that more murders might occur, which resulted in heightened anxiety and panic. The world would never feel safe to me.

With the alarm system in place and the house checked out, I could sit down and take a deep breath. The familiarities and charms of our old warm home wrapped their arms around me like a familiar shawl hugging me tightly. After all, there were nothing but happy memories here when our family was all together. Maybe I could make it through the first summer in Michigan without JonBenét. I wasn't looking forward to it, but I was ready to try.

18

SNOOKERED ... AGAIN

The gentle breezes blowing off Lake Michigan and Grand Traverse Bay often gave a paradise quality to our summers at 112 Belvedere in Charlevoix. Northern Michigan is fabulous this time of year. John's dad had had a small summer cottage on an inland lake in central Michigan for over twenty-five years, and John cherished his childhood memories of those family vacations in Mecosta, Michigan.

Charlevoix, an upscale Lake Michigan hamlet, had been a summer sanctuary for the work-weary well-to-do since before the turn of the century, and it's a thriving year-round home to eight thousand residents today. In the 1800s Charlevoix had been a rough-and-tumble logging town, where the virgin forests of northern Michigan were cut down to build cities like Chicago at the southern end of the Great Lakes, and to provide the tall masts for sailing ships. In fact, the Great Chicago fire indirectly did more to decimate the forests of northern Michigan than any other "natural" event, because so much wood was needed to rebuild the city.

With our house perched up on a bluff on the south side of Round Lake, we had an expansive view of the small harbor, which served as a refuge for boats of all sizes coming in off Lake Michigan. The lake's waters could be more treacherous than any ocean. The summer air was invigorating, and the retreat from the constant madness unfolding in Boulder helped restore some of my peace of mind, but there were still unexpected "blips" that kept popping up in our little paradise.

Of course the tabloid media followed us in droves to our summer retreat. We knew it would not be easy to spend time here this first summer, since we had so many happy memories of summers with JonBenét. But that's how we wanted to remember her: walking down to the beach together, with her riding on John's shoulders and grabbing leaves from the low-hanging elm trees. Unfortunately, the media stalkers were waiting for us when we arrived, making that first summer even more difficult.

No matter where we went, the media were there. Outside our house, across the harbor, in the Edgewater Hotel, and hanging out at Whitney's Oyster Bar; these stalkers stayed poised to strike at any time with their trusty cameras.

One of the tabloids came out with a picture of the Stines and John and me standing on the upper deck of the house with wine glasses in hand, enjoying the view. The caption under the photo said, in effect, that we were celebrating our escape from the police. We broke into laughter as we heard about the story, because we realized that the photographer who took the rather docile picture of us relaxing with wine glasses had missed the jackpot photo of the century, had he arrived twenty minutes earlier.

Susan Stine and John had been out on the deck, joking about setting up a machine-gun turret to pick off the paparazzi if they crawled through our bushes. It was always good to laugh at our problems when we could. Stored in the house was a collector's 12-gauge shotgun that my dad had given John; we had never fired it. Jokingly, John brought the gun out on the deck and was standing there, playfully aiming it toward the water. Susan had said she needed a gun, so John gave her one!

However, he quickly put the gun away, realizing that photographers might be lurking somewhere within camera range. If the tabloids had gotten a picture of John with that shotgun, no telling what kind of headline and accompanying story they would have run. Whoever was sneaking around out there with his zoom lens was just twenty minutes too late!

One afternoon Burke, Doug Stine, and I were visiting garage sales in Charlevoix when a particularly foul character from a tabloid started stalking us. Burke was always on the lookout for old toys and games, and I kept looking for a treasure somewhere in the stacks of junk. However, when the photographer obviously wasn't going to stay away, I went up to him and said, "Why don't you leave us alone and go home?"

Immediately the photographer started snapping away while shouting obscenities at Burke and me. Of course, the experience of his vulgarities ruined my day, and I felt so terrible that Burke and Doug had to be a witness to that.

Sometimes, however, these tabloid people were not always so obvious. On one of those glorious summer afternoons in Charlevoix, I noticed a woman around town who seemed to be quite friendly. Susan Stine was staying with me at the time and was rather skeptical, but I didn't buy her reservations.

"Quit being so doubtful," I pushed Susan. "I think Kathleen Keane is a nice person."

Susan shook her head. "I don't trust her," she said definitely.

"Oh come on," I objected. "Lighten up."

Susan mumbled and grumbled but I didn't agree with her doubts. In fact, over the next couple of days, I kept running into the woman and she seemed genuinely friendly. Later she positioned her easel at the bottom of the hill and said she wanted to paint the lilacs that were blooming near our house. I told her to go ahead and come into the yard, but that's where Susan drew the line. She politely but firmly asked Kathleen Keane to leave.

Susan returned home to Boulder, and my mother came up for a visit. That afternoon, Kathleen came to our door and begged me to go painting with her.

"Go on," mother urged. "You need to get out and get some fresh air."

"I won't take no for an answer," Kathleen insisted. "Let's go paint some watercolors. I've even got another new friend to go with us."

"You're sure?" I felt rather inadequate and really not in the same league with this woman's painting abilities. "I mean . . . after all . . ."

"Sure," Kathleen assured me. "I've been planning to do some sketching at the herb farm at the edge of town. Let's go down there and see what we can find to paint."

I was hesitant, but I loved to paint and hadn't done anything since JonBenét and I had started to paint together the winter before.

Kathleen smiled again. "Let's go."

Much to my delight we spent most of the afternoon together, talking and painting. Another woman who lived at the Belvedere Club brought lunch, and we had a wonderful few hours eating and painting the large beautiful sunflowers. Kathleen seemed to be a warm, friendly sort of person whom I could get to know. She even brought me a copy of the book *Chicken Soup for the Christian Soul* as a gesture of friendship. Abruptly, the owner of the farm came running out back, where we were painting.

"I think a photographer is following one of you girls," the owner told us. "Any of you know why?"

"Oh my gosh." I jumped to my feet. "It's probably me."

"Why?" Kathleen asked.

"Look. I don't have time to explain." I started packing my gear. "I've got to run."

I looked up front one more time and knew that a tabloid photographer had found us. I had to get out of sight as quickly as possible.

"Thank you for a delightful time, Kathleen," I said as I started packing up my stuff to beat a hasty retreat. "Goodbye."

Soon the Charlevoix police came and detained the photographer.

A week later the story of my day painting appeared in the *National Enquirer*. Much to my horror, I discovered that Kathleen Keane was the wife of the tabloid's editor. I had been completely snookered . . . again. Keane was quoted in the article several times, saying things about me.

Susan Stine was right. I should have been much more suspicious. And even worse, I had shown Kathleen Keane's work to my friend and home decorator Linda Mason, who had purchased some of the imposter's paintings to carry in her shop in Charlevoix! How badly could I be taken? My faith in my fellow human beings had been shaken once again.

Unfortunately, the media seemed to be everywhere. Even tourists were driving by and pointing at our home, some stopping to pose in front of our house for pictures, and our lawyers were calling every day. We were also constantly wondering what was happening in the police investigation. Were they looking at other suspects, or were they still just concentrating on us?

I felt as if I had no control over anything that was happening to me. I could stand up on a soapbox and say, "Listen to me. I *didn't* do this. I loved my child. I'm hurting," and yet it wouldn't change anything. This was like a giant tidal wave sweeping down on us.

One day I was driving through the small downtown area in Charlevoix and all these thoughts were playing over and over in my mind. I pulled into the corner 7-Eleven, where Jon-Benét had often walked with twenty-five cents in her pocket to buy gum or candy, and I went inside to buy a pack of cigarettes. I had smoked once at a slumber party in the ninth grade and a little bit when I worked at Hayes, but not since then. Now I said defiantly to myself, *I'm going to smoke until they find the killer.*

I knew this was pure rebellion. I felt so out of control. People were telling me what to do, where to go, whom to talk to, whom not to talk to. They meant well, but I felt less and less like an adult who could manage her own life.

After that I smoked occasionally for about a year or so. Then I finally realized I was not hurting the killer or the media. I was hurting no one but myself. I quit.

I felt the same frustration and fear that Patsy was feeling. Early one morning Melinda and I were returning to the dock from sailing when a boat started pursuing us. I knew what was coming and got prepared for the assault. As we pulled up to the dock, a camera crew from a nearby van ran out on the dock with boom microphones, cameras, and all their paraphernalia.

Melinda and I quickly ducked down below, and I called 911 on my cell phone. (One of the nice things about a small town is that the 911 operator was also one of our neighbors.) In spite of the "Keep Off" postings on the marina, the camera crew kept coming at full speed. Minutes later a sheriff's patrol boat pulled up from the lake side, and the Charlevoix police converged on the van from the street side. It turned out that these people were from *Hard Copy,* the tabloid television program. They had to leave the dock without getting a picture, and the sheriff's boat took us to another dock so we could get to our car without being photographed.

Unfortunately, we weren't the only Charlevoix residents bothered by the media. We hated that the media hounded all our friends. Certainly our friends in Boulder had suffered from this invasion. And Charlevoix was no different, as the *Traverse*

City Record Eagle reported in a story called "Charlevoix
Under Siege!" The paper noted that signs posted at the city
limits proclaimed "Charlevoix the Beautiful," but during this
summer the name could have been changed to "Charlevoix
the Besieged."

Yet the townspeople showed a loyalty to us that was heart-
warming, even when they were offered money for any tidbit
they knew about the Ramseys. Rumors were that you could
make a quick twenty dollars by reporting whether or not our
car was in the driveway. And Scott Vollmer, manager of the
Harbor Wear T-shirt shop off Bridge Street, said friends of his
were approached by tabloid reporters in Whitney's Oyster
Bar. "They were willing to pay those girls that night anywhere
from $500 to $2,500," Vollmer said. "Whatever gossip, whatever they could get, they would be willing to pay into the
thousands of dollars for it."

A former manager at Whitney's, where the third-floor covered porch offers a bird's-eye view of our front porch, recalled
throwing reporters out one night. "The Ramseys deserve some
privacy. This is their home, and they deserve some peace," she
said.

Laurie Lounsbury, editor of the weekly *Charlevoix Courier,*
said that she had refused multiple offers of payment for pictures she'd taken in previous years of us and JonBenét. "I just
said no, good-bye," Lounsbury said.

Lanie, one of Jon Benét's very special friends and baby-sit-
ters, who was fourteen when JonBenét was killed, was called
directly by the television program *Extra* and offered seven
hundred fifty dollars each for any photos of JonBenét. Lanie
told them she would not part with her photos of JonBenét for
any amount of money. Her dad, Carlos, later told the callers to
leave his daughter alone, or else.

One family whose daughter participated with JonBenét in
the 1995 Little Miss Charlevoix Pageant was offered "a bundle of money" for their pageant videos and pictures, according to Charlevoix County Sheriff George Lasater. But the
family, who according to Lasater could have used the money,
refused. The mother said, "I will not profit from this tragedy."

Charlevoix protects its own, Sheriff Lasater said. "The community, at least in my perspective, seemed to kind of close
quarters, kind of rally behind the Ramsey family."

Charlevoix's overwhelming support of us was a welcome change from some of our other experiences where people with less integrity had sold their recollections, photographs, and videos for profit.

One of the funnier incidents that first summer was when our good friend and neighbor, A.J. Witthoeft, whose daughter Mikaela was a playmate of JonBenét's, noticed a couple pointing their camera toward our house and taking pictures. A.J. got out his camera and started taking close-ups of them, saying, "Let's see how it feels to have your picture taken."

It turns out this couple was from Germany and was innocently taking pictures of the harbor, not our house. They immediately went to the police station and reported the "assault" by A.J. Police Chief Dennis Halverson called A.J. and told him, "Well, I guess these people won't be coming back to Charlevoix anytime soon!"

The love the Ramsey family, and JonBenét, felt in Charlevoix can be best described by a quote from a letter written to JonBenét after her death by the Witthoefts, who said:

> We miss your silly smile and grass-stained knees. We miss your flag dance routines and the way you would plead for fireworks after dark. We miss playing on the swing set and picking blueberries by the driveway. We miss riding decorated bikes, swimming in the pool, and swinging on sky chairs. We miss going to the beach to watch the sunset and skipping rocks in Lake Michigan. We miss sliding down the hill in cardboard boxcars after spending hours decorating them with crayons and markers. We miss roasting hotdogs and marshmallows with you in the fire pit. Sister Socks, our cat, misses you too.

One day in mid-June my secretary walked hesitantly into my office. "I'm sorry to bother you, John," she said slowly. "But are you getting ready for your speech at Keystone?"

I glanced at my calendar. Only a few weeks left.

"Remember, you agreed to be the keynote speaker for the New Frontiers event coming up in Keystone. Hate to tell you, but time is running out."

"You're right." I nodded my head. "There will be a big

crowd this year." Each year we hosted this week-long event for all of our customers, vendors, and employees to build relationships and hopefully increase business. This year we expected around a thousand people.

"And plenty of media," she added.

I could feel the lump in my throat, but a deadline was exactly what I needed to pull me out of the grief that still overwhelmed me. "Thanks for the reminder," I said to her.

She left the room and I faced up to my tough assignment. I had to prepare to speak to a large crowd about business, and every one of them would really want to know how things were going with me and my family.

When that July morning came, I walked into the packed conference center at the Keystone resort. Walking to the podium, I knew I first had to begin by talking about how I felt and where I was personally. I drew a deep breath and started thanking people for their compassion and support. I told them our family had received a near-fatal arrow to the heart, but we were surviving because of the love and support of all the good people.

A unique letter came to mind. A gracious lady had sent a letter from Tenerife in the Canary Islands, to express her sympathy and compassion. She didn't know our address so she sent it to the Ramsey Family, Boulder, Colorado; the letter was soon returned to her, marked "Incomplete Address." Undaunted, she returned the letter to the United States, writing on the envelope, "Boulder Postmaster, Please try harder." Eventually the letter arrived in our mailbox.

As we read her tender condolences, she became a symbol of a multitude of deeply caring people whom we didn't know but who helped carry our burden. A horrible evil had struck us, but we began to realize that the world was filled with good, caring people, like this wonderful woman in Tenerife, who cried with us. I wanted the group to know that Patsy and I weren't bitter, and, in fact, were overwhelmed by all the positive encouragement we were receiving from good people out there in the form of those many compassionate letters.

Once I had talked about our personal situation, I turned my attention to the industry and our business. After my speech, a man came through the crowd and offered his hand. "I want you to know I read the papers, and I'm sure you can imagine what I thought." He shook my hand kindly and looked into my eyes. "Now I just want you to know that tonight there is one more person who will be praying for you." I was deeply touched and grateful.

In early July I left Patsy and Burke in Charlevoix and went to Atlanta to meet with security system installers to talk about our particular and unique needs in our new home there. Above all, I didn't want anyone to be able to enter our home while we were sleeping. The fear of the killer returning remained a formidable one for both Patsy and me.

We discussed halogen lights in the yard that would light up the outside of our house like a football field. I wanted video monitoring equipment that could detect anyone hiding in cars along the street or around the bushes surrounding our house or approaching the house. The experts prepared to install video cameras in the upstairs and downstairs hallways. I wanted to make sure the house was completely secure. *Why hadn't I been more diligent with my family's safety in Boulder?* I asked myself.

When I returned to Charlevoix, Patsy and I attended a silent auction for "Keep Charlevoix Beautiful," which is held to raise money to pay for all the petunias that line the streets in the summertime. At this particular benefit they were auctioning one of the small, manmade lakes on the golf course of the new country club, which has become the heart of the city's social activities. The highest bidder got to name the lake in front of the clubhouse. JonBenét had been the first person to step into the swimming pool when it was built at the Charlevoix Country Club, and she had her picture taken by the local newspaper. *How nice it would be,* we thought, *to commemorate her life beside this small lake.*

Patsy and I won the auction with the high bid of five hundred dollars, and the lake there is now named Lake JonBenét. In the future we hope to place a big rock beside the lake with a little plaque to remember Little Miss Charlevoix.

Early in July Patsy had to return to Boulder with me to meet with the DA's investigator, Lou Smit. He had contacted our attorney and requested a meeting. We went to Mike Bynum's office for the private meeting, which was attended by Smit,

Detective Tom Wickman, Bryan Morgan, and ourselves. Lou looked thoughtful as he carefully considered what he would tell us. "Is it possible for us to talk with complete confidentiality?" Lou began.

"Of course," I answered. "You can feel free to ask Patsy and me anything you wish. What you say stays in this room."

Lou nodded his head. "I need to be able to know that this important information is kept in a limited circle," he began. "When we find the killer or killers, it's important that certain facts be known only to us and the killer. That's how we will know we've got our man."

"Absolutely. We understand completely," Patsy confirmed.

Lou went on. "Do you know what a stun gun is?"

"A stun gun?" I frowned.

"You understand what I'm talking about?" Lou asked.

"Sort of," I said. "I only know about stun guns in general. I believe it's an electrical device. I don't have any idea what one looks like."

"Do you know anyone who owns a stun gun?" Smit pushed.

We thought for several moments and had to respond that, no, we did not.

Smit nodded his head. "I'm going to ask you not to discuss this matter with anyone, but I think a stun gun was involved in what happened to your daughter."

I stared at him, speechless.

"Please keep this completely in this room," Smit continued. "Think about it, and if any other thoughts come to mind, please let me know."

After the meeting we learned that some of the cops had previously resisted Lou's request to even ask us about the stun gun. This evidence clearly would point to an intruder, and that didn't fit the police theory that we had killed our daughter. Lou felt this information was so significant that he appealed to Boulder police detective Tom Wickman, who finally agreed to let Lou meet with us.

We also learned why Smit had asked us these questions. Back on April 11, Lou Smit, Trip DeMuth, and Steve Ainsworth had gone to John Meyer, the Boulder county coroner, with a single question. "Could the marks on JonBenét's body have come from a stun gun?" The investigators felt they had discovered a significant clue, and Meyer evidently agreed that the small red marks he observed on JonBenét's body could have come from such a weapon.

Following this conversation, Smit had spoken to Peter Mang and Sue Kitchen of the Colorado Bureau of Investigation about a stun gun causing the same marks. Could a stun gun leave the red welts found on our daughter? Both Mang and Kitchen believed it was possible. In turn, they suggested that Lou pursue the issue with Arapahoe County Coroner Mike Dobersen. In the past, Dobersen had dealt with crimes involving a stun gun. His experience was first-hand and practical, and he should be able to offer some insight.

During Lou's talk with Dobersen, the autopsy photos were studied from every possible angle. After a careful examination, Dr. Dobersen believed that the marks in the pictures did appear to have come from a stun gun. However, Dobersen wasn't ready to make a definite public statement unless the body was exhumed. Because the exhumation didn't occur, Smit couldn't obtain the conclusive statement he was seeking. However, the evidence was mounting that JonBenét had been knocked unconscious by a stun gun while she slept in her bed on the night of December 25, 1996.

Lou Smit had pursued this line of evidence in every possible direction. Working with Ainsworth and DeMuth, Smit had narrowed down the potential weapon to an Air Taser stun gun, which could have left the exact marks photographed on JonBenét. The detectives found a distributor of these guns not far from Boulder. The Upper Edge Company in Greeley, Colorado, carried the type of weapon the DA's investigative team was seeking.

Later in July I learned that stun guns could be bought at spy shops. I remembered that Patsy and I had attended a Super Bowl game in Miami in 1994 as guests of Sun Microsystems. On Saturday morning we had gone out for a walk in the small village of Coral Gables with no other intention than doing a little window shopping, and happened to pass by a "spy" shop that sold goods for security and monitoring.

Several times in the past I had wondered if a competitor might tap our telephones at the office and get sensitive information that could be used against us in business. (Not that our competitors would do that, but I didn't know that they wouldn't, either.) This particular shop in Coral Gables carried hidden cameras, bugging equipment, security devices, and everything under the sun that a person concerned with security might want. I learned that it was not easy to detect a phone tap on a complex phone system, such as the one we had at Access. I also got a sales pitch on some of the other things they had to sell.

As we left, the clerk gave me a videotape catalog to take home. When I returned to Boulder, I threw it into a drawer and completely forgot about the tape. I surmise that as the police went through everything in our house, they found the video catalog, which apparently turned out to have an advertisement for ... you got it ... stun guns! Not too long after that the police reported to the media that they had found a stun gun "instructional video" in the Ramsey house. So on the one hand they were supporting the stun gun theory, but on the other hand they were now indirectly saying that I had used this weapon on my daughter. Of course, for a period of time the video created a significant uproar and cast further suspicion on me.

Later we got a copy of the video catalog from the store in Coral Gables, and found it was recorded in Spanish! Not only had I never reviewed the tape; if I had, I wouldn't have understood it.

19

FOLLOWING UP LEADS

August 6, 1997. JonBenét's seventh birthday. John and I had always done special things on our children's birthdays, but when the first empty birthday came after JonBenét's death, I was completely undone. Facing the memory proved to be an almost overwhelming task.

In JonBenét's preschool class, they always celebrated summer birthdays by selecting a day near the end of May and making that day a special celebration, since school would be out on their real birthdays. JonBenét was able to bring cupcakes, refreshments, and go through the whole school birthday celebration that first year of school when she was approaching six years old. And before we left for Charlevoix, we'd always had a birthday party for her friends at our home in Boulder. Of course, when we would go to Atlanta, there was another celebration with Grandma and Grandpa and all of our Georgia friends. We had so many birthday celebrations that JonBenét had gotten confused about how old she was, assuming that every birthday party added a year to her age. At five, she had thought she must be at least eight years old!

No matter what anyone might want to do to ease my pain, there was no avoiding the first birthday, the first Halloween, the first Christmas, the first Easter. The "firsts" have to be lived through.

When Beth had died, I asked our minister, the Rev. Dr. Frank Harrington, "How are we going to get through this time? How can we face another birthday? Another Christmas?"

Dr. Harrington had answered me with the best advice anyone could have given. "All you have to do is to be responsible for today," he advised. "You get up, you go through this one day as best you can, and you don't think about tomorrow."

His words came back to me in that dark hour, reassuring me that all I was responsible for was getting through the day until bedtime that night. If I had to go to bed at 7:30 P.M. and call it a day, then that was the best I could do for that *one day.* Jesus Christ told us not to worry about tomorrow because today has enough problems of its own. *Today was my only concern.*

As devastating as it was, somehow I made it through that first birthday. Not long afterward I was walking alone by Lake Michigan, enjoying the peace and quiet beside the rippling blue water. The lake looked just like the ocean with its surf and sandy beach. I reached up and felt the chain around my neck. A friend had lovingly placed this cross, with a little pendant attached, around my neck sometime during the frenzy in Boulder after JonBenét's death.

As I felt the little charm attached to the cross, I wondered, *What is that?* I had never looked closely at the pendant.

When I got back into the house, I looked at the charm up close in the mirror. It was a tiny porcelain figure of the baby Jesus and his mother, Mary. I felt a warm flush and tingling come over me as I stood in front of the mirror. Suddenly I had this immediate empathy with Mary. I thought to myself, *She watched them kill her child. She lost a child too.* Tears welled up in my eyes.

I was raised in a Methodist church, so we usually only thought of Mary at Christmastime. A few days later I mentioned this tingling to a Catholic friend, who explained that the feeling was called the veil of Mary. "We believe she puts a veil of protection and love around us," she said. "You are very blessed." And I knew it was so.

Charlevoix had always been a magnet in the summertime, drawing people from downstate to the souvenir and shirt shops that dotted the downtown area of our little town. John and I enjoyed wandering through the shops there and looking at the boats parked at the city marina. On the weekends, multitudes of people surged in to shop, walk down the quaint streets, and watch the big powerboats and sailboats coming in off Lake Michigan. The Beaver Island ferry was docked in Charlevoix and in the summer took hundreds of people back and forth to Beaver Island.

The peace we sought there that first summer would frequently be interrupted, directly or indirectly, by the media. On August 13 Dennis Halverson, chief of police, came to our door and asked for John.

"He's not here," I said. "He's down at Irish Marina, I think."

"Are you sure?"

"Yes. I talked to him a little while ago on his cell phone."

The chief looked directly into my eyes and said softly, "We have just been notified that he has hurt himself."

I didn't quite understand what the chief was saying.

He could see the questioning look in my eyes, so he explained further. "The rumor is circulating . . . several media people have called me, saying that John has killed himself."

I immediately dialed John's cell phone, but he didn't answer. If I hadn't just talked to him, I would have really panicked.

Chief Halverson and I drove down to the marina, and sure enough, John was standing on his sailboat, *Miss America,* getting ready for the local Wednesday race.

"Looks like a false alarm," I said.

Later that day I walked down to the end of the street to visit with one of our favorite ladies in Charlevoix, eighty-four-year-old Evelyn Seger, who baked and sold the best pies I've ever had (next to my dad's, of course). She did this to fund her weekly Bingo night forays at the VFW.

I picked up the lemon meringue pie she had baked for us, and as I walked back to our cottage I noticed a news station car parked in front of our house. A young female reporter jumped out of the car as soon as she saw me and asked, "Do you know the Ramseys? I need to talk to somebody at the Ramsey house."

I was amazed that she hadn't recognized me. "Well, I'm Patsy Ramsey," I said.

She stammered a little and looked quite surprised. Then she said, "I just heard that your husband . . ."

"He's fine," I said. "I just saw him."

The reporter quickly got her big video camera out. For once I welcomed the interview. If this erroneous story got on the national news and our parents or friends heard it, I knew how devastated they would be. John's brother, Jeff, had already called in a panic, until I assured him it was not true.

I stood there for the interview, holding my lemon meringue

pie, and told the reporter and her viewing audience, "He's fine." The reporter was actually very sweet and was a recent graduate of Northwestern. *What a business you've gotten yourself into,* I thought.

A few hours later, Evelyn came to my house all excited. "My granddaughter from downstate just called. She said, 'Grandma, I just saw your pie on national television.'

"I asked her, 'How did you know it was my pie?' And she said, 'Because nobody does meringue like that but you, Grandma.'"

Who could believe it?! Even pies associated with the Ramseys received national exposure.

The visibility of our house in Charlevoix and its openness to the street on both sides made it easy for people to walk up to our door. One afternoon Burke came out to the back porch and told me that someone was at the front door, wanting to speak to me. Susan Stine had gone back to Boulder, and I didn't have any choice but to go to the door myself. I looked out through the screen and saw a man in his late fifties sitting in a wheelchair on the sidewalk. The man appeared disheveled and his clothes were pretty worn.

"I have information for you," he said and then started to cry. He had long gray hair and an unattractive growth of beard. "I must speak to you."

"Okay?" I stuck my head out of the door. "What do you want to say?"

"I know something important," the man blubbered. "Very important." The man had sad eyes and needed to comb his hair.

"I don't understand." I blinked several times, trying to decide if I knew the person. I was sure I'd never seen him before.

"Please listen to me. I know important information on your daughter's murder."

"Excuse me a moment." I darted back in the house as quickly as I could because I wanted to find the telephone and call for help.

I had no idea who this strange man was. Was he legitimate? A nut case? Could he hurt me? Could he help? I didn't know what I was dealing with, but the man scared me. He could be a panhandler, a man looking for a handout, or a tabloid reporter. Or he could be totally legitimate. All we needed was for one person to come forward with information. Then again, the stranger might have more frightening ideas in mind. He could be the killer.

I immediately called my neighbor, Vicki Emery, and asked for her help. Vicki was a native of Charlevoix and knew everybody . . . including this man. As it turned out, she recognized him as a local resident.

The man wheeled his chair to the porch side of the cottage, and asked us to help him out of the wheelchair so he could sit on the porch. As he was getting set to talk, I went back into the house and called Lou Smit on his direct line in Boulder. I needed someone in authority to tell us what to do.

"Mr. Smit, I need your help!" I caught my breath. "This is Patsy Ramsey calling from Charlevoix, Michigan."

"Of course," he answered in his gentle way. "What can I do for you?"

"I've got this man outside on the back porch and he says that he knows something about the killing." I shook my head. "I don't know what to do. Can you talk with him?"

Lou said, "Call the local police and have them come over and take his statement. They will take it from there."

The Charlevoix police came immediately and the man began telling a long, winding yarn. The heart of his story was that during the previous summer (1996) he had been driving down Belvedere Avenue, which ran in front of our house, when he saw a young man run down the hill from the direction of our house. The man flagged him down and asked if he could get a ride. When the young man got in the car, he suddenly blurted out, "I hate the Ramseys and I'm going to hurt their daughter."

The Charlevoix police wrote down the entire story and took the man's picture. This man said his conscience had overwhelmed him for having done nothing about reporting this incident for an entire year. I thanked him for coming forward now with the information, and the police took him home. I have no idea what became of him or of the information he provided. But the whole episode left me terrified.

When I heard about the story of the man in the wheelchair and discovered how frightened Patsy was by this incident, I was upset and concerned. I knew that the media had descended on Charlevoix and were following us around, trying to get pictures of every family member possible. I had no way of knowing the difference between overly intrusive media and what might be a killer following us, lurking close by for another attack. The man in the wheelchair could be anyone.

As I heard more about the story, I discovered that the frantic young man was also supposed to have said that I had contracted with him to build a secret room in the Charlevoix house and that I owed him thousands of dollars. He went on to claim that he had a green Pontiac parked in our neighbor's driveway, which he wanted to sell, as "he wouldn't be needing it anymore." The whole story was confusing and bizarre, but extremely interesting.

As the gray-haired man's story wound down, he had made a concluding remark to the effect that, "Well, you know, the tabloids would pay a lot of money for this story." His final comment hit all my alarm buttons. While he was talking about something that could be very important to us, the man sounded as if he might be preparing to go fishing for cash in the tabloid stream, seeing what his story might be worth.

I knew the tabloids had a history of sending false information to the Boulder Police Department, which regrettably wasted its time in following dead-end leads. We didn't need any more cranks putting out nonsense that only made the investigation more difficult.

By now anyone who knows John and me will agree that if there's anything we avoid, it's the tabloids. When I pass the magazine rack in the grocery store, I literally try to look the other way. Unfortunately, the tabloids certainly don't go out of their way to avoid the Ramseys. One of their most creatively written stories came out in August, claiming that they had obtained a copy of the taped conversation when I called 911 early in the morning of December 26, 1996, asking the police to come at once to our house. The tabloids had come up with a new twist.

The *National Enquirer* ran a story saying that our telephone had not been hung up properly and the police had heard additional voices on the 911 tape. The tape, the story said, had been enhanced technologically to produce a mes-

The Days of Innocence
Atlanta, August 1991

*Pretty Baby
in a Buggy . . .*

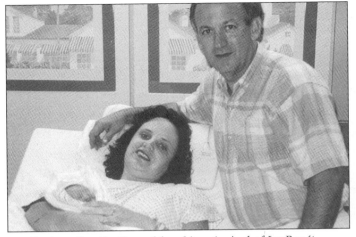

*Posing after the Record-breaking Arrival of JonBenét—
Atlanta, August 6, 1990*

Some Father-Daughter Time

*Biggest Sister Beth
Holding JonBenét*

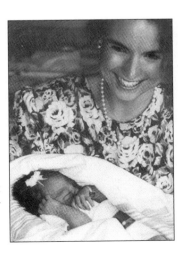

Burke selects JonBenét's first Christmas tree Atlanta, 1990

Making Pancakes with Burke

Best Buddies

First Birthday

*Out for a Spin
in Charlevoix,
Summer 1991*

Beach Buddies

Daddy's
Pardners!
New Frontiers
Business
Conference

Look what the Easter Bunny
left in Mommy's basket!—Boulder, 1993

Burke,
the Ninja Turtle
JonBenét,
the Pink Bunny
Pearl Street Mall
Halloween, 1992

The Princess and
Her Frog Prince
Going to Quinn's
Birthday Party

Growing Up Together
Summer 1993

JonBenét with Gingerbread Replica of 755 Fifteenth Street, December 1994

Holiday Shopping with Melinda Atlanta, November 1995

Palm Sunday Parade Boulder, 1995

JonBenét skied from atop Ajax Mountain. Aspen, Colorado, January 1996

*Family Talent Show
at Summer Hill*

*Like Mother,
Like Daughter*

*JonBenét Sitting
Pretty in Pink
on the Porch
at Summer Hill*

*JonBenét
with Santa
and Jacques*

*"The Queen
of Our Hearts"
Valentine's Day,
1996*

JonBenét . . .
A Real
Sweetheart . . .

. . . in any
Language!

*Visiting Olympic City
Atlanta, July 1996*

*Swimming at the
Grand Hotel
Mackinac Island,
July 1996*

*Playing Ball in
the Backyard
Boulder,
Spring 1996*

Best All-Round Camper, Burke; Camper of the Week, JonBenét Camp McSauba, Charlevoix

A Scenic View along the Mackinac Island Bike Trail, July 1996

First Day of Kindergarten—
JonBenét and Jacques, 1996

The Picture
of Innocence . . .

Decorating the Big Tree
December 1996

Ice Skating at
Rockefeller Center,
1996

Out on the Town with Grandpa and Grandma Paugh
Boulder, December 1996

sage, which supposedly occurred in the hallway area near the kitchen, just after I "thought" I hung up the telephone. According to unnamed sources, the *Enquirer* claimed that you could now hear Burke on the tape saying, "Please, what do I do?" and John replying, "We're not speaking to you." Obviously, if this were true, then John and I had been inaccurate when we testified that we had not awakened Burke or talked with him until later in the morning. Their scenario ran along the lines that we couldn't have possibly forgotten such an important conversation. Therefore, the enhanced tapes would represent a major flaw in our explanations. We must have done *something* we were trying to cover up.

John and I saw the story as another one of those crazy accounts the tabloids kept running on us. We knew it was probably a police leak that in time would be viewed as misinformation. As a matter of fact, an accurate account was later published in *Newsweek*. The magazine reported that some of the people who had heard the tape—the police— thought they heard Burke's voice, while others said no conversation was heard, even after the tape was enhanced in the lab. *Why would the police have had to enhance the tape if the wall phone was off the hook?* we wondered.

Meanwhile, our investigators, after months of struggle and requests for help, had identified a number of credible and substantial leads. No matter what was happening or not happening with the police, we were finding promising leads, but we couldn't do much without the authority of the police.

John and I were both amazed at the number of transients who lived in close proximity to our Boulder house. We had learned that the house across the alley was occupied by a house-sitter during that Christmas. This man disappeared within days after the twenty-sixth. Who was he? Why had he left so quickly? The young CU art student who had created the "Daddy's Little Hooker" display had once lived only four doors to the south of us in a student rental house for a period of time. Unfortunately, we were realizing how transient our University Hill neighborhood really was. Some neighbors rented their extra rooms and basements to students and others who moved in and out frequently. We could only hope the police were paying close attention.

Summer was quickly drawing to a conclusion, and we knew

that our time at Charlevoix was nearly over. We had to get Burke back for school, and we had a new home that needed our attention. In mid-August, with heavy hearts, we closed up the house and prepared to go south.

Once we arrived in Atlanta, the tabloid media drove up to our house within thirty minutes of our walking through the front door. It looked like the circus had come to town. Whether they had been tipped off or it was a coincidence, their appearance was not an encouraging sign for what we might expect in the future. We would have to make some provision to keep them off our property. A nice gated wall would help insure our privacy. We decided to make this our first order of business.

One morning, as we started to leave for a meeting with our contractor, John discovered that he had a flat tire on the 1984 Honda he was driving. He had given it to Beth as her first car when she was at Miami University. After her death, both Melinda and John Andrew had used the car. Because it was Beth's, the automobile meant a great deal to John as a sentimental bridge to the past, a way of still keeping in touch with her. I watched him changing the tire out in front of our house, and hoped the media got a good picture of him down on his hands and knees fixing the car. That view ought to put things back into perspective!

Their front-page stories had painted us in silver and gold, implying that we were filthy rich. How untrue that was. John had built a business from scratch and made some money when it was sold, but now everything we'd been through since JonBenét's death was draining us dry. The expense of the investigation and the legal bills had proven to be astronomical. John Douglas had told us that most families experiencing a tragedy like this end up broke. Justice is expensive. Our assets were rapidly dwindling, but I knew that John didn't care. He and I had only one commitment: if it took our last dime, we would find JonBenét's killer.

On Saturday, August 16, Patsy, Burke, and I attended an all-day picnic at Big Canoe, north of Atlanta, with our old friends and their children. This was an annual event we had missed during our years in Boulder. We returned home at dusk to find Pam and Nedra sitting in their car in our front driveway.

Our house had been broken into, or at least it seemed so. Apparently the alarm had gone off at 4:30 in the afternoon, but Pam and Nedra didn't discover the problem until 8:30 that night when they had arrived at the house. What had happened to our security system?

After growing tired of waiting for the police, I entered the house, armed with a cast iron frying pan (the only weapon I could find), and went through every room. I admit I was frightened as I opened closets and stuck my head into the attic, but I was buoyed by the thought that if the intruder were JonBenét's killer, I would have an opportunity to finally face him myself.

I found a basement window unlatched, right over our newly installed telephone junction box. Normally the phone company wants these boxes outside the house so they can get at them, but we had moved it inside so our phones couldn't be easily tapped. Was this window unlatched by someone for a later return to tap our phones? Or worse, to get into the house? We never knew. After several calls to our security monitoring service, which should have dispatched a call to the police at 4:30, they finally told us there was a note in our computer file that said not to call the police if an alarm were detected! Where did that come from? Again, we will probably never know.

Later that evening, as we were trying to relax, we received a call from Pam, who said she had just gotten off the phone with a lady in Boulder. Jacqueline Dilson had reported to the Boulder police that she believed her thirty-seven-year-old live-in lover, Chris Wolf, might be the person they were seeking. When she couldn't get them to respond, she finally called Patsy's mother, Nedra, and she in turn called Pam, who immediately called Jackie back.

Jacqueline Dilson owned the Dakota Ranch, a small retreat and conference center near Lyons, Colorado, which pushed New Age experiences. She had allowed Wolf to move into her trailer in 1995. Chris Wolf turned out to be a reporter for the *Colorado Daily* and the *Boulder County Business Report* with a master's degree in journalism. His strange behavior before Christmas and early on the morning after Christmas raised Dilson's concern about what Wolf had done all night.

Apparently Dilson spent Christmas Day with Wolf, but he would not have supper with her and her family. He told Jackie that he might go out that night. If you wake up and I'm not here, he said, I'm just driving around. Somewhere around 10:00 P.M. Jacqueline went to bed alone. At around 5:30 A.M., sounds from the bathroom woke Jackie up, and she realized that Wolf was getting out of the shower. His navy blue sweater and jeans were lying on the floor dirty.

Later the next day, Dilson and Wolf watched the television news reports of JonBenét's death. To her surprise, she observed him becoming quite agitated. Wolf cursed and said he believed JonBenét had been sexually abused by her father. For the rest of the evening, Wolf brooded over the case.

According to Dilson, Wolf hated big business and had a fascination with world political disputes and political violence. He told her that John Ramsey's company designed parts for guns, which were then sold to third-world countries to kill people. Wolf was extremely upset every time the Ramsey case was discussed on television, Dilson said. We considered this a very significant lead and gave all the information we had to the police.

We also learned that on January 30 police officers had stopped Wolf at 11:00 A.M. as he drove into Boulder; they discovered he was driving with a suspended license. The woman officer took him to the police station for further questioning when Wolf abruptly told her that the police would make better use of their time by chasing the killer of JonBenét Ramsey. He definitely caught everyone's attention with that remark. Detectives Ron Gosage and Steve Thomas started interrogating Chris Wolf with hard questions about our child.

When they asked Wolf to write some of the words from the ransom note, he refused. The police put him in handcuffs, but he still refused. Finally the two detectives put him in jail, pending the resolution of his suspended license. Later that day Wolf was released.

Wolf later reported that Steve Thomas and John Eller called him a few weeks afterward to come down to the police department. Once there, they told him, "We have no interest in you." But they did confirm that someone had given his name to the police.

Whatever the police's intentions, Wolf represented too many unanswered questions.

At the end of August, I left Patsy and Burke in Atlanta for a business trip to Boulder. While there I talked with Father Rol Hoverstock, seeking his counsel on what to do with the house we still owned in Boulder, but which sat vacant. I simply couldn't figure out what to do with the property. I could try to sell it, but that would be nearly impossible, now that it was the scene of a murder.

"Let me ask you, John." Father Rol looked me straight in the eye as he spoke. "Isn't that house a stone around your neck?"

I nodded my head. "Yes, it is."

"And you're never going to move back in again?"

"Absolutely not," I said firmly. "That would be impossible."

"Then you need to get rid of the place, John. Do whatever it takes, but get rid of it."

Father Rol always made sense, and I knew he was right. I needed to do something about the house fairly soon.

The truth was that we had never been back inside the house at 755 Fifteenth Street after December 26 because of the horror that had happened there. For a period of time, the police had kept everything under seal and no one was supposed to enter. Neither Patsy, Burke, nor I ever spent the night in the house again.

Eventually the police had turned the house back over to our lawyers and investigators. Even though the house was secured, the property was broken into, so our investigators suggested installing a video monitoring system in case someone broke in again. Perhaps it would help us capture the killer. One evening the police went in the house and discovered the video surveillance system. They accused us of trying to monitor their actions and acted as if they had caught us spying on them. A big flap followed, and they confiscated the equipment, taking everything to the police station. I couldn't believe that the police interpreted our attempt to protect our house and perhaps catch the killer as having *anything* to do with them. They seemed to be paranoid! Eventually the police department's legal advisor decided that the equipment should be returned to us.

Mike Bynum and his paralegal assistant, Lucy Hale, took care of everything related to the house for us. Eventually Lucy packed up JonBenét's toys and articles and carefully put them in boxes. Lucy later told us that this job was one of the hardest tasks of her life.

From time to time, Lucy had checked on the supposedly locked house and noticed that objects had been moved. One logical deduction I could make was that the police had been back inside, even though they did so without seeking or receiving permission. Without surveillance equipment we couldn't determine what was going on, and it worried me. Could the killer have been back? Probably not, but something had to be done. Father Rol's advice seemed a logical solution: sell the house, at any price.

One of my first thoughts was that the house was within walking distance from the University of Colorado. Maybe if I offered the house as a gift, they would accept the place for their use. Surely a university could use an additional residential facility close by. However when I approached the university foundation, which handles such gifts, they were told by university officials that the house was "too hot." To my amazement, they turned the gift down!

The market for larger homes at that time was reportedly good because of the limited supply and the growing high tech industry up and down the Front Range. Our real estate agent, Joel Ripmaster, said the best way to try and sell the house was through word of mouth. Put up a for-sale sign, and we'd have every photographer within a hundred miles going through it.

I did get some offers on the house, but their suggested price was only pennies on the dollar. Our appraiser told me that the house was stigmatized and worth no more than half of its original value. I was not surprised. But even getting that much seemed like a long shot now.

In the end, Mike Bynum and several of our attorneys and investors put up the money to buy the house. Mike was concerned that some promoter type might acquire the place and turn it into a circus, selling tickets to go through it or using it to make a movie about all this. As the months went by, Mike's group rented the house to students, some of the coaching staff, and other individuals at CU, just to keep it occupied. Mike later told me that their plan was to sell the house in a

few years, and should there be a profit, the money would go
to the JonBenét Ramsey Children's Foundation. I was overwhelmed with gratitude when Mike shared their intentions.
What a special group of men!

20

TABLOID TACTICS AND
POLICE RUMORS

As September began, John and I were trying to get situated in Atlanta and get Burke settled into a new school. We had hopes that the move back to our home turf would leave behind some of the chaos we had experienced in Colorado. At least we were near our family and old friends, who would be close by if trouble erupted.

On the evening of September 2, I went over to my sister Polly's home in East Marietta, a bedroom community north of Atlanta. Plunking down on the family room couch, I switched on the television. As luck would have it, I happened upon Larry King, who was embroiled in a discussion with Tony Frost, the editor of the *Globe*. They were discussing the paparazzi's stalking of Princess Diana and Dodi Fayed the night the two were killed in an awful car accident in Paris. Tony Frost was saying, "If we could turn the clock back, and I really wish we could, and if that tragic accident had not happened, and I walked into my office on Monday morning and had been presented with photographs of Di and Dodi leaving the Ritz in the back of a Mercedes, I wouldn't have considered them for publication."

I couldn't believe what I was hearing. The *Globe* a bastion of ethics and integrity? I don't think so. Neither did Whoopi Goldberg, who was on the phone to Larry from Europe. She said, "Well, I wish that Tony had let them know that he wasn't interested. I mean, part of the problem, you know, is that you guys forget that these people, who are out there doing this stuff, really believe that you're going to buy these pictures."

Frost objected. "These photographers were not there on the *Globe*'s account. Let's be quite, quite clear on that. These were freelance photographers. But, Larry, I want to make the point that the *Globe* just turned down a heck of a lot of photographs for reasons of taste, for reasons of ethics, for legal reasons."

"You turned down photos of the accident?" King asked Frost.

"Larry, that's a very easy question to answer. The *Globe* was never offered photographs of Princess Diana and Dodi Fayed in the crashed vehicle. We never entered into negotiations for them. We do not want them. We would never publish them."

Who is he trying to kid? I wondered. The *Globe* is the worst of the worst.

"Now when this terrible tragedy happened," Frost went on, "I was in the Bahamas on vacation with my family. I got a call at 9:30 in the evening from my deputy telling me there's been this awful crash . . . I immediately ended my dinner, went to my hotel room with my family. As we watched, and there was mention of the paparazzi in hot pursuit, my wife turned to me and said, 'If there are any photographs of Diana in that car, I don't want you to buy them.' And my two sons turned to me and said, 'No, Dad, you mustn't do that.'"

As Larry King cut to a commercial, I thought, *Tony Frost, you fraud! You published illegally obtained autopsy photos of our daughter on the front page of your filthy rag. How dare you come out with this inane position of piousness!*

At that moment I didn't know what I would do—but I had to in some way or the other respond and refute this imposter. I got up and paced back and forth a few times and then grabbed the telephone. I found the number and dialed the CNN offices in downtown Atlanta, and a man answered.

"Is this CNN?" I asked.

"I'm the night security guard at CNN."

"This is Patsy Ramsey," I said. "I would like to talk to Larry King."

"Who?" The man sounded like he was having a hard time hearing.

"Patsy Ramsey. JonBenét Ramsey's mother."

"O-h-h-h." The security man finally sounded like he understood. "I see. Oh, my! Well, just you wait a minute."

For the next several minutes my phone call was passed around the building to different people, asking me questions and trying to make sure I was who I claimed to be. Finally, a woman got on the line and started asking me more questions to clarify my identity.

"You know that CNN interviewed you and your husband earlier this year," she stated. "Do you remember who the interviewer was that evening?"

"I don't remember his name," I said in an exasperated voice. "But he had glasses and they picked us up in the most rundown taxi I have ever seen in my life."

"Yeah," the woman answered. "That's us."

Within a few minutes, the lady patched me through to the *Larry King Live* show, which was still in progress. I was sitting in Polly's family room with the phone to my ear, listening to the television across the room as Larry King said, "We have someone on the phone. They told me we ought to take a break and come back and have her join us."

My mother was sitting on the other end of the sofa. She looked at the television, and then at me and asked, "What in the world are you going to say?"

"I don't know," I answered, "but I'm praying that God will give me the right words."

"Me too," she said. "I can't wait to see this."

Suddenly I was talking on live television, launching first into an attack on Larry King for having the *Globe* editor on the air and thereby giving him credibility, along with his trash tabloid! I wanted to know how a legitimate program could let this money-grubbing, immoral editor who represented all that was evil so presumptuously say that he would never publish Princess Diana's pictures as she lay dead in the car when he had already published the stolen autopsy photos of my daughter, JonBenét.

As a good television host, King turned to his other guests, Tom Selleck and Joan Lunden, for an opinion. They discussed the issues I'd laid before them for a moment, but I wasn't through.

"Let me tell you what happened the other day, Larry . . . I took my son to a local department store to buy school supplies. As we were checking out, he looked to his left at his eye level, there was a photograph of his murdered little sister with the most horrible headline accusing his parents . . . I didn't know whether to cry or be angry.

"I mean, do they think my friends, my family, my neighbors,

people I know don't shop at these places? You know, even if they don't buy them, they see them. And it is hurtful."

"Are you thinking of suing them, Patsy?" King asked.

"I don't know. You know, I hope they're not even around to be sued. I mean, if everyone would stop tomorrow and boy-cott these publications . . . I would love to see them off the face of the earth."

"What was the effect, Patsy, on your son?" King asked.

"The effect was horrible. I mean, he tried to keep a stiff upper lip, but he looked at me like . . . you know. He tried to pretend he didn't see it. But how can you not see it, when it is at a child's eye level?"

The other guests started in again, discussing how difficult it is to sue the tabloids. If nothing else, at least I had gotten to make my point about Tony Frost and the *Globe*. After I fin-ished saying my piece, I hung up and left Polly's to go back to our house.

A few minutes after I walked through the door, Polly called. "You're not going to believe this," she began. "But Larry King just called my house."

"Really? What for?"

"He wanted to talk with you, Patsy. To thank you for being on the show and ask you if you'd come and do a show with him."

"No kidding."

"And since he had me on the line, King wants me to come with you."

"Really?"

"I'm ready to go! I'd love to give them a piece of my mind!"

I had to laugh at my sister's enthusiasm, but the truth was that there is no end to the lengths to which the tabloids will go, and my family knows that fact well. Whether it was Larry King who had called her or a tabloid imposter, we never knew for sure.

One evening, months earlier, while we were still living with the Stines, I had called my mother in Roswell, Georgia. My sisters happened to be there too. While we were on the phone, the doorbell rang and Mom answered it. A woman stood at the door with a big bouquet of flowers in her arms, explaining she was a representative of Princess Diana and the British people, who were sending their condolences and expressing their grief. Mom told me she would call me back so she would be free to talk to this woman with the British accent. Mother was very honored and innocently let the woman in as she explained how distraught Lady Di was over JonBenét's death. My mother took the flowers, thanked the woman, and talked to her for quite a while. Later she called me back.

Sure enough, in the next week's *Star* there was my grieving mother's picture. The British "representative" was a tabloid writer, and flowers and sympathy were just a ruse for these tabloid types to pry their way into my mother's home and get a horrible picture of her in tears as she reminisced about her granddaughter. What the tabloids do is nothing but cruel! At least I'd gotten my opportunity to tell the world on the Larry King show what I think of those muckrakers!

Ironically, Tony Frost, who is a Brit, is permitted to work in this country with what is known as a "critical skills" green card. In other words, he is supposedly working here because there is a critical shortage of people with his particular skill. How I wish there *were* a shortage of people like Tony Frost! We don't need his kind of skills here at all, it seems to me.

Even though we were 1,092 nautical miles from Boulder as the crow flies, news from Colorado still made it quickly to Atlanta, and the problems in the police department seemed to persist. However, Patsy and I didn't know much more than anyone reading a daily newspaper could learn. We were completely on the outside and could only watch the smoke rise as the explosions happened.

One of the constant problems that compromised a legitimate hunt for the killer was the intentional release of information apparently leaked out through the police department's back door. On the front page of the Thursday, September 4 edition of the *Boulder Daily Camera,* an article ran from an "unnamed source," which complained that the district attorney had nixed a search warrant of my Access Graphics' offices and the Access hangar space where I supposedly stored my airplane at Jeffco Airport. As I read the article, which was filled with errors, I couldn't keep from responding with a letter to the editor protesting these "unnamed sources" as being also "uninformed."

The truth was that I'd have gladly given permission at any

time to the police to look at our offices, the hangar, or anywhere else. As a matter of fact, we had agreed to all their requests for access and information. We had given them free access at any time to our house in Boulder and offered them a key to the cottage in Charlevoix. The really wrong part of the article was the inaccurate statement that my airplane was stored in the Access hangar. If the police thought my airplane was stored there, they simply hadn't done their homework very well; it wasn't. Even their leaks seemed flawed.

The next morning, my letter to the editor got front-page coverage in the *Boulder Daily Camera*. Not a bad response. However, the distressing side of it was that our hot line began to get hate calls—and hate mail was also coming in. The situation increased my already very high concern for the safety of our family. Nine months had now passed since the murder, and no one in an official capacity would say anything except, "The parents are under an umbrella of suspicion." We would eventually call it "a parasol of persecution."

Thinking about this possibly dangerous situation prompted me to see if I could do anything to move things ahead and get out of this bureaucratic quagmire. We knew a killer was out there, and we were frightened. It also threatened our safety for these veiled accusations to continue against us. I pulled out a piece of paper and started writing, "Dear Mr. Hunter . . ."

At that moment, I felt that I needed to tell District Attorney Alex Hunter and the police to either fish or cut bait. If the cops thought they had a case against Patsy and me, let them bring it on so we could deal with it in an open and fair court of law. If they didn't, then say so! Either bring us up for trial, or let the world know that the evidence didn't support their original quick conclusion. After all, we in the United States were supposed to be innocent until proven guilty! In my letter, I detailed the many security precautions we had taken, including the elaborate system in our new home in Atlanta. For the first time in our marriage, we had even brought firearms into the house and were armed should an intruder break in. A good friend had loaned us a couple of handguns, and even though Patsy had never fired a pistol before, a Fulton County police officer who was working for us as a part-time security guard had offered to instruct us. The point of my letter was simple. I asked the district attorney to take a stand in order to disarm the crazies who were running around, threatening bizarre actions against our family. Either try us in court or quit inciting the public against my family. I got no response.

Friday evening, September 5, a friend from Boulder called to tell Patsy and me the latest rumor he'd heard.

"I hate to bother you with this," he began cautiously, "but I need to tell you something unpleasant."

Great, I thought. *Here comes another bombshell.* I gripped the phone more tightly and said, "Let's hear it."

"There's a rumor out here that seems to be fairly widespread, suggesting that Patsy will be arrested either tonight or sometime this weekend."

"Where did you hear this?"

"The news media in New York has it . . . I don't have any indication that it's true, but I don't know for sure that it's false."

"I see," I answered and took a deep breath.

"Sorry to ruin your weekend, but I felt I had to tell you. You can't be caught unprepared."

As I hung up the phone, I thought I knew what was happening. This was a perfect time for the police to float a rumor, trying to make us sweat it out until Monday morning. They were trying desperately to get us to "crack." The fact of the matter is, you don't crack if you are innocent and have been telling the truth all along.

Wanting not to believe this garbage, but also wanting to be prepared, just in case, Patsy and I kept a card with all the phone numbers of Jim Jenkins, the kids' attorney, who lives in Atlanta. If either of us were arrested over the weekend, we'd be able to get hold of Jim with the one phone call we had a right to make. We believed that if one of us were arrested, the police would very likely arrest the other person as an accessory. We had already drawn up a legal document appointing my brother, Jeff, as a custodian for Burke. I couldn't think of anything more horrible than having my son, whose sister had been murdered and whose parents were in jail, thrown into a foster home or put under the protection of the county in some public facility. At least my brother would have legal custody of Burke if the unspeakable happened.

For the rest of the evening, Patsy and I watched our security monitors out of the corner of our eyes, looking for a blue-

and-white flashing light on top of an Atlanta police car. It was almost impossible to rebuild our lives with bombshells like this going off all the time. I guess that was the intent. Obviously, we weren't arrested that weekend, and the attempt to torture us didn't succeed in "cracking" us as the cops might have wished.

The ongoing battles with the Boulder PD erupted publicly again on September 7, when Police Chief Tom Koby traveled to Boston to talk about the problem of police integrity. Apparently Koby was concerned and upset over where the press leaks were coming from within his organization. The investigation leaks had obviously spilled out across the American landscape like water through an old dam. Koby's intentions were to stop the constant dribble by requiring polygraph tests of the rank-and-file officers. His announced intentions did not sit well, and a backlash followed.

Greg Perry, the president of the Boulder police union, reminded Chief Koby that the officers didn't have to cooperate. In fact, Koby's request was illegal unless he had already named a suspect. Apparently Koby wasn't ready to put any names on the table and had to back down. Koby's life wasn't getting any easier, either.

We also heard that around the middle of September an internal investigation was started to look into allegations of misconduct against Chief of Detectives John Eller. The bullheaded leadership style that came from Eller's office was apparently catching up with the man. As the searchlight of public opinion and media coverage turned its focus on the police, the picture that we had seen for months was starting to become apparent to the public. The question being asked on many fronts was why this investigation had gone so poorly.

On September 16 I returned to Access Graphics in Boulder and, as seemed to happen almost every day, another bombshell went off. I learned that Glen Stine, our host for the last five months—an Ed.D. from Harvard, and chief financial officer for the University of Colorado—was under fire from Peter Boyles, the local radio talk show host. Boyles had gone so far as to demand the removal of Glen from his university job because he had taken us in. The idea that one of the finest people we knew was being attacked—and by one of the lowest gossip commentators I'd ever heard—was disgusting to me. Glen and Susan had saved our sanity and probably our lives.

At the same time Bill McReynolds, who had been Santa Claus at our family Christmas party, was becoming of interest. On the day before Christmas, JonBenét had spent a good part of the time playing at her friend Megan Kostanick's house. During this time JonBenét told Barbara, Megan's mother, that Santa was going to make a special visit to her *after Christmas.*

Barb had challenged her about this, thinking JonBenét had just gotten mixed up. Barb told her, "No, Santa Claus comes on Christmas Eve. Tonight is Christmas Eve, and Santa comes this evening."

JonBenét had repeated, "No, Santa told me that he is making a *special* visit to me after Christmas. And it's a secret."

After the murder occurred, Barbara Kostanick called the police, trying to get them to listen to her story about what JonBenét had said. The police wouldn't pay any attention to Barbara; apparently they were still focused on their theory that "the parents did it." As a trained engineer and highly educated person, Barbara knew that the comment JonBenét had made to her was possibly of critical importance. She finally called Susan Stine, expressing her frustrations with the lack of response from the police. Susan in turn called our investigators, who encouraged the police to take a second, more careful, look.

While we were interested in this type of information, we did not want to do a "Boulder police" and rush to erroneous conclusions.

Any time I was in Boulder, I would try and spend time with Father Rol Hoverstock. This time we arranged to go for a walk and have lunch together. We met at the church, and Father Rol naturally asked how Patsy and I were doing. Since we had joined St. John's Church, nearly four years earlier, he had been a real spiritual mentor to me as well as a good friend. I felt a special kinship with him because he had owned a successful business himself before he went to seminary to become an Episcopal priest. He had done well in the secular world and yet chose to serve the Lord in a full-time capacity. Father Rol brought the element of a real-world experience to the priesthood.

That afternoon I related to him my struggle with the concept of forgiveness as it is defined for us in the Lord's Prayer. How could I ever forgive the man who had brutalized my daughter and killed her? I knew we were supposed to forgive others, just as we expect God to forgive us, but I didn't think I could ever forgive what had been done to JonBenét. At this point I still thought, *Give me five minutes in a room with this creature, and there won't be a need for a trial.* I felt so much rage and anger that I could have ripped the person from limb to limb.

Father Rol really didn't have any easy answers that day, but he helped me talk through my struggle. "Eventually you will find the answer to that," he said, "but I can't sit here and tell you how or when to forgive the person who murdered your daughter."

I continued to do a lot of reading and thinking about forgiveness, and I came across a quote that crystallized things for me. It basically said, "Forgiveness to the victim doth belong." I really wasn't the victim here, I decided. JonBenét was the victim. An obvious analogy occurred to me. Suppose I were sitting in my car at an intersection when a drunken driver ran through the red light and smashed into a school bus. And suppose I got out of my car and walked over to the drunk and said, "I forgive you. You ruined my day, I'll be late for work, but I forgive you." Such nonsense. The maimed or dead children in the school bus are the victims, and if forgiveness were to be given, it would come from those injured in the accident. Comparatively speaking, I was not the victim, and for me to offer forgiveness would be shallow and meaningless.

The crime committed against me was nothing compared to the crime perpetrated against my precious daughter. I finally concluded that the only ones who could forgive JonBenét's killer were JonBenét herself and God. I couldn't forgive her murderer on her behalf.

The next Wednesday morning I attended the midweek Eucharist service at St. John's. It was always a good pick-me-up in the middle of the week. All I ever had to do was walk in, and five minutes later I was brought close to God and my burdens would be lightened. As I knelt to pray that day, I noticed that a good friend of ours was also in worship. She was on her way to Assisi, Italy, to attend a worldwide retreat of the Catechism of the Good Shepherd, a spiritual program for children that brings the meaning of the church down to a level they can understand. Patsy and I had sponsored the atrium setting for the program at St. John's in Beth's memory as well as covered the cost of our friend's training as an instructor of the program.

After Beth died, we wanted to do something that would be an ongoing, memorable way of honoring her life. As we considered a number of possibilities, this program settled as an idea that was needed at the church and also represented Beth's devotion to God. Patsy helped work out how the program would be set up for children ages three to six. JonBenét was in the first class and spent one hour each week for nine months participating in this learning experience.

The Good Shepherd program is a classroom situation set up in the Montessori style of learning, with different centers placed around the room for insight and developmental experiences. For example, in one section is a little table to teach children about the Last Supper of Christ. In addition to a chalice, little figures can be placed around the table as the children learn the meaning of this event while the leader tells them the story of what happened on Maundy Thursday. Another area in the atrium has a baptismal font where children learn about their entry into the Christian life.

In the beginning, Patsy hung JonBenét and Burke's christening gown on one of the walls near the baptismal font. Our former baby-sitter, Suzanne Savage, and her parents carved and hand painted many of the little wooden figures used in the teaching, and Father Rol made a large wooden map of Jerusalem. Another man in our church built little work tables as well as a beautiful replica of our altar with everything child size. As I saw what they were learning, I thought, *Boy, I would like to take this class myself!*

Often, near the conclusion of an atrium class, the children would kneel to form a prayer circle in front of the little altar. An adult would lead them in prayer and then they would blow out the candles on the altar. JonBenét always said that the smoke rising from the snuffed candles was taking her prayers to Jesus in heaven. The program truly helped these little ones develop not only an awareness of the church's meaning but a sense of the closeness of God.

As I sat in the worship service that Wednesday morning, I knew we had helped put something in place that was a lasting tribute to Beth and would be helping children for years to come. Teaching children about faith is a significant way to positively impact their entire lives. It had been an important part of JonBenét's life. I smiled as I prayed. The gentle quiet felt good.

21

SAME TRAIN, SAME TRACKS

On Monday morning, September 29, I flew back to Boulder from Atlanta on an early flight. I was in my office, preparing for the day, when I received a phone call from my boss at Lockheed Martin, Gary Mann.

"I've got some disturbing information for you," he said.

Disturbing? For a moment I pondered what he might mean. "Humm, doesn't sound good. But let it rip."

"Looks like General Electric is working on a deal with our corporate people at Lockheed Martin that would result in our selling Access Graphics to them."

I caught my breath. "You're serious?"

"Afraid so."

"Boy, Gary, I sure didn't see this one coming."

"Well, it's been something of a surprise to a number of people. Let me share some things you might expect in the immediate future." He began outlining details of what might happen if the deal went through. Gary was a great person and a compassionate and forthright boss who had a way of making bad news seem not so bad.

As I hung up the phone, I realized that everything in my world had again changed radically. The potential deal was disappointing to me for a couple of reasons. Lockheed had recently expressed an interest in divesting themselves of our company because it didn't fit their current long-range strategy. I had been working to accomplish this, either through a management buyout or an Initial Public Offering, which would have been any entrepreneur's dream: to be able to sell the same company twice! In our case it would have been first to Lockheed, then to the public. Apparently GE had a considerable amount of Lockheed Martin preferred stock, and Gary explained that the companies had agreed to an asset swap for the stock, in which Access Graphics was one of the assets to be traded.

A more personal reason also troubled me. I couldn't help but believe that General Electric would see me as a liability because of the accusations leveled against me in the press. I figured that most people in America had seen me labeled as a child killer on the front of the screaming tabloids. Lockheed knew me and believed in me, but GE did not. I could guess what the top executives at GE must be thinking and saying about John Ramsey.

"This Ramsey guy runs a good business, but man, think about the bad publicity!" one of the executives might say. "Look at the media reports. Read them. He is one bad guy."

Someone at the other end of the long conference table would probably respond, "As part of our purchase of the company, you need to get rid of Ramsey."

Even though Gary Mann didn't say so, I knew my days at Access Graphics were numbered. I called in the six people who reported directly to me and told them the news about a possible GE takeover. As I looked around the room, I could see that everyone was stunned and disappointed.

Gary had told me that the GE people could possibly come in on Thursday or Friday to conduct due diligence, and we would need to be ready for them. The changes would probably go into effect quickly if the agreements between the two companies went through; I didn't have any choice but to begin getting "our" business ready to become "their" business.

Shortly after I made the announcement to our executive staff and put the necessary actions into gear, I left to attend a meeting with David Williams and Ellis Armistead to see how our private investigation into the murder was going. I had to keep our costs down or I would quickly run out of resources at the rate we were going, and we needed to cut back in order to sustain our activities over the long haul. Bryan Morgan, Hal Haddon, and Pat Burke told me that getting paid for their time was not an issue. Catching the killer was everything to them. I was truly grateful. No question that these are not only top people in their field but also very principled men, and I couldn't have been more thankful for their dedication. We were all united in the number one goal of finding the killer, even though they would remind me from time to time that their number one goal had to be to protect our innocence.

By this time Chris Wolf captured our renewed interest. Jacqueline Dilson said that Wolf had some photographs of Jon-Benét out of newspaper articles, some military magazines—the soldier of fortune kind of stuff—and some pornographic photos of himself. Public records showed that he had once been arrested for public indecency.

Much to my surprise, the district attorney's office called Hal Haddon with a lead they wanted us to check out. While I was delighted that the DA had called us and was indeed working to find the killer, I was surprised that the county had asked our team to follow up the information. Obviously the DA was becoming as frustrated with the lack of an objective police investigation as we were. All of us continued to be concerned about the problem of the "unnamed sources" that kept appearing in the newspapers with false or misleading information that in some cases continued to hamper a legitimate investigation.

As we were discussing the request from the DA's office, another action by the media produced more headline material. In an effort to learn what was in the search warrant issued by the police for our property in Charlevoix, the *Denver Post* sued for full disclosure of the warrant's contents. Of course, it was the big story on the Tuesday front page. In the newspaper account was a picture of one of our exterior doors at the Boulder house that looked like it had been pried or forced open. The police later publicly stated that an "expert" locksmith had said there were no signs of tampering with the doors, apparently to discount the picture that had appeared. The police's locksmith told us, "I never said such a thing." The police had apparently made up the story and put it out publicly to further discredit the intruder theory.

We discovered other deficiencies that surfaced in the official investigation of our neighborhood around 755 Fifteenth Street. All of the neighbors living close to our former home had not been interviewed after the murder. In effect, some of the people in the closest concentric circle to where the murder occurred were simply written off as possible sources of information. We understood that one of the Boulder detectives had justified this omission by telling Officer Steve Ainsworth, who was on special assignment to the DA's office, "We don't need to do that. We know what happened. The Ramseys did it."

While John traveled back and forth to Boulder, Burke and I stayed in Atlanta. Burke had always been a good student and quickly adjusted to life in his new school. I knew he would do well and that the fifth grade would be a challenging but significant learning experience. And I knew he was glad to be back in Atlanta, close to my parents and some of his old buddies.

On October 8 I discovered that Judith Phillips had finally made her big sale. The *National Enquirer* was running photos she had taken of JonBenét and me. Despite our attorney's warning not to sell them, her persistent efforts to profit from the old pictures finally paid off at the cash register. Shortly after the tabloid hit the streets, Judith showed up on the television program *Hard Copy*, describing our past friendship and expressing dismay about why I had dropped her as an "old friend." However, I was pleased that she described my personal relationship with JonBenét as loving.

Friends of mine began seeing Judith on a number of other television talk shows, describing her relationship to me. Apparently she was on the talk-for-pay circuit and making all the stops. We were pleased that she truthfully reported *never* seeing us hurt the children or being abusive in any way. Rather, Phillips described us as a loving, close-knit family. On one of these occasions, Judith said that she hated even to think that we might be guilty, but she couldn't understand our hesitation to talk about what happened. Evidently she expected us to make the same talk show circuit, discussing our daughter's death. This was not an entertainment issue, in our minds. We were in the midst of a serious murder investigation and did not feel compelled to share our investigative tactics or our excruciating pain with the press and the public.

On October 10, 1997, newspapers reported a story that gave Patsy and me new hope that better days might be ahead. We had been praying for a long time about the struggle and confusion at the Boulder PD, hoping for a change in leadership because we sensed that Commander John Eller was very much at the center of the problem that inhibited the capture of our daughter's killer. For a long time we didn't see much hope on the horizon and then, as though our prayers were answered, a lead story appeared in the *Boulder Daily Camera*.

Police Chief Tom Koby announced that John Eller had been removed from JonBenét's case. Undoubtedly, Koby would take a significant number of hits from the media, but we knew that he had done the right thing in adjusting the leadership. The change was long overdue. Koby indicated that he was adding two investigators and moving Mark Beckner to oversee the investigation of JonBenét's murder.

Mark Beckner graduated with a degree in criminal justice from Ferris State University in Big Rapids, Michigan, and immediately started with the Boulder Police Department in 1978. During the years that followed, he worked in a wide range of positions. In 1994 he had been elevated to the rank of commander.

As Patsy and I read of his new responsibilities, we hoped that Beckner's new role would also be a new day for JonBenét's case. However, there was always the possibility that while Beckner might be the new engineer, the train was on the same tracks and traveling in the same direction the police had been going since December 26, 1996. Their destination? *Get John and Patsy Ramsey.*

At about the same time the police chief made this announcement, we learned that a major media source came to Koby's office with a totally presumptuous offer: we know you think the Ramseys did it, and we want to help you get them. Chief Koby apparently threw these people out, telling them they ought to read the United States Constitution. The Ramseys, he said, are innocent until proven guilty! His act of courage really lifted our spirits. Koby seemed to understand how the justice system is supposed to work.

Patsy and I were encouraged by Koby's action, and in an effort to put past mistrust aside, we extended an offer through Father Rol to meet Beckner in our home in Atlanta. I thought the best way to get this "new" investigation off on the right foot was to sit down and talk. Rather than contacting us personally, Beckner chose to respond publicly: No, he would not meet with the Ramseys, as that would be to their advantage.

It appeared we had been right: the investigative train was still traveling the same old tracks.

In the ten days since Gary Mann had called me to say that Access Graphics was for sale, the deal with General Electric had gone off and then on and then off again. Several times I felt that the deal probably wouldn't happen. However, on Monday morning, October 13, Gary called to let me know that an agreement with General Electric had been finalized and would be announced to the public on the coming Thursday morning. As I had suspected, Lockheed would put together a severance package for me because GE didn't want me to be part of their company. I was to be gone as soon as the deal closed.

There was no question in my mind that I had been asked to leave primarily because General Electric didn't want a tarnished CEO in the front office. The real issue behind my termination was that Patsy and I had been painted guilty by the cops, the city government, the media, and the public.

Later I learned that my father-in-law, Don Paugh, our vice president of operations, would also be released. I couldn't imagine anyone questioning Don's ability. Before joining me at Access, he had a thirty-five-year career in management with the Union Carbide Corporation. I couldn't help feeling that GE was making a mistake. People buy products and services from those they like and many, many people in our business liked and respected Don. It was simply another case of tarnished goods. Isn't it ironic that Patsy's father and I were the only casualties of the buyout? Where Lockheed had demonstrated compassion throughout all this, GE showed the cold cruelty for which big corporations are despised. Of course, Don accepted his removal with grace, but I wished that I could do something to change what had happened. Unfortunately, I couldn't.

The two of us were being shoved out the back door of a business we had worked for years to develop and build. In 1991, when we had moved the business to Boulder, the company was doing around fifty million dollars in annual revenues and had a net loss of over three million. At the time Don and I were discharged, Access Graphics was poised to gross 1.5 billon in annual revenues, with operations in twenty countries.

I was proud of that, but what a price I'd had to pay! I would have given up every position or material possession to have JonBenét back. Family was all that mattered, I now realized. Money and material things could lead to great unhappiness, because you run the risk of limiting the time you have to focus on what's really important: your children, your spouse, your spiritual growth. Why had I been so driven? Where had it gotten me? A murdered daughter and the loss of my livelihood.

At least now I would be back in Georgia full-time with Patsy and Burke. The silver lining, I suppose.

I knew from the erroneous accounts in the newspapers that the problems with information leaking out of the police department had escalated over the months. Each day seemed to bring some new tidbit of trouble or disorganization from Boulder. Back in August, John Eller had announced that his detectives were looking at about thirty-five sex offenders who had been forced to register in Boulder. Now that number had been revised upward to seventy-one people in the area, more than twice Eller's original estimate. Obviously, the town had far more potentially dangerous pedophiles than I would have dreamed possible. We had lived innocently without the slightest idea that perverts resided in the shadow of our home. The world is a harsh place. We would never lose sight of that again.

Another important piece of evidence surfaced in the *Denver Rocky Mountain News* about this same time and was sent to me in Atlanta. The newspaper had identified "unnamed sources" who reported that unlocked windows and doors had been discovered at our home on the morning of December 26 but had gone unreported. Obviously someone had either come in or gone out one of the exits during the night. Peter Schild, a Boulder attorney without any association to Jon-Benét's case, expressed the opinion that unlocked windows and doors could clearly indicate the existence of an intruder. The release of this material further supported our claim about what must have happened during Christmas night.

Late in September, as John and I settled into a routine in Atlanta, I learned that Vicki Chabol, my good friend and roommate from the National Institutes of Health, was in the final stages of her battle with cancer. Her CA 125, the marker in your blood that indicates the presence of ovarian cancer, was escalating rapidly. NIH could no longer help her, and she explored alternative treatments, some as far away as Mexico. Even though we were getting short on money, John told me we could help pay for those trips if she needed us to.

I made plans to go to Pittsburgh, where Vicki now was, on October 30, but her mother told me that Vicki probably wouldn't last that long. Travel for me was now complicated by the threat of media stalkers and fear for my safety. People thought we had killed our daughter, and our security adviser had cautioned us not to travel alone anymore. He was afraid someone would think, *The Boulder police can't take care of this, so I'll do it myself.*

I decided to leave on Tuesday, October 28, accompanied by my mother. She suffered from severe arthritis and weighed about a hundred pounds at the time, but as John always said, "I wouldn't want to pick a fight with her." We both knew I would be quite safe with her at my side. Besides, Mom wanted to see Vicki again too.

I went to Pennsylvania with a bottle of oil blessed by one of our ministers at Peachtree Presbyterian Church. While there I would anoint Vicki in a healing service, just as Father Rol had anointed me years before. Vicki and I were especially close, since we had shared so many hospital stays together.

After a couple of sad days with Vicki, Mom and I started driving south toward Parkersburg, West Virginia, in the late afternoon to visit Linda McLean. When we reached Morgantown that evening, I said, "Let's stop here for a moment and take a look at my old alma mater." It had been almost twenty years since I'd visited the campus of West Virginia University.

First we drove up Spruce Street to the Alpha Xi Delta sorority house, and I asked Mom to double-park on the steep incline, which was like parking on the edge of a ski jump. I had lived in the sorority house in 1977 and 1978, so I wanted to take a look inside to see how it had changed over the years. Unfortunately, the doors were locked, but I chatted with the house mother on the sidewalk as she waited for her ride.

Then we drove through the main campus. We swung into Woodburn Circle where Martin Hall, which housed the School of Journalism, and the other two oldest buildings on campus are located. Again we double-parked, and I jumped out of the car. "Where are you going?" my mom asked.

"Just sit here for a minute. I want to see if I can get into the J-School." Ironically, I had been a journalism major at WVU, and now I was one of the media's biggest critics.

The building was unlocked, so I peeked into a room on the first floor where I had taken an advertising class. The professor saw me and opened the door. "May I help you?"

"Oh, no. I'm sorry. I didn't mean to bother you."

I turned and walked up the stairs, which were at the end of the hallway. Once I reached the second floor, I opened the door to one of the smaller rooms, and there sat three students, working at their Apple computers. "I don't mean to interrupt you," I said. "I'm just going down memory lane."

One young man turned to greet me. I nodded hello to him, then pointed to his keyboard. "I would have loved to have had a personal computer when I was in J-school," I said. "What are you doing?"

"I'm writing a story for the AP wire."

"Really?" I said, amazed. "Right here in the journalism building you can do that?"

"Yes," he said, "I—"

Another student interrupted him before he could go further. "You look familiar," the girl said. "Where have I seen you before?"

I hesitated and stumbled a bit before I answered, "I'm Patsy Ramsey, JonBenét's mother."

The third student stopped what he was doing and looked straight at me. I now had their full attention.

"Okay," I said as I sat down. "I'm going to help you get your career off to a good start. Everybody and his brother wants to interview me . . . You've got five minutes. Fire away."

The young man paused a minute, then said, "Is there anything you want to tell people about what you've been through?"

"I would like to tell aspiring journalists to be truthful and always check their sources—and don't write by the seat of their pants! . . . It's not guesswork when you are dealing with people's lives. It's not fiction. The truth is everything."

The next morning my friend Linda McLean woke me up with the newspaper in her hand. "You're on the front page of the *Parkersburg News*," she said. Obviously, those students had gotten their scoop published.

Later that afternoon I learned that the story was also on all three news stations in Atlanta. John was surprised to hear the reports, seeing as I was supposed to be keeping a low profile while traveling. His response to those who questioned him about this latest news was typical of my gentle husband. "Oh well," he said, "Patsy doesn't know the meaning of the words *low profile*."

22

TELL IT OFTEN, TELL IT LOUD

Although ultimately defeated, Adolf Hitler and his reign of terror left a lasting legacy in the United States, according to commentator Thomas Sowell, a senior fellow at Stanford's Hoover Institution. The Nazi dictator and his propaganda minister, Joseph Goebbels, had refined the theory that people will believe any lie, if it is big enough and told often enough, and loud enough.

Sowell sees this doctrine increasingly practiced in the American media. In an article titled "The revenge of Goebbels and Hitler," he cites the smears against Robert Bork, who was nominated for the Supreme Court, and Clarence Thomas, who was finally confirmed for a place on the high court. As Sowell notes, a new verb, which emerged from the Bork nomination, now appears in the dictionary: *to bork.*

Certainly John and I felt we'd been borked a lot throughout the first year after JonBenét's death. We often referred to the "urban legends" that had been created by the police and then broadcast repeatedly and loudly by the media.

One particularly difficult moment occurred on October 22, 1997. We have never watched much television, but John liked the Weather Channel, and Burke and JonBenét liked to watch Nickelodeon and Discovery. After her death I rarely watched television because I was never sure what I might see. It was too easy to be channel surfing and run into accusations being leveled against us by the talking heads.

One afternoon I decided to rest for a moment and happened to turn on a local station, where the program currently airing was the *Geraldo Rivera Show.* Rivera was interviewing a short, chubby guy named Mike Walker, who was an editor for the *National Enquirer.* He claimed that John had been in a Denver porn shop within a few weeks after JonBenét's death. Claiming he got his information from police sources, Walker said that John had visited the porn shop several times, and that while there John had purchased a sex toy and a video about transvestites.

I couldn't believe what I was hearing. The accusation was totally false. The closest John had been to adult magazines would have been at a magazine stand at the Denver airport, which is typically how the tabloids would justify such a statement. Actually, John had never spent much time in Denver and had told me when these rumors first started that he couldn't find a porn shop there if his life depended upon it.

At the end of the show Rivera asked Cyril Wecht, a forensics pathologist and an "expert" who frequently appears in the tabloids, if he thought the case would ever be solved. Wecht replied that he didn't think so, but that the police should continue the investigation and that criminal charges should be brought against both John and me.

At this the studio audience erupted in cheers, applauding and yelling their approval. The sound rang over and over in my ears. "Crucify them, crucify them, crucify them" was what I was hearing. I was horrified. Welcome to America. Land of the Free. More like Land of the Freaks, and they all seemed to be on national television.

I could not believe what I had heard. How could people, who did not even know us, hate us so much? That night I couldn't sleep for hearing those jeers in my mind.

Later, in July 1998, Cyril Wecht published a book, *Who Killed JonBenét?*, in which he pointed the finger directly at John and me. This man was becoming prominent—at least on the tabloid circuit—because of the death of our daughter.

A month after I had seen the *Geraldo* show, I again fell prey to the lies being broadcast on national television. We had been in our Atlanta house for a few months, and on November 24 plumbers were working outside because the main water pipe to the house had burst. I was tired and decided to rest on the sofa in the family room that afternoon. I turned on the TV, just to relax and use its monotony to put me to sleep. Unfortunately, the dial was set to MSNBC. That day Geraldo was conducting a mock trial of the Ramseys! At the end of the two-day broadcast, a volunteer jury would be asked whether they thought that one or both of us had committed this dreadful act. I couldn't believe this was happening in a civilized country!

As in any trial, the prosecution went first. Raoul Felder, a former federal prosecutor who now specialized in civil litigation, told the jury that JonBenét would speak through him and tell them what happened. He ended his opening statements by making derogatory comments about John's character and repeating the claim that John frequented porn shops.

And then the show replayed *National Enquirer* editor Mike Walker's statement from the October broadcast that my husband had been seen buying pornography not long after JonBenét's death. I thought of Hitler and Goebbels' legacy: people will believe any lie, if it is big enough and told often enough, and loud enough. Certainly Geraldo Rivera was allowing that to happen to us on national television.

Just then John came into the room. He took one look at my face and turned the television off. "You shouldn't be watching that garbage," he said.

I tried to turn it back on, and nothing happened!

"Well, fine," John said, "we don't need the TV anyway."

We later learned that the contractors outside had accidentally cut the cable line, just at this moment. (Could it be God's intervention?)

That night I went to bed in tears. This shouldn't be happening in America. Whatever happened to the Ten Commandments? Specifically, "Thou shalt not bear false witness." Am I mistaken, or don't they predate the First Amendment by several thousand years? How much better our world would be if we would just observe those ten simple statements laid down 3,500 years ago.

Later we learned that the *Geraldo Rivera Show* actually has a guideline for the program, a "bill of rights and responsibilities," if you will. "Integrity and honesty" are the first items mentioned on their list. Yet they had allowed their "paid-for-performing experts" to make statements that were totally false—without checking them for accuracy. Lives are destroyed by this kind of flagrant abuse of media power. If it weren't so tragic, it would be laughable.

"Children may be watching" was another responsibility on Rivera's list of rules. I've mentioned some of the topics covered during the two-day mock trial. Others were even more graphic and salacious. Children could be watching such an exhibition.

Yet another responsibility in their pious guideline was "accentuating the positive." The statement said, "While taking hard looks at hard topics, we will emphasize the positive aspects of our life and times, rather than dwell on the negative or the bizarre. We will emphasize solutions, values, and community spirit." Not dwell on the bizarre? What in the world does Rivera consider bizarre, if this isn't? Certainly the shows on October 22 and November 24 were the most bizarre programs I have ever witnessed.

Several months later, John got a call from the cable company that we hadn't paid the bill on time. "We're going to cut off your service if you don't pay by tomorrow," the person said. What an answer to prayer. For a couple of months John had been trying to get through to a human being at the company to terminate our service, but the wait on hold each time was so long, he had finally given up. Now they were going to send a real person out to get the forty dollars due them and shut off our cable.

We would miss a few channels, like the Weather Channel and the Discovery Channel, but everything else now seemed like trash TV. Why had we let this stuff come into our home? We were also worried about Burke accidentally seeing some of the shows that were talking about his sister and his parents. When the man came to collect our bill, John paid it, then told him, "Please discontinue our service." The man was amazed that we could possibly live without cable television, but he followed John's instructions.

We have never reinstalled television since then. We feel as if we have kicked a very bad habit—plus we save four hundred dollars a year, do a lot more reading, and spend a lot more family time together. Not a bad trade.

December unfolded in Boulder without the Ramsey family but certainly not without the effects of JonBenét's death remaining in the community. Wherever people turned, the ominous atmosphere created by her murder hung in the air. One could not escape how the unsolved crime affected everyday life in the town; the fallout simply kept coming.

On December 6, 1997, an article in the *New York Times*

brought an issue to light on the national scene that should have started to unravel the police mask of competence. A University of Colorado history professor, Patricia Limerick, who lived directly across the street from our house at 755 Fifteenth Street, was interviewed. In this particular story Patricia said, "My husband and I have never been interviewed by the police. For weeks I assumed it was a measure of how well the police were doing. Now, I am not so sure." Eleven months had passed since the murder, and the neighborhood around our former house had never been completely canvassed. Where were the police? Patricia Limerick was asking the right question.

A few days later, another telling story hit the newspapers, reporting that the police had been asking our friends if they owned shoes or boots with the brands SAS or Hi-Tec. We did not own either brand, and the police were trying to explain away the footprint they had found in the cellar near Jon-Benét's body. Obviously, the SAS or Hi-Tec footprint could be an important piece of evidence.

The police also began the task of collecting palmprints and mouth swabs to follow up on the prints and genetic material found in the basement and on JonBenét's body. Our friends and their children were approached by the cops and asked to give samples. It had certainly taken the BPD a long time to get around to gathering this important evidence, Patsy and I thought. Yet we felt sorry for our friends. Many of them had to submit to this kind of examination, which obviously was an annoyance. (We wondered if the police were doing the same sampling on the suspects we had given them.) The police, we were later to learn, were mostly trying to explain away the evidence they had found that contradicted their theory that "the Ramseys did it," in order to eliminate any defense strategy.

Our concern deepened when we saw what happened when the police showed up at the Stines' home. Once the detective had taken a swab sample from Doug Stine's mouth, the officer discovered that he had forgotten to bring any sort of container for carrying the sample back with him to the police department. Somewhat befuddled, he pushed the original wrapper he had torn off the swab back on it and left, carrying the swab in his hand, walking down the sidewalk into the wind and exposing the sample to possible contamination. Susan watched him drive off, wondering how many other samples of important evidence might be lying around in unusable condition.

In the early part of December 1997, our friends came to us with the idea of a remembrance service for JonBenét. John and I wanted to travel to Boulder to attend, but we came to the conclusion that we couldn't show up without the media making the event into a circus. We knew from experience that wherever we went, the photographers followed, no matter how discreet we tried to be. Their intrusive picture-taking could turn the solemnity of any occasion into a nightmare and make everyone feel like caged animals in a zoo. With reluctance, John and I decided not to attend the special memorial service.

The idea of a one-year remembrance began with Margaret Harrington, Roxy Walker, and Susan Stine. Their lives had been caught up in this tragedy, and they felt it would be helpful to spend a few moments reflecting on our daughter's life and thanking God for this beautiful child. Because JonBenét had gone to preschool at the First Presbyterian Church and it was Margaret's home church, that congregation seemed to be the right place for the service.

When our friends approached the church with the idea, the ministers were supportive and plans were put in place. However, as soon as word got out, Fleet and Priscilla White, who also attend First Presbyterian, protested holding a service for JonBenét there. For reasons we didn't understand, the Whites apparently demanded that the church back off and refuse to allow the service to take place.

Roxy turned to her congregation, the First United Methodist Church of Boulder, and received a warm welcome. "Of course," the minister responded. "We'd be glad to have the service here."

The pastor of the Wesley Foundation, Tracey Hausman, graciously helped prepare the service. As we later discovered, Tracey had lost an infant child and knew firsthand the impact of such a loss. She worked to find the right words and liturgy to thank God for JonBenét's life and give support to those who loved and missed her.

Margaret Harrington worked on the service and came to the conclusion that something special ought to be done to give people a genuine sense of involvement. She inquired if we had any ideas of what might lend a touch of meaning for people coming to the service. As I thought about it, an image came to mind. In the canyon just west of Boulder was an "angel tree," which had always seemed like a lovely idea to me. Unsolicited, people brought angels and left them hanging on the beautiful pine tree. With time, the little images grew in number and inspired people passing by. Of course, environmentalists and antireligious groups had protested. One month the angels would be there. The next month they would have disappeared, taken down by one of the politically correct groups. Soon after, the angels would mysteriously reappear, one by one.

As I thought of that tree and the beautiful old dogwood that reached out over JonBenét's grave, I could see angels moving in the breeze, testifying to her life and watching over her. Maybe people could bring ornaments to the memorial service that would be like those angels on that pine tree, and we would hang them in Atlanta on the old dogwood. I relayed the thought to Margaret, and she passed along the idea. Friends who attended the service brought angel ornaments of every shape and size. Some were made by little hands, and all were given in love to remember JonBenét.

We were grateful for the wonderful group of people who came to the First United Methodist Church on December 14 and paused during the busiest time of the year to thank God for our child and ask his blessing on JonBenét's memory. Many of the attorneys involved in our struggle attended, and we wished that it had been possible for us to be there with them.

John and I wrote a message of appreciation to our friends to be printed on the back of the liturgy of the day. We thanked the people for their support throughout the past year and expressed how much their love had meant to us. We also commented on the meaning of the Christmas season and why it was important to remember the real reason we celebrate this time of the year. In composing this expression of appreciation, John and I had each written a version. With both copies in hand, John dictated and I typed at the computer as we merged the two into one. Later Susan Stine and Roxy Walker made a few edits as they typed it into the liturgical program.

This edited version included the phrase *and hence*. Those two words turned out to be the next bombshell!

Much to our amazement, John and I discovered that some people were literally watching and checking every word that came out of our mouths! The expression *and hence* had also appeared in the ransom note, and some people saw that usage as unusual. In the eyes of the lynch mob, the use of *and hence* in the memorial message clearly made us guilty. Immediately after the service, newspapers exploded with the story that our inspirational note to the First United Methodist Church service contained these words. The tabloids went crazy with the inference that they had found the ultimate evidence that "the Ramseys did it!" They interviewed schoolteachers who said that *hence* was a transition word by itself. You didn't need to use *and* with it, these teachers proclaimed.

Actually, I have no idea why we used that phrase. Maybe we'd seen it so many times in reading the ransom note—and having to write it over and over again for the police—that it became a part of our subconscious vocabulary. Who knows? Then again, maybe people everywhere use the phrase *and hence* every day of the week, because it's a normal part of the English language. The fact we used *any set of words* in our statement meant nothing more than an attempt to convey our personal feelings at the moment we were writing.

The uproar over *and hence* made it painfully clear that many people were scrutinizing everything we did and said with suspicion. In that vein, we realized that we needed to accelerate the permanent monument for JonBenét's grave before December 26, 1997, lest the media sensationalize the absence of a marker. The problem was that we really weren't sure what we wanted to say on her headstone. Nothing seemed exactly right. I've talked to other parents of children who have died, and they relate similar difficulties in deciding what they want to say on their child's gravestone for generations to see. John and I thought about it a lot, but we hadn't yet come to the exact wording that we wanted on that stone forever. In the fall of 1997 we had finally decided on what we wanted and picked out a two-piece headstone that would accommodate the wording. We had a little angel carved into this stone, fashioned after one given to me by Gary Mann's wife, Pam. We wanted the Episcopal cross on the stone to remind people that JonBenét understood and loved God.

I found that I just couldn't emotionally handle buying and arranging for the headstone, so John had to go by himself. He picked out the marker from the Roswell Monument Company, the same people from whom we had purchased Beth's gravestone. Ronnie Stewart, the owner, told John he expected to have the headstone completed sometime in January. That was okay with us, but we began to realize it wouldn't be okay with the media. They were bound to slam us for not erecting a headstone before the first anniversary of her death.

John called Ronnie, and he called the Georgia Marble Company quarry, who said they would do their best to get at least the upright portion of the marker to Ronnie so he could engrave it and get it in place, even if temporarily, by December 26. Then we felt we could short-circuit the anticipated media hullabaloo. We installed the top piece of the marker on December 23.

We had already decided to spend Christmas in Florida in an attempt to stay secluded from the media. We knew they would do everything possible to get a picture of us during the anniversary of JonBenét's death, and that was the last thing we wanted. Susan Stine and our friend Cathy Sanford arranged for our family's trip, and by the grace of God the media never found out where we were until after we left.

After we returned to Atlanta, Regina Orlick and I went out to St. James Cemetery and hung the angels on the tree next to JonBenét and Beth's graves. With time, the custom has grown and many other people who visit JonBenét's grave have added to the beautiful ornaments swinging from the tree. Every time we visit the cemetery, we pause to look at all the angels glistening in the sunlight. It reminds us that a lot of people have been touched by a little angel named JonBenét.

By the middle of December 1997, so many lies had been told by the tabloids about the Ramsey family that these yellow newspapers had definitely gone way out on a limb and were now exposed legally for extremely misleading, false, and defamatory stories. If Patsy and I were not indicted, these tabloids would be vulnerable to libel lawsuits from us. If we were indicted, they were off the hook. It didn't matter if we were later found not guilty. That's the way the system works. Consequently, it appeared to us that they were doing everything possible to make sure we got indicted. Now it was all about money.

During this struggle, another strange figure appeared, pushing the indictment issue as hard as possible. Darnay Hoffman was a New York lawyer who filed a lawsuit against District Attorney Alex Hunter in a grandstanding effort to try and force an indictment of Patsy under an old, unused Colorado law. His motives for doing so remain suspect.

During this fray, a letter from Hoffman to a tabloid attorney named Tom Miller ended up on the Internet. Miller, who lived in Boulder, was probably getting involved for the money. Hoffman's admission in his private letter to Miller is very interesting, since Hoffman was claiming in his suit that he had experts who would testify that Patsy had written the ransom note.

Hoffman told Miller that he had spoken with handwriting expert Paul A. Osborn, who said he refused to touch the Ramsey case. Why? Because Osborn knows the handwriting experts who gave their reports to our defense team and to the Colorado Bureau of Investigation. Hoffman admitted that these experts had impeccable credentials, and their verdict was that the similarity between Patsy's and the ransom note writer's handwriting was at the very lowest end of the spectrum. No basis for a match.

The elder Osborns originally worked on the Lindbergh ransom letter in the 1930s. Hoffman's private admission obviously signaled that the tabloid knew that Patsy had nothing whatsoever to do with the ransom note, but that fact didn't matter one bit. This was about money and protecting themselves from what could be huge damage awards if we were not indicted and later chose to sue them.

In stark contrast to tabloid people, I have met with reporters like Clay Evans from the *Boulder Daily Camera* as well as Dan Glick and Sherry Keene-Osborn of *Newsweek*, Lisa Ryckman of the *Denver Rocky Mountain News*, and Paula Woodward of Channel KUSA in Denver. I was very impressed that these were legitimate journalists who worked hard to separate the facts from hearsay and gossip, attempting to uphold the traditions of good journalism. We respected them and what they did, or what they at least tried to do, within a broken system. That probably isn't where the big money is, but it's the last bastion of integrity in the media.

As December wound down, I began to realize that I was running out of ways to raise cash and would be forced to sell my airplane to pay our mounting debts. I'd owned this airplane for nine years, and enjoyed fixing it up much like bikers like to tinker with their Harley Davidsons. It was my hobby, and I had made it pay for itself by chartering the plane to Mike Archuleta's company, Mountain Aviation. After nine years I'd finally gotten this airplane exactly the way I wanted it. I'd installed Pratt and Whitney PT6A-110 turbine engines, which made this Beechcraft C90 the only one in the world with the more powerful 110 engines. I had also added four-bladed Raisbeck props, Frakes speed cowlings, Frakes slim-line exhaust stacks, and finally a new interior. It was fast, as King Airs go, and easy to fly. Now that customized plane, which was named for Beth, would have to go. I also began the process of selling our summer home in Charlevoix. The damage being done to our family by the continuous police and media persecution simply kept expanding in ever-widening circles.

23

You Need Christmas More Than Anyone

In the services in *The Book of Common Prayer,* which is used in worship in the Episcopal Church, we remember the death of the innocents during the Christmas season. This rite recounts the grotesque and horrible spectacle of King Herod of Judea slaughtering innocent children immediately following the reports of the birth of Jesus, who was being called the king of the Jews. Herod savagely murdered all the little babies in hopes of killing a future king who might rival him.

The world was a brutal and dangerous place then, and it really hasn't changed much since. Evil continues to confront all of us with awful and seemingly endless randomness and tragedy. For our daughter to be killed immediately after the Christmas Day celebration seems to be part of this diabolical madness that shakes our foundations to their very depths. *Where was God,* I wondered, *when my own innocent child was murdered?*

The first of everything is so hard after a death. John and I had experienced it with the loss of Beth and the death of his father, Jay Ramsey, who died only three months after Beth's accident. You cannot help but remember how things were before your loved one was lost. Still, we tried to make the holiday a joyous time for the other kids. We always baked cookies, sang all the Christmas carols, had parties, built gingerbread houses, and did the thousand and one things children love to do on special occasions.

My memories of Christmas Eve 1996 were still vivid. The four of us had attended the family Christmas Eve service at St. John's and had gone to Pasta Jay's afterward for dinner. Then we drove up Baseline Road all the way to the star the city erects high on the rocky face overlooking Boulder. Jon-Benét had wanted to get out and walk to the center of the big star, outlined in white lights. Since she was wearing her black velvet Sunday school shoes, I suggested that we'd better wait and come back next Christmas with boots on. She was sorely disappointed. "Well, what's the use of coming up here if we're not going to stand in the middle of the star?" she had asked.

Now the anticipation of the first Christmas without Jon-Benét was a far heavier load than I thought I could bear. In some ways, the months since Christmas 1996 dragged by like a chain pulling behind us, and then, in a much different way, the months leading to Christmas 1997 seemed to accelerate.

This Christmas we received a handmade ornament from Quinn, one of JonBenét's friends from preschool at First Presbyterian Church, with her name and JonBenét's written on it. She had also written a poem about JonBenét:

> The important thing about JonBenét is . . .
> She was always there for me.
> She had golden hair.
> She was never mean.
> She helped me.
> She knew how to treat a friend.
> She was generous.
> But the most important thing about JonBenét is . . .
> She was always there for me.

John and I were touched that Quinn had remembered us this Christmas and remembered her friend JonBenét in such a special way.

Of course, Christmas for us would be forever tied to the date of JonBenét's death, and this connection presented us with an inevitable twofold burden: how could we celebrate Christmas as a day of joy when we still had vivid nightmares of that night of death?

In a way that I did not recognize at the time, there had been strange premonitions of ill during the previous Christmas season. I had ignored them. Yet now, some of those "nudges" came back to haunt me.

One of these strange events had occurred while I was decorating the big Fraser fir tree in our living room. I kept making trips back and forth downstairs, where most of the decorations were kept. Greenery, silk poinsettias, and ornaments were stored on shelves in the back room of our basement. As I unloaded the cabinets, getting everything out for the Christmas tree decorating, I had noticed a large roll of beautiful purple velvet ribbon on one of the shelves. I reached up and took it down. Usually I decorated with gold, red, or green, but on that day the color purple particularly caught my eye.

Why not? I thought. *Purple would be a different look this year. The family won't expect it. And it could be beautiful.*

For a moment I held the roll of ribbon up to the light, noticing how striking it was. *Perfect*, I said to myself. *I think this will be a nice touch.* With the ribbon in hand, I started back upstairs to trim the tree.

I took the roll into the living room and started interweaving the ribbon through the branches. I liked the effect so much that the richly colored velvet sort of took over in prominence and gave the Fraser fir a decidedly purple cast. The family loved the look of the beautifully decorated tree. *Maybe I'd started a new tradition,* I thought.

Now my mind wandered back to that moment, and I began thinking about that one large Christmas tree. The velvet ribbon suddenly flashed into my mind. I could once again vividly see the purple strands running from branch to branch around the tree. At that moment, another image opened up before my eyes.

Purple was always used at St. John's Episcopal Church during the season of Lent. I remembered that on Good Friday, the cross in the center of the altar was draped with a sheath of purple cloth. Father Rol and the ladies of the altar guild adorned the altar in purple to remind us that Christ had died on this profoundly significant day. Suddenly the two seasons blended together in my mind.

Advent and Lent. Both are marked with the color purple!

In a strange and unexpected way, I had unconsciously woven death into the fabric of our Christmas celebration, and, of course, couldn't have imagined in my wildest nightmare how that 1996 Christmas season would end for us. I couldn't help but feel that there had been a premonition in my selecting purple ribbon for our Christmas tree. Without an awareness of its significance, I had placed the meaning of Lent in the midst of our celebration of the nativity. Beckoning to the future, the use of the deep purple ribbon suggested that what began in the cradle would end on the cross.

When I later shared my premonition with a friend, she told me that purple is particularly significant to Christians because it blends the colors of red and blue. Anglicans often think of blue as the color that symbolizes mankind or humanity. Of course, red represents our redemption through the shed blood of Christ. As the red and blue come together in purple, it becomes a symbolic way of telling the world that "God is present" with mankind. As those ideas worked in my mind, another connection began to form. An assurance had been handed to our family with the presence of the color purple. As God was present in the crucifixion of Jesus, in ways that we couldn't grasp or understand, he was also present in the tragic death of our daughter. In the extreme pain of our loss, God the Father was standing near with his hand upon the Ramsey family, as interwoven in our lives as the ribbon on the tree.

Purple did have a place after all . . .

Another strange experience happened on that 1996 Christmas Eve. I had seen the My Twinn doll advertised in the Denver airport terminal before Christmas and ordered one for JonBenét. The craftsmen groom and mold the doll so that it looks as close as possible to the picture sent to them.

As John and I had placed the gifts under the tree that Christmas Eve, I hurried about the house putting the final touches on the room so that when the children got up the next morning it would be perfect. JonBenét's My Twinn doll had been hidden on a top shelf in the laundry room in the basement for several weeks. After I had everything else in place, I went to get the doll, which was packed in a rectangular white shipping carton.

Carefully I pulled the box down from the shelf and set it on top of the washing machine. I lifted the lid slowly. The doll lay silently in the long white box with her eyes closed. For a split second, I had a horrible feeling. The beautiful doll with golden hair looked like JonBenét lying in a coffin! I was so shocked that I caught my breath. I had to blink several times. It was a momentary, but horrible, feeling.

I quickly put the lid back on the box. The unexpected strangeness of the moment was disconcerting, but I dismissed my silly feelings. I shook my head, picked up the box, and hurried up to the living room to place it under the tree.

The weight of these memories and premonitions became heavier and heavier as December 25, 1997, approached. I found that my normal preparations for the season were roughly shoved aside by the darkness that had settled over my heart. I didn't want to see a Christmas tree or hear a Santa Claus's jolly laugh. Only one thought took precedence. My mind kept saying over and over, *I will never, ever celebrate Christmas again.*

I felt torn to pieces. For as long as I could remember, Christmas had been the crescendo of happiness that concluded a year. Our family had enjoyed everything from the colored lights to the cold, wintry nights. We annually watched the Chevy Chase comedy, *Christmas Vacation,* and laughed every time. Usually I spent an entire month decorating and getting ready for the holiday. Christmas was in my blood.

But on this first anniversary of JonBenét's death, I was mad at God and everyone else. The only thing I wanted to do was get rid of everything in our house that even slightly reminded me of Christmas. I wanted all the ornaments and greenery dumped into trash bins! I had already given a lot of my decorations to the men who helped us move to Atlanta. From the depths of my soul, I could have yelled out our front door at the world that I didn't want *anything* whatsoever to do with this day *ever again!*

As the boiling anger in my soul came to a head, I rushed into the bedroom and slammed the door. "I hate Christmas!" I screamed. I dropped on the bed and yelled at God or anyone else who would listen, "I absolutely don't want to ever hear about Christmas again!" I beat on the bed and broke down sobbing uncontrollably.

I have no idea how long I cried, but eventually the frustration subsided and my mind cleared a bit. In the silence that followed my anguished outburst, I looked at the ceiling, mindlessly staring and sighing.

From somewhere in the stillness at the center of my being, a thought arose and drifted into my mind. *Patsy Ramsey, you need Christmas more than anyone.*

I blinked several times. Where did that come from? Not from me. That idea was the farthest thought from my mind. I took a deep breath. I simply couldn't have dreamed up that conclusion. With great hesitancy, I realized that I had received a message from God.

The thought returned. *You need Christmas more than any-one, Patsy. If you didn't have Christmas and the real meaning of this day, you would live without the promise of ever seeing JonBenét again.*

I sat up slowly and took another deep breath. I knew that the God of this universe was giving me a very important message, and I wanted to understand every word he had to say to me.

I had always tried to hear God's voice, but no one ever told me quite how to listen for it. Many times I thought I was sup-posed to hear him speak as if a big microphone suddenly boomed, "Hello, this is God. Can you hear me? Is this micro-phone on? Testing 1, 2, 3."

Well, that's not the way it happened that day.

Now I began to realize that God often speaks quietly to us through our minds, in the form of thoughts and ideas. And often those little strains of thought are the complete antithe-sis of what we are thinking or feeling at the time. That's cer-tainly what happened to me that Christmas. In my mind I could hear God saying:

> *Patsy, without the miracle of Christmas, you would never have the hope of spending the rest of time and eternity with your precious child. Yes, you need Christmas . . . not Santa Claus and all the bright trimmings . . . You need what is real about this special day. Sure, it's hard walking by the pretty holiday dresses for little girls. Of course, seeing all the Bar-bie dolls in the stores is absolute torture. Those are not pleas-ant moments. But if you don't celebrate Christmas—if you deny this day—then it's all over. There is no hope. Patsy, you of all people need Christmas.*

I slowly stood and dried my eyes. A very different perspec-tive had seized my mind and turned my anger into wonder. No longer could I let my pain-filled emotions rule me. I had to let the facts of God's larger plan keep my thinking fixed on the most important truth in the world. *Because of what hap-pened on that first Christmas day—because a baby was born who would change the world—John and I know that we will see JonBenét again. Now, like never before, we need Christmas.*

24

A New Year, A New Process

A number of times in the months after JonBenét's death, I dreamed about her. One night the dream didn't disappear on awakening, as dreams usually do. Patsy lay asleep next to me as I glanced at the luminous alarm clock and realized that it was 5:00 A.M. I knew I couldn't go back to sleep quickly; the warmth of the dream still clung to me like a gentle comforter.

In each of these dreams JonBenét was the same, about three years old, filled with affection, always smiling and happy. In this dream she ran enthusiastically into my arms and crawled up on my lap. I could feel her tenderness as she cuddled close. JonBenét laid her head on my shoulder, and in a few moments quietly went to sleep. In my dream I was overjoyed and yet at the same time crying. That dream brought to the surface the unconditional love parents feel for their child. The dream was so strong that I awoke with a jolt and knew there was no hope of drifting back to sleep and returning to that wonderful dream.

As I lay in bed, staring into the morning darkness, I couldn't help but remember what a spark plug JonBenét always was for our family. If she saw me frowning or looking concerned, she would say, "Dad, I don't like that face." Of course, I would put on a big smile and then she'd say, "That's better, Dad." That was her personality. I looked forward to those random dreams of JonBenét now. It was like going back in time to more joyful days.

Unfortunately, this day and others like it were far different from those dreams. A number of events had happened in real life just before the beginning of January 1998 that foreshadowed much that would come later. Police Chief Tom Koby had already announced that he would resign at the end of

1998, having been the subject of a no-confidence vote by the city's police organization. Koby's announcement was encouraging to us, since we continued to hope for strong, experienced leadership for JonBenét's investigation.

The fundamental flaw in the whole investigation, I believe, was the leadership provided by Commander John Eller. As chief of detectives, he seemed to direct his people in a bullheaded manner that led everyone right over the cliff. And the wrong cliff at that. Another reason the investigation failed was the police tradition of the so-called "code of silence." Eller, as chief of detectives, had proclaimed the parents did it, and no one thought, or had the courage, to tell the emperor he had no clothes.

The airlines had a similar problem a number of years ago, which they corrected after several tragic accidents. In the past, the flight captain had absolute and unquestioned authority. If the captain wanted to fly the plane into a mountain, the copilot couldn't intervene—or he would lose his job. Several copilots lost their lives before the airlines introduced cockpit resource management. As the airline companies had studied this problem, they realized that such authoritarian control was foolish. Not only the captain, but the co-pilot and the flight engineer also had brains and expertise. The best way to fly an airplane safely was by using a team effort, not following one solitary person with unquestioned authority.

Police organizations do not have this team approach. Commander John Eller was the captain, and no one thought to question his wisdom, at least openly. Obviously, the problems of this type of system are too numerous to list here. What the police needed to come to grips with was that this was a murder investigation, not a military assault. Everyone's input was essential. Police departments need their own version of cockpit resource management in the squad room. I'm certain there are Boulder police officers who think we are innocent, but to speak up could cost them their jobs.

Unfortunately, our distrust of the BPD influenced all our decisions. In the winter of 1998, the media began reporting that Patsy and I had hired attorney Jim Jenkins in Atlanta to represent Burke. We didn't announce that to anyone, so we could only suppose the police chose to leak that tidbit to their favorite reporters. We brought Jim in because we had learned that the Boulder police intended to interrogate Burke further about JonBenét's death. We weren't sure what the cops had in mind, but by this time we had to suspect the worst possible motives. We knew Jim would serve as an adequate wall to protect Burke's civil rights.

Jim Jenkins talked to Mark Beckner about a third interrogation for Burke. Beckner required four conditions, all of which were acceptable to Jim, except one. That one condition was that Burke keep the interrogation a secret from his parents. Jenkins advised Beckner that would not even be legal under Georgia law. More important, Jim felt, was that this is not the kind of wedge that should be put between a child and his parents. Beckner said he would think about Jim's objection and get back to him in a few days.

Within five minutes of ending that phone call, Jim received a call from Marilyn Robinson of the *Denver Post*. She had all the details of the conversation, and in particular, his refusal of Beckner's condition.

Jim immediately called Beckner and said, "What is going on there? How could the media know about our private conversation within five minutes?"

"Well, I didn't tell them personally," Beckner answered.

"Whoever did needs to be reprimanded and reminded that this is a murder investigation," Jim said. "You're in charge out there—can't you call your men in and do something about the leaks?"

Beckner replied, "I'm not sure they would tell me the truth."

Jim Jenkins was flabbergasted that Beckner couldn't count on his own staff telling the truth if he asked them a question. Jim told Beckner he would not subject Burke to any voluntary questioning as long as Beckner could not assure him that Burke's answers would not be leaked to the press.

In addition to hiring Jim Jenkins to protect Burke's legal rights, we also took Burke to Dr. Steven Jaffe, an Emory University professor and child psychiatrist. We wanted him to spend some time with Burke to evaluate whether another intense police interview would harm him emotionally. We concluded that Burke would be okay as long as people who knew how to interrogate children conducted the interview.

During January Patsy and I found ourselves in another

strange twist in this saga. We went to Madrid, Spain, to talk with Jose Martin, one of the owners of Jaleo Software and Consultores de Comunicación Integral, about bringing the company's video postproduction software to the United States. Jaleo had developed a very sophisticated digital editing and compositing application that ran on Silicon Graphics workstations. The expenses in our investigation of JonBenét's death had been high, and I needed to start producing an income again. Jaleo looked like a good bet.

Much to our amazement, we discovered that the *Globe* had received word of this business trip, probably because we charged the tickets on our credit card. (To be on the safe side, we quit using our American Express card for airline tickets.) They sent their senior editor, Craig Lewis, and several photographers to follow us. A somber-looking guy, Lewis maintained a casual look in jeans and a black leather jacket. Unbeknownst to us, he followed us around Madrid and even witnessed Patsy weeping as she looked at the painting *Las Meninas* by Diego Velázquez in the Prado museum. The Infanta Margarita looked like a seventeenth-century replica of JonBenét, with beautiful long blond hair.

During this time, Lewis apparently jumped to the conclusion that Spain and the United States must not have an extradition treaty. At that moment he made a quantum leap of imagination and decided that Patsy and I were fleeing to Spain to escape extradition. On the flight back to the United States, Lewis broke his cover by sending a note to us via the flight attendant. He said he believed in us and wanted to tell our side of the story. *Oh, great!* I thought. Here we were, trapped on an eight-hour flight with a tabloid reporter!

Upon arriving in Boulder, Lewis got an appointment with Alex Hunter to report that Patsy and I were getting ready to flee to Spain. When the story reached us, I was surprised that Hunter would even allow *Globe* personnel into his office. Moreover, I wondered how Lewis explained that we had fled *back* to the United States after our visit. The story made tabloid headlines—based solely on a short business trip, in which we left on a Wednesday and came back to the United States the following Monday. The *Globe* reported that we stayed in a cheap hotel in Madrid. As best as I can tell, that's the only fact Lewis got right. He apparently bribed the hotel staff and came into our room while we were gone and took pictures. (By the way, I think Lewis stayed at the Ritz.)

On February 18, 1998, Police Chief Tom Koby made an unscheduled public appearance before Boulder's City Council to explain the stress that the department had faced in dealing with a number of difficult cases. It was kind of a "you need to feel sorry for us" speech. Yet in his speech Koby predicted a resolution of JonBenét's case within three months. While he missed that prediction by a mile, five days later the *Boulder Daily Camera* released the story that the fifty-one-year-old chief of detectives, John Eller, was quitting to move to Miami to be closer to his and his wife's families. He had not been selected for the position of chief of police in Cocoa Beach, which allowed us to put Cocoa Beach back on our list of safe vacation spots.

Eller left behind a rather telling statement: "I wanted to be chief. I wanted to do it my way." That's the only way we ever experienced Eller's behavior.

Our concern about the condition of evidence in the murder investigation was heightened when the newspapers reported that interviews and printed evidence had been "misplaced" in JonBenét's case. The police were now asking for friends and members of our family to resubmit samples given earlier. The obvious conclusion was that the *police had actually lost* important data in the case. Who knows what else had fallen through the cracks?

At the end of February, forty-two-year-old Mark Beckner, who had previously been in charge of the patrol division, was promoted to take Eller's place as chief of detectives for the Boulder PD. The *Boulder Daily Camera* noted that JonBenét's case had been like a minefield, leaving the bodies of what the paper called the BPD's "best and brightest" littering the area. They mentioned Commander Eller, who was retiring, Detectives Linda Arndt and Larry Mason, two of the original Ramsey investigators who had left the case, and Police Chief Koby, who announced that he would leave at the end of the year. No one, not even the police, had escaped the horrible effects of our daughter's murder.

In his typically low-key manner, Beckner indicated he was ready to take on the hard challenge. He obviously knew that solving JonBenét's case could be very important to his career.

Beckner had no reluctance in admitting that he was interested in pursuing the chief's position. He said, "Yeah, I'm interested in being chief. I haven't decided yet to put in for the opening, but certainly I'm giving it consideration."

Throughout the winter we continued to wonder about the condition of the evidence in JonBenét's case. By March, the district attorney's office was still not privy to all of the evidence obtained by the Boulder police. We could tell that the police were not eager to turn their case over to another group of investigators who weren't already committed to their theory that someone in the Ramsey family was the murderer. Conversely, investigators in the district attorney's office desperately needed all the material in the original police files in order to move forward.

A final example of the poor leadership problems within the BPD was the manner in which the police department failed to use the protocols supplied by the FBI. In November, before JonBenét's death, the Federal Bureau of Investigation had produced a seminar to teach small towns like Boulder how to respond to a kidnapping. Unfortunately, the protocols were not relayed to Boulder's detectives. In fact, on the morning of December 26, one of the detectives had to track down a copy of the "how to" book from the Boulder sheriff's department sometime after the ransom note was found. One of the most significant aspects of the protocols is that a good investigative plan must be prepared ahead of time. If this isn't done, there is a strong possibility that a case will never be solved. The ultimate responsibility for the lack of training of people like Linda Arndt had to lie with their supervisor, Eller, and the chief himself, Tom Koby.

Patsy and I had listened carefully when Mark Beckner, now chief of detectives, announced that the police would eventually come out with one of three possible conclusions: an arrest would be made, the case would be placed in an inactive status, or a grand jury would become operative. We hoped for an arrest, of course, although I'm sure Beckner was only thinking of the two of us at the time he said that. As for the case becoming inactive, Patsy and I weren't about to let that happen. We knew JonBenét's killer was lurking about somewhere, and we would not rest until the creature was found.

As the spring began, the third option—a grand jury—became fairly certain. After fourteen months of working on Jon-Benét's case, on Friday, March 13, 1998, the police petitioned the district attorney's office to convene a grand jury. Detective Commander Beckner made the veiled statement: We think we know who did it, but we can't prove it. Because the police did not have the substantive evidence to prosecute anyone as the killer, they had turned to the grand jury as a way to get what they wanted: an indictment. Once someone is indicted, the police consider the case solved and closed.

During the preceding fourteen months of their work, the police had named no suspects and not made a single arrest. We were not even official "suspects." They continued to maintain that Patsy and I were "under an umbrella of suspicion," that proverbial parasol of persecution. The grand jury could well be their next ploy in an attempt to indict us. If honest evidence wouldn't make a strong case, then try another route.

Back when grand juries were established in the 1300s, their purpose was to protect the common people from overly aggressive prosecution by the crown. Now many legal commentators believe grand juries are often just servants of prosecutors.

Grand juries have the capacity to compel testimony by subpoenaing witnesses, even those outside the state, which was probably important to the police since we were now living in Atlanta. The proceedings are totally secret, and surprisingly few leaks come out of the grand jury process. It is possible for the target of a grand jury investigation not to even know he or she is under investigation until an indictment is handed down. Since a grand jury takes the place of a preliminary hearing in a criminal case, the defense is not allowed to present evidence.

The basic reason for calling a grand jury is to create an environment in which decisions can be made about filing cases for legal prosecution. When the evidence is not decisive, a grand jury can explore the diverse aspects of the case unimpeded by many of the restraints placed on a regular legal panel. Such a jury doesn't establish guilt or innocence, but merely determines if there is "probable cause" for bringing charges, particularly in cases where the penalty requires that a significant amount of time be served in jail. If the grand jury believed there was limited but "probable cause" that Patsy and/or I could have committed the crime, then we would be indicted and stand trial.

Patsy and I knew the grand jury process could be stacked any way the prosecutor chooses. The one-sided way in which the procedure operates makes it comparatively easy to charge people with a crime. (There's an old joke that a grand jury could indict a ham sandwich if it wanted to.) Nevertheless, we wanted the opportunity to tell our story. We were prepared and anxious to testify.

Some authorities pointed out that we might invoke the Fifth Amendment to avoid self-incrimination. The last thing we were worried about was struggling over any form of privilege or immunity. We had already submitted to several major interrogations by police and the DA's office.

As time went by, rumors of what the grand jury might be asked to do began circulating. One of these rumors was that Mark Beckner thought the grand jury system could be used as an investigative tool. The district attorney's office apparently had to spend a significant amount of time clarifying to Beckner that once the grand jury session began, the grand jurors were the ones in charge. Both the police and the DA's office would become subservient to the jury's decisions.

By the middle of April, the former grand jury for Boulder County had completed its term and was disbanded. Another grand jury would be called, and speculation began that this group would address JonBenét's murder. One hundred forty-five people were summoned from the Boulder community to be questioned for possible inclusion in such a jury, yet only fifty-seven showed up.

Rather than make the process closed and secret, the judge pressed for an open selection, as the media would find out who the jurors were anyway. On April 22, 1998, Chief District Judge Joseph Bellipanni's courtroom was packed with the potential grand jurors and the media. Reporters were there from NBC, ABC, and CBS as well as the *New York Times, USA Today, Time* magazine, the tabloids, and local newspapers. During the selection process, Judge Bellipanni asked the potential jurors if they were aware of the conflict existing between the police department and the district attorney's office. Obviously, Jon-Benét's case was a strong option for this grand jury.

In order to start the examination process, Alex Hunter had developed a questionnaire fashioned after what had been used in the O.J. Simpson case and the Oklahoma City bombing trials. On the first page were general questions that clarified the prospective jurors' backgrounds; the second page had issues relevant to JonBenét's case. Four questions specifically dealt with her murder. For example, "Are you involved or do you know anyone who is presently involved in any current criminal investigation (including but not limited to the investigation into the death of JonBenét Ramsey)? Explain." And, "Please describe any opinion you now hold based upon what you know of the investigation into the death of JonBenét Ramsey."

On Wednesday, April 22, the prosecutors in JonBenét's case were hard at work selecting citizens who might comprise a jury to consider JonBenét's murder. Of the fifty-seven people, eight women and four men ended up qualifying to sit on the grand jury. In addition, four women and one man were selected as alternates. The *Boulder Daily Camera* reported that those selected ranged from a University of Colorado graduate student to a licensed pyro-technician. Interests, they said, ranged from outdoor activities such as fishing and hiking to more indoor fare, such as listening to National Public Radio, which encouraged us to think that they would be thoughtful in their deliberations. By the end of the day, the legal components were in place. Although District Attorney Alex Hunter hadn't officially announced that this panel would pursue JonBenét's investigation, we believed they would do so.

In order to appease the police and the governor, on May 5 Hunter hired Michael Kane, Denver's former assistant district attorney, who had also served as an assistant U.S. Attorney and was now working for the Revenue Department of the Commonwealth of Pennsylvania. Kane would work for Hunter's office as a grand jury specialist. Forty-six-year-old Kane had the reputation of being a no-nonsense prosecutor.

Patsy and I weren't afraid of the grand jury process. We strongly believed that eventually the truth would win out. In fact, in March we had publicly stated that we were "eager to assist" a grand jury investigation into JonBenét's death. At the same time, our attorneys strongly believed that this panel should also examine how the Boulder Police Department had handled the case. Our primary concern was that this be a fair and objective proceeding. Our first disappointment came when two Boulder police detectives were named as investigators for the grand jury. It started to look like "fair and objective" might be wishful thinking.

On the first of June, the police department finally presented their case to the district attorney. Several "experts" were in attendance, but they left after the first day of the Tuesday presentation. Like a mountain moving into town, the enormous quantity of paperwork came thundering down on Alex Hunter's offices. The case file contained thirty thousand pages of material and indicated that the police had investigated 119 possible suspects. Potential evidence samples were ponderous, amounting to 1,058 pieces of collected material. And yet, no one had been indicted, restrained, arrested, or even named as official suspects. Once this data was in their hands, the district attorney had to immediately begin assimilating it, and we hoped, conduct his own investigation. Hunter's plate was full.

On June 23 the news broke that Mark Beckner would replace Chief Tom Koby as the new chief of police or "director of police services." Beckner opted for the title "chief" and immediately moved into the responsibilities of the office. Tom Koby had his departure accelerated and would be working for the rest of the year in the Boulder city manager's office. In turn, Alex Hunter praised Koby for his work.

While John worked on his new business and the constant grind of the legal issues, I tried to go about establishing our home in Atlanta. Much of the time John was with us, but he did spend time in Boulder, trying to help our investigators as much as possible. I worried as he traveled back and forth.

I knew about many of the issues and struggles within the Boulder Police Department. However, I tried to avoid much of the public discussion because the reporting was often slanted and inaccurate. Every time one of these stories hit the newspapers, I would get upset. I didn't need any more trauma. The continual struggle had its own insidious way of gnawing and chewing on me, undercutting my will to rebound, day after day, week after week. John and I were trying to rebuild our lives, but mentally we kept getting the legs knocked out from under us.

Thomas's interview had failed to move what we all knew about the murder forward. After all the media uproar about our being reluctant to be interviewed, we were left with the feeling that we had accomplished nothing. Another urban legend came out of the interview, and that was that we had refused to take a lie detector test. The truth is that the police have never asked either of us to take one.

The authorities said they felt the interviews went well, and that the investigation was moving right along. Of course, Patsy and I were glad when the experience was over.

During the months that followed this 1997 interview, the police continued their internal squabbles and conflicts, including a public charge by Commander John Eller that the DA's office had stolen information from the cops' "war room," the command center for the JonBenét investigation. Eventually, long overdue changes were made in police leadership. Out of the shuffle, Commander Mark Beckner, who had not been involved at all, came to the top as the person responsible for solving JonBenét's case.

The changing of so many key players in such strategic positions only added more problems to the chaos in JonBenét's case. On January 23, 1998, in an attempt to move the investigation into competent hands, our attorney wrote to Commander Beckner:

> . . . At our meeting December 19, 1997, we told you that we did not trust the Boulder Police Department to conduct an objective or competent investigation. Our distrust is rooted in the incredibly unprofessional conduct of the police investigation over the past year. It serves no purpose to detail the numerous incidents which led to our conclusion. What must be said, however, is that nothing has changed under your leadership: you continue to "negotiate" requests for information from the Ramseys by resorting to press release and leak, and the "focus" of your investigation continues to be what Commander Eller called "the elimination of defenses" rather than an objective search for the real killer. The hate media continue to be fed smears which demean the Ramseys and the monster who committed this murder is treated to information courtesy of your agency.
> . . . The Ramseys are desperate to participate in an honest,

*objective, and professional investigation. Contrary to your
letter, they have frequently met with, and provided information to, law enforcement agents, including Detective Lou
Smit, who has apparently been banished from active participation in "the investigation" because of disgraceful internal
politics. In this context, your reliance on the narrow phrase
"formal interview" is extremely disappointing, deceptive,
and counterproductive. Because the Police Department investigation is wholly compromised, it is time that it be concluded and turned over to the persons or agencies who have
the competence and objectivity to salvage any hope of finding the real killer. Until that day comes, we have no hope for
justice or even common decency. We will no longer deal with
the Boulder Police Department, except to honor our previous commitments.*

The police did not ask Patsy or me for further interviews,
although rumors of our lack of cooperation continued to
swirl. One day in April, out of sheer frustration, while sitting
in our investigator's living room trying to figure out how to
move the investigation forward, I grabbed a pen and piece of
paper and wrote a letter to District Attorney Alex Hunter. I
wanted him to know my position exactly, without being
passed from our attorneys to his attorneys for interpretation.
I was getting stronger emotionally and could start to deal with
these issues myself. I finished the handwritten letter and gave
it to Bryan Morgan, who hand delivered it to the DA. The letter said:

April 11, 1998

Dear Mr. Hunter,
*I am writing this letter because it seems difficult at times
for us to communicate through attorneys who are focused
on protecting my rights as a citizen.*
I want to be very clear on our family's position.
*1.) We have no trust or confidence in the Boulder Police.
They have tried, from the moment they walked in to our
home on December 26, 1996, to convince others that Patsy
or I or Burke killed JonBenét. I will hold them accountable
forever for one thing—not accepting help from people who*

offered it in the beginning and who could have brought a wealth of experience to bear on this crime.

2.) We (myself, Patsy, Burke, John Andrew, Melinda) will meet anytime, anywhere, for as long as you want, with investigators from your office. If the purpose of a Grand Jury is to be able to talk to us, that is not necessary. We want to find the killer of our daughter and sister and will work with you twenty-four hours/day to find "it."

3.) If we are subpoenaed by a Grand Jury, we will testify, regardless of any previous meeting with your investigators.

I am living my life for two purposes, now. To find the killer of JonBenét and bring "it" to the maximum justice our society can impose. While there is a rage within me that says "Give me a few moments alone with this creature and there won't be a need for a trial," I would have succumbed to behavior which the killer did. Secondly, my living children must not have to live under the legacy that our "entertainment industry" has given them based on false information, and a frenzy centered on our family's misery to achieve substantial profit.

It's time to rise above all this pettiness and politics and get down to the most important mission—finding JonBenét's killer. That's all we care about. The police cannot do it. I hope it's not too late to investigate the case properly, at last.

Finally, I am willing and able to put up a substantial reward ($1 million) through the help of friends if this would help drive information. I know this would be used against us by the media dimwits but if it would help, I don't care.

Please, let's all do what is right to "get" this worst of all killers in our midst.

> *Sincerely,*
> *John Ramsey*

Now there should be no doubt in Hunter's mind that our family would cooperate fully to find the killer of our daughter and sister. Yet the DA couldn't interrogate us until our case was completely in his hands, and that wouldn't happen until the police made their formal presentation of the evidence to the district attorney's office.

On Saturday, May 30, with the transfer of the investigation imminent, I called Alex Hunter's home to share with him our concern and to stress our desire to cooperate with his office. With responsibility now shifting completely to the DA's staff, I felt our response to their questions might be of significant help as they examined the evidence. After a struggle to get Hunter to the phone, I finally succeeded and told him who was calling. I sensed that the DA was surprised to hear from me personally, but he responded forthrightly. Hunter told me that the canon of ethics made it impossible for him to talk to me without the approval of my own attorneys. I told Hunter I would get the lawyers' formal approval as quickly as possible, because I didn't want anything to get in the way of the investigation. I told him that Patsy and I were available for questioning at any time. The conversation seemed positive and a step forward. I hoped that my lawyers could respond immediately.

I believe Hunter met with his staff the next day and related our conversation. Detective Commander Mark Beckner of the Boulder PD was there and heard what I had told the district attorney. To our astonishment, in a few days the story of the possibility of our interrogation was reported in the *Globe*. Once again, leaks were the standard mode of operation.

On June 1, 1998, the police made their formal presentation of the murder case to the district attorney's office. We were hopeful that now the case would be looked at by experienced investigators. And the pace of the investigation did pick up again with the involvement of the DA's office.

About a week later, Peter Hofstrom of the DA's office and Dan Schuler, a witness interview specialist from the Broomfield Police Department, requested an interview with Burke. We agreed, and the two men came to Atlanta. *Why couldn't Beckner have done the same thing months ago?* I wondered. Hofstrom and Schuler conducted these interviews as true professionals; they came to our home to meet Burke first, and helped him to understand what would occur when the interrogation began. It was obvious that they were objectively looking for information and wanted Burke to be comfortable enough to remember and verbalize everything he could. Their interview with Burke was videotaped at the district attorney's office in suburban Atlanta.

Hofstrom and Schuler talked to Burke in two-hour sessions

for three days as his psychiatrist, Dr. Stephen Jaffe of Emory University, observed. Burke's attorney, Jim Jenkins, was with him during the interviews. We had placed no conditions on what these men might ask Burke, and as far as we know he answered all of their questions to the best of his ability. After all, his sister had been murdered, and I'm sure he wanted to help find the killer too. When the questioning was complete, Hofstrom and Schuler thanked Burke.

On Tuesday, June 23, Patsy and I flew to Broomfield, Colorado, for the first interviews since I had written my letter to Alex Hunter. We landed at the Jefferson County Airport, which wasn't far from the Broomfield Justice Center, where we would meet. The media was still surrounding Boulder, so we couldn't meet there. Yet the fact that we were in Colorado answering questions was eventually leaked to the press, and reporters and photographers soon had the Justice Center surrounded. Alex Hunter's team of prosecutors and investigators came to Broomfield to talk with us. Grand Jury Specialist Michael Kane and Special Investigator Lou Smit as well as Homicide Investigations Supervisor Thomas Haney, on loan from the Denver police, were there along with Senior Trial Deputy Trip DeMuth. We were told the interrogation would be videotaped.

While I was not entirely sure of all the motives operating in the district attorney's office, I did feel that they had a fundamental commitment to the truth and to a solution of the case. Whatever happened, I knew they would attempt to bring the facts to light and find the killer. I believed they could be trusted.

The district attorney's office had developed a two-team approach so that Patsy and I could be interviewed simultaneously. Lou Smit and Michael Kane would talk with me while Tom Haney and Trip DeMuth would interview Patsy. By talking to us at the same time, there would be no way for us to confer. We knew the interrogators would be extremely well prepared.

The process proved to be arduous. The videotapes were changed in two-hour intervals and sent back to the Boulder Police Department, where detectives viewed them throughout the day and evening to determine what we would be asked next. Seven Boulder police detectives who had been in-

vestigating the case for the past eighteen months also provided questions for the interviews. Our personal lawyers were
with us during the questioning; Bryan Morgan accompanied
me, and Pat Burke was with Patsy. We were told to take all the
time we needed to answer the questions.

The room where I was interviewed was a small, square interrogation room that held five people at most. A round table
approximately three-and-a-half feet in circumference sat in
the center, and the video camera was aimed at me through a
camera port at the other end of the room. We sat in cafeteria-
type chairs with hard seats and backs. If someone left the
room, at least one or two people would have to get up to make
space for them to move. The interview broke at lunchtime, and
the police sent out for pizza. Once we were through, the
process started again with Lou Smit and Michael Kane conducting my interviews.

Kane spent a considerable amount of time sitting in the
corner listening. He asked how much I had spent on my private investigators, and my attorney pointed out that that
didn't have any bearing on the murder and wasn't an appropriate question. By and large Kane's few questions seemed to
come from what he had read in the tabloids. I got tired of his
repeating the gossip and hearsay from the papers and finally
told him that I could answer everything that the tabloids published with one statement: It is all BS. After that response,
Kane quit asking me much of anything.

Detective Smit showed me crime scene pictures, taken at
our home, and led me through an investigation of rooms in
the house. As I looked at the photographs, I pointed out pe-
culiarities when I saw them. They had pictures of the broken
basement window that I had found open, and I wondered if
they had fully checked out what this window offered in the
way of clues. I saw pictures that to me clearly showed that the
grate above the window had been recently removed and replaced. They also questioned me at some length about the 911
call and wanted to know where Burke was during this time. I
told them that he had been asleep in bed until I got him up to
go to Fleet White's house.

The investigators spent a great deal of time talking with
me about a large diagram of the house on the wall behind
me. I later learned that they also used the same diagram with

Patsy. I was shocked to see that they had found the butler kitchen door, which led to the outside, open. This was reported by one of our friends when he arrived shortly after six in the morning. I'd never even noticed that open door as we frantically rushed around making phone calls, and yet there on the police diagram of our home was the note: "Door found open."

Of the interrogators, I found Lou Smit to be the most professional and skilled. He often allowed long pregnant pauses to pull more information out of me than I even knew was there. In turn, he put information before me that I didn't know existed. During the interrogation, I actually learned there was a significant amount of unanswered evidence. For the first time, I learned that someone had drawn a heart on JonBenét's hand.

Who had drawn that heart? The killer? JonBenét? I doubted that my daughter had done so. Certainly as a younger child she might have drawn things on her hand, but at almost seven years old she was beyond that stage, in my opinion. She cared about her appearance and was not likely to have done so. And if she had, she would have had to draw it with her right hand. Which hand was the heart on? I don't know the answer to that.

Lou Smit showed me an October 1995 issue of the *Boulder County Business Report* that included the article "People vs. Profits" with my photo along with those of Mary Ellen Vernon, Jirka Rysavy, and Jeffrey Kohn. We had all received Esprit Awards, given by the Boulder Chamber of Commerce, the journal, and other organizations. The other people's pictures were crossed out, but mine was circled by a crudely drawn heart. Smit asked if JonBenét could have drawn this heart. I was sure she hadn't. I had never seen this marked-up article before; we hadn't even kept any papers about the award around the house. Later I remembered that Chris Wolf had worked for this newspaper at one time.

Then the questioning turned to the public receptions following the award. Those of us who had been recognized by the Chamber were obligated to open the doors of our businesses to the public and host receptions for people who were interested. Access Graphics had hosted a couple of sessions where about thirty or forty people came into our offices. I gave a short explanation of our business, and then answered the visitors' questions.

Smit wanted to know now if I remembered anyone strange or unusual in those sessions. Sure, I answered. They came in off the street, and there were a few odd ones in the crowd. At the time I had even wondered about some of the strange questions one or two of the people had asked. Now I didn't remember any of those questions specifically—nor was I able to give a description of what the people who asked them looked like.

But I was encouraged by this new information. Could this heart circled on the newspaper photo be connected to the heart drawn on JonBenét's hand? Was this another clue the killer had intentionally left behind?

In addition, I learned during this interrogation that there was unidentified DNA evidence. I was encouraged. This could be the clue we hoped for. The investigators had found samples of DNA material on JonBenét's underwear and under her fingernails. I was getting the impression that the killer had left a ton of evidence behind when he left our house, which would finally lead to this person if carefully and objectively analyzed. At the conclusion of the three-day interrogation, I was excited. Maybe the killer could be captured after all.

As my interview began, I knew that John was undergoing the same process at that same moment. The interrogation room was small, maybe ten-by-ten-feet. With such limited space, we were going to be very close to each other, making me almost sit in the face of my questioners again. I sat on a small office furniture-type love seat with Tom Haney to my right and Trip DeMuth to my left, sitting on side chairs. A small coffee table was in front, ready for the investigators to lay out photos or whatever they wanted to show me. In fact, the space was so crowded that we all could barely fit. I was told that on one wall, directly facing me, a pinhole camera lens would be staring at me through an opening in what looked like a heating-and-cooling thermostat. I also knew that District Attorney Alex Hunter was in another room to listen and watch everything I would say or do in the ensuing hours.

The interrogators asked me to begin by trying to recall the events of the morning of the twenty-sixth. Starting with the moment I awoke, I tried to recall each and every step I had taken that morning. With blue and red markers I made dashes and *x*'s on a diagram to show every place I walked or stood: where I dressed, where I stepped on the second floor, where I found the three-page ransom note, and where I saw John. Then we would start all over again, further probing what we had just discussed. It seemed like we spent most of the first day laboriously tracing every step and turn and movement I could remember.

We took a break sometime just before lunch, as I recall. I remember as I walked to the ladies' room seeing computer-generated signs on white 8½ x 11 sheets that read: QUIET, INTERVIEWS IN PROGRESS. They were stuck on doors and cubicle panels, everywhere you looked. I smiled at some of the office workers, and they returned a smile, trying to pretend that it was just another day in the life of a justice center employee. I knew they were silently sizing me up.

When the interrogation resumed after lunch, Tom Haney pushed me to describe any secrets that John and I kept from each other. I said something about smuggling in some shopping bags every so often so John wouldn't know I'd been on a shopping spree. He kept repeating that to me as he implied that I might hide other things from my husband. I could tell he was trying to discover if I would avoid implicating John in the murder. I looked the man squarely in the eye and told him that if I thought John Ramsey had committed the murder, we wouldn't even be having this conversation right now. I would have brought the curtain down on him long ago. Don't even go there, I told him. That, of course, was the sound bite leaked to the press by the police. It revealed my capability to become enraged, the report went, and in the police's opinion, fully capable of bringing harm to my daughter.

Haney once more covered the story of what had happened on December 25 and 26, asking me to detail everything I could remember. He asked why I had called 911 when my husband was the big CEO. I explained that John was on his hands and knees, reading the note, and I was standing right by the phone. Once again, I tried to be as forthright and factual as I could be.

During my discussion of what occurred, they questioned me about JonBenét having eaten pineapple, and I said I couldn't remember exactly what she had eaten on that day. Haney kept pushing me by saying, "Stay with me, stay with me, stay with me," and then conjuring up the possibility that I might have fed pineapple to JonBenét after we returned from the Whites'. I kept telling Haney that I had no idea if she had any pineapple that day. The children were always free to help themselves to things in the kitchen, I told him. But I absolutely did not feed her when we returned from the Whites'. She was sound asleep!

Then Haney produced a picture of a white bowl and asked me if I recognized it. He kept pushing, asking me what I would say if he told me that Burke's and my fingerprints were the only ones found on the bowl. I told Haney as forcefully as I could that whatever they found on the bowl was irrelevant *because I had not fed JonBenét any pineapple!*

Apparently during the autopsy, an issue was raised about the possibility of JonBenét's having eaten pineapple. Our understanding had been that this was nothing but a conjecture, not a fact. As far as we know, the coroner had said that the substance in her intestine could have been fruit or vegetable. Some thought that Linda Arndt, who had been present during the autopsy, might have asked the coroner if the substance could have been pineapple, since Arndt had seen the bowl on the kitchen table. The coroner had replied that it was possible. Amazingly, this too was leaked to the press and became another urban legend.

The detectives then asked me about the ransom demand and why I hadn't known that 118,000 dollars was the amount of John's bonus that year. I told them that the household finances were John's department. It wasn't that I wasn't permitted to know about financial matters, I just chose not to. You might say I operated on the "as long as I have checks, I have money" system.

During the interview, photographs of JonBenét's bedroom were shown to me, and I saw a red-and-white stuffed bear in a Santa suit lying on an adjacent twin bed. I said I didn't remember seeing that bear before. My comments started a nationwide search for the bear.

I found it difficult to look at many of the pictures; I could see little things that evoked memories. The detectives pointed to some circles on her bedroom carpet, wondering what they were. The potholder frame wasn't there, but I could tell the circles were cloth rings that JonBenét would weave into potholders. They showed me a picture of JonBenét's blanket and wanted to know if it was hers. The blanket looked pink in the picture, so I told them no. Her blanket was white. That's just the tint of the photograph, they assured me.

Then they turned to her Barbie nightgown, which had been in the windowless room where she was found. I had no idea how it could have gotten there. It certainly was not supposed to be there. I couldn't say for sure if the blanket had been on her bed that night. Often we would wash our bedding in the large washer and dryer, which were in the basement, rather than use the smaller stackable unit on the second floor. Could the blanket and the nightgown have been removed from that dryer?

At one point, Tom Haney started insisting that JonBenét had been sexually abused and began speaking very harshly. I told him that no one had ever said that this claim was a fact. I would have known if she had been sexually abused. I shot a horrified look at Pat Burke, my attorney. "This just isn't true," I cried, with tears spilling down my face. Pat intervened and told Haney that sexual abuse *was not* a proven fact and that they were unduly upsetting me. After that, Haney backed off this subject.

Then Haney asked if I remembered what JonBenét had gotten me for Christmas, and I became very emotional. I remembered a little green construction paper ornament JonBenét had made in her class at school. When I had opened it on December 25, 1996, I saw her school picture with the message: your gift is ME. How true, how very, very true. I had thought the ornament was lost in the shuffle, but Trip DeMuth assured me they had it in their possession. Of all the hundreds of items that were confiscated from both of our homes, that is the one item I most want returned.

During much of the interview I felt emotional and overcome. In fact, by the third day, I was so tired that I retreated to the bunk beds in the Broomfield police's nap room to sleep for an hour or so during the lunch break. The whole ordeal had been mentally and physically exhausting, but I would do it again in a heartbeat if I thought it would advance the search for JonBenét's killer.

When the three days were over, no stone had gone unturned. No topic had been off-limits, and the interviews had been a no-holds-barred experience for both Patsy and me. We were honoring the commitment I made in my letter to Alex Hunter. The time had been very, very laborious. District Attorney Hunter released a statement saying, "Mr. and Mrs. Ramsey have been cooperative. Questioning was not restricted in content or length. The Ramseys have agreed to continue to cooperate and to provide certain documents."

To our amazement, the content of the interviews was immediately leaked to the press. Details that we had absolutely held confidential appeared on the front page of the newspapers, on the Internet, and later in a best-selling book. We were beginning to see the correlation. If the police were involved, the media seemed to know it all.

A while after the interrogation, Patsy and I left for Charlevoix, Michigan, where copies of the videotapes had been sent to us to review in anticipation of being called before the grand jury. As we started to watch them, I realized that Patsy's interview was far more brutal and accusatory than what I had experienced. The interviewers meticulously tried to break her emotionally and even called her a liar. At one point, Haney persistently hammered Patsy on the point that he knew one of us was the killer. She firmly held her ground and insisted that they were absolutely going down the wrong path. Haney was in her face, pushing her hard, and she stood up to him. Later, the police leaped on that stern dialogue between Haney and Patsy as evidence that she had the ability to kill JonBenét. The truth was simply that Patsy wouldn't be bullied by the belligerent cop.

I couldn't stand to watch the videotape of the interrogations. When I saw for myself how Tom Haney had attacked Patsy with such unrestrained force, I simply got too angry to watch anymore. I told the attorneys they would have to review these materials themselves.

No one can ever say that we avoided answering any questions the authorities have ever asked us. The truth is that we have always been ready to respond. I returned to Boulder several times after those interrogations and always let the DA's office know I was in town, in case they had more questions. Not cooperating? Baloney!

26

JonBenét's America

As the months following JonBenét's death turned into years, countless media outlets requested our participation on their programs in one way or the other. They couldn't seem to understand that to us, JonBenét's death was a tragic blow, and we did not feel obligated to fill their time slots as macabre entertainment. They didn't really need the parents anyway; the programs went on without us.

One of the most thoughtful programs, and one in which we did agree to be interviewed, was *JonBenét's America,* produced in 1998. John and I felt this two-hour documentary was particularly significant because it thoroughly exposed many of the myths the media had perpetrated about our family and Jon-Benét's death. The main objective of the documentary, in fact, was to expose the tabloid mentality taking over our main-stream information system.

Back in the fall of 1997, the *Boulder Daily Camera* had run an article written by Dr. Michael Tracey, a journalism professor at the University of Colorado. Though we had never met the man, we were impressed by the keen insight the professor had into the new and frightening posture the media had taken in reporting JonBenét's story. Much of what they reported and talked about was fundamentally gossip. Tracey believed that the media was spiraling downward and had lost its basic sense of purpose. His article painted an extremely accurate picture of what the Ramsey family had seen firsthand. We were glad somebody was finally saying, "Hey, there's a problem here."

John and I felt that Michael Tracey was so much on target that we wrote him a letter thanking him for speaking out. "Being on the receiving end of this problem," John told him, "in our view you are absolutely correct in your assessment of what's going on in the media." We later discovered that Tracey had been a media critic for many years.

Several months following our correspondence, Professor Tracey approached us with the concept of using our situation as a real-life example of what was so tragically wrong with the media in the United States.

"It's very difficult to do this as a professor standing in front of a classroom just talking hypothetically," Tracey told us. "Your case has given us the perfect example of how the media has overstepped its boundaries," he continued enthusiastically. "I'd like the documentary to also demonstrate how our justice system has been dangerously influenced by the media."

John and I looked at the U.S. media as a hopeless case, but it sounded as if Michael Tracey wanted to try and make a difference. Of course, we had to talk with our attorneys, but the project seemed like a worthwhile effort.

"I'm a little concerned," John admitted to me one evening, "since our attorneys do not want us talking to anyone in the media, let alone appearing on television."

I nodded my head. "Sure, they'll be opposed, but we have nothing to hide, and this is a great cause. If we don't stand up and speak out, then we don't have any right to criticize."

"You're right," John said. "I think we should call Michael Tracey back and let him know we'll work with him on this project."

As the documentary began to take shape, Tracey was adamant about maintaining the editorial control necessary to give the program impeccable credibility. Rather than look for a producer in this country, he went to a former colleague, David Mills, in London. Mills was excited about the proposed documentary as well and saw the same possibilities for effecting change. Mills and Tracey began looking for funding and approached several U.S. networks as well as the BBC and Channel 4 in London. To avoid losing editorial control, Mills ultimately financed the project himself.

In talking with Mills we learned that the media is required to operate very differently in England, where, by law, they are not allowed to prejudice the legal process. They cannot discuss a case publicly until the court decision has been rendered. They can report what's happened in an actual crime, but a suspect cannot be tried and convicted on television (à la Geraldo) or in the newspapers. If what happened here had happened in England, Geraldo and company would be in jail by now.

John and I had no problem in agreeing that Tracey and Mills would have complete editorial control. We would place no restrictions on the project except one. We reserved the right to ask them not to run the final production until the grand jury was over, if the jurors were actively working before the film was ready to be broadcast on television.

When the production was completed, it aired in England on Channel 4, a large well-respected station in London. The response was very positive. In Colorado, Channel 9 in Denver ran the documentary in the local market on August 5, 1998. Rather than let the television audience view the piece and draw their own conclusions, Channel 9 felt it necessary to feature a panel of talking heads to analyze and comment on the documentary after it aired. Most of them, like Peter Boyles, were doing exactly what the program was chastising. This panel was analogous to airing a documentary on drugs in America and then inviting prominent drug pushers to comment on it.

CBS had turned down the program before it ran in London. However, after the first showing in England, they took another look and then backed out a second time. None of the other major U.S. networks expressed any interest. Then the A&E Network decided to pick up the show to run as part of their *Investigative Reports* series. The original British version was reformatted to include Bill Kurtis, the host of *Investigative Reports,* as the commentator. As part of this A&E series, the show proved to be a big winner, drawing the largest audience ever for this network.

Patsy always has a good, strong sense of the issues. She believed, as I did, that the A&E documentary could be important for far more people than just the Ramseys. Of course, I knew that some people would consider the film to be "proRamsey" because it would criticize the media, and we'd take a lot of flak for it. However, the documentary wasn't about JonBenét's case *but how the media was failing to report with accuracy and objectivity.* And if this had happened in our case, what else was the American public being spoon-fed that was untrue or misleading? Today six major corporations control virtually everything the U.S. public sees on television or at the movies or listens to on the radio. And it's all for profit.

The documentary would publicize the all-too-frequently-used "sources say" as a cover-up for the media's failure to accurately validate and qualify the originator of the reported event. Citing unnamed sources, they were "off the hook" by just repeating information given to them by another reporter.

To help focus on the issues that needed to be addressed, two journalists from *Newsweek*, Sherry Keene-Osborn and Dan Glick, became advisors to the Mills and Tracey production. They had both thoroughly covered the case from their location in Colorado as stringers for the magazine, so they provided a great deal of substantive information and helped develop the questions to be asked. Then Tracey, Mills, and a camera crew from London came to our house in Atlanta to conduct the interviews. One of the most enjoyable characters they brought with them was the sound man, who had been an actor in Monty Python's *Flying Circus*. He was hysterically funny and provided a bit of comic relief throughout the rigorous three days of taping.

The 260,000-dollar A&E television special began with announcer Bill Kurtis saying that for millions of people who had watched television over the past year, there was no question but that Patsy and I were guilty. As the program unfolded with music and scenery, Kurtis explained how JonBenét had been killed and the way in which this murder had gripped the interest of the American public. He said that in this program Patsy and I would respond to the accusations, issues, and evidence in the case, as we knew it. The story began with the taped video of JonBenét singing "God Bless America."

Geraldo Rivera was the first TV "journalist" featured. The documentary presented a clip from his show where he was seen proclaiming our guilt. He said that no real evidence in the case pointed in any direction *other than straight into the faces of John and/or Patsy Ramsey*. (How in the world would Geraldo know anything about the real evidence?) Immediately following this clip, Mike Tracey asked Patsy if she had been involved in JonBenét's death. She answered firmly, "No!"

I added, "I would have given my life for JonBenét, and I

will regret for the rest of my life that I wasn't able to that night. No! To answer your question, no we did not."

Many people had heard our denial before, because we had stated it over and over again since December 26, 1996. What they hadn't heard was the truth behind many of the urban legends in the case and admissions by members of the press that stories they had reported were later proven to be false.

As the production continued, it detailed what had happened when JonBenét was found missing, and how the day of December 26 had evolved. We also talked about Beth's death and Patsy's battle with Stage IV ovarian cancer. As the story was told, key issues arose.

Kurtis questioned Charlie Brennan, a reporter with the *Denver Rocky Mountain News* who early on had written a story suggesting that *only* a family member could have murdered JonBenét. Brennan defended himself by saying, "I had a trusted law enforcement source tell me the first officers there noted that it was rather strange, they thought, that there were *no footprints in the snow,* and this is a source that has been infallible, in my experience . . .

"When the police first arrived, at least one officer thought it was worth noting in his report, strange—no footprints."

A bit later in the program, Kurtis interviewed Julie Hayden, a reporter for Channel 7 in Denver. Hayden said, "We looked at the videotape, once the relevance of the footprints in the snow became an issue, and one of the things I observed was, there did not seem to be snow going to all of the doors. So in my opinion this no-footprints-in-the-snow issue has all been much ado about nothing. It seemed clear to me that people could have gotten into the house, whether they did or not, without traipsing through the snow."

Of course, that initial observation by the patrolman was meaningless. It wasn't snowing when we returned home that night, and even if it snowed at all during the night, the killer could have easily come in and out of the house without ever getting near any snow. "No footprints in the snow" was a non-issue and meant to implicate us.

Kurtis continued to bear down on the media. He said, "Soon another story appeared. There had been no break-in." Reporter Charlie Brennan had covered that too.

Again Brennan defended himself in the documentary by

saying, "That was coming from law enforcement sources, and you know, I know that you know this is a story that was heavily reported through unnamed sources, and I'm not going to name the source now. But law enforcement was telling us from December that they saw no signs of forced entry." (Why were the police talking to Brennan at all? This was a murder investigation!)

Later in the documentary Bill Kurtis again returned to this issue. "Would it be reasonable to assume that the information about 'no forced entry' was false information that was being leaked by the authorities?"

Brennan replied. "False, false, wrong, misstated, mistaken. Yes, that would be fair to say. Particularly in light of where you can start at least from the broken window in the basement. In January '97, February '97, March '97, we didn't know that there was a broken window in the basement." (No one in the police department had bothered to leak *that* bit of information or the information about the open door either.)

Bill Kurtis noted that curiously it took a year for this story to be corrected when, in fact, the unlocked and open basement window and the open butler's door had been discovered early on the morning of December 26. Kurtis further noted, "The reality of the situation is that an intruder could easily have gotten in, and once in, moved around undetected and unheard. From her parents' bedroom on the third floor, it is no less than fifty-five feet below to where JonBenét was sleeping. There are thick carpets, sound does not carry . . ."

Yet the national media also picked up the story of "no forced entry." This urban legend was so well publicized that many people in the United States still believed there was no forced entry and no footprints in the snow, despite the few corrections that were issued later. Remember, people will believe any lie, if it is big enough and told often enough, and loud enough.

The real problem was that these incorrect stories, which were reported by a local reporter, were soon picked up by the national news media. The national press relied on the local boys to feed them news, and nobody took the time to check the validity of the information.

Bill Kurtis further noted that national television reporters had hammered away on the theme that JonBenét was found

in a "hidden room." A clip of our cleaning lady, Linda Hoffmann-Pugh, was introduced with her claim that "When I
cleaned the house, I cleaned that basement many times and I
didn't even know that the room was there."

The truth was that Linda could not have missed knowing
the room was there. Far from hidden, we called it the wine cellar, although we seldom used it for more than storage. It was
originally probably a coal room. Besides, Linda and her husband, Mervin, had taken our Christmas decorations out of
that room, including several artificial trees, while we were
gone during the previous Thanksgiving holiday.

The A&E program noted that Chief Koby had been in-
censed by these leaks of material, and he was quoted as saying, "I have never in the twenty-eight years I have been in
this business seen such media focus on an event and it is, in
fact, intrusive and is making it much more difficult to work
through this."

Kurtis then went on to another false story, which had been
printed in *Vanity Fair*.

Boulder television reporter Julie Hayden spoke to this
issue. "It was reported in *Vanity Fair* that John Ramsey left the
house to get the mail for about an hour. That looked suspicious
to me, frankly, and I think it looked suspicious to a lot of people. And I know it looked suspicious to the police who believed that initially to be the case. It is my understanding that
the police initially believed he left the house, but very soon
thereafter they learned he did not leave the house. However,
the police never bothered to correct the *Vanity Fair* article. I
don't know why the police and the law enforcement in Boulder would allow things they knew were not true to continue to
be widely reported. I can speculate that they didn't mind having stories like that out there because it put some pressure on
the Ramseys."

Patsy and I had been accused of faking our grief and only
acting as if we were in anguish. While I have no idea how one
puts on that sort of performance, I discovered that *Vanity Fair*
quoted a policeman as saying that he caught Patsy appearing
to be weeping, but she was actually looking at him through
"splayed fingers." Of course, such accusations raised people's
suspicions about us. The documentary responded by presenting a statement from my brother, Jeff, describing Patsy's state

of shock. He said that she "couldn't sit up, couldn't stand up, couldn't walk, could barely talk. I spent most of the nights up out there [in Boulder] with John—he couldn't stop crying for ten minutes at a time."

Later in the program Kurtis explored the "fact" that I had flown my jet from Boulder to Atlanta for JonBenét's funeral.

Again Charlie Brennan, who had first reported the story, backpedaled. "I was told he flew it, so I reported he flew it."

Michael Tracey asked Brennan, "Did you subsequently follow up on that story?"

"I didn't subsequently follow up on that story because in the early days that did not stand out as something in my mind that needed a lot of scrutiny. And as soon as I say that, I suspect that what one's concern might be is that creates an image of a man that maybe is the wrong image. I mean maybe—perhaps you can tell me it wasn't his own plane or that he didn't fly it."

Tracey then told Brennan the facts: it wasn't my airplane and I didn't fly it. My employer, Lockheed Martin, graciously provided a corporate jet and pilot to get us to Atlanta. Isn't it a shame Charlie Brennan hadn't bothered to check this out before reporting it to the world. (Charlie Brennan should have asked his mother about Patsy and me. After all, Janet Brennan and Patsy taught Sunday school together at St. John's.)

Later the documentary showed a piece of our CNN interview, in which Patsy had said, "There is a killer on the loose."

This was followed by a cut to Leslie Durgin's press conference where she had said, "People in Boulder have no need to fear that there is someone wandering the streets of Boulder as has been portrayed by some people." This clearly implied to the world that the city officials of Boulder thought we did it.

Finally, in an interview Tracey conducted with the mayor, she tried to explain her earlier statement. "It was done in large part," she said, "to allay the fears of the children in our community and to let people know that the information I had at the time was that we did not have some crazed person wandering the streets of University Hill."

Michael Tracey asked her, "And who did you clear it with?"

"The police chief," Durgin answered.

Probably one of the most explosive issues the Tracey-Mills production addressed was the allegation of sexual abuse. The collective innuendo in all this was that Patsy or I had killed Jon-Benét, and we had sexually abused her in the past. Of course, lurking in the shadows was the "fact" put out by the *National Enquirer* that I had visited a pornography shop after Jon-Benét's death. In the documentary Mike Tracey asked me point-blank if I frequented pornography shops in Denver. I answered, "I couldn't tell you where a pornography shop was in Denver, Colorado, if my life depended on it. That's false. Absolutely, totally false."

Then Michael Tracey interviewed JonBenét's pediatrician, Dr. Francesco Beuf. He asked the doctor, "JonBenét was brought to see you on twenty-seven occasions. Does this number of visits strike you as excessive?"

"No," Dr. Beuf replied, "I don't think it's excessive under the circumstances. I went through her chart and summarized the types of visits she had in the office in the few years prior to her death. She was here three times for annual well-child visits, one time for stomach ache, one time for vaginitis, one time for a bruised nose from a fall at a local market, and twenty-one times for colds, sinusitis, ear infections, bronchitis, pneumonia, hay fever, and possible asthma. A pretty wide spectrum of generally allergy and respiratory system-associated problems, which are not uncommon with kids her age."

Earlier, on a September 10, 1997, *Prime Time Live* program, Dr. Beuf had talked to Diane Sawyer about JonBenét's visits and the vaginitis. "Would that be unusual?" Sawyer had asked him.

"For a child that age, certainly not," Dr. Beuf had replied. "They don't wipe themselves very well after they urinate. And it's something which usually is curable by having them take plain water baths or learning to wipe better. But if you have four-year-old kids, you know how hard that is. The amount of vaginitis which I saw on the child was totally consistent with little girls her age."

On the A&E documentary Tracey turned directly to the issue of sexual abuse when he asked the doctor, "Did you see any signs of any kind of sexual or physical abuse of JonBenét Ramsey?" he asked.

"No," Dr. Beuf replied. "Absolutely no signs of sexual abuse. I had no suspicion of it."

Beuf had said much the same thing earlier to Diane Sawyer. She had asked him, "If there had been an abrasion involving the hymen, you would have seen it?"

"Probably," he replied. "I can't say absolutely for sure, because you don't do a speculum exam on a child that young, at least unless it's under anesthesia."

"Did you see in any of these examinations any sign of possible sexual abuse?" Sawyer queried.

"No, and I certainly would have reported it to the social service people if I had. That's something that all of us in pediatrics are very acutely aware of."

As she ended the interview, Diane Sawyer had said, "Dr. Beuf says he has turned in people he has suspected of physical and sexual abuse in his career, and that he not only looks for physical evidence, but personality changes in the children involved. And he says he saw none of that with JonBenét Ramsey."

In the *Investigative Reports* special, Bill Kurtis also said, "Other media stories have suggested that vaginal inflammation released in the autopsy report suggests previous sexual abuse. This suggestion is not supported by the balance of medical opinion."

His statement was followed by an interview with Denver Medical Examiner Dr. Thomas Henry. "From what is noted in the autopsy report, there is no injury to the anus, there is no injury to the skin around the vagina and the labia. There is no other indication of healed scars in any of those areas. There is no other indication from the autopsy report at all that there is any other previous injuries that have healed in that area."

My first wife, Lucinda Johnson, also appeared on the documentary and strongly stated that I was not a child abuser. In contrast, she described me as kind and gentle. My son John Andrew gave his statement that there had never been any sexual abuse in the Ramsey family, and my daughter Melinda strongly seconded what John Andrew had said. Melinda added, "He is the most caring father in the world."

As the production continued, suddenly a picture of Geraldo reappeared, followed by a clip from the *Hard Copy* program claiming that Patsy had killed JonBenét because she wet the bed. The implication was that there was such a significant problem, it finally drove Patsy over the edge.

"That is absurd," Patsy responded. She answered this issue by saying, "She had accidents but children do. It is so minuscule in the big picture. Does someone actually think I would kill my child because she wet the bed? I have lived through Stage IV cancer, and in the grand scheme of things, bedwetting is not important."

After the documentary was released, I was often asked if Patsy and I were pleased with the results. Of course, we weren't happy that we had to do such a production in the first place. Rather than explain to the world on national television that we didn't sexually abuse and kill our child, we would much rather have been riding bikes with her around University Hill. On the other hand, the documentary needed to be done, and it felt good to be working with objective people who didn't peddle gossip. Maybe there were a few ethical people in the television world after all.

We weren't paid a dime for our part in the documentary. London's Channel 4 bought the first rights to the film from Mills and Tracey. Approximately a month after they ran our piece, the same English channel reportedly paid Monica Lewinsky six hundred thousand dollars for an interview. It occurred to me that they might have made a donation to Jon-Benét's Foundation. Yet the fact of the matter was that we weren't doing the project for money. Our interest was to expose a system that had run amuck. We knew a number of fraudulent rumors had been circulating through the media during the first year and a half about JonBenét's murder, and the lies and rumors needed to be corrected. Many of these ugly accusations were addressed by the Mills-Tracey production.

Boulder Mayor Leslie Durgin made a concluding statement to her part in the documentary. She said, "I've learned an important lesson and that is, I don't believe what I read in the press or listen to on talk radio anymore."

We hope so. At least, we hope that anyone watching the A&E program clearly understands the implications of an unchallenged, unaccountable, and reckless system of reporting information.

27

THE MONTH OF RESIGNATIONS

The day after the *Investigative Reports* documentary on the
Ramsey family appeared on Channel 9 in Denver, Detective Steve Thomas angrily and publicly resigned from the
Boulder police force. Patsy and I could not help but conclude
that these two events were connected.

As people in Colorado watched the program with its various interviews, the errors of the police quickly became clear.
I felt that these allegations must have pushed Thomas over
the edge. We didn't dislike him personally but had come to
believe he was a loose cannon. As noted earlier, Steve
Thomas was a very inexperienced young detective who had
been a patrolman and then a narcotics cop. I don't believe he
had ever successfully investigated a murder. Unfortunately,
both for him and for us, he simply lacked the wisdom, which
comes from years of experience, to handle such a complex
and weighty case.

Recently Patsy's high school teacher and friend, Linda
McLean, told us about the questions Thomas had asked when
he and Ron Gosage interviewed her in Parkersburg, West Virginia. Linda said, "I could tell that Detective Thomas had targeted Patsy and was trying to dig up anything negative he
could find in her past." According to Linda, Thomas didn't
seem very experienced or professional. "I wondered why the
business card he gave me said 'Narcotics Unit,'" she said. "I
wished at the time that I could have talked to someone who
would have been neutral and remained objective. He seemed
to have jumped to a conclusion and wanted to justify it.

"Evidently he didn't want to hear anything good—only to
try to find some dirt. He asked how John treated Patsy when
she had cancer, and if Patsy ever told me whether they had
sex during that time. Why would he ask such a crude ques-

tion? Later I realized that he might have been implying that John had used JonBenét instead. How sick!

"He wanted to know if Patsy was promiscuous in high school. Was I aware that one of the dramatic readings Patsy did for our high school speech team (*The Prime of Miss Jean Brodie*) was about lesbians? Did I know if she had seen a psychiatrist when she was in college? What was her relationship with her father? Was she distraught when I was with her the night of the funeral? How did I know it was real? The tone of his voice seemed to drip suspicion."

After a while, Linda didn't want to talk to Thomas anymore. She got physically sick from the things he implied about Patsy and me, and was frightened by the whole experience. "When Thomas acted like he did," Linda said, "it made me realize that if the authorities make up their minds that they want to target somebody, it's not easy to make them slow down and listen to all the facts."

Linda was especially surprised by the way the police handled the handwriting samples she provided them. "Detective Thomas told me that they hadn't been able to get a 'real' handwriting sample from Patsy because she had been sedated. He asked if I had any samples of Patsy's handwriting. *Good!* I thought. Here was something I could do that would really help. I always kept the Christmas cards Patsy sent with the kids' picture and a handwritten note. I gladly gave them the originals. Imagine my surprise when, for several weeks after that, the police kept saying, 'We don't have any handwriting samples.' I wanted to tell somebody, 'I gave them plenty!' And they never returned them as they promised."

Patsy's sister Pam had a similar experience with Thomas when he came to Atlanta to question her. The police made a tape recording of the interview. However, they refused to let Pam tape the session. She was told it was against the law in Georgia and that she would have to get permission from the state's attorney general. Patsy's other sister, Polly, was also outraged by Thomas's questions. He started out her interview by asking Polly if she was the black sheep of the family.

By August of 1998 we knew that Steve Thomas had been upset at the way his view of the case was received by the district attorney's people. Apparently the DA's office let him know that the case he tried to develop wouldn't float in court, and this greatly angered the detective. It seemed that in Thomas's mind the DA was getting in the way of the hanging. Just as Linda Arndt was convinced I was the murderer because she saw it in my eyes, Thomas was equally convinced it was Patsy.

During the past year Thomas had lost nearly thirty pounds and was struggling with medical problems; for a time he had taken a medical leave of absence. With this in mind, I believe that Thomas watched the A&E special and wrote the letter of resignation in a fit of anger.

Rather than submit a quiet, confidential, "I'm quitting" letter, Thomas aimed his response at the world as if he were screaming from a rooftop, which seemed to be immature. Written on August 6, 1998, which would have been Jon-Benét's eighth birthday, the letter was also sent to ABC News and to Governor Roy Romer of Colorado. Thomas's letter had to be an embarrassment to professional law enforcement officers; his stance basically was "I'll take my ball and go home if you don't play my way." Even though the letter was sent to Police Chief Mark Beckner, it was clearly addressed to anyone in the media who would listen and televise or print it. And, of course, they did.

Thomas began and ended the resignation letter by continuing the war that had gone on for almost two years between the BPD and the district attorney's office. He said that he was surprised when Beckner suggested that there was renewed cooperation between the two groups "at the very time the detectives and those in the DA's office weren't even on speaking terms." Thomas said that he was surprised "that there had not been a fist fight."

In addition, Thomas attempted to defend Detective Commander John Eller's resignation and tried to cover the many mistakes Eller had made when he was in charge of Jon-Benét's investigation. Thomas complained that the DA had not embraced every bit of data that he and the detectives brought in as being valuable for a trial. Thomas did not like making sure that his theories and the evidence collected fit the legal grid that a judge and jury would demand from the district attorney's staff. He even hinted that the necessary litmus test of legal viability that the DA's office required was prejudicial to the detectives' work.

Thomas sounded obviously miffed that he would not be asked to perform in a significant role in the presentation of the evidence to the grand jury and would not be asked to be a grand jury advisory witness. The detective concluded that the district attorney's office had been compromised by these issues and was a hindrance to solving JonBenét's case. After a long and rambling redress of these basic issues, Steve Thomas resigned from his job and career as a law officer.

As Patsy and I thought about Thomas's resignation, we remembered his passionate proclamation in Patsy's April interview that he wouldn't quit until he'd found the killer. We really felt that Thomas had been sincere in his desire to avenge our daughter's death, and we were grateful for his passion. He truly wanted to serve JonBenét. But what if we hadn't killed her? How did he think she would feel about his unfairly accusing and persecuting her parents for so many months?

Throwing a big rock in a small pond always creates ripples. The Steve Thomas resignation letter immediately became headline material for the bloodthirsty media. The contents were before the public, and reverberations began to occur.

On August 8 Governor Roy Romer asked four metro-area district attorneys—Bill Ritter (Denver), Bob Grant (Adams County), Jim Peters (Arapahoe County), and Dave Thomas (Jefferson County)—to evaluate the possibility of appointing an independent prosecutor. On August 12 the governor met with these district attorneys to evaluate how Alex Hunter had handled JonBenét's case. After a lengthy discussion, Romer reaffirmed his faith in Hunter and announced that the murder would be heard by a grand jury.

Five days later, and just two weeks after Steve Thomas's resignation, Fleet White—the friend who had been with me when I found JonBenét's body on December 26, 1996—sent a fourteen-page, rambling letter to "the people of Colorado" and to Governor Roy Romer, asking him to remove District Attorney Alex Hunter from JonBenét's case. White claimed that various relationships between the Boulder County district attorney and the legal community (our attorneys, specifically) may have impaired the objectivity of the DA. He also cited the atmosphere of distrust and noncooperation between the district attorney and the Boulder police. Finally, he said that Hunter had been criticized in the past for not being an aggressive prosecutor of homicide cases.

A few people spoke out about this letter. For instance, in an interview with the *Boulder Daily Camera*, Colorado University Professor of Legal Ethics Dan Vigil said the relationship between Hunter and our attorneys, mentioned in White's letter, was inconsequential because "in a legal community this size, people are going to interact."

Then, on August 20 Governor Romer's spokesman, Jim Carpenter, said the governor was standing by the decision he had made the previous week not to intervene in the Ramsey case, which was now headed for the Boulder County grand jury. He would not remove Hunter. Carpenter said that the governor saw nothing in Fleet White's letter that would lead him to change his mind.

Fleet White had tried to get Romer to replace Hunter before. He had met with Governor Romer on December 18, 1997, and when his request was rejected, White had sent an earlier letter to the *Boulder Daily Camera*, making many of the same allegations as his present letter.

Why was White so adamant about ousting District Attorney Alex Hunter? Chuck Green had given one theory in a *Denver Post* article back on January 16. "Her death and the year-long investigation has become a daily obsession for the Whites, according to friends," Green said, "and they are determined to follow every twist and turn to its conclusion. It was primarily that preoccupation with the murder case that caused them to ask Governor Roy Romer to personally intervene in the investigation by replacing Boulder District Attorney Alex Hunter with a special prosecutor. But there was a lingering animosity toward Hunter's office, sources said, that helped fuel the Whites' anger."

Green went on to explain that in the summer of 1997 the Whites had asked to be "publicly cleared as potential suspects in the case, demanding that Police Chief Tom Koby issue a statement of exoneration." The DA had advised the police "to limit the statement to the current status of their case." White, Green's sources said, resented this.

Still, Fleet White's protests continued. On Monday, August 24, White wrote another letter to "the people of Colorado," this time suggesting that Lt. Governor Gail Schoettler had influenced the governor's decision. White said that Schoettler's husband had made several telephone calls to me in the days right after JonBenét's murder. Yes, he had, although I never received any of them. As a former fraternity brother at Michigan State University, Don Stevens (Schoettler's husband) had called to offer his condolences and to inquire about funeral arrangements.

Lt. Governor Gail Schoettler replied to this accusation in an interview with the *Boulder Daily Camera,* "The governor and I have never discussed this case," she said.

The Whites were apparently trying to show that the Democratic "family" had somehow closed ranks to protect us. It was absurd and a bit mad. Plus, I was never an active Democrat.

On August 20, 1998, the Whites commented to a *Camera* staff reporter, "The district attorney and the Ramsey attorneys have simultaneously rebuked the police for 'focusing' their investigation on the Ramseys when in fact the police were simply following evidence."

The innuendo here was obvious. Why had our former friend turned against us?

As Patsy and I thought about this, we went back to the days right after the murder. On December 26, 1996, the police had naturally asked me a lot of questions. I learned that the officers had interrogated Fleet for a long time on the twenty-seventh. I had no idea what was said, but after this session, Fleet returned upset and confused. Suddenly this close friend became tense and acted very strange.

As was the case with most of our social friendships, Patsy had met Priscilla and her children first. Their kids were almost the same ages as JonBenét and Burke. Later Fleet and I were introduced into an already blooming friendship. When we first met, they were renting a small house, two doors up the street from us. The Whites told us that they had left California because they felt the fast life around Newport Beach was a poor place to raise children. They had originally thought of moving to Aspen, where Fleet's parents had a home and where Fleet and Priscilla and their children had spent considerable time. But even Aspen didn't suit what they were looking for. Ultimately they settled in Boulder after Fleet drove there one day and decided it was the perfect community for them. Our children became instant friends and enjoyed frequent trips to and from each other's houses, which they could accomplish on their own with complete freedom, via backyards or front sidewalks. That was one of the benefits of a small town, I thought.

Priscilla was a fun-loving California girl who liked to entertain and had a good sense of humor. She and Patsy quickly hit it off, and they enjoyed each other's company. The moms soon discovered that Fleet and I shared a penchant for sailing, as well. It's rare that dads and moms and both children synchronize so easily. Both sets of parents were older, and that added to the similarities.

The newspapers later would refer to Fleet as an oil magnate. His father, Fleet White Sr., was reported to have had a natural gas drilling company in California. He may have worked for his dad for a period of time before coming to Colorado, but as far as I know, Fleet did not work at a steady job during the time I knew him in Boulder. At one point he was trying to help his dad clean up some environmental issues at a gas station they owned in California, and he spoke of trying to get something started with some Denver businessman.

Fleet was mainly my sailing buddy. He occasionally talked of being an ardent sailor in the Newport Beach area and proudly displayed many models of the sailboats he had raced. He spoke of a silver loving cup, which bears his name and is on permanent display at the Newport Beach Yacht Club. He was a very experienced sailor. I was not. I could learn a great deal from him. Whenever we were together, sailing was our singular topic of conversation. Since he didn't have a nine-to-five job as I did, Fleet was free to be the coordinator of logistics for our sailing ventures.

After JonBenét's murder, the Whites had arrived in Atlanta for JonBenét's funeral the day after we did. They were scheduled to stay at Rod Westmoreland's home. Each of our Atlanta friends had graciously adopted a family from Colorado to host during the funeral. As an unspoken courtesy, our closest friends in Atlanta were to host the Whites, our closest friends from Colorado. For some reason, shortly after the Whites arrived at the Westmorelands', Priscilla got into a tiff with Rod's wife, Kimberly, and refused to stay in the Wesmorelands' lovely home. The Whites said they would check into a hotel instead.

When I heard what had happened, I attributed the incident to the fact that everyone was distraught, tired, and easily upset. I assumed they must have had reason to be on edge, and I mistakenly thought everything would subside.

As is customary in the South, the Westmorelands hosted a brunch in their home immediately following JonBenét's funeral for family, friends, and children. Apparently the Whites interpreted this gracious act as a horrible display of opulence and ostentation. In the Whites' view, the Westmorelands were acting totally in bad taste, a view which was not shared by any other friends in attendance.

Eventually, Patsy and I suggested that the Whites stay at my brother's house. We didn't know what had happened at the Westmorelands', but we didn't want them staying in a motel. After all was said and done, they were our good friends and my brother, Jeff, is probably the most calm and under control person I know. Suggesting the Whites stay there was the logical thing to do. Unfortunately, nothing worked out there either.

Following the funeral Jeff remembers giving the Whites a ride to the Westmorelands' for the reception, and afterward, bringing them back to his own home. Fleet began complaining about the Westmorelands' home being in an exclusive area of Atlanta. Priscilla apparently was offended that the family had a maid. They persisted with these demeaning statements and ridiculed the Westmorelands' lifestyle. Fleet and Priscilla left Jeff's for a walk around the neighborhood.

When they returned, Fleet had become even more upset and kept talking about the need to keep "outsiders" from getting in on the investigation. He was rambling on and on, saying things like "We can't hurt the reputation of the people of Boulder . . . JonBenét is gone, we have to protect Boulder now . . . One hundred years ago people on farms took care of themselves. They didn't need cops or lawyers." His behavior seemed irrational to Jeff.

In short order, Fleet became more and more animated. He was periodically jabbing Jeff in the chest with his index finger and putting his hands on Jeff's neck. Jeff thought Fleet was on the verge of being out of control.

"How many people have you made really, really mad at you?" Fleet said, very agitated. "Ten or twelve maybe?"

"No, I don't think so," Jeff said, trying to remain calm.

Fleet continued pressing. "How many people have you made mad enough to want to kill you, or a member of your family? Two or three?"

"No," Jeff responded. He didn't know how anyone could think that way.

But the altercation didn't go away. Fleet's behavior seemed so unreasonable and out of place that it was frightening. Even though Jeff, who had been a high school quarterback, was perfectly capable of defending himself, Fleet scared him. Fleet and Priscilla left Jeff's home to talk to me, and Jeff decided that without a doubt he didn't want the Whites staying in his house that night.

Later that day at the Paughs' house, Priscilla sat me down and told me she had talked to the police for hours. Then she abruptly said there was semen found on JonBenét's body. I was so shocked, I couldn't speak. I just walked away. That urban legend was later proven untrue.

Before the Whites left Atlanta, Priscilla called Patsy's father on the phone from the airport and argued with Don that she knew things that nobody else knew, telling him that he must persuade Patsy and me not to get attorneys. With that Priscilla hung up the telephone, and she and Fleet flew back to Boulder.

After we returned to Boulder, we experienced another strange incident involving the Whites. Patsy and I had been meeting with Father Rol Hoverstock in his office at St. John's and were in prayer with him when we heard a commotion outside. Fleet White pushed past both Patsy's father, who was waiting for us in the reception area, and Father Rol's secretary, demanding entrance to his office. Fleet barged in, unannounced, and dropped down on one knee, flashing a reporter's business card in the air.

"Now they're after me, John!" Fleet shouted at me. "You know what I have to do, John." He looked crazed and shaken.

Father Rol kept trying to calm him down.

"What is it, Fleet?" I reached out for the card. "Let me see it."

He kept waving the card but finally gave it to me. I looked on the back and realized that a reporter had scribbled a question about who had removed the tape from JonBenét's mouth. Was it Fleet or was it John? she had asked. Fleet kept yelling at us, as if Patsy and I had some sort of command over the media. I told him not to pay any attention to the press and offered to take the card and have one of our investigators call the reporter. Fleet said, "No, I'll take care of this in my own way."

What can I say? Fleet and I never had friction in our friendship prior to JonBenét's death. Clearly, something happened to the Whites between the time they were with us on the morning of December 26 in Boulder and when they arrived in Atlanta. Because Fleet and Priscilla claimed they knew things that no one else did, we had to surmise that the Boulder police must have planted fear or suspicion in their minds. Maybe the police told Fleet and Priscilla that we had turned on them and named them as suspects; but that simply wasn't true.

Friends later told us that the police tried to bias them against us in an attempt to force some sort of confusion and anger that would crack a locked door and reveal information about us. The Whites' abrupt break with us seems to fit into that pattern. Whatever the case, their sudden outbursts left us no choice but to retreat from them for a period of time.

How do we make sense out of what happened? We don't. Fear of something unknown created an unsafe world with people reacting to the specters they feared might be hiding from them, rather than the genuine realities standing in front of their eyes. Some people obviously felt implicated by the circumstances, and the Whites were two of them. Throughout the days after the murder, hysteria began to take its toll on everyone.

Circumstances like these demonstrated how important it was to stay objective and go with the evidence. We were really disappointed when Lou Smit, who was committed to this principle, submitted his resignation to District Attorney Alex Hunter on September 20, 1998. Steve Thomas had crashed because of flying by the seat of his pants. In contrast, Lou Smit had proven to be a sage, thoughtful, and highly experienced investigator. He kept his eyes on the evidence and followed it wherever it led. Having spent many years tackling difficult cases, Smit understood how important it was to follow the clues. Rather than pursue his feelings and impulses, Lou's approach was to allow the evidence in the case to lead him where he needed to go. His feelings, theories, hunches, or prejudices didn't count if they didn't add up with the data found at the scene of the crime. He also said he had the best "partner" in this of all, God.

In many ways, the paradoxical differences in Thomas and Smit became a mini-study in why JonBenét's case had not been solved to date. Both men had the same evidence at their disposal. Yet they took two entirely different paths. Thomas and company believed that when they came to the end of their investigation, they would be able to prove that either Patsy or I was guilty. In other words, they came up with the answer first and then tried to prove it. In contrast, Smit's careful assessment of the facts, which led him to find evidence overlooked by the police (such as the marks on JonBenét's body that indicated a stun gun), produced the conclusion that at the end of his path, he would arrest an intruder who killed JonBenét.

Some felt that Smit exonerated us because we were Christians. Not so. After the grand jury was over and Lou could speak to us, he told us, "I have sent many 'Christians' to prison in my time. It's not your and Patsy's faith that has influenced me. It's the evidence."

In March of 1997 when Lou Smit was hired, our impression was that the district attorney had already determined that the police weren't pursuing the investigation in the right manner. The DA needed an investigator to review what the cops were doing, and Smit, whose reputation for diligence and integrity was known throughout Colorado, was the right man for the job. Lou moved in and set up the "war room" at the Justice Center. However, Smit soon discovered that the police wouldn't really listen to him. In fact, his considerable wisdom was ignored. Once Lou revealed the thought that perhaps Patsy and I weren't the killers, the police saw Lou as the enemy simply because he didn't buy into their "group theory." We heard the rumor that Steve Thomas had even called Lou Smit "a delusional old man." The locks to Smit's war room were changed, and he was not issued a key.

In fact, the way that Smit was treated exposed one of the major flaws in the police establishment. Their lack of teamwork polarized the department. On an authentic team, people do what needs to be done without worrying about who gets the credit. The overriding objective is to solve the problem and do the job right. Unfortunately this wasn't the attitude of the Boulder police.

On September 20, 1998, in contrast to Steve Thomas's noisy media-oriented resignation, Lou Smit quietly turned in a two-page, private letter of resignation, addressed only to District Attorney Alex Hunter. He wrote:

> *It is with great reluctance and regret that I submit this letter of resignation. Even though I want to continue to participate in the official investigation and assist in finding the killer of JonBenét, I find that I cannot in good conscience be a part of the persecution of innocent people. It would be highly improper and unethical for me to stay when I so strongly believe this.*
>
> *It has been almost 19 months since we talked that day in your office and you asked me to assist you in this investigation. It has turned out to be more of a challenge than either of us anticipated. When we first met I told you that my style of approaching an investigation is from the concept of not working a particular theory, but working the case. Detectives collect and record information from many sources, analyze it, couple that with their experience and training and let "the case" tell them where to go. This process may take days, weeks or years, depending on the direction the case tells you to go. Sometimes you must investigate "many paths" in order to find the killer. It is not a political speed contest where expediency should outweigh justice, where "resolving" the case is solving the case.*
>
> *Alex, even though I have been unable to actively investigate, I have been in a position to collect, record and analyze every piece of information given to your office in the course of this investigation. I believe that I know this case better than anyone does. I know what has been investigated and what hasn't, what evidence exists and what doesn't, what information has been leaked and what hasn't. I am a detective with a proven record of successful investigations. I have looked at the murder of JonBenét Ramsey through the eyes of age and experience and a thorough knowledge of the case.*
>
> *At this point in the investigation "the case" tells me that John and Patsy Ramsey did not kill their daughter, that a*

very dangerous killer is still out there and no one is actively looking for him. There are still many areas of investigation which must be explored before life and death decisions are made.

When I was hired I had no agenda one way or the other, my allegiance was to the case, not the Police Department nor John and Patsy Ramsey. My agenda has not changed. I only desire to be able to investigate the case and find the killer of JonBenét and will continue to do so as long as I am able. The chances of catching him working from the "outside looking in" are very slim, but I have a great "Partner" who I'm sure will lead the way. There is no doubt that I will be facing a great deal of opposition and ridicule in the future, because I intend to stand with this family and somehow help them through this and find the killer of their daughter. Perhaps others who believe this will also help.

The Boulder Police Department has many fine and dedicated men and women who also want justice for JonBenét. They are just going in the wrong direction and have been since day one of the investigation. Instead of letting the case tell them where to go, they have elected to follow a theory and let their theory direct them rather than allowing the evidence to direct them. The case tells me there is substantial, credible evidence of an intruder and lack of evidence that the parents are involved. If this is true, they too are tragic victims whose misery has been compounded by a misdirected and flawed investigation, unsubstantiated leaks, rumors and accusations.

I have worked in this profession for the past 32 years and have always been loyal to it, the men and women in it, and what it represents, because I believed that justice has always prevailed. In this case, however, I believe that justice is not being served, that innocent people are being targeted and could be charged with a murder they did not commit.

The law enforcement Code of Ethics states it very well. My fundamental duty is to "serve mankind; to safeguard lives and property; to protect the innocent against deception, the weak against oppression or intimidation, the peaceful against violence or disorder. To respect the constitutional rights of all men to liberty, equality and justice." This applies not only to JonBenét but to her mother and father as well.

I want to thank you and the others in the office for the wonderful support and treatment I have received. You have a great DA's Office and the men and women who work with you are some of the most honest and dedicated people I have ever met. My life has been enriched because of this memorable time together. I have especially enjoyed working closely with Peter Hofstrom and Trip DeMuth, who also have dedicated so much of their lives to this case. I have never met two more fair, honest and dedicated defenders of our system.

Alex, you are in a difficult position. The media and peer pressure are incredible. You are inundated with conflicting facts and information, and "expert" opinions. And now you have an old detective telling you that the Ramseys did not do it and to wait and investigate this case more thoroughly before a very tragic mistake would be made. What a double travesty it could be: an innocent person indicted, and a vicious killer on the loose to prey on another innocent child and no one to stop him.

History will be the judge as to how we conducted ourselves and how we handled our responsibilities.

Shoes, shoes, the victim's shoes, who will stand in the victim's shoes? . . .

The press obtained this letter, although that was not Smit's intention, and it was published in some newspapers about a week later.

With Lou Smit's departure, most of those in the district attorney's office who had seriously considered the intruder theory were no longer directly involved with the case. On August 21 Boulder County Sheriff George Epp had asked investigator Steve Ainsworth to return to the sheriff's office. During the six months that Ainsworth worked for Hunter, he had not been allowed to interview witnesses, much as Smit had not, since the police department had kept the DA's men at bay.

By September 4 District Attorney Alex Hunter had added two more prosecutors to his staff for the sole purpose of pushing the case to the grand jury. Adams County Chief Trial Deputy Bruce Levin and Denver Chief Deputy District Attorney Mitch Morrissey would work with attorney Michael Kane, who had now been assigned the responsibility of having major oversight in the grand jury proceedings. It did not appear that either regular DA staff members Trip DeMuth or Pete Hofstrom would be involved in the presentations to the grand jury, even though they had worked on the case from day one. The result was a further deterioration of effectiveness as the knowledgeable prosecutors in Hunter's office were pushed aside and replaced with new attorneys who had no background on the case.

When University of Colorado law professor Christopher Mueller was asked about Smit's and Thomas's resignations, he said, "If you look at the case as a type of case that is seen with some regularity—that is to say where a child is dead and the killing happened when the parents were home—then statistically, there's a great chance that the parents did it.

"If you view the case not as a type, but on its own precise facts, it's easy to see why you could have doubts as to the parents' involvement."

Of course, we agree with Mueller's assessment, but there are important exceptions to the common notion that many children are killed by their parents, and often even "experts" cavalierly throw around statistics that are misleading or downright wrong.

In an overwhelming proportion of cases where family members commit child homicides, there is a history of one or more of the following characteristics: poverty, abuse in childhood, drug or alcohol abuse, mental illness, young parental age, domestic violence, single parenthood, and "family members" who are not the biological parents (such as step- or foster parents or live-in boy or girl friends). In addition, as the age of a child moves beyond the toddler stage, the likelihood of his or her death being caused by a family member decreases considerably. The statistics also show that normal, natural parents with no history of these dysfunctional characteristics simply do not get up one day and go berserk and kill their children.

For instance, in a recent Georgia study of eight small children who were murdered by their parents, all had been well known to the child protection agency. In other words, there was a documented history of violent behavior leading up to the killing. None were from perfectly normal families who suddenly murdered their child, and then returned to normal.

Lou Smit ended his resignation letter with a quote from an

article he had written years earlier on how the investigation of a crime ought to occur. He wrote, "Shoes, shoes, the victim's shoes, who will stand in the victim's shoes?"

Patsy and I have the same question. Who will help us find JonBenét's killer?

28

RUMBLE ON THE INTERNET

T he death of innocence aptly describes our experience during these last three years. As we look at why Patsy and I were not afforded the presumption of innocence guaranteed by our Constitution, I've concluded that three primary factors led to the quick presumption of our guilt when, in fact, the police have never officially labeled either of us as suspects. First, of course, is the police themselves. The difficulties created by an inexperienced police force operating on hunches rather than evidence—and talking freely about those hunches with the media—started the avalanche. Second, the infotainment media were eager for a juicy soap opera-style story, since the O.J. Simpson trial had just ended, and they had lots of talking heads sitting idly by and lots of tabloid talk shows to fill with gossip. I was even less prepared for the third factor resulting in the loss of our presumption of innocence, and that was the new world-class gossip machine: *the Internet.*

Because I was in the business of selling high-end computers and network equipment, I didn't view the Internet as a high-tech chat room, but rather as a revolutionary new tool for commerce. The Internet really propelled our business when it began to emerge.

However, the Internet has become a publishing tool for anyone with a Web site to express their opinions to the world—a kind of giant collage of editorial newspaper pages. JonBenét's murder is probably one of the first cyberspace crimes that hundreds, probably thousands, of people discussed, vented, and in some cases tried to solve with the use of this vast network of computers.

During the time that Patsy, Burke, and I lived with the Stines in Boulder, every morning Susan Stine got up, turned on her computer, and started surfing the Internet to learn the latest rumors and allegations. Susan constantly discovered both cruel and startling comments that we hadn't seen coming from any of the more conventional media. We were surprised to realize the amount of time and attention being given to this subject by anonymous people with absolutely no connection to the case beyond their curiosity. But they all had an opinion, and it was usually that the evil Ramseys were guilty.

Susan soon discovered the anonymous chat rooms and networks of people sending e-mail back and forth on this subject. The vast web of people with opinions astounded us—and these people were totally unknown, at least as far as we could tell, since they all used aliases to post their messages! Were they writing from their living rooms, a public library, their office, or a prison cell? Who knows?

During her Internet searches, Susan Stine discovered a Web poster called "Jameson." While most of the opinions floating through cyberspace were hostile toward Patsy and me, Jameson maintained a straightforward approach to reporting information that was generally factual and correct.

Sometime in the fall of 1997, we received a letter from a person named Susan Bennett. Mrs. Bennett wrote to tell us that she had been following JonBenét's case and was interested in how the crime would be solved. To our surprise, Susan Bennett disclosed that she was, in fact, Jameson.

Six months later, Patsy and I met Jameson for the first time. She and her husband, James, brought their son to Atlanta for a vacation visit to Six Flags Over Georgia. Jameson had contacted us, and we agreed to meet for coffee at the Moonbean, a coffee shop not far from our home. I wanted to thank her for being one of the very few supporters of our innocence. We expected to just meet briefly, but it ended up that we talked for over three hours.

Jameson looked like a regular mom with her long dark hair, big eyes, and broad smile. She had a good sense of humor and wasn't sure how she had gotten so wrapped up in all this. If anything, Jameson was on the quiet and shy side. Among other things, she wanted us to know who she was and what she looked liked, because anyone could show up at our door and proclaim herself to be "Jameson." After all of the problems we'd had with the media, we appreciated her genuine concern to protect us from intrusion.

I wondered how in the world Jameson ever got hooked on our story and became so involved in the Internet. (I was also amazed by the amount of data she had assembled, once she described it to me.)

For a moment, Jameson looked thoughtful. "I saw the story about JonBenét, and for some reason this story touched me," she answered. "It just didn't seem to me that this was a parental crime. You have a nice Christmas, carry a sleeping child to bed, go to bed yourself, and then get up and kill her? It just didn't fit."

"But how did your interest turn to cyberspace?" I asked.

"I went to the Internet to see what people were saying about the crime," Jameson said. "It was idle curiosity. I had no idea I'd get caught up in the issue, but I was shocked at the way people were jumping to conclusions. The presumption of your guilt was already forming, and people were saying horrible things. How could these people make such terrible statements?" Jameson shook her head. "Intuitively I didn't believe that you and Patsy did it, and I decided that somebody had to be a voice of reason in this great big avalanche of hate."

That evening Jameson gave us a quick lesson on the Internet, since we were strictly amateur users. She described the three distinct types of Web sites: bulletin boards, chat rooms, and home pages. A bulletin board, which is often referred to as a forum, is where people post messages that can be read by anyone and the reader can respond at any time, much like a slow-moving discussion group. A chat room is a real-time discussion; only the people signed on at that moment can participate. When it's over, the conversation disappears, unless a participant has saved it. Home pages are not interactive, like the first two areas, but the broadcast work of one person.

Patsy and I listened in amazement as Jameson described how she had developed her Web site. She had started reading articles and leaving messages on the *Boulder Daily Camera News* site on February 4, 1997. This newspaper site was the first Ramsey bulletin board, and the computer keyboard world began congregating here. During the month of February alone, Jameson told us, she had posted 670 separate messages.

Initially most of the people on the *Boulder Daily Camera News* site proved to be new to the Internet and were civil people. They didn't steal anybody else's "hat" (cyber lingo for logging on with someone else's name). At first the forum was monitored and moderated, but after a while the moderator was frequently called to delete entries that were personal attacks, pornographic, even threatening. Soon the newspaper realized that to do this properly, they would need to hire someone twenty-four hours a day, seven days a week. This site had gotten out of hand and become a "Jell-O forum," one that is a free-for-all.

A lot of untrue and contradictory information flooded these forums. The police knew who had killed JonBenét, some posters said. They had the evidence, and it was just a matter of days before the father/mother would be arrested. I was ready to turn Patsy in, others said. Still others said that Patsy was ready to turn me in.

Some posters claimed I had been an "ice man" toward my family; I was abusive, they said, and my marriage was falling apart. Others suggested that Patsy had been having an affair and had left the house on the twenty-fifth to go to the park with her lover. Still others said JonBenét had been the victim of abuse all her life, and the evidence against us was undeniable. It was live tabloid journalism in a brand-new medium.

Jameson told us she repeatedly said, "The Ramseys are innocent. I challenge you other posters to prove that they are guilty." She was "flamed" (screamed at or called names) because of her position. Dozens, hundreds, of messages attacked her. These reactions from the "lynch mob" really pushed her into putting her TimeLine on a private home page. She hoped to present accurate information about JonBenét's case, using information taken from credible news sources and supplementing it with any official documents that became available. It wasn't long before she decided to present her own point of view there, where it would not be met with the onslaught of negative responses. She color-coded the material so there could be no mistaking what was official (blue), what came from news stories (black), and what was her opinion (brown).

After a while the Jameson TimeLine was so large that it covered more than three thousand pages. In addition to the Jameson site, there are hundreds of others that do nothing but circulate rumors and information about JonBenét's case and the Ramsey family.

Jameson soon found that other forums would ban her involvement because they had decided she was too pro-Ramsey. Her attempt to identify pertinent facts had pushed her into the "enemy camp" simply because she wasn't part of the "get Ramsey crowd"—the BORG, as they became known. She informed us that some Internet users assumed that BORG was an acronym, which stood for "Bent on Ramsey Guilt." Once again, they had missed by a light-year. The term *BORG* comes from *Star Trek* and refers to a civilization of people linked to a collective consciousness; the BORG followed one mind-set and were incapable of independent thinking. Their mantra was, "You will be assimilated; resistance is futile." Believe me, I was stunned. Real-life BORGS!

Most of the BORGS, Jameson said, completely ignore the fact of foreign DNA on JonBenét's underwear. Jameson always asks them, "Where do parents get foreign DNA? If they kill their child and it's twelve o'clock at night, they can't run out to the nearest drugstore and ask for 'one small vial of foreign DNA, please.'" Jameson told us she usually paused to let that reasoning sink in. Then she continued, "Patsy couldn't go down to the Pearl Street Mall and ask some bum if she could give him a back scratch. How do you get the DNA home and under JonBenét's nails and in her panties without mixing any of your own with it?" None of the BORGS want to deal with that reasoning.

Jameson had followers as well as detractors. They formed a group and set up an area of the Web where people could click in daily and become part of a discussion group. That forum fell prey to "hackers" (people who disrupt or destroy an area) time and again, and the owner of the site often wanted a voice in how things were run. Eventually Jameson bought her own space to prevent hacking and to maintain full control of the bulletin board. That bulletin board can be found at <www.jameson245.com>.

As interest in Jameson's Web site grew, Internet people became obsessed with her true identity. There were allegations that she was an agent or employee of the Ramsey family or business. Her last name was Bennett, and my mother's maiden name was Bennett, so we must be related. Of course, this was nonsense. One anonymous guru even posted the idea that Jameson was a person inside the police's war room, sending out theories to sway people's opinions. These folks ought to have stuck with reading tabloids and collecting empty beer cans. This Internet stuff was obviously much too taxing.

One of the most bizarre twists in the Internet spectacle came from an enthusiast who is a professor in the English Department at Vassar College. Donald Foster considered himself an "expert" in linguistic text analysis. He claimed that he could identify a vast multitude of facts about people—their age, sex, religion, politics, and level of education, for instance—merely by examining the words they choose to write and how they put them together.

In May 1997 Donald Foster went online looking for John Andrew Ramsey. He had determined that John Andrew was the most likely suspect in JonBenét's murder, and he felt that a college-aged boy whose father's business involved computers would be online. He found the Boulder News Forum and concluded, after applying his magic formula, that the murderer was Jameson, and that Jameson was JonBenét's half brother, John Andrew Ramsey!

On May 22, 1997, Foster made his first contact with Jameson, applauding her for reminding the anonymous Internet "voices" that the Ramseys were innocent until proven guilty. He placated her with the idea that he wanted to write a book on people who were "anonymous hats." However, Foster asked Jameson nothing about her family or personal data. The next step for this guy was to contact the authorities in Boulder and clue them in on the "big secret" that John Andrew was on the Internet posing as Jameson. He let them in on his "grand conclusion" that John Andrew had killed his sister. The final step was to alert his literary agent that he, Donald Foster the great, had not only solved the crime but was ready to publish a magazine article entitled "Paging JonBenét's Killer." Ah, such modesty. He had no idea that his fax to the literary agent in New York City would eventually reach the hands of Jameson and the producers of television's *48 Hours*.

Foster had also written a full-page letter to Patsy proclaiming his belief in her innocence and stating that he would both stake his reputation and faith in humanity on the fact of her not being guilty. In addition to this magnanimous sweep of generosity, Foster had another motivation for writing. He wanted Patsy and me to use him to find the killer. When we didn't respond, he went to the Boulder police with a similar offer, only he must have left out the part about Patsy being innocent.

Foster then gave Jameson his home phone number and asked her to call him. When she called, he heard her soft, obviously female voice and was shocked. Foster quickly became quite uncomfortable with the information he was being given but believed his analysis of "Jameson's" writings was correct. He was convinced that he had not spoken to the Internet poster "Jameson" (whom he believed to be John Andrew) but to an accomplice named Susan Bennett, probably a cousin who had been hiding John Andrew in her North Carolina home. Foster refused to admit that his assessment of Jameson's writings was off.

As Jameson posted on the Internet almost a year later, "The guy is *nuts!*"

How far can you miss the target? Oh, by quite a bit more, we were to see later.

In a fax to his literary agent, dated June 10, 1997, Foster stated, "In the ten years I have done textual analysis, I've never made a mistaken attribution. If I'm not sure, I bite my tongue."

What an ego! He should have bitten off his tongue, but it looked okay to me when I saw him on television. Foster missed guessing Jameson's age by a quarter of a century, had Jameson's educational background in Georgia, not Massachusetts, and obviously had her gender wrong.

On June 29, 1997, Foster sent a long certified letter to Mrs. Susan Bennett, offering to go between her and the police if she would turn herself in to the authorities for her part in the Ramsey crime. Foster now was convinced that Susan had been allowing John Andrew to use her computer to send out information. He still hadn't gotten the point that Susan Bennett *was* Jameson.

Bennett didn't tell anyone about the Foster interaction. She had initially agreed to keep their private e-mail confidential and later was embarrassed to admit that she had been turned in as a suspect because her writings were interpreted by an "expert" to be the words of a child killer. She didn't know about the fax to Foster's literary agent, but the certified letters were enough to seal her lips. Jameson didn't speak to anyone about Foster until a year later.

In the summer of 1998 Jameson had possession of a fax that Foster had sent to his literary agent. She was upset to find out how sure Foster was that Jameson was the killer, and she was even more upset that the authorities had been told so. Still she said nothing.

Late that summer, Jameson learned that the Boulder police intended to introduce Foster as an expert witness for testimony in the grand jury setting in an attempt to get an indictment against Patsy. By that time Foster had decided he was wrong about Jameson. Instead Foster now believed that Patsy clearly was the only one who had written the thirty-one-sentence ransom note, and he would testify for the police as an "expert." (See Appendix B.) Textual analysis is not a recognized science, and therefore is not permitted in a normal trial, but Foster could be used as a witness in a grand jury setting where there would be no way for anyone to challenge his opinions. Foster's "expert" testimony was crucial to the police's case against Patsy, we later learned.

Jameson took the story of Foster's claims against her to the district attorney's office. Donald Foster, she said, was anything but a credible witness, but the DA never contacted her. With the help of Colorado University professor Michael Tracey, one of the producers of the *JonBenét's America* documentary, Jameson brought her story to CBS. In April 1999 she appeared on *48 Hours,* which in part exposed Foster for what he really was.

As I listened to Jameson speak, I realized just how big a story JonBenét's death had become. Instead of reading a good book, people were spending hours and hours speculating in the dark about a subject of which they knew nothing! This is exactly how rumors come to life and then grow into urban legends, and then grow into fact.

One of those alias e-mailers intruded into our lives in April 1999. Out of the clear blue, somebody started sending e-mail letters signed "Patricia" and implying that she/he was Patsy. This person claimed that she/he needed someone to talk with and wanted a friend. People receiving these e-mails reported to Jameson that they were talking to Patsy. Jameson told them that Patsy wasn't on the Internet and had no e-mail address. Then she gave them specific questions to ask "Patricia" the next time they talked to her, like what was Jameson wearing when you met with her? "Patricia" refused to respond to those questions, and got angry at her integrity being challenged.

Patsy and I first became aware that her name was being used in these e-mails when a woman from Wisconsin wrote Patsy a card, expressing concern for her well-being and indicating that they had been communicating through e-mail. She said, "Your last e-mail sounded like you were very down." At first I couldn't figure out the strange card, but later I put two and two together and realized that someone was on the Internet anonymously posing as Patsy. That, by itself, wasn't particularly disturbing until I was able to get hold of some of the e-mails. They were extremely bizarre. We turned these e-mails over to our investigators to try to locate the sender but found the mysterious "Patricia" was clever enough to hide her/his tracks by using aliases and routing the e-mails through a computer server at MIT, which then rerouted them to a different part of the country.

One of the e-mail communiqués described a letter from a man, which was supposedly sent to Patsy's parents' home at the time the grand jury convened for the first time. "Patricia" said that in his letter this man . . .

wrote with the promise that he could tell me all about the murderer. He described the killer as a person who is obsessed with little girls fitting JonBenét's description; a person with a definite preference. In a twisted way, he falls in love with his victims. It is debatable what he considers love, but it can be certain; he becomes obsessed with his young victims. This person possibly stalked JonBenét for some time prior to making his final move. He is a pedophile, but his sickness runs deeper. He slowly becomes consumed with bringing his young victim as close to death as possible, without actually killing her, until she ultimately dies in his arms; becoming his perfect possession forever.

In great depth, the writer of the letter described a bizarre sexually deviant practice he said he had researched for several years, among other things, including pedophilia. He de-

*scribed individuals who torture their victims to near death
through various methods; one known as erotic asphyxiation.
He believes that JonBenét's killer was a cross between a pedophile and a person who is sexually aroused by bringing
his victim to the point of death, or asphyxiation and other
forms of deviant sexual torture.*

The "man" whom Patricia claimed sent the letter was, I suspect, "Patricia." This person's description of the killer and the
crime was sickening to us, but it was plausible.

In another "Patricia letter" sent on Saturday, July 17, 1999,
the writer, claiming to be Patsy, says of JonBenét's killer, "He is
not bound by my attorneys . . . He has no family that would
think evil of him to kill another little girl like JonBenét."

While the letters had a chilling, soap opera sound, the un-
dertone was threatening. We seriously wondered if this person could be the killer, a schizophrenic who was teasing us
with his clues. We couldn't find out without the intervention
of the police or some other government agency with the legal
power to subpoena subscriber information from Internet
service providers. We don't know if the BPD ever followed up
on this lead, but all this information was turned over to them.

We are also disturbed that a "Burke Killed JonBenét" home
page still exists on the Internet. One of our researchers sent us
a copy of this bulletin board in 1999, long after Burke had
been exonerated. At the time the Web site (http://www.geoci
ties.com/Athens/Forum/7615) had received over 72,708 hits
since January 20, 1998. In graphic detail the poster of this site
portrays how Burke murdered his little sister. How could anyone so malign a boy who was nine years old at the time? As we
have said, evil is alive and well and breeding on the Internet.

Of all the opinions offered on the Internet about Jon-
Benét's murder, Jameson's have been some of the most in-
sightful. Considering that, her thoughts on the killer are
haunting. She said, "I am convinced that our killer is a true-
crime buff and has modeled parts of this crime after other
crimes he has studied." She cites similarities between Jon-
Benét's murder and the slaughter of the Clutter family in
1959, which became the basis for Truman Capote's book, *In
Cold Blood.*

"The killers in the book specifically bought white nylon

cord and tape for the crime, they went to the house prepared. The cord around the neck had a long 'tail' in both cases. One killer in this book was very interested in obscure words; he worked hard to develop a strong vocabulary. He was also interested in movies, and we know the murderer in the Ramsey case was a movie buff, since he used so many movie quotes in the note."

During our meeting at the Moonbean, both Patsy and I were moved almost to tears as we talked with Jameson. At times when the topic of our conversation would bring up sad memories, she tended to change the subject to something lighter. As we ended our conversation, Jameson looked both of us straight in the eyes. "While I totally believe you are innocent, I will continue to look at any evidence the other side shows me . . . If anyone proves that you were involved in the murder of your baby, you will find me as tenacious an enemy as I was a friend."

"An open and objective mind is all we have ever asked of anyone—the police, the media, and the public," I replied, "but I can promise you, Jameson, we are innocent."

Just before we parted, Jameson said to Patsy, "I know nothing can bring JonBenét back, but if anyone asks what they can do for you as a sign of caring, what could they do?"

Patsy thought for a moment and then said softly, "If someone wanted to place an angel on the tree by the grave, it would be appreciated."

As we were leaving Jameson was so conscientious that she didn't want me to pay for her coffee, lest it appear that the Ramseys were in some way or the other "buying" her off.

Once Jameson returned home, she went online and posted the suggestion that people might want to hang angels on the tree at the grave site. It wasn't long before more angels began appearing at JonBenét's grave. Some posters who couldn't get to the cemetery sent their angels to Jameson, and she hung them when she visited the grave on JonBenét's birthday, August 6, 1998.

On the back of her own angel Jameson wrote, "Happy Birthday, JonBenét from Jameson," and placed it on a branch of the dogwood above the grave site. Before long someone who had knowledge of the Internet went to the cemetery, took it down, and then put a photograph of that stolen angel and its inscription on the Boulder News Forum site to boast of what they had done.

What Patsy and I have lived through might go down in history as the first cyberspace lynching, administered electronically with a huge anonymous mass of keyboards eager to shout out their accusations while knowing few facts about what actually happened to our daughter. The Internet has given the twenty-first century a massive party line, much like the party line telephones our parents had to deal with before private lines were available. Anyone connected could pick up the phone and listen or talk while someone else was using the line; there was no anonymity, and the network could only extend to a dozen phones at best. Today the Internet party line connects the world, and Patsy and I turned out to be the neighbors who were targets of the gossip.

Anonymity on the Internet is a debatable quality. While it seems to invite participation, the unknown aspect begs the slanderous, destructive, and hateful elements in our society to speak out without fear of accountability. We seem to act differently when we can speak without having to take responsibility—or even be known.

We, as a people, are lazy and won't spend the time necessary to check out the information being fed to us. Instead, opinions fly as fact like an unaimed machine gun. People don't stop to make sure that what they are about to say is the truth. People don't listen with a critical ear. What's missing? At the very least, a good editor to check the facts before they are "published" on the Internet.

On February 8, 1998, the *Boulder Daily Camera* ran a story by Everette Dennis, a professor at Fordham University, on the loss of the editing function in national life. The account notes that in the 1880s American newspapers invented the copy desk and copy editing to bring greater objectivity to stories being prepared for publishing. Today we stand at a similar place, needing an editor out there in cyberspace between the readers and the writers of data.

"Now in the age of the Internet, rumors, false information, and even malicious lies travel freely on graphically impressive, professional-appearing Web sites," says Dennis. "They have an audience of their own, of course, and have also become sources for other news organizations, hungry for updated material and leads." Dennis makes the point that the Internet needs some device to separate anonymous nonsense from important truthful information.

Patsy and I understand. Through the Internet, we were victimized by harsh, damaging, and untrue information disseminated about us across the world of cyberspace.

29

THE GRAND JURY INVESTIGATES

The grand jury finally convened on Tuesday, September 15, 1998, at 8:00 A.M. at the Justice Center in Boulder. Of course, the media were there in full force. Huge satellite trucks crowded the parking lot, and television crews, photographers, and reporters had begun congregating in front of the center as early as seven. The *Boulder Daily Camera* had already published copies of the jurors' pictures, obtained from the Colorado Department of Motor Vehicles. Anyone picking up a newspaper would know who they were. Still, sheriff's deputies forced the television and newspaper reporters to keep their distance as the jurors walked past the media. There was a scuffle as one juror pushed away a photographer who had gotten too close. With the sun beginning to shine against the face of the Flatirons, today was going to be a typical Colorado fall day—except that the circus was back in town.

The next day, the judge ordered all journalists to maintain a distance of at least twenty-five feet from any of the twelve jurors and four alternates. Apparently some jurors had been chased to their vehicles the evening before, even though they had left by a side exit. It appeared that all the players involved with the grand jury had rehearsed their parts well, and they were at least prepared for the media assault. The pieces were in place, and now the grand jurors would see if they could put the complex puzzle together. Our only hope was that they would be given all the pieces. A grand jury proceeding can be like a one-sided debate if the prosecutor chooses to run it that way.

Shortly after the jurors started working, Patsy and I began talking about what the grand jury could mean. She was really frustrated, thinking how this would delay the hunt for JonBenét's killer. "Look," I said, "we all know that our common mission is to find the killer, but something else is very much afoot here."

Patsy paused for a moment, as if unsure what to say. "I don't quite understand," she answered.

"You need to recognize what's happening," I explained further. "The number one job of our attorneys and investigators has always been to keep the two of us out of jail." My words had a cold, hard ring.

"You've got to be kidding," she stammered.

"The police department has the sole intent of putting us in the gas chamber. You and I now have to focus totally on making sure that doesn't happen."

"Okay," she answered and took a deep breath. "I think I get the picture."

"We've got children and will have grandchildren. We've got to get through this now, so we can live to be with them."

"Yes," Patsy answered.

"For the moment we have to make sure that you and I aren't sent to jail. Once the grand jury is behind us, then we can return to our number one goal, finding the person responsible for this."

Based on our experiences over the previous two and one-half years, it was hard for me to feel that the grand jury would be a fair proceeding if the number one objective of some of the prosecutors was to indict Patsy and me. I felt as if someone had strapped me in a straitjacket, pushed me in a corner, and told me to wait for several months until the grand jury decided what to do with me. The only silver lining I could see was that if we were indicted, then we'd have the right to see all the evidence the police were accumulating. And if all the evidence from the case were in our hands, we'd be able to pass it on to our investigators, who would then be able to pursue the killer with all the information. We were just sure there had to be lots of evidence the police had considered unimportant, which might furnish significant clues to an experienced eye. The promise looked rather tarnished, but at least some good might come if the worst happened.

What I said to Patsy was direct and frank, but I knew that was how we had to think now. The trail was growing colder and colder, and the grand jury would put everyone on hold, including the police.

The expectation that the prosecutors would do everything possible to present a compelling case against Patsy and me was frightening. The grand jury can indict based on *probable cause*, which is the lowest standard required to bring an indictment. In the case of JonBenét's murder, probable cause might simply mean that the cops thought we could have committed the crime, but couldn't put together enough evidence to prove it. So they say, "This is probably what happened." Alex Hunter had stated publicly that his office would not take to trial a murder case based only on probable cause, because the regular courtroom system required a much higher standard of proof: *reasonable doubt*. That's where innocent-until-proven-guilty-beyond-a-reasonable-doubt starts to work. We had absolutely no fear of what the outcome of a full-blown trial would be, but we sure didn't want to be submitted to that tortuous process.

The truth was that politics and the intense media scrutiny had thrown JonBenét's proceedings into a no-man's land, so we were faced with a grand jury proceeding that seemed as if it had to operate with a lynch mob standing outside the courtroom door. The best we could hope for was that the grand jury would say the investigation was flawed; what was needed were competent, seasoned homicide investigators. The worst was that both Patsy and I would be indicted for the murder of our daughter.

We had already lived through almost two years of unwarranted attacks. If we stood back and looked at the big picture, we had maintained our ground while the opposition had crumbled. A chief of police fired. A lead detective removed. A chief of detectives quit. A city manager left. We were battered but still standing. I tried to remember the knight in Monty Python's *Search for the Holy Grail*. This knight met a formidable foe on a bridge and was ruthlessly chopped to pieces. The last scene of the confrontation showed the thoroughly defeated knight, minus arms and legs, shouting defiantly, "Come back here. I'm not finished with you." I felt like that knight. Remembering that hilarious scene and applying it to my situation kept me going.

The entire grand jury procedure was threatening. Each morning as the sun rose, we had to wonder what more would happen to us and our reputations that day. Moreover, we had no idea how long the grand jury would sit. A month? Three months? Surely not six months. We had no way of knowing the outcome. In a short while, many of our investigative efforts would come to a standstill; otherwise, we would be loudly accused of trying to influence the grand jury, and that would put the whole process in jeopardy.

On September 25, the *Boulder Daily Camera* reported that Detective Linda Arndt and Sergeant Larry Mason had been called to testify. We wondered what Arndt would say, since our initial opinion that she was very supportive of Patsy had changed during the past year. Rumors were that Arndt would actually be a very negative witness. (We later learned that was accurate when she told her story to *Good Morning America* in October 1999—coincidentally?—just before the grand jury made its final decision.) We had also heard that Arndt had reported that Patsy and I were not together throughout the morning of December 26, but stayed in separate rooms. The implication was that we were not functioning like normal parents caught up in a terrible crisis. Therefore, I must be the cruel father/husband and Patsy, the battered wife.

The truth is that Arndt totally misread the situation. Patsy was mostly in the sunroom with women friends and two victim advocates who were trying to comfort her. She was distraught and near shock. Periodically, I came in to check on her, as I was concerned for her well-being. However, the total focus of my attention had to be on getting our daughter back. With her friends helping, I knew that Patsy didn't need my constant attention. The best thing in the world I could do for her was to get Jon-Benét back into the safety of her arms.

I suppose the most troubling statement by Arndt on *Good Morning America* was her claim that after she told me that JonBenét was dead, she feared that I would explode and kill everybody. She claimed to have mentally checked to see if she had enough bullets to stop me. Of all the strange things the cops said and did, that claim had to be right up there at the top of the list. When I heard her tell me, "She's dead," I went into shock. Anything that Arndt saw or thought beyond that response was purely her own projection, which she placed on me. Of course, Patsy and I had to worry about how Detective Arndt would present these bizarre accusations to the grand jury.

We also knew that the conflict between Lou Smit and Steve Thomas's resignation letters had to cast a shadow over the grand jury proceedings. According to news reports, both men had seen the same evidence but come to completely different conclusions. What the media never pointed out, however, was that Thomas had been a detective for only a few months and his previous experience was as a narcotics and patrol cop. Smit was a thirty- year veteran homicide detective who had investigated over two hundred homicides. To put those two men on equal levels was absurd. Smit's quiet and reasoned assessment should have been the counterbalance to Thomas's childish public outburst.

Even outsiders knew the grand jury was faced with a heavy burden to try and sort all this out. When the *20/20* television show reviewed the case on the evening of September 27, reporter Elizabeth Vargas questioned well-known Los Angeles prosecutor Vincent Bugliosi. He said that "the strongest evidence against the Ramseys in this case is nothing that directly implicates them." After discussing several other aspects of the case he concluded, "Even if you could prove beyond a reasonable doubt that Patsy Ramsey wrote the ransom note, that doesn't mean that she committed the murder."

We were surprised that the talking heads were now questioning the police, but we knew that these same people had earlier placed us into a guilty status. Throughout the time after JonBenét's death, Patsy and I could not fathom how anyone could doubt our innocence. Now the debate was, should we be tried for murder? Would the next debate be whether or not we should be executed? I had often thought I would rather be executed than sentenced to spend the rest of my life in jail.

The issue of who I really was versus the hated character the media had created me to be would, indeed, continue to haunt me. In March 1998 I had become the president of Jaleo North America, a company formed to handle the sales and support of Jaleo video editing and compositing software in America—a result of my earlier trips to Spain. Glen Stine planned to leave the University of Colorado and join me in this business venture later that year. My main partner, our vice president of sales, Jeff Cavins, was based in Seattle. We had what some would call a virtual company. I was optimistic that the Jaleo product would do well in the United States, and Patsy and I were back in business in a manner that could help us cover the staggering costs of all this.

Yet in the fall of 1998, my partner in Seattle called me and delicately brought up the subject of my personal reputation, which wasn't good for business.

A few potential customers had asked Jeff, "Hey, isn't this the same guy who killed his daughter?" Others might venture, "Isn't Ramsey the man who won't cooperate with the police?"

The implications were clear. While I had hoped that my business reputation and experience would instill confidence in the customer base, my reputation, as created by the media, was scaring our customers away.

Now Jeff and I could see that I needed to back away from the business. If I remained as president of our little operation, my tattered reputation might kill the company and put our thirty or so employees out of work. I resigned my position and told Jeff I would help him in the background if I could. I also offered to give my stock to the other key employees who could make the company successful. Once again my feet had been knocked out from under me. Perhaps ever working again was out of the question.

Around October 1, on the sixth day of the grand jury's work, Darnay Hoffman surfaced again with his so-called handwriting experts claiming that Patsy had written the ransom note. He offered David Liebman and Cina Wong, who were eager to point the finger of guilt at Patsy, to the prosecutors. But apparently Michael Kane was not interested; he later sent Hoffman a letter refusing to allow his "experts" to appear before the grand jury. Kane had the backbone to call a sideshow what it was and not let it interfere with the seriousness of the grand jury.

Near the end of October, the grand jury and the alternates toured our former home at 755 Fifteenth Street, carefully looking the place over for two hours as prosecutors waited in the backyard. Neighbors could see the jurors walking around inside the house, examining windows and checking doors. The group must have given extra attention to the grate and basement window where the killer could have entered or left. I wondered if the suitcase were still standing below the window as I had found it on the twenty-sixth. Apparently the jurors also spent a considerable amount of time walking in the back-yard. By court order, photographers and reporters had to stay at least one hundred feet away from the house, so they weren't able to intrude on the inspection.

I suppose that the jurors checked out all the rooms and looked in the cellar where I had found JonBenét. I'm sure they found that area of the house to be a difficult experience, knowing that they were probably standing on the exact spot where this terrible crime happened. In that same area, the ju-rors must have also tried shouting through the pipe that was probably the source of a neighbor's report of hearing a scream in the night. Could a scream have been heard across the street when we hadn't heard it three stories above? At each point, this group of people must have tested the theories that were being presented to them in the courtroom.

I wondered if, as they walked through the basement, any of the jurors brought up the issue of Burke's red Swiss army knife, which according to the media had been found on the countertop near a sink, just a short distance from where Jon-Benét's body was found. The implication was that the killer could have used the knife to cut the nylon cord used to tied JonBenét's wrists together. The cord was also used to make the garrote placed around her neck, which ultimately resulted in her death by strangulation. Linda Hoffmann-Pugh, our cleaning lady, had said on a TV talk show that she thought the issue of the knife was relevant to the murder.

Patsy and I never quite understood why she'd made those statements except that we knew she was mistaken about a number of other issues when she spoke on national television. The truth was that we had no idea where someone might find Burke's knife at any given time; he has a tendency to leave things lying around when he loses interest in them. The knife could have been anywhere in the house. And we had no idea if the knife had any relationship to anything that happened in the crime.

The October 30, 1998, edition of the *Boulder Daily Camera* quoted former Denver prosecutor Craig Silverman about the jurors' visit to our house. "It's rare, because most grand juries hear the DA's version of the scene . . . If there's a question about distances, then Detective Joe Blow is called in to say how far it was and what was possible at the scene and what, was not . . . I think this demonstrates what the DA's team has been saying, that this is not a prosecutorial jury, but an investigative grand jury."

Maybe this careful inspection showed that the members of the jury were going to think for themselves and not simply rubber-stamp the police's theories.

As best we could tell from the outside, the legal proceedings were moving along slowly. However, on November 19, the grand jury took a break from JonBenét's case and considered another case for a period of time.

While John worked with the attorneys, I spent time thinking about something more pleasant for a change. As the months had gone by, our daughter Melinda's relationship with Stewart Long was becoming more serious. I was hopeful because we all loved Stewart and felt that he would be a wonderful match for her. Finally Stewart proposed and Melinda said yes. A wedding was coming!

Melinda's birthday is on November 14, a date that had come to have special meaning in our family. John's father and his stepmother, Irene, got married on this weekend years after John's mother died; John and I also married on the same weekend in November of 1980. What a perfect time for a wedding. I found that helping plan for this event lifted my spirits.

Unfortunately, the wedding was like a two-edged sword. JonBenét had always talked about being in Melinda's wedding someday. In some way or the other, I wanted to do something that would include JonBenét in the wonderful festivities, but I wasn't sure how that could be done. After all, I didn't want to do anything that would detract from the joy of the great day.

Finally an idea struck me. I gathered up my friends Regina Orlick and Susan Stine for a special trip. We stopped by a nursery and picked up several flats of pansies and spring bulbs before heading for the St. James Cemetery. We planted the pansies around JonBenét's and Beth's headstones, and Regina spent quite a bit of time clipping one of the boxwoods into the shape of a heart. That was the best way I could think of to get the girls ready for the wedding.

When I went over to the hose to fill my watering can, the caretaker came over and introduced himself. "Lots of people come out here to visit those particular graves," he said, wiping the sweat from his forehead.

"That's wonderful," I said. "I'm Patsy Ramsey, JonBenét's mother."

He looked surprised. "Oh!" he said. "Don't believe we've met." He offered his hand.

"Glad to know you." I shook his hand. "Thanks for everything that you do."

"Don't you worry." He winked. "I'll take good care of her."

I thanked him for his compassion and went back to watering the flowers, feeling just a bit better.

John did everything possible to keep the media out of the wedding, but it wasn't easy. We had special passes that the guests were to present prior to entering the church. Gene Matthews helped with security and showed up with a staff that included seven off-duty policemen, many of whom had worked security at our house in the past months.

Sure enough, the press got wind of the wedding early on. Someone even put a copy of the wedding invitation on the Internet! That Saturday evening, November 14, the press was out in force, but our security people demanded that they stay off church property. At least one newsman had the courtesy to come to the front door of the church, dressed in a tux, and introduce himself as being a reporter. He politely asked if he could come in.

"Sorry, afraid not," we said. "This is a family affair, and we want to keep it private."

At 6:05 P.M., minutes after the wedding was to have started, a busload of out-of-town guests who were shuttled from their hotel pulled up in front of the church and started filing in. In the rush to get everyone seated, a well-dressed couple pressed by the usher unchecked and quickly disappeared inside. When the wedding started and Burke walked me down the aisle, suddenly this same woman leaned over the balcony and started taking pictures. The security guys were beside her immediately, and I don't know what they said to her, but she willingly handed over her roll of film. She and her partner were promptly escorted out of the church.

Because the Ramsey family's heritage is Scottish, a bagpiper and drummer in full regalia preceded the nine bridesmaids into the sanctuary. Stewart's middle name is

McLendon, after his Scottish ancestors, so the bagpipe music also honored his heritage.

I wore a black, full-length satin ball gown because Melinda had wanted the evening wedding to be very formal. The *National Enquirer* later reported that I wore a pink-and-white checked suit with white shoes! Didn't they know that no self-respecting southern lady would be caught in white shoes after Labor Day?

The First Presbyterian Church of Marietta, a very old structure that had been used in the Civil War as a hospital, had special meaning to Melinda; she and John Andrew and Beth had grown up going to church there. Salmon-pink walls with white molding and the pine plank floors tied the past and present together in a way that would forever bless Stewart and Melinda's life together.

It was raining that evening, so to protect the guests—and to prevent the paparazzi from getting pictures—we collected a dozen or so large golf umbrellas. Every time someone had to go outside, they'd raise the umbrella, and all the cameras could get was a view from their knees down. At least the photographers didn't succeed in getting shots of anyone's faces. The tabloids later reported that the "umbrellas of suspicion" were part of the wedding!

John wanted a great band for the reception, and we came up with an outstanding '60s hits group called the Swinging Medallions. We gathered at the Capital City Country Club in Brookhaven, and the band kept everyone on the dance floor throughout the incredible evening. As the night progressed, I finally got Burke to dance with me. As we swirled around the floor, something within my mind clicked and I realized that for the first time in many months I was truly having a wonderful time. I looked down at my young son with so much pride and could feel the joy and love rising up within me. I was happy, really happy. I had thought I would never feel that way again.

After a month-long break, the grand jury reconvened on January 5, 1999. Patsy and I heard that Mike Archuleta was subpoenaed to testify, and I knew he would clarify one of the urban legends that had been floated by the media, if he were asked. They had reported that I had called Mike on December 26, 1996, to arrange a hasty trip to Atlanta. Of course, that wasn't true. I had called Mike to tell him what had happened. He took the responsibility of contacting Melinda and John Andrew, who were already en route to meet us.

We also learned through the grapevine that Barb Kostanick had been asked to testify. The mother of one of JonBenét's friends, Barb had talked to our daughter on Christmas Eve, after JonBenét had said that Santa was going to make a special visit to her on the twenty-sixth. We hoped Barb's testimony would open a new door for the grand jury's inquiry, because we considered that statement to be a significant piece of information.

One evening Patsy put down the book she was reading and looked at me for a moment. "Five months have elapsed," she said slowly. "The grand jury has been in session quite a while. What do you really think is going to happen?"

I could feel the weight she was carrying, and I knew the pain bearing down on her. "I don't know," I answered honestly. "I just hope this will not go on much longer."

Unfortunately, it did.

30

THE INTERMINABLE WAIT

The grand jury hearings continued on and on, and we had no idea when they would actually come to an end. Patsy and I agonized as the time seemed to drag by. Of course, the Christmas season was painful, and the coming New Year didn't promise much joy. Because we could do virtually nothing to find the killer, what was most important to us seemed to have been put on hold.

Near the end of January, we realized that the grand jury must still be struggling with the handwriting issues. The *Boulder Daily Camera* reported on January 19, 1999, that Vassar College professor Donald Foster, the self-proclaimed linguist detective, had been talking with prosecutors about how he could best present his conclusions.

Foster's work was reported in the press to be a critical ingredient in the case developed by the Boulder Police Department against Patsy. Recognizing Foster's position with the cops gave us a sense of how much trouble the police must be in, since we knew Foster's theories and methods were junk science, at best. The police had clearly run down the wrong alley.

The grand jury finally asked the handwriting experts our attorneys had consulted to testify, and these experts willingly complied. While they couldn't tell our lawyers what was said in the hearing, we were left with the impression that the prosecution treated these analysts pretty harshly. Patsy and I discussed two possible explanations for the rude treatment. On the one hand, we could envision the prosecution as leaders of a lynch mob intent on indicting us and trying to destroy the credibility of experts who did not support their theory. On the other hand, the tough examination could have been done so that no one could later say the prosecutors had been friendly to the Ramseys. At this point, the latter possibility was the one I chose to believe.

Unfortunately, Michael Kane expected us to pay for the experts' time to testify before the grand jury, including their expenses for flying from California, all their meals, and their lodging while in Boulder. Money was getting very scarce for the Ramsey family. The mounting costs worried me; I was getting close to running out of cash. Everything we owned, except our home in Atlanta, had been put up for sale. I knew that if something didn't sell quickly, I'd be out of funds in thirty days or so.

The accusations leveled against us had been so tough and cruel that often Patsy and I found it difficult to even talk about them. For example, we heard rumors that hand lotion had been found next to JonBenét's bed with the lid ajar. Immediately some in the media jumped to the conclusion that this was a sign of sexual abuse. Such sick allegations were disgusting to us. Virtually every bedroom in our house had lotion of some kind. Colorado is a very dry place; chapped lips and dry skin followed quickly if you didn't keep your skin moist. I couldn't think of anything wrong with JonBenét having lotion next to her bed. Nevertheless, the crude allegations infuriated me.

Another really outlandish allegation was made that Patsy was a born-again Christian who had killed her daughter because she would be better off in heaven. Dale Yeager with a company called Seraph put such a claim in his report to Detective Ron Gosage. Sure, we are Christians who believe in Jesus and read the Bible. But who would suggest that a mother might brutally and savagely murder her daughter to get her to heaven quickly? Such a thought is an affront to a human being, much less a Christian.

As the grand jury heard evidence, we wondered how these accusations against us were being handled by the jurors. One question that had to trouble some people was why we didn't have the security system armed on the night JonBenét was killed. The truth was that we hadn't turned the alarm on for a long time because of an experience we had had about three years earlier, just a year or so after we moved into our Boulder house.

It was one of those late Friday afternoons when all you

wanted to do was sit down, kick up your feet, and just relax. The week had been demanding, and I had come home from work tired. Patsy and I were wondering what we might do to have a fun weekend. Suddenly an ear-splitting siren filled the house. I bolted forward in my chair. Patsy's eyes widened as if she'd just grabbed a 220-volt wire. I realized that the unbearably loud noise was the burglar alarm going off.

Patsy ran for the back entry hall, and there was three-year-old JonBenét standing on a stool with her fingers on the alarm system panel. Apparently, she'd been reaching for the button to open the garage door and hit the buttons on the alarm system instead. One button automatically summoned the police, another called the fire department, and the third key alerted emergency medical services. She had hit them all.

"This makes my ears loud," JonBenét said, putting her hands over her ears.

Patsy grabbed her and tried to turn the system off, but she suddenly realized that she didn't have any idea what the numeric code was to disarm the system. We both tried, but nothing stopped the terrible clamor.

Within a few minutes a fire engine pulled up in front of our house, followed by a squad car. Then an ambulance came roaring down the street. Patsy had already put JonBenét in our car inside the garage to protect her ears.

One of the police officers immediately asked, "If you live here, why don't you turn the alarm off?"

"We don't know the code," I explained.

"You don't know it?" The cop's mouth dropped.

"I'm sorry." I grimaced. "My daughter set off the alarm. I didn't even know it was working. We've been remodeling."

By this time the neighbors were out on their lawns, staring at our house. Patsy was digging through my briefcase, trying to find something that would give us the code to authorize the alarm monitoring service to turn the system off. Thirty minutes later the deafening siren finally timed out and quit. Silence. The quiet was overwhelming.

After that experience, we didn't want the system turned on because the sound was simply so debilitating. We were apprehensive of it going off unexpectedly again in the middle of the night and frightening us to death. The concept behind this particular alarm system, which had been put in by the former owners, was that it would be so loud that an intruder couldn't stand to be in the house and would be forced out. We looked at it more as a fire alarm, a function it was always armed for, so we fell into the habit of not turning the system on at night. For these reasons the alarm hadn't been on for several years, and it wasn't armed on Christmas night, 1996. In hindsight, of course, we should have changed the interior siren for a more conventional outside siren.

During this difficult time when the grand jury was meeting, I began to read the book of Job in the Bible. I wanted to try to understand how this man dealt with all the tragedy in his life. Job was a man with a great number of oxen and sheep, and he had seven sons and three daughters. Life was good. And Job was a good person. Yet, tragically, everything was taken from him, including the loss of all of his children. After Job had suffered for seven years, God gave him favor and doubled everything Job had lost . . . with one exception. Job was only given seven sons and three daughters.

I am sure Job must have thought, *Wait a minute, God! You miscounted. If you were doubling everything I had before, why didn't you give me fourteen sons and six daughters?*

To this question God might have replied, "But you *do* have fourteen sons and six daughters. It's just that half of them are with you and half are with me."

In the eyes of God, the children who died were already *at home* with their Father. Far from being "lost," the first group of children were very much alive. When I really listen to that subtle message of promise, I find almost more consolation there than anywhere else in Scripture. I know that my "lost" children, Beth and JonBenét, are waiting for us in heaven. That gives me profound encouragement.

My Thursday men's Bible study group also began discussing the book of Job. Some of the men felt that throughout their lives they had been blessed so greatly and suffered so little, they feared what could be ahead for them. It certainly has been my observation that every person receives a burden at some time, and we must learn how to be prepared to carry whatever happens to us.

The question our group was trying to understand was why God permits suffering when he loves us so much. I don't think anyone can answer that question with authority until we cross over the line and are in God's world permanently. Maybe the best answer we can give for suffering in this world is that our time here is like going through "boot camp." We are exposed to all the struggles an evil world places at our doorstep, and they become the obstacles along the journey. Anyone who was been in the service knows that boot camp is a testing ground and ultimately a builder of men. Though mentally and materially destroyed, Job was brought closer to God and to a better understanding of His love.

Job suffered for seven years, and I realized that it had been more than seven years since Beth had died. Following her death a string of unexpected tragedies had fallen on my house, just as it did on Job's. I had hoped that seven years would wrap up our problems, but the clock simply kept on ticking. I knew that we had no hope but to trust in God and his grace.

By March of 1999, the *Boulder Daily Camera* reported that Patsy and I *might not be called* to testify in front of the grand jury out of a fear that we could "win over" some of the jurors. I was stunned! What could that possibly mean? The only term I could think of to describe this situation was "kangaroo court."

I had told Alex Hunter in my letter that Patsy and I were eager to testify before the jurors. Being subpoenaed was an important part of protecting our rights. If the prosecutors subpoenaed us, we would have the right to see all the statements they had collected from us.

Producing a witness's statements helps keep him from becoming vulnerable to deception or the misuse of past testimony in a way that would cause him to appear to be making contradictory remarks, and therefore make him a possible target for a charge of perjury, or worse. Our position was very clear: when subpoenaed, Patsy and I and all the members of our family would be eager to testify. We wanted to do so. All of our children—Melinda, John Andrew, and Burke—had been subpoenaed, so we felt we would surely be next. After all, we were the parents of the murdered child. We were in the house the night JonBenét was murdered, and as far as we knew, we were also the cops' only suspects. The fact that they wouldn't subpoena us was sending a message, but we weren't sure what it was. It almost seemed that they were not allowing us to speak as a part of some strategy, but we didn't have a clue what that strategy might be. Several rumors quickly followed.

One speculation was that the police had treated the evidence so poorly that important statements had been lost. In other words, they couldn't give us everything they had collected because they had lost some of the materials. If this were true, the problem would only magnify if we were indicted. Still another story floating around was that some of the transcribed conversations the police had of us had been illegally obtained. If wiretaps were used without court approval and they had bugged the places where we lived following the murder, then the police would be held accountable for illegal activities. They may have backed themselves into a real dilemma.

Patsy and I didn't know what to believe, but the persistent story was that the prosecutors didn't want us to appear because the grand jury would be convinced after hearing us that we didn't kill our daughter, and the prosecutors didn't want to risk such an appearance. I simply couldn't imagine that after all these months of investigating the murder of our daughter, the grand jury wouldn't have called the parents and/or the prime suspects—and we were both. It seems that we should have been the first people through the door when the grand jury began.

Slowly I was able to prepare myself mentally for the possibility of being jailed and tried for murder. I knew we could try to face such an ordeal with dignity, yet it would be the ultimate disgrace. We would be faced with permanent public humiliation. Our children's children would be branded forever. Moreover, the costs would be staggering. My estimate was that a trial would cost at least seven hundred fifty thousand dollars. I found myself lying awake in the middle of the night, worrying about what was ahead.

On March 3 Boulder PD detectives Gosage and Harmer came to Atlanta to talk to our home security company to verify that we had, in fact, installed a sophisticated security system in our home there. I guess they thought if we hadn't that would be additional proof that we were guilty. Of course, they discovered that we had. After our experiences with Jon-Benét's murder, we did everything we knew to do to protect ourselves and our son.

During the whole grand jury period, the media kept a constant eye on us. At one point, they parked trucks in front of our driveway twenty-four hours a day, watching everything that was going on and listening with high-sensitivity boom mikes. They became increasingly belligerent to our visitors. The camera crews would set up their tripods in the street, hang boom microphones outside the trucks, and confront anyone coming to our house. While it was true they were a royal pain in the neck, I tried to look at them as free security guards and was sort of disappointed when they changed from twenty-four-hour-a-day coverage to merely 6:30 A.M. to 8:00 P.M. Everyone knows you need security mostly at night!

Detectives Gosage and Harmer also talked to Merrill Lynch—more than two years after the murder—to verify that we did attempt to raise 118,000 dollars on the morning of December 26, 1996, to meet the demands of the ransom note. Once again, obviously, we had. The money was in Boulder within a few hours of our finding the note. As hard as the cops tried, they could not come up with one instance where we hadn't told the truth. By now they should have started to figure out that we had been telling the truth all along, and that maybe we weren't the killers, after all. Unfortunately, they were in way too deep to change courses now.

As I occasionally followed the details of the grand jury and listened to John's description of what was unfolding, I also began to understand that there was a distinct possibility that things would not go well. The thought of being separated from John frightened me, and the threat of going to jail crushed any hope I could muster for the future. We had done nothing but be the parents of a child who had been murdered, and yet we found ourselves being destroyed by the justice process. Sometimes it seemed as if it were just John and me against the world. How I loved this husband who had been so good to me throughout the years. So gentle, so kind. Often during this difficult time I would realize how lucky I was to have such a supportive husband, and I liked to think back to our early days together.

When I was young my aunt Naomi had always told me that I would hear bells ringing when the right man came along. In July 1979 I moved from West Virginia, where I had lived all my life, to Atlanta, and I met John through my friends Dan and Claudia McCutcheon. Shortly after our meeting, John invited me to a cocktail party with him. While he and I made small talk, the front doorbell kept ringing as people arrived for the party. It seemed like the bell would ring every ten seconds or so. I finally realized that John was standing right next to me, and I was hearing *nothing but* bells. And here all this time I'd been expecting church bells or something of that order!

After that party, mutual friends got us together at a cookout. I soon learned that John was thirty-four while I was only twenty-two. I wouldn't have planned to get close to someone that much older than I was, but it turned out that the age difference really didn't matter. That night he asked if I'd like to go on a picnic, and I said yes. The next day John came roaring up to get me in his Porsche 911. I got in and complimented him on his cute little Volkswagen. Bad start! Cars just hadn't been a big thing with me. In the back of the Porsche, to my surprise, was John's three-year-old son, John Andrew! I thought this little boy with his blond Dutch-boy haircut was adorable. I then learned that John also had two daughters from his previous marriage.

John didn't have to tell me that his children meant the world to him; he showed it. After dinner every night, regardless of where in the world he might be, John was on the phone to them. I lost count of the number of times he would excuse himself from whatever was going on and then return about thirty minutes later, having talked with John Andrew, Melinda, and Beth. I can still see the two little girls the first time we met, with their white anklets and black patent leather shoes. I loved all three of these darling children immediately, and I think they came to feel the same way about me.

Later that summer, John and his children were flying to Atlanta after a visit with Grandpa Jay Ramsey in Michigan. On the way back John stopped in Charleston, West Virginia, to pick me up at my parents' house. After socializing a bit with my family, we all took off for home. Later, as we neared Atlanta, severe thunderstorms stopped us short, and we had to detour to Gainesville, Georgia, to wait out the storms. Even when we were safely on the ground, all three little ones were rather shaken up due to the rough ride. I remember gathering them near the candy vending machines in the Gainesville terminal and conjuring up a plan of how fun it would be to spend the night in the snack bar! Kind of like Willy Wonka's Chocolate Factory, I told them. Soon we were all laughing and eating dinner out of the candy machines. They were sorely disappointed when the weather cleared and we didn't have to spend that night in the candy shop!

My mother had always championed this sage advice: "Observe how your boyfriend's mother and father treat each other. You'll learn a great deal about how this man will be in his later years." I knew this was very wise insight. As I observed John's father, Jay Ramsey, I discovered that he was one of the most gentlemanly men I had ever met. He was an old-fashioned, Ozzie Nelson kind of man who always had a pipe nearby. If John turned out to be anything like his dad, he would be all right. I never knew John's mother, since she had died before we met, but I found Jay to have the same endearing qualities that I was beginning to find in John.

When we had dated for more than a year and a half, I had a feeling that John was getting close to asking me to marry him. At that time I was still working in an advertising agency in Atlanta. As one afternoon slipped away, I tried to call him about our dinner plans, but I couldn't get him to answer the phone. Little did I know that John, the potential son-in-law, was talking with my dad, the possible father-in-law. It was the proper thing to do in the South: before he asked me, he had to ask my father. John wasn't about to put my father on hold to answer the call-waiting signal at that moment.

When John did ask me to marry him, I was so flustered I could only answer, "I'll have to ask my mother." John wasn't quite sure how to take that.

My parents' only advice was that I fully understand the commitment involved in a ready-made family. John's devotion to his three children would guarantee that our new family would include them. As soon as my grandmother Janie Paugh heard I was thinking of getting married, she looked me straight in the eye and pronounced, "You know, we don't divorce in this family!" And she meant it too. I've often thought if more grandmas would say that, the divorce rate in this country wouldn't be so high.

Now, during the difficult days of the grand jury period, I looked back on these earlier times and remembered all the

wonderful things we did together. Nothing could lift my spirits like the knowledge that I would always have this gentle
man by my side.

On March 23, 1999, the Boulder County Commissioners
granted the prosecutors' request for another 62,000 dollars to
keep the grand jury operating through the end of June. To
date, the city, county, and state of Colorado had spent more
than 1.7 million dollars on JonBenét's case. A couple of weeks
later, on April 8, the district attorney was granted a six-month
extension on the grand jury's term. If the jury's work was
done before then, the jurors would be released, but now Patsy
and I had a more solid picture of how long this jury would sit.
The process was far from over.

The issue of Burke's testimony became our next concern. We
didn't object to his testifying before the grand jury; nevertheless, we worried about subjecting our son to a process that
might prove emotionally damaging. We discovered that the police had interrogated Burke on the morning of December 26,
1996. We didn't know about that until the subpoena came from
the grand jury with a record of when the police had talked to
Burke. As we reviewed the documents, we wondered, *What interview occurred on the twenty-sixth?* As we put two and two together, we realized they had interrogated Burke at the Whites'
house, while we were desperately waiting to get JonBenét back.
In fact, they had questioned Burke for forty-one minutes. The
interrogation had been without our permission or awareness,
and that is illegal under Colorado law.

In addition, we were concerned that Burke's appearance
before the grand jury would require him to go through a
wall of photographers as he entered the building to be
seated in the courtroom. We knew that we would have to secretly get him into town and then into the Justice Center. It
simply wasn't right to subject a twelve-year-old child to such
a barrage.

Our plan was to leave from our house in Atlanta at the
same time we left every morning to take Burke to school. At
the school we would drive through the car pool line and meet
Susan Stine, then we'd exchange cars with her and head for
the Marietta airport. After we left town, Susan would wear
one of Patsy's wigs as she drove our car in and out of our

driveway several times a day so the media watching our house would think we were still in Atlanta.

That particular morning, May 19, 1999, the media people showed up later than usual, but we still had our security system surveillance cameras focused on the spot where their trucks always parked. For some reason, they parked farther down the street that day. The thought struck me that I needed to put up a sign near the driveway saying, "Please Park Here for Best Photo Op!"

The plan worked flawlessly, and we were able to depart Atlanta without any picture takers. We refueled in Salina, Kansas, and then flew on to the Fort Collins airport, where Mike Archuleta picked us up and flew us to the Broomfield airport—kind of a switching-cars-with-airplanes routine. Ellis Armistead met us at Stevens Aviation and whisked Burke away for downtown Boulder. We had worked out a rather complex scheme: Armistead drove Burke to a parking lot where a van from the district attorney's office was waiting. Then Burke was driven to the Justice Center and into the sally port right under the noses of the horde of cameras waiting outside.

When Burke's full day of testimony was finished, he left the same way. No pictures. In fact, I'm not even sure they knew Burke had been there. Pam Archuleta drove us from Boulder back to Fort Collins, where we immediately took off for Sidney, Nebraska, since it was too late to fly back to Atlanta that night. We figured Sidney was far enough away that the media would have a hard time following us or running us down.

In Sidney we checked into a motel near the small airport and went over to Cabella's, a big sporting goods store near the airport. It was Burke's treat for putting up with all this. He loved Cabella's. After they closed, we had a great steak dinner in downtown Sidney, spent the night, and the next day headed back to Atlanta. We had actually pulled the whole trip off without giving up any photographs.

Burke's testimony went unnoticed until it was leaked several days later. The following day the prosecutors publicly reaffirmed that he was not a suspect in his sister's death. Later it was leaked that John Andrew and Melinda would be interviewed as well, and the report even gave the day they would testify. That would complicate getting John Andrew and Melinda in and out of Boulder about tenfold.

Abruptly the grand jury adjourned for the summer. We wondered if the adjournment had been due to the grand jurors' wanting clearer answers on the DNA evidence. They knew that foreign DNA—which did not belong to anyone in our family—had been found on JonBenét's body. Patsy and I felt that if they insisted on an answer to the question, "Whose DNA is it?" then the jurors would seem to be fulfilling their appointed role of preventing groundless prosecution. Maybe the grand jurors thought that the DNA found on JonBenét's clothing was a potentially significant clue. Our belief continues to be that this DNA is the killer's. Match the DNA and you've found the murderer.

Almost immediately, the Boulder police appeared in Atlanta and started taking DNA samples from all our family members. Even Patsy's young niece gave a sample. Melinda's husband, Stewart, became a target for the testing, even though he had not been in Boulder more recently than eight months before JonBenét was killed. We wondered if they were also testing the 119 suspects they claimed to have investigated as thoroughly.

Once the grand jury adjourned, we began to think about going back to Charlevoix. Losing our summer home there was difficult, but Chip and Vicki Emery helped John and me face the hard transition by allowing us to move some of our furniture into their house. They insisted that we be their guests in their lovely old home on Michigan Avenue, so we sought refuge there during the summer of 1999.

One afternoon I was sitting on Vicki's front porch, talking with her mother, Edna, and her aunt Marguerite. I was feeling blue as I remembered the fun times we had with JonBenét during our summers in Charlevoix.

"I know how it feels to lose your daughter, Patsy," eighty-two-year-old Marguerite observed. She took a deep breath. "It's been forty years. Forty years since I lost my Sandy."

I turned and stared at this lovely older woman, dumbstruck. I had no idea that Marguerite had lost a daughter.

"Still hurts," Marguerite said softly.

"Forty years?" I asked.

"Just about as fresh as if it happened a few weeks ago. Sandy was twenty-one when she died."

I could feel the tears gathering in my eyes. "How have you dealt with her death over all these years?"

"You simply tuck it away, Patsy. And try to remember the good times ... But it never gets any easier. You just try to keep on going."

I sat there staring straight ahead. Her child had died forty years ago; mine had died two and a half years ago. Age, circumstances, length of time, place—nothing made any difference. I realized that the deep pain of losing a child remains the same ... regardless of the passage of time. In fact, no one can lose a child and live without the constant apprehension that it could happen again.

Burke loved to ride his bicycle around the small town with his buddies Chad, Taylor, and Ian because he couldn't do that in Atlanta. Before we sold the house on Belvedere, I always knew his whereabouts instantly because he would be within shouting distance. Now that we were just "visiting" Charlevoix, and now that he was older, Burke was frequently out of my line of sight when he took off on his bike.

In the beginning, I had tried to keep tabs on him with a portable walkie-talkie, but discovered that it simply wouldn't reach far enough. To be able to find him whenever I wondered where he was, I had broken down and bought him a cellular phone. Even though the calls could be expensive, it was a small price to pay for peace of mind. Burke was always good at checking in with me; the more often he touched base, the more autonomy I gave him. Being able to get hold of him at any moment helped me feel comfortable with letting him have some freedom to roam.

One afternoon in Charlevoix, Burke and his pals, including his friend Ian, a diabetic, wanted to go to a friend's house in Norwood. I drove the boys because it was way out in the country, but they could ride their bikes for miles there without seeing a car. Ian's mother wasn't concerned, because the boys had Burke's cell phone if Ian had any problems. One of the boys' dads would pick them up around 5:30.

However, later in the afternoon I discovered that Burke had left his cell phone in the backseat of our car. *Oh well,* I thought, *it's only a couple of hours. I'm sure they will be okay.*

Around 5:30, it started to rain, and suddenly darkness fell and thunder started cracking. I usually enjoy a good rainstorm but not this time. The sky looked more than a little threatening.

As I worried about where the boys were, sirens began roaring off in the distance, cutting into the claps of thunder. An accident had happened somewhere close by. My heart started to race, and I began to pace back and forth across the front porch. Of all the times for Burke to have forgotten his phone! The rain came harder, the thunder boomed, and the sirens continued. A million "what ifs" raced through my mind. I tried to tell myself that there was no problem. Surely by now Burke was with a responsible parent, and I was just imagining things—but I couldn't stop myself. I was starting to panic.

The same panic-stricken feelings I felt the morning I discovered that JonBenét was gone from her bed swept over me. I started to tremble. An incredibly helpless feeling brought me to my knees. I began having a difficult time breathing and struggled to take deep breaths. Panic was squeezing the oxygen out of me. *Maybe Burke has been in an accident,* I thought, *and if we lost him, too, I couldn't live.*

Oh God, I cried out into the rain, *please let Burke be okay!*

Suddenly, as if in answer to that prayer, the van load of kids pulled up in front of our house. *Thank you, God!*

Burke was okay. Even after he returned home, it took quite a while for me to get over the sickening feeling in my stomach. Even today, I don't want to do anything that would inhibit my son from having a normal childhood, and I know that many of these feelings are my problem. Still, I have to force myself to let Burke be just a normal kid.

Patsy and I spent the rest of the summer at home in Atlanta. On August 5, 1999, the Boulder County Commissioners granted an additional 56,999 dollars as a final funding to keep the jury seated until October 20. It certainly appeared that the end of this particular tunnel was in sight.

As September drew to an end, John Andrew and Melinda were subpoenaed to testify before the grand jury. Getting them in and out of Boulder was a big concern since the media knew they were coming on September 30. We decided that both John Andrew and Melinda would travel on a commercial flight because I had sold my plane by that time. I took them to the gate in Atlanta, and Jim Jenkins met them in Denver with a Denver police escort who took them off the back stairs of the Jetway and drove them to a safe zone of the airport. There they switched cars and went on to Boulder. That night they stayed in the home of our friends. The next day they did a shift of cars as we had with Burke, and they got to the Justice Center without being photographed.

We don't know what they were asked, but it made me very proud that my children were fighting for their dad and step-mom. Anyone who spent five minutes with them could tell these two fine young people came from a loving family. They were both strong kids who were outraged at what was being done to their family. A number of friends asked us why the grand jury had called John Andrew and Melinda to testify. I had to conclude that perhaps the members of the grand jury had insisted on hearing from them, and the prosecutors were forced to let them testify.

Once John and Melinda were finished testifying, they left by the same musical-chairs car routine, except that John Andrew went on to Seattle to visit a friend, and Melinda flew back to Virginia. There were no problems. We knew October 20 was only weeks away, and the grand jury would be required to finish its work. For over a year this group of twelve people had explored every aspect of the case, and now they had to respond in some way. As the final day drew closer, we became more and more apprehensive.

I could hope for the right thing to happen, but I had to prepare myself in case the grand jury leveled the ultimate reproach against our entire family. I was not worried about the outcome of a regular jury trial; there was absolutely no doubt in my mind that we would be found not guilty. Patsy and I were innocent, and a thorough, objective exploration of the facts would demonstrate the truth. What frightened me was the degrading spectacle that would accompany a trial. What if the grand jury did indict us, and the police came with hand-cuffs? I could see Patsy and me being led to the police station in chains, taking the perpetrator's walk toward a jail cell. Photographers would be on each side snapping their cameras. Appalling pictures of us would flash across the national head-lines, and our children, our relatives, and our friends would see them. Torturous pain chewed on my imagination and kept me awake at night, worrying about the worst. I would remind myself that worry was a sin, that Christ had told us not to be anxious but to trust in him. Yet I just couldn't keep the "what ifs" from returning to my mind over and over again.

Patsy and I had to start formulating some plans on how we would respond if indicted. We had to be ready emotionally, financially, and legally for being arrested and taken to jail.

"What will we do?" Patsy asked me as we reviewed the possible alternatives. Her voice sounded strained and tense.

"We will probably need to leave our home in Atlanta," I explained, "and eventually go back to Colorado. We have to be prepared to turn ourselves in immediately if we are indicted."

She shook her head. "Totally and completely horrible."

I pulled her close to me. "Yes," I said softly. "I can't imagine it." I knew that we were both faced with the most difficult of tasks. We had to prepare to be charged with a murder we did not commit.

31

THE FINAL MONTH

Friday, October 1, 1999, was all too typical a Friday since JonBenét's murder—unlike the old days when my spirits would be high, looking forward to a weekend with Patsy and the kids. Fridays now meant we had to prepare for what the Boulder justice system and the media might do to us over the weekend, especially now, when the "Ramsey Grand Jury" was nearing its completion date of October 20. What would happen this month? No one knew. We only prayed that those twelve jurors would be objective and judge the case by the evidence, and that they would not have seen only "selected" evidence.

If indicted, Patsy and I could expect the police in Atlanta to publicly arrest us and jail us here. In that situation it would take our attorneys several weeks to arrange for a bail bond hearing. If we were in Boulder, however, it might only take a couple of days to get a hearing. The last thing we wanted to do was to spend two weeks in Atlanta's Fulton County Jail, despite the fact that we had gotten to know and like a number of Fulton County police officers. If an arrest warrant were issued, we wanted to be in a position to quickly and voluntarily turn ourselves in to the sheriff in Boulder, rather than being put through the humiliation of detention in Atlanta.

That Friday afternoon, October 1, Patsy and I spent some time looking through past issues of the tabloids, trying to decide if we would put our family through the additional court proceedings necessary to sue the papers for defamation. We had not seen many of these stories before, so we were amazed that anyone could print such lies, particularly about our twelve-year-old son, Burke. How could such vulgar, irresponsible journalism thrive in a civilized society?

That evening Melinda and her husband, Stewart, were in

town from Virginia and took us out for dinner to a small, but great, Mexican restaurant. As we sat on wooden chairs at a small table, waiting to order our meal, they said, "We've got a surprise for you, and we want to celebrate."

I was secretly hoping the surprise was the announcement of my first grandchild. Amazing! I was actually wishing to be a grandfather. *Must be getting old,* I thought. Instead, Melinda laid a set of Land Rover keys on the table and proudly told us they had bought a new car. They were really excited, and I tried to be excited for them. Their first new car as a family. Certainly that was a proud moment; they'd only been married a year and were already able to buy a new car to replace Stewart's old Oldsmobile, which he had driven throughout medical school.

Later, as we were having coffee after dinner, Melinda looked me in the eyes and said, "Dad, there's a reason we got a big 'family' car."

Bingo! I was going to be a grandfather. A lump rose in my throat as I realized that not two days ago, I could barely muster the will to hang on to life. Now I was reminded of why it was so important to persevere. This tiny one would need a granddad who could give a grandparent's unconditional love. I determined to go on fighting for our reputation—and for JonBenét. I couldn't imagine bringing another child into our family without battling with all I had to restore our good name.

During the last few months I had seen a number of stories about the Sam Sheppard case, which had also been surrounded by a media circus in the 1950s. Sheppard's son, who was seven at the time his father was indicted for murdering his mother, feels that the *Cleveland Plain Dealer* newspaper probably convicted his dad. Dr. Sam Sheppard, who always maintained his innocence, spent twelve long years in prison. A young attorney named F. Lee Bailey took up Sheppard's cause in the late '60s, and after a new trial, Sheppard's conviction was overturned. He was freed, but not before his life was ruined.

This former neurosurgeon quickly slipped into alcoholism and eventually died of liver disease at the age of forty-six. The justice system and the media had destroyed an innocent man and who knows how many future generations of his family. For thirty years his son has tried to absolutely clear

Dr. Sheppard's name, and that now seems possible because of DNA technology. I didn't want my kids or grandkids to have to spend thirty years of their lives trying to clear my name. I renewed my commitment to my primary objectives: enabling my living children—and future grandchildren—to live a normal life and be proud of their name, and finding the killer.

That evening as we finished our coffee, another emotion quickly surfaced. My daughter had endured traveling to Boulder under difficult circumstances where a prosecutor, who was trying to indict her parents, had interrogated her for three long hours in front of a jury of strangers. At the time she was three months pregnant, carrying this new life who needed protection. Melinda, I realized, had been abused by the system too, at a time when she needed rest and peace. Yet at exactly the moment I needed it most, God had delivered this wonderful reminder about the sacredness of life. I vowed to endure until I was called home.

The next two weeks were unbelievably stressful for John and me. On Monday, October 4, we were planning to drive to Waldorf, Maryland, to visit my friend Mary Ann Holt, who was in the final stages of her bout with ovarian cancer. She and I had shared many rough days of therapy during our participation in the program at NIH. She was ahead of me in the treatment program and had been a real cheerleader for me. Two days earlier, Ann's husband, Mike, had phoned me in Atlanta. "Things are not going well," he had said. "If you want to see Ann alive, you'd better get here in the next few weeks."

Yet I'd still been too late. On Sunday, October 3, we were sitting in my friend Lin Wood's living room, discussing our strategy to fight the tabloids, when my cell phone rang.

It was Mike. "Patsy, Ann passed away last night," he said. "There's no need to hurry now."

I felt so bad. Here I was, letting the tabloids continue to invade my life when I should have rushed to spend time with my dying friend.

Now I needed funeral clothes instead of visiting clothes. I borrowed a dress from Susan Stine and ran out to Steinmart for a pair of black shoes and a hat. That would be okay. Ann wouldn't care. She was a solid, down-to-earth person and knew that death was a new beginning. I mainly wanted to be there for Mike and to see Ann's son, Patrick. She had told me she wanted to live long enough to get Patrick out of high school. She did. Patrick had graduated that past June.

Until JonBenét died, I didn't know Ann had also lost a young daughter. Julie was only days old when doctors realized she had a problem and wasn't going to make it. As Ann had shared her sorrow of losing her baby girl with me, she had assured me that JonBenét and Julie were in heaven and that we would be with them again one day. Before Ann's death she requested that Mike move Julie's body so she could be buried with her mom. Mike had worked hard to grant Ann this final request.

Now Julie's tiny casket lay next to Ann's at the cemetery. They were finally together again. A part of me envied Ann. No more pain, no more sickness, no more tears. Only Julie and heaven. I quietly hoped Ann was checking on JonBenét for me.

I stood there a moment longer, remembering my chemo sisters who had lost their fight: Humberta Sylveria, Peggy Fairchild, Vicki Chabol, and now Ann. Only Colonel Barbara and I remained of the roommates. I never thought I'd live this long. God saved me from cancer for a reason. I only wished he would speak a little louder and let me know what that reason might be.

Following the service at the Catholic church, Ann's father and mother invited us to a luncheon at the community hall. Many of the Charles County sheriff's officers were there in dress uniform to support Mike, a deputy who had been with the sheriff's department for years. Several of the officers approached John and me to offer their sympathy for what we had been through since losing JonBenét. How could these law enforcement officers be so thoughtful and compassionate and the Boulder officers seem so cruel and vindictive? Never once had the chief of police in Boulder, the sheriff, the mayor, or any of the detectives said to us, "We are sorry for your loss." Now perfect strangers in the same profession were looking deep into our eyes with such empathy from beneath their wide-brimmed hats. We were very touched and ashamed, at the same time, that we had been so angry at police in general when our issues were really with just a handful of bad apples in Boulder.

Back at Mike's house, he took me by the hand and led me to Ann's room. He opened a small jewelry box and gently removed a gold bracelet. "This is the matching bracelet to the necklace Ann is wearing," he said. "I'd like you to have it." He carefully clasped the bracelet on my left wrist, where it shall remain. Mike had no idea that his tender gesture was also flooding my heart with a special memory of JonBenét.

I had given her a tiny gold bracelet on the evening of December 23, 1996, placing it on her wrist in much the same way Mike was doing now. It was the evening of our family Christmas party, and since she was all dressed up, I had decided to let her open the gift early so she could wear it during the holidays. The bracelet was inscribed with her name on the front and on the back with the date she was actually supposed to receive it: 12-25-96. I hope I can someday get that bracelet back. It's part of the vast number of items still in police custody.

For the moment, John and I knew we had to stay away from home so the *National Enquirer* or CNN wouldn't catch us on video being arrested if the Boulder cops orchestrated a surprise visit. A daunting thought. We couldn't go home. But where should we go? Michigan? West Virginia? Sightseeing in Washington, D.C.? Or Dahlonega, Georgia, where John had been invited to attend a Christian men's retreat? If we weren't supposed to go home, how did we keep ourselves busy for a week or so with absolutely nothing to do, except fret over whether we'd be indicted? After all, these could be our last few days as free citizens.

The next morning we decided to go to Dahlonega, in the North Georgia mountains relatively close to Atlanta, so John could attend the men's retreat. News from Boulder was that the Ramsey grand jury might finish its work as early as the following day and announce a decision next week. I knew we were supposed to stay out of sight, but I was already missing Burke terribly and really wanted to spend the weekend with him, especially if this might be our last weekend together.

The Stines agreed to drive up from Atlanta with Burke, who had been staying with them while we were in Maryland. *Best to keep him focused and in school,* we had thought, *despite our unknown future.* He was really comfortable with the Stines because we had lived with them for so long after JonBenét's death.

So even though we were now looking forward to a nice get-away weekend in the Georgia mountains with friends, we still had to plan for the worst-case scenario. We had alerted Burke's school, where he was enrolled in the seventh grade, to the possibilities of all this taking place, and told them who would pick Burke up in our place. It was embarrassing for both parties to even talk about such things, but we had to face reality.

It was a long drive back to Georgia from Maryland, nearly twelve hours. We used a new Earthmate Global Positioning System (GPS) hooked up to John's laptop as our travel guide for the trip through the back roads of Georgia. He had bought it for 149 dollars before leaving Atlanta, and I dubbed it "the marriage saver." It gave precisely correct directions and eliminated the typical squabbles that develop on a family car trip when a husband won't stop to ask for directions.

But along about midnight we pulled into the parking lot of the sheriff's office near Ellijay because we were lost, in spite of our high-tech navigational tool. John waved down an officer who was pulling out onto the road in his squad car and asked for directions to the retreat, which was somewhere in the vicinity of Waters Road (we couldn't remember the exact name of the place).

The officer mentioned a name, and John said, "Yeah, yeah, I think that's it." So the policeman started to give us directions but stopped short and said, "That's the nudist camp."

"Nudist camp? No! That's not what we want! This is a church retreat," I retorted. I could just see the tabloid headlines: "Ramseys Escape into North Georgia Nudist Camp before Grand Jury Indictment!" That's the kind of stuff the tabloids go wild with. Give them a sensational idea or picture, and they'd run with it—true or not. I didn't even know nudist camps still existed. Wasn't that a '60s thing?

The policeman finally figured out where we wanted to go and gave us the right directions to the camp where the men's weekend would be held. An hour later, we checked into our one-bedroom cabin. Exhausted, we dragged our bags in and got ready for bed. I popped my usual two Benadryl to insure a good night's sleep. Dr. Beuf had suggested them back on December 26, and I'd been taking them ever since. My insides were probably hot pink from taking so many. On nights when I forgot or ran out, I didn't seem to get deeply enough asleep to prevent the wild dreams and continual searching for JonBenét.

That night I slept well and by mid-morning hadn't rallied. John, of course, had been up for hours, made coffee, had breakfast, and checked out our surroundings. Finally he decided to come check on me. I awoke suddenly to find him leaning closely over me, trying not to awaken me. I screamed and he jumped. I'm not sure who scared whom the most! He apologized and said I was so still, he just wanted to make sure I was breathing.

Guess I'll never get over being afraid, I thought. *I'm afraid of the night. I hear noises. I see shadows.* Over and over my mind had relived the fact that a murderer was in my home that night and I didn't know it. *Where had he hidden? Would he return? Would someone else pierce the sanctity of my home? Why didn't we have the dog there that night? Why, why, why?*

I had to remind myself that fear is not of God. He wants us to feel safe and secure in his presence, and assures us that he will never leave us or forsake us. But where were the ten thousand angels the night that creature slipped into our home and committed the unthinkable? God never said he would always protect us from suffering, but he promised he would always be near us when we are suffering.

Sometimes I thought of the prayer I'd said so many times in my childhood.

> *Now I lay me down to sleep.*
> *I pray the Lord my soul to keep.*
> *If I should die before I wake,*
> *I pray the Lord my soul to take.*

I had taught Burke and JonBenét to say that prayer each night before going to sleep. Then, after we lost Beth in the automobile accident, I disliked saying the third phrase, so I modified it.

> *Keep me safe all through the night*
> *And wake me in the morning light.*

Now I couldn't say the prayer at all. It made me shudder. *Please God, help me with my fear of the night.*

I got out of bed, and John went with me over to the lodge. While I ate breakfast, he updated me on the news from Boulder. The grand jurors had spent several hours the previous day working alone, which could indicate the beginning of their deliberations. For over a year now we'd been living under the shadow of the grand jury. When would it end? Next Monday or Tuesday? The end of the week? Who knew? It couldn't be much longer, though, since this grand jury's term was about to expire.

The newspapers said some people were beginning to speculate what steps would be taken next if there were no indictment. I hoped that was a positive sign. For so long the published rumors had been, "They'll indict Patsy this week" or "They'll hold both Ramseys responsible."

John told me he had spent the morning sitting in the swing on the front porch of the little cabin, enjoying the peace and quiet of the natural surroundings, thinking, *Next week I might be in jail. I might only have these few moments left now to enjoy my freedom.* He'd found that a very strange feeling. It made him appreciate freedom more than ever before.

On Friday we drove to Amicalola State Park for lunch, and then toward Ellijay, where preparations were well under way for the fall Apple Fest. John and I were both very somber under the heavy weight of what the future might bring. It was terrifying, particularly since we were innocent.

In Ellijay I began poking into little shops as John went to the barbershop to get a haircut. I was just about to allow myself to feel good about the beautiful day when an Atlanta television truck, complete with a satellite dish, turned the corner. I froze. For a split second I thought, *Oh no, they've found us!* I quickly turned my face toward the storefront window, which was decorated with all things apple.

The Apple Festival! Of course, I remembered. *Big weekend in Ellijay. They're probably just covering the Apple Fest.*

I hurried over to the barbershop to meet up with John, who was in the chair with hot lather spread all over the back of his neck. The lady barber was using a fierce-looking straight-edged razor, which she cleaned off on the palm of her hand after each swipe. It looked as if she were going to slice her hand wide open with that thing!

She was talking a blue streak while she shaved. John, in turn, was commenting on all the pictures of her family taped on the wall by her barber chair.

I stepped up to have a closer look at the photos of this woman's kids and grandkids.

"That little girl there is my granddaughter," the woman proudly announced, pointing the lather-coated razor at the wall.

I looked over to where she was pointing, and there was her six-year-old granddaughter in tap shoes. And there was another photo, probably taken at Olan Mills or Wal-Mart, of the same sweet little girl posing with a pink feather boa, wearing gold, jewel-laden sandals. She had a beautiful, innocent smile. Little did she know that the media considered such outfits scandalous for a six-year-old.

"I bought those shoes for her," Grandma boasted.

"Beautiful, just beautiful," I whispered. The lump in my throat was choking me. Fortunately, John had his chin buried in his chest as she was finishing the shave, so he didn't notice my distress.

Her granddaughter was not unlike millions of other little girls who tap-dance and dress up in fancy clothes and like to have their pictures taken. Not unlike me when I was a little girl. Not unlike JonBenét. And I am no different from that doting grandma who was so proud of her little granddaughter.

We left the old barbershop both thinking it was nice to be in a small town in the South. John also said it was the best seven-dollar haircut he'd ever had.

Late Friday evening, the Stines arrived with Burke and Doug. They had had a hard time finding the place too.

John spent the next day attending the Christian men's retreat. This was the eighteenth year this group of men from all over the United States had met together, and it was John's second year to attend. Gayle Jackson, John's spiritual mentor, had started the conference to bring men together to study the Bible, and it had grown to around one-hundred-fifty men.

Even though it rained most of that Saturday, I decided to enjoy this time with Glen, Susan, and the boys and tried to avoid thinking about what might happen to us the next week. Occasionally Glen would walk over to me, put his long arm around my shoulder, and give me a hug. He's a gentle man of few words, but very perceptive. He could tell my thoughts were elsewhere. "It's going to be all right," he assured me. "We've come this far, we can't let it get us down now." I really didn't know what would have become of us if it hadn't been for Glen and Susan Stine shepherding us through the last two years.

On Sunday, October 10, the Stines told us they had heard on the news that Alex Hunter was meeting with nationally known forensics expert Dr. Henry Lee to discuss the DNA evidence. What did that mean? We weren't sure. We knew that the DNA stain on JonBenét's underwear had not been linked to any family members—or anyone else for that matter. We thought this was the seventh time Hunter had met with Lee, the most recent being on September 21. What were they discussing now? And at this late date?

The Stines also reported that Suzanne Laurion, Hunter's spokesperson, announced that the grand jury would not reconvene until Tuesday, October 12. We had watched patiently—and without fear—for the past thirteen months as the grand jury had investigated us. Now that it was getting down to the wire, we became very anxious. A year ago I wouldn't have been able to stand such humiliation. Now, we both were prepared to accept whatever happened and to deal with it with dignity.

That morning we started back to Atlanta. We decided we could sneak back home for a day, since the grand jury wasn't going to meet until the twelfth. I don't remember exactly why, but both boys rode in Glen's car. Seems as if John and I were going to be on the car phone for a good part of the way with the chaps in Colorado, and I didn't want the boys exposed to all that talk. Susan was riding with us. It now looked as if we needed to be in Boulder (or somewhere close by) no later than Monday night, October 11.

As we neared the suburbs of Atlanta, it started to rain. Susan thought it might be prudent to stop by my parents' house in Roswell and change cars, since we knew the paparazzi would be looking for us. (Glen would drive directly back to their home with the boys.) We called ahead, and my parents assured us that no "picture takers" were lurking about. Dad said he would open the garage door so we could quickly pull in and get our car out of sight.

Once there, we loaded our things into Dad's old white Grand Prix, the car he had bought to drive when he was working in Boulder. Now it had become the floating loaner

(FAB-RENT-A-CAR, we called it) when somebody's car was in the shop.

As Susan pulled slowly out of my parents' driveway, John glanced to the right and saw the photographer instantly. Down the hill, on the opposite side of the street, sat a car with lights on, wipers going. It was parked in plain view, between two other driveways. We watched him pull out behind us as we turned left toward the neighborhood entrance. We turned right onto Hardscrabble Road, and here he came, right behind us, though staying some distance back.

Susan loves a good chase scene, and she happened to be driving. We pulled up to the traffic light at Mountain Park Road and waited until the left-turn signal was just about to change. As it turned red, Susan quickly made a U-turn. She jammed the gas pedal and went racing east on Woodstock Road. The follower was left at the red light—which usually wouldn't stop the paparazzi, but in this case, the oncoming traffic did.

Susan made a quick right at King Road and headed south. Meanwhile John was leaning over in the front seat, and I was down in the back, peering out just enough to issue directions. I knew these little side roads well, so we easily lost the would-be photographer. We made a snap decision to head for John's brother's house rather than to the Stines', so we doubled back.

Still crouching down in the backseat, my mind flashed to Princess Diana, who had been killed in a car chase. It is foolish, really, to allow the paparazzi to get under your skin so much that you risk your good driving sense. Yet it is so natural to want to outrun them, to outsmart them, to keep them from getting a photo and writing the next front-page story to smear you.

Again we called ahead to make sure that Jeff and Peggy were home so we could slip into their garage. Then we phoned Glen and the boys, who were waiting at the Stines', wondering what in the world had happened to us.

Days later we heard that the stalker was probably Scott McKiernan, the photographer who had purchased JonBenét's pageant videos and resold them. McKiernan bragged to *Newsweek*'s Sherry Keene-Osborn that he knew *exactly* where the Ramseys were hiding out in Atlanta. Apparently he and a few others hung out at my parents' the next week, waiting for John and me to try and sneak out. A couple of times they came up to the front door, and Dad told them in not-so-polite terms to stay off his property. At night they would illuminate the house with floodlights. They just knew we were in there! But we were already headed to Boulder.

As was frequently the case, an encouraging word had arrived just before we left. Margaret Harrington wrote us this note:

> As we wait for the end of this chapter, not knowing what the next one holds, please know that there are many, many people who are quietly standing with you, coming before God's throne on your behalf daily.
>
> I pray that you will continue to stand firm, trusting that our God is all-powerful, perfectly just, rules, and overrules. In Isaiah 41:9–10 [NIV], God says, "You are my servant; I have chosen you [Patsy and John], and have not rejected you. So do not fear, for I AM WITH YOU, do not be dismayed, for I am your God. I will strengthen you and help you; I will uphold you with my righteous hand." At his right hand, is, of course, Jesus who is with you always, and will never, ever leave you nor forsake you.

32

A Jury of Our Peers

As the grand jury deadline of October 20, 1999, approached, Patsy and I felt as if our lives were like a wall clock that would stop at twelve midnight. We could see the hands on the clock inching forward, but after midnight we didn't know what lay beyond. Each tick seemed to resonate with an ominous sound. We were standing on the verge of being unjustly whisked away at any moment.

The grand jury had begun on September 15, 1998, and stayed at their work far longer than we imagined possible. We didn't know when they would conclude, but their inquiry had to end by the twentieth of October, when their term of service would be up. In order to proceed further, a new grand jury would have to be seated. More than a year had been spent assessing every aspect of the case against us. The jurors had pondered at least some of the thirty thousand pages of data from the case files and, according to the media, had heard many witnesses. We were anxious to know what really was going on, but our only source of information was the media.

On Tuesday morning, October 12, 1999, the *Denver Rocky Mountain News* reported that special prosecutor Michael Kane had worked late on Sunday night and into early Monday morning preparing for his final conclusion to the grand jury. Patsy and I had no doubt that he would ask for our indictment. As far as we knew, that had been his mission from the beginning. If this grand jury functioned like we had heard most grand juries do, undoubtedly we would be indicted and soon be arrested and jailed.

Former detective Steve Thomas weighed in with the newspapers and publicly declared that, in his opinion, probable cause to indict us had existed since 1997 and had only grown stronger during the past year. We clearly knew where his vote was. But we knew that from the first days, rookie detective Thomas had made his mind up, and had refused to let facts and evidence deter him for almost three years.

Sunny weather settled over Boulder with the usual crispness of fall. The feeling of football and Halloween was in the air. Naturally, the media were also settling in around the Justice Center, jockeying for the best positions to report and photograph the conclusion of the grand jury the moment the jurors stated their position. The television cameramen and reporters were outside pacing up and down on the grass or conversing with one another. The grand jury's decision would be announced to the country in a week at the most.

Police Chief Mark Beckner knew that the decision would also have an impact on the Boulder Police Department. He noted that if there were no indictment, then the BPD would receive more criticism to be piled on the enormous heap already in front of their door. Apparently, the police seemed to have some concern about what could come out of the jury room, despite the fact that they had demanded a grand jury.

One of the accusations that had been leveled against Patsy and me was, "If the Ramseys are innocent, why wouldn't they agree to appear before the grand jury?" The truth was that we had done everything we knew how to do to get the prosecutors to subpoena us so we *could* testify. We wanted to testify. They wouldn't allow it. Throughout the process, we had been excluded from testifying by the prosecutors who were running the hearing. We were never called, and are not sure why. Now we saw ourselves confronted with the prospect of a dead investigation, financial devastation, standing trial for murder, as well as passing on a blighted family reputation to our children and grandchildren.

During these last days, I realized how the entire process had squeezed the innocence out of Patsy and me. On the morning of December 26, 1996, we were typical Americans who believed that America was a great country, and we had been blessed by its bounty. In our view, the guilty always went to jail and the innocent didn't. How naive we were! The song that JonBenét used to sing, "God Bless America," was now forever tainted and overshadowed by what we had learned about the potential injustice in this land. When an innocent child is killed in her own home and the response of the justice system is as defective as it had been in JonBenét's case, hope dies as well. A killer, compounded by a defective police department, a rampant Internet gossip system, and an irresponsible news industry willing to print and say anything that makes a story, had destroyed our dreams for the future. Our innocence had died.

On Monday, October 11, John and I had decided that we must return to Colorado immediately in anticipation of the jury's decision. To complicate matters, the media was hunting for us like we were their only story. Regardless of what it took, we needed to be in Boulder, ready to turn ourselves in if an indictment came down.

John worked out a plan with Mike Archuleta to fly one of his charter airplanes to Chattanooga, Tennessee, to meet us the next morning. We picked Chattanooga because we were certain the media would be watching for us at the Atlanta airports. John's brother drove us the two hours from Atlanta to Chattanooga, and we met the plane at Krystal Aviation. Mike's pilot, Chip, had already filed a flight plan listing the destination as Jeffco Airport, but we knew that the media had access to these flight plans. (Another bad aspect of the Internet.)

During the four-and-a-half-hour flight, we had a lot of time to think about what might be facing us. When you start thinking about not being free anymore, things come into perspective. You start to realize the value of freedom and begin to imagine what a horrible experience prison would be, particularly when you are innocent. I wondered how I would find the strength, if that's what was waiting for me in Colorado.

I thought back to something that had happened to my youngest sister, Paulette. Mom always considered Polly to be the most emotionally delicate of the girls in our family. Yet, after JonBenét's death Polly had turned out to be the most composed of the three of us. The unexpected calmness was the result of something very unusual that had happened on the morning of December 26, 1996, as the Paugh family gathered at my parents' home in Roswell, Georgia, waiting for information on what was unfolding in Boulder.

Mom, Dad, my sisters, and their families were highly distraught. They hugged each other and tried to offer support and comfort as they waited by the telephone. No one knew what would happen, and they were as terrified as we were in Boulder. While my sisters paced the floor, Polly's husband, Grant, sat down and started reading the Bible, seeking guidance and direction. As people talked of different aspects of the kidnapping, Polly walked over to the Christmas tree and pulled off two small angel ornaments. She walked through the house from the kitchen into the sunroom, looking at the angels she was holding. Suddenly an awesome presence settled around her.

Polly realized that the Holy Spirit was abruptly doing something unique and special. At that moment Grant looked up and said later that he saw a brilliant light radiating around her. Polly stared straight ahead as an unexpected sight filled her mind. JonBenét was running toward her through a field of tall grass and wildflowers, her hair blowing in the wind.

"Hi, Aunt Polly!" JonBenét called and waved. "Tell everyone I'm all right." She kept smiling and waving.

Polly stared. She had never seen JonBenét look more beautiful. Polly blinked several times and felt overwhelmed as she watched her niece.

A few seconds later the phone had rung, jarring Polly out of her extraordinary experience. Polly listened in stunned silence as John told my family that JonBenét had been found and that she was dead.

As time went by, Polly often thought about what had happened to us and tried to make sense out of this very unusual experience. She came to the conclusion that God had done something special in her life because she was the weakest of the sisters. Yet the experience did something extraordinary: Polly was the only one of us who didn't have to struggle with depression or grief. Within her soul, she believed that she had definitely seen JonBenét in heaven. Her experience always strengthened me when I became depressed during these rough moments.

As we approached the Denver area, Patsy and I worried that the media might have learned we were en route and be awaiting our arrival. So we canceled the flight plan and made a last-minute diversion to Erie, Colorado, where there was a small landing strip. Large private airplanes don't usually land in

Erie's small airport. When the King Air 200 touched down, it created a bit of a stir with the local guys who hang around watching the planes. (I know, I've been a plane-watcher myself many times.) One of the local "hang-arounders" came up to inspect the airplane and was standing right in front of the door when we needed to exit. Chip had to encourage him to look at the front of the airplane so we could sneak out the back. Whatever the media might have expected, it appeared that we had outsmarted them. No one was in Erie, waiting with cameras—that, at least, was good. We quickly sped away for Mike Archuleta's house in Boulder.

After we got settled there late Tuesday afternoon, Mike wanted to take us out to a Mexican restaurant for supper. We really wanted to go, because this could be our last supper in a restaurant for some time (and we love Mexican food), but we decided it wasn't a wise thing to do. We had Pasta Jay's pizza delivered instead.

As the evening progressed, Mike turned on the television, and we started watching the commentary on the grand jury. The talking heads speculated about what Patsy and I might or might not do, and we listened to the whole bizarre spectrum of opinion—from where we might be hiding to whether we would run if indicted. The idea of sitting at ground zero and preparing to present ourselves to the jailer, while news commentators surmised that we were probably fleeing the country, left me with a strange "from another planet" feeling.

Abruptly Alex Hunter appeared on the television screen and said he would be making an announcement the next day. Our initial understanding was that he would speak in the morning. Later it was announced that Hunter's statement would not be made until the late afternoon. We had no choice but to wait and see what followed. We seemed to always be waiting . . . waiting . . . waiting, and every painful minute seemed like hours.

The next morning, October 13, we were trying to determine what was going on. We figured we would probably be arrested first and then the DA would make an announcement of the fact. Announcing on television that someone was about to be arrested would generally not be done because it would serve as a warning for the suspect to flee. Surely Hunter wouldn't do that. Every once in a while the doorbell would ring, and we'd wonder if the Boulder police had arrived to take us away.

Throughout the day we tried to joke about spending time in the slammer. Humor can be good medicine, even if it's forced. Patsy asked if she would be allowed to bring her favorite pillow with her to jail. She joked that the black-and-white stripes on her prison uniform would have to be vertical; horizontal stripes would make her look fat.

The early afternoon hours seemed to drag by slowly. I paced back and forth and Patsy tried to read a bit, but both of us found it hard to concentrate. Finally, we sat down together in front of the television. Hunter's announcement would be made momentarily. We held hands and thanked God for his comfort and strength as we felt very much at peace. It was a wonderful feeling—the peace that passes understanding.

Hunter walked to a microphone and made a terse statement. "The Boulder County grand jury has completed its work and will not return," he said. "No charges have been filed."

As we heard Hunter's words, we squeezed each other's hands.

"I must report to you that I and my prosecutorial team believe we do not have sufficient evidence to warrant the filing of charges against anyone who has been investigated at this time," Hunter concluded.

I couldn't believe my ears. The battered justice system had creaked and shuddered, but it had worked! *We had not been indicted!*

Patsy hugged me and we stood there in relief, staring at the television screen. People would have to finally see the jury's decision as our vindication. I was so choked up, I was about ready to cry. We weren't going to jail!

Needless to say, we were extremely relieved. Even though it was wonderful to be in the home of our friends the Archuletas, we wanted to get out of Boulder as quickly as possible. But I realized we hadn't made any plans for returning to Atlanta. We were so mentally prepared for indictment, we simply hadn't thought about the possibility of being free to leave!

We quickly decided we wanted to drive to Colorado Springs before we left Colorado. We'd been unable to speak with Lou Smit since June of 1998 because of police politics and then an order forbidding him to do so during the grand jury tenure. Now that the grand jury was finished, we could have an open, full discussion with him. We wanted Lou's perspective on what we needed to do to get the investigation going again. Whatever time had been lost with the grand jury hearing must be made up quickly.

As we were getting our things together, a van pulled up in Mike's driveway. Out jumped a camera crew, and they started running up the driveway. Instantly I ducked behind a wall. I certainly didn't want these people to catch us, after all we had done to remain out of sight.

Mike answered the door and then sat in his living room and gave an interview to Dan Abrams of MSNBC about his perspective on the outcome of the grand jury. Of course, Abrams had no idea that we were only a few feet away. After MSNBC left, another television crew pulled up, but Mike kept them outside. Mike later joked that when Abrams asked him how the Ramseys felt about the outcome, he should have said, "Hey, they're sitting in the other room. Let's go and ask 'em!"

Finally we were able to leave undetected and started south. We had called Lou Smit earlier and asked if we could meet with him. Lou agreed, and we met at a motel on the highway between Denver and Colorado Springs at Castle Rock. Lou's house had been surrounded by the media, but he had also been able to get out of town without a tail. He brought his wife, Barbara. We had known about her struggle with cancer and were glad to see her. For the next couple of hours Lou gave us important insights on where we ought to go in our search for the killer. He emphasized that ultimately the Boulder police would have to be the ones who would catch him. Somehow we needed to get them on the right track. I felt we could now get back in gear and start going down the right path. Finally!

Patsy and I had planned to rent a car at the Colorado Springs airport and drive at least part way back to Atlanta. We didn't want to risk getting on the airlines, only to be delivered to a waiting bank of cameras at the other end. We'd experienced that one too many times already.

When we arrived at the airport, we rented a car from Alamo. Using a lesser-known company bothered me a bit, because we were going to drop off the car in Tulsa, Oklahoma, but it was the last car available anywhere. We were soon on our way south toward Texas. What a great feeling! By night-fall we were in Trinidad, Colorado, which is a neat little town. We stopped for a great Mexican dinner. (I might like to go back there sometime. On second thought, I don't want to ever go back to Colorado, except to be at the killer's trial.)

Then we drove for several more hours and ended up spending the night in Conway, Texas, in a thirty-nine-dollar roadside motel. It was the best night's sleep both of us had had in ages! The next morning we had a five-star breakfast in the motel diner and headed out east.

Our plan was to drive to Tulsa, drop off the car, and fly on back to Atlanta privately. However, when we started looking for the closest Alamo dealer, I discovered why I had been apprehensive. *Alamo didn't have a car drop in the entire state of Oklahoma!* We were already way out of Texas so we didn't really have any alternative but to continue driving through Oklahoma to leave the car in Little Rock, Arkansas, the nearest Alamo drop point. It took a little shuffling and four or five extra hours of driving, but we worked it all out and by ten that night we had landed at the Marietta airport, just outside of Atlanta.

Never had I been so grateful to be home!

A few days after the grand jury ended, some unknown person spray painted on JonBenét's grave marker, "No justice in the USA." As disgusting as the graffiti was, we suspected it was done by the tabloids. We felt that if the painted inscription showed up in a tabloid photo, we would have a good idea who was responsible. Sure enough, the *Star* soon came out with a big picture of the marker and a tabloid reporter kneeling over JonBenét's grave, marked with the graffiti. They will do anything for a headline.

Well, there had been some justice in America, at least for us. After looking at the evidence—or lack of it—a jury of our peers had not indicted Patsy and me. It seemed the system had functioned as our Constitution had intended. We were truly grateful.

On the media front it was also starting to appear that justice would prevail. Tom Miller, a *Globe* gofer, was indicted for attempted bribery. *Globe* editor Craig Lewis was indicted on bribery and extortion charges. Lewis would now have to explain to a court why he offered an envelope with thirty thousand dollars in cash to a handwriting expert in Evergreen, Colorado, while trying to persuade him to "share" a copy of the ransom note. The expert had integrity and refused to sell. Lewis's lawyers are also trying to keep him from having to explain his reported attempts to "blackmail" former detective Steve Thomas in exchange for inside information. The crimes charged against Lewis involve the buying and selling of confidential information for illegal or improper purposes. Other indictments may follow, and the cavalier approach to information gathering taken by the print and broadcast media may finally be thoroughly examined in court.

Patsy and I have endured three years of slanderous insults from the media, the police, and the political leaders of various institutions of the state of Colorado. We have been investigated and maligned, perhaps more than any other individuals in the history of this country. If we do not attempt to hold these groups accountable, how can we expect the future climate to improve for our children and theirs?

33

ANOTHER YEAR GOES BY . . .

So much has happened in the past year since the grand jury concluded and yet so little progress has been made. After thirteen long months of looking at all the evidence presented by the special prosecutors and police, the Boulder grand jury said no to an indictment. It takes a mountain of evidence to convict, but only a paltry amount of evidence to indict. Yet in the eyes of the grand jurors, even that did not exist. Nor was there anything in our backgrounds that would indicate even the slightest potential for such a horrendous crime. The police were devastated.

Of course, in the months that followed the grand jury's secret decision, there was much speculation by the media on what the grand jury really did conclude. To suggest that it voted to indict and that the D.A. refused to go along, as some of the media speculated, is pure folly. If that had been the case, the police would certainly have leaked it to the media before the grand jurors even arrived home.

We know now that Michael Kane, the lead special prosecutor, had what can only be described as an obsession to indict us. Kane was at the beck and call of the Boulder police and was therefore the kind of prosecutor the cops love.

In hindsight, I guess, we should have seen Michael Kane coming. When he arrived on the scene in May 1998, regular prosecutors who had worked full-time on the case for sixteen months were pushed aside and not allowed to have any further involvement. Sixteen months of knowledge and hard work were summarily discarded.

The United States has become a country that is devaluing the concept of justice because of a growing number of unqualified and undertrained police who are too eager to make arrests, overzealous prosecutors who seek to win cases at any cost, and politicians who use a "tough on crime" message to garner votes. Of course, the media is right in the thick of it, using the justice process as made-for-TV entertainment.

The Boulder police, following the grand jury conclusion, continued to focus on our family to the exclusion of all others. Trying to break into their frozen minds has proven to be virtually impossible. For example, in January 2000, we requested that the Boulder police and the special prosecutors meet several well-respected medical experts to discuss what they had concluded after examining the medical facts of JonBenét's death. We were devastated when the special prosecutors and the police insulted such highly regarded professionals by refusing to meet with them. A wealth of credible information was being offered to them, no strings attached. Their minds were locked shut out of fear of the possibility of hearing something that threatened their conclusion. Winston Churchill called this type of rigid consistency "the hobgoblin of small minds."

The months following the conclusion of the grand jury were spent working on our book. The initial release of *The Death of Innocence* was scheduled for March 2000. We had a lot to do in a short amount of time, but the book was very important to us. We wanted to tell our story as only we could tell it. We wanted people to know the real JonBenét, not what the media had made her out to be. We wanted to expose the horrible faults of the Boulder justice system, and above all, we wanted to find the killer by spreading the word and keeping the case alive.

To promote the book, we would have to appear publicly. We were not anxious to do so and insisted that this be as limited as possible. At the advice of our publisher, we agreed to do our first interviews with Barbara Walters and Katie Couric. Colorado's Governor Owens would later criticize these two women journalists by saying that we should have been interviewed by a male television personality. A man would have been tougher on us, according to Owens. (I wonder what Owen's female constituency thought of that remark?) He might feel differently if *he* had to spend six hours being questioned by Ms. Walters and Ms. Couric.

We arrived in New York the evening before the Barbara Walters interview. The next morning we were taken to a large old house in Manhattan that ABC had selected for the taping. The crew was already set up when we walked in, and we were shocked at what we saw. We expected a camera, microphones, and a couple of chairs. What we found were at least thirty technicians, ten cameras, and an extensive control room, all set up on a temporary basis in this big old house. It looked to us like preparations for a Super Bowl telecast. Knowledgeable people had told us that this first interview was worth millions of dollars to the networks. Unlike some of their other guests, we were never paid a penny.

Barbara Walters' production, to be aired on *20/20,* was well orchestrated. She was polished and very clearly in control. To top it off, she seemed to genuinely know about the case. It was obvious to us that she hadn't just walked in and been handed a script. At one point during the interview, Barbara Walters said, "Did the Boulder police ever ask you to take a lie detector test?" We both answered an emphatic no. Then, of course, Walters' follow-up question was, "Would you take one?" We both automatically answered, "Yes, of course."

We discovered in these first television interviews, as well as all the subsequent media interviews, that we would be repeatedly challenged to defend our every action and, in fact, ourselves. Each interview was almost like a police interrogation all over again. It was as if the interviewers felt they had to be "hard" on the Ramseys or they wouldn't be credible. Even the Christian television show, the *700 Club,* couldn't resist billing us as "perhaps the world's most hated couple."

A few days later on CNN's *Larry King Live,* we were asked to elaborate on whether we would actually submit to a polygraph. We told Larry that we would most certainly take a polygraph but that we would expect it to be fair, independent, and conducted by someone of national repute. We said we would also expect the results to be made public.

Within days, in response to our comments, the police released a public statement saying that they would take us up on our offer to take a lie detector test but the FBI must administer it. Already the battle lines were drawn. Our civil attorney, Lin Wood, responded that we had said "independent" and we meant independent. We would gladly have put the names of six qualified, truly independent polygraphers in a hat and drawn one at random, but the FBI had been anything but independent from the Boulder police. Detective Steve Thomas even disclosed in his book that the FBI's Child Abduction and Serial Killer Unit, headed by Agent William Hagmaier, had been egging the police on in their vendetta against us.

Lin Wood reminded us that it was the FBI who tried to illegally trick Richard Jewell into participating in a so-called "training video" on how to deal with suspicious packages in order to get him to unknowingly waive his right to counsel and be interrogated without a lawyer present. It was also the FBI that erroneously "profiled" Jewell as someone who might create an incident in order to be praised as a hero. The government can be very dangerous when it empowers less than competent people to wield its vast power. It is extremely dangerous when it is out to "get" somebody. Lin told us that he did not let Richard Jewell take an FBI polygraph and he would not let us do so either.

As if in answer to our prayers, we received several letters from former FBI polygraphers who told us to stay away from the FBI; its sole purpose was to "interrogate the hell out of you" and shake us up so much that the tests would indicate deception. A former state attorney general even wrote to tell us that under no circumstances should we participate in a FBI "test." The FBI, he said, only uses polygraph tests to interrogate and intimidate.

Since it was apparent the Boulder police were only interested in an FBI interrogation, Lin Wood contacted a former FBI official he knew to get recommendations of highly qualified, fair polygraphers who were located relatively close to Atlanta. Jerry Toriello was recommended. In our polygraphs with Mr. Toriello, both Patsy and I tested "inconclusive but tending toward truthfulness." We didn't understand why the tests were inconclusive when we were telling the truth. This was disappointing and frustrating.

There are several categories of polygraph results based on a complex scoring system. "Truthful" is the top category and is the strongest result. The next score is "Inconclusive but tending toward truthfulness." The next is "Inconclusive but tending toward deception," and the lowest result is "Deceptive." The only meaningful results to a polygrapher are "Truthful" or "Deceptive." "Inconclusive" indicates that the tests produced no meaningful results. "Inconclusive" results can be due to a number of extraneous factors such as physical movements, mental or physical fatigue, anxiety, or animated gestures. They can also be a result of the choice of questions asked by the examiner. The media, true to its previous track record, reported that Patsy had "failed" the first two tests. This was totally incorrect.

Putting aside geographic proximity as a criterion, Lin decided to find out who the experts thought was the best polygrapher in the business. Everyone agreed that he should call Dr. Edward I. Gelb of Los Angeles. Gelb is the foremost polygrapher in the country, having administered over 30,000 tests in his career. Past president of the American Polygraph Association (APA), he regularly trains law enforcement agencies and has been honored with three major awards from the APA. We later learned that the APA made an offer to the Boulder police to furnish an independent examiner for our test and *its* first choice was Dr. Gelb.

Before approaching Dr. Gelb, Lin had also made an offer to the Boulder police suggesting Gelb as a possible compromise. After all, Dr. Gelb's credentials are impeccable and no honest person could challenge his integrity. Above all, why would he risk his world-renowned reputation on the Ramseys? Dr. Gelb is honest, qualified, experienced, and truly independent. I guess that explains why the Boulder police rejected him.

Dr. Gelb explained that it was very important that polygraph questions not contain multiple issues, such as "Did you arrive home at 10:00 P.M. and did you take the money from the cash drawer?" Our earlier tests had contained multiple issue questions that Dr. Gelb felt might have been the reason the results, while not indicating deception, nevertheless were inconclusive. To insure complete clarity, Gelb's polygraph tests were developed around three single-issue questions:

"Did you administer the injuries that resulted in JonBenét's death?"

"Do you know who did administer the injuries that caused JonBenét's death?"

Patsy was also asked, "Did you write the ransom note?"

These were not the only questions asked of us during the examination, however. Each session lasted for several hours and included a long question-and-answer period before we were actually connected to the electronic polygraph equipment. The entire polygraph process is much more complicated than either of us had previously understood. A very methodical process for the examination ensures that answers are focused on key issues and don't get "muddied" by poorly worded questions. Consequently, a skilled examiner can be very certain of the results. The tests can be either hand scored or computer scored. Dr. Gelb scored our tests both ways.

Because Dr. Gelb knew these test results would be challenged, prior to releasing them he contacted Mr. Cleve Backster to blind score the tests, as a quality control measure. Seventy-six-year-old Backster is considered the "Father of Modern Polygraphy," having developed the zone comparison polygraph procedure that is now the standard used worldwide. He has taught polygraph procedures and techniques to hundreds of law enforcement agencies, including the FBI and the CIA.

A few days later, Backster informed Dr. Gelb that his blind-scoring analysis was in full agreement with Gelb's scoring of our tests. In fact, he had scored our results even higher than Dr. Gelb. Our tests results showed we had responded truthfully when we answered an emphatic no to each of the three key crime questions. It was the professional opinion of both Gelb and Backster that our truthful answers were conclusive when we said we had nothing to do with JonBenét's murder.

We announced the results of the polygraph examinations at a press conference on May 25, 2000, to a large gathering of media assembled in Atlanta. Dr. Gelb and Mr. Backster were there because they had full confidence in their results and they felt strongly that a great injustice had been done to us. But even these two experts were not prepared for the hostile and skeptical reaction to their test results.

One of the two Boulder police PR persons (yes, they actually have two PR people) publicly discredited the test results as "meaningless"—even before the results had been announced. The TV talking heads were all saying that these tests really didn't mean anything since they were "self-sponsored." *Rocky Mountain News* columnist Bill Johnson wrote a highly unfair and inflammatory piece headlined "Ramsey's paid, so of course they pass." This is the kind of media libel that has contributed so much to the viciousness that has been unleashed on our family.

Adams County District Attorney Bob Grant, who has been the Boulder DA's TV spokesman throughout this case, made the rounds of the talk shows saying that polygraph tests are "easily beatable. . . . You can learn responses." Police Chief Beckner said taking the tests from Dr. Gelb may have ruined any chances for the Ramseys to take a polygraph that would be meaningful to the police because taking "too many polygraph tests can ruin the reliability of future tests." Steve Thomas declared authoritatively that it was "too late" for a polygraph to work.

Real polygraph experts will tell you all of these claims are completely false. In fact, people can't improve their chances of passing by practicing. Taking more tests cannot ruin the reliability of the results. Test results only get worse for a guilty person with repeated testing, and taking the test one week after or twenty years later will not change the results. Dr. Gelb explained, "The clean get cleaner and the dirty get dirtier."

Ironically, no one was critical of Dr. Gelb or Mr. Backster. No one dared question their credentials. The media and the FBI knew they were the best and couldn't be bought, as the *Rocky Mountain News* reporter had so flippantly charged. We wondered what all these talking heads and the police would have said had we *failed* the tests?

Confirming our suspicions, a source inside the Boulder justice system told us that it was a good thing that we had refused to take the FBI polygraph as demanded by the Boulder police. "It was a total setup," it was confided.

On May 31, 2000, we again appeared on CNN's *Larry King Live;* this time to confront, face-to-face, our primary accuser, former Boulder policeman Steve Thomas. Thomas had become a momentary TV celebrity and author. Boulder DA Alex Hunter said it well when he described Thomas as one who "had never handled a homicide case, and wasn't a very experienced detective, even in narcotics". . . . He was "mostly a patrol officer during his stay at the Boulder Police Department."

Thomas had written a gossipy, tell-all book and by doing so violated the most basic code of conduct for a professional police officer. He used access to confidential case material in order to cashin personally. DA Hunter reportedly described Thomas as a tormented soul whose motivation was financial. "This is just pure-and-simple blood money," he said.

This appearance on Larry King was the most distasteful media appearance I have ever experienced. I was so angry with Thomas because of all the harm he had caused my family, I could barely stand to be in the same room with him. Patsy was more comfortable with confronting Thomas and told him she honestly felt sorry for him and his single-minded blindness to the truth. Talking with Thomas was like talking to a mechanical robot. There is an old axiom that "one should never argue with a fool in public" and now I know why! Patsy kept trying to get him to tell her and the audience what he thought actually happened the night JonBenét was murdered. Even Larry King pushed Thomas to tell everyone what he thought had happened, step by step. But Thomas just couldn't do it. All he was able to say, five times, was his memorized mantra challenging us to talk about our "convoluted, sex-crime, pedophile, kidnapper-turned-murderer theory." Without looking at Patsy, he stammered, "I think you're good for it."

It was interesting that the only public comment made by Chief Beckner regarding his former detective writing a book about an ongoing case was that his book would probably have more detail than the Ramsey book. (Was that an endorsement?)

According to Thomas, and confirmed by our recent exposure to the police and prosecutors, the police theory is that on the night of December 25, 1996, Patsy went to bed with her clothes and makeup on, was somehow awakened, and found that JonBenét had wet her bed. In a fit of rage, Patsy accidentally killed JonBenét by struggling with her in the bathroom and causing her to fall and strike her head and then, to make it *look* like an intruder killed JonBenét, staged an elaborate cover-up by strangling her with a professional-style garrote, writing a three-page ransom note virtually disguising her handwriting to even the most skilled expert, and then going back to bed to await the morning. According to their theory, she also was able to leave stun gun marks on several locations on JonBenét's body and plant still unidentified male DNA under her fingernails and in her underwear.

Logical, thinking people can't believe this is actually the

cops' theory—but it is! They came up with this bizarre story-line within days of Jon Benét's murder. There is absolutely no evidence of bed-wetting that night, because it didn't happen. The police have known all along the sheets had no trace of urine and had obviously been recently slept in. Fibers from the cord used to tie JonBenét's arms were found on the bed-sheets. Despite the amount of tangible evidence indicating an intruder, to accuse a mother of murdering her young child be-cause she wet the bed is an insult beyond measure to any par-ent.

Of course, you recall, the other Boulder detective originally working this case, Linda Arndt, appeared for five straight days on a nationally televised morning show (just before the grand jury was expected to vote) to publicize *her* theory that I was the killer—talk about jury tampering! The announcer introduced the highly publicized segment by calling Arndt the "one who could now tell us what really happened in the Ram-sey house that night." She stated that when she saw JonBenét lying dead on the living room floor, her mind "exploded." She "saw black with thousands of lights" and could see in my eyes that I had murdered my child. Thomas and Arndt. Two cops. Two theories. Both theories formed totally independent of the evidence and the facts.

The most hurtful thing Steve Thomas did was to disgrace JonBenét by using her beautiful name as the title of his slan-derous book. We truly felt he had stolen something from us to which he had no right. Despite all the books that have been written on the subject, no one had stooped so low as to use JonBenét's name as the main title. I guess Thomas has suc-cumbed to what the media has known for four years: Jon-Benét sells.

During this appearance on the King show, we said we were still willing to sit down with the Boulder authorities. Chief Beck-ner had recently stated that the police had new questions about new information that had surfaced since our interviews in June 1998. Surprisingly, the police never asked to meet with us in over two years and didn't even bother to subpoena us before the grand jury. Based on their refusal to meet with the medical ex-perts we had assembled, we assumed they were unwilling and uninterested in meeting with us and our very experienced in-vestigators. Could the police be turning over a new leaf?

"Would you meet again with Beckner and the cops?" King asked. We said that we would gladly welcome the opportunity to bring our investigators and theirs together with us for a roundtable discussion to get everyone's questions answered. It was something we had asked for in the past. This response started the next round of confrontation with the police, to the media's delight.

A few days later, a terse letter from Chief Beckner arrived, requesting yet another interrogation, not a meeting, and instructing us to respond within three days. During our subsequent telephone conversation with Chief Beckner, one of the special prosecutors seemed to be threatening us by suggesting that if we didn't submit to these new interrogations, they would subpoena us before a new grand jury. We were to be grilled by seven interrogators. (Lin Wood said it sounded like a firing squad to him.) They were adamant that we be questioned separately with no time limits. Patsy must go first, Beckner insisted; otherwise it was a "deal breaker." They insisted the interviews be videotaped, "for evidence," as Chief Beckner candidly admitted. Our investigators, Ollie Gray and John San Agustin, would be allowed to sit in the room, but could not ask any questions.

Despite serious doubts on our part about what their objectives really were, it would be the first time Chief Beckner had been willing to meet with us. Perhaps a face-to-face meeting would make him realize they were "barking up the wrong tree," as John Douglas, the best-known crime profiler in the country, had told them several years ago. We agreed to all their conditions and told them we were available immediately.

The police and special prosecutors were finally ready for the interrogation on August 28, six weeks after our appearance on *Larry King Live*. They arrived at nine A.M. to a barrage of media cameras outside Lin Wood's downtown Atlanta office building. After a few pleasantries, the questioning began. Patsy went first, as Chief Beckner demanded.

The police participated very little in the questioning. On the other hand, the special prosecutors came with a well-rehearsed sequence, which seemed designed to discredit us for the benefit of the camera and whoever would ultimately "study" our verbal and physical reactions (probably those independent guys at the FBI). For example, almost a hundred questions were asked of Patsy about her concern for Burke's security after JonBenét was murdered. The intent of this questioning was to somehow prove that Patsy wasn't concerned about Burke's security at all, because she knew there really wasn't a murderer out there. Michael Kane clearly could not disguise his insulting insinuations about Patsy and the network of volunteer moms and dads that our friends had arranged to carry out the "Burke Watch." These wonderful parents took shifts throughout the day at High Peaks Elementary School so that someone was watching Burke at all times. They were equipped with an elaborate emergency response security system that we had paid to have installed in the school prior to Burke's return. This gave us comfort and still allowed Burke some freedom to return to his school. Michael Kane further challenged Patsy about these parents when he asked skeptically, "Were these people trained in self-defense?"

That is when Lin Wood stopped Kane and said, "What in the world does this have to do with finding the killer of Jon-Benét?" Kane erupted and got up to storm out of the room, claiming that Lin was obstructing justice and this whole interview was a "sham." It was a sham, all right, conducted by the government at the expense of the Colorado taxpayers and us!

We took a break and the other members of the "Boulder Seven" persuaded Michael Kane to calm down and continue with the questioning. Patsy spent a total of eight hours over two days in front of the firing squad from Boulder. She patiently answered all of their questions even though they nearly all seemed to be rehashing old ground. As she later commented in a *USA Today* article, "It became readily apparent that it was all about me."

Soon after Patsy left the conference room, I entered and sat down across from the now six interrogators. (Prosecutor Mitch Morrissey had returned to Colorado the previous evening.) I was asked questions about events that had taken place over three years ago. Did I get JonBenét ready for bed that night? Yes. Did I remove her underwear? No. Kane then slipped into a different line of questioning. He questioned the foundation we established to honor JonBenét and accused us of sponsoring fund-raisers. How much money was in the Jon-Benét Ramsey Children's Foundation bank account? What was the highest balance?

I explained to him that we set up the foundation to honor JonBenét with the intent of doing good works in her name, and we hoped to fund it handsomely with proceeds from civil libel suits against the tabloid media. We had no intention of soliciting money from the public. In fact, IRS rules do not permit active solicitation of money under our tax-exempt private foundation status.

I did lash out at Kane and criticize him for continuing to ridicule the foundation, as I knew he had already spent countless hours investigating it during the grand jury proceedings. We had set up a similar charitable foundation in my daughter Beth's name when she died in 1992. I suppose for grieving parents it is a way to keep their child's memory alive. To be held in such suspicion for this was quite unbelievable and only added to my contempt for the Boulder justice system.

I was prepared to undergo questioning as long as the police and prosecutors wanted. After about an hour and a half, they looked at each other and Bruce Levin, the only prosecutor remaining, said, "Well, I guess that's it. No more questions."

Just like that? It was over? That was all they had for me?

Michael Kane had earlier dashed out the door to catch his noon flight back to Pennsylvania. The others made references to running to catch the flights they had booked back to Colorado.

As Patsy, Lin, and I were saying good-bye to Chief Mark Beckner, he made a casual, yet seemingly preplanned comment: "Well, we actually had a lot of questions that we didn't get answered." Wham! We were being set up! Even Lin was caught off guard.

Lin challenged Beckner: "How could you say you have more questions after you told us you were completely finished and half of your inquisitors have already rushed out the door?" Instead of thanking us for meeting with them voluntarily and hopefully setting the stage for further cooperation, he was simply setting the stage for another smear of the Ramseys. I could just see the next day's headlines: "Ramseys refuse to answer all the questions!"

Sure enough, that was the public spin the police would put on the interrogations within hours of leaving Atlanta. Unfortunately for the police, the transcript of the conclusion of Patsy's interrogation supports quite a different story.

MR. BECKNER: Anybody got anything else?
MR. LEVIN: I do not.
MR. WOOD: Okay, are you all done with Patsy?
MR. LEVIN: We are. Thank you, ma'am.
MRS. RAMSEY: Thank you so much.

We had given the police our trust again, and once again, they forfeited it. Deceive me once, shame on you. Deceive me twice, shame on me!

While the police continue to investigate us, Boulder continues to be plagued with bizarre attacks on girls and women. In 1997, a serial rapist stalked the south part of town, striking virtually at will. One of the local news organizations criticized the Boulder police for "serial incompetence" since they couldn't seem to lay a hand on this dangerous criminal. They did finally arrest a man and put his picture on the front page of the *Boulder Daily Camera,* but later they had to recant and admit that this poor soul was innocent. Too bad the police had already ruined his reputation.

Highly significant was information exposed in August 2000 through the efforts of journalists Charlie Brennan and Frank Coffman. This information appears to have been intentionally kept from the grand jury prosecutors and the public by the Boulder police for almost three years.

In September 1997, nine months after JonBenét was murdered, an intruder attacked a young girl at 3 A.M. in her bedroom in Boulder, while the mother was asleep in the house. The man entered the house sometime before 11 P.M. when the burglar alarm was set. He waited, quietly hidden in the house, for over four hours until he was sure all were asleep. After creeping into the child's bedroom, he began to sexually assault her. He covered her mouth and told her that he knew her name and not to scream or he would "knock her out." Thankfully, he was interrupted by the girl's mother, whose room was nearby and she sprayed him with mace. He fled through the house, into the mother's bedroom, where he exited through French doors onto a lower roof and jumped to the ground. All this occurred within two miles of our home in Boulder. Similarities to our case? You bet.

1. He waited for hours in the house until the family went to bed and were asleep. We stated early on that we be-

lieved this is what happened the night JonBenét was assaulted and murdered. People in authority scoffed at us. "Who would do that?" they asked.

2. He knew the layout of the house well.
3. He sexually attacked the girl and threatened to knock her unconscious if she made a noise. The final act of JonBenét's killer was to violently strike her in the head.
4. The police reported there was no sign of forced entry, just as they had reported in JonBenét's case.
5. This young girl and JonBenét had both performed publicly in Boulder in the fall of 1996, and they attended the same dance school on Pearl Street.

Does all this sound interesting? It would to any legitimate detective trying to solve a murder and now a possible attempted murder in the same town. Successful criminals rarely change their M.O. (Modus Operandi) and this is usually how police are able to attribute multiple crimes to the same perpetrator. Could this have been the same creature who killed JonBenét? That possibility needs to be examined very seriously. It should have been looked at as a possible link to JonBenét's murder three years ago!

We know for a fact that as of September 2000 the police had never questioned anyone at the dance studio both girls attended. The young girl's parents were so dissatisfied with the Boulder police performance they hired their own private investigator, just as were forced to do.

Chief Beckner quickly brushed aside any possible connection between the two crimes, saying that this couldn't have been the same person who killed JonBenét because there was no ransom note and the girl wasn't killed. He also stated that he could find thousands of cases with similar circumstances. He concluded by saying that whether you thought these two crimes were related depended on your "perspective." Perhaps to be clearer, he should have said it depends on your bias!

In another incident in August 2000, a man was arrested near Denver for repeatedly attacking a young girl with a stun gun in her home. We are now able to prove conclusively that an AirTaser stun gun was used in the attack on JonBenét. The arrested man was charged with attempted murder and held under a million dollar bond. Police in the Highlands Ranch community found cord, duct tape, panty hose, and rubber gloves in a box in his home and theorized that he had other victims. Could one of his other victims have been JonBenét? This known criminal needs to be seriously considered as a suspect in the murder of JonBenét because of the stun gun if for no other reason. Based on previous performance, we can only assume that the Boulder police will do all they can to refute any possible connection. I hope we are wrong.

As frustrating as it is, life goes on for our family. What is our alternative? We try to lead as "normal" a life as possible, whatever that has come to mean now. We try to get some enjoyment out of things although it feels like we're just going through the motions.

We attended Patsy's 25th high school reunion in Parkersburg, West Virginia, over the summer. JonBenét had been with us at her 20th reunion, so even this visit was difficult for us. We didn't go to the family picnic as we had five years ago because it would have been too hard for us without JonBenét. Instead, we attended a gathering of friends planned by Linda McLean and some of Patsy's former teachers. Many friends and classmates were there and brought along old photos and notes of support to leave behind in a "Memory Basket." One man brought in his old yearbook for Patsy to sign. Even her former high school principal dropped by to say hello and lend his hometown support. The get-together meant a lot to us even though the media was waiting outside with their cameras to catch us on tape. The local newspaper had incorrectly reported that we would not be going to the dance that evening so we were able to go and have a great time, sans media.

Since JonBenét's death, we have been asked to speak to various groups including churches and universities. We try to accommodate as many as we can and are eager to talk about our experience with the justice system, the problems in the media, how faith endures a tremendous tragedy, and family security in a dangerous world. Patsy has been able to talk to a number of people about fighting ovarian cancer. I know she has been an encouragement to many women experiencing the same killer disease she faced.

The most consistently asked question is: "How do you go on?" People tell us that they don't think that, under the same circumstances, they could have survived the loss of a child to murder, the indictment in the press, financial devastation, and the outrageous police misconduct.

We respond that even though we have seen the underbelly of humanity since JonBenét's murder, we have also seen the good, as well. We get dozens of e-mails and letters each day, the vast majority of which are thoughtful, compassionate, apologetic, and supportive. They almost all begin by asking for our forgiveness because they believed we were guilty based on what the media and the police had told them. We are overwhelmed by the good people in this world who have come forward and reached out to us. That gives us faith in humanity.

Ultimately, we tell them, the only way you can go on is to have hope for the future. For a long time after JonBenét's death we felt as if we had no hope. We had lost our precious child, we had lost our home, our life's savings, and the Boulder police continued to pursue us with blind vengeance. When you have no hope at all, life becomes nearly unbearable to face.

Hope doesn't come from money or possessions, as so much of our culture ascribes. These things can be destroyed in a moment. Over time, the immense grief, which has been so physically debilitating, begins to subside and we realize that a faint flicker of hope still burns within us. It had been there all along, just smoldering in our tears. Lifesaving hope comes from realizing that this difficult and flawed world is not all there is to live for. We have two futures ahead of us: our immediate future, and our infinite future throughout eternity with Christ. We understand that now, better than ever. With this eternal perspective, we take things one day at a time.

The Boulder police seem to be content to let us twist in the wind under their umbrella of suspicion for the rest of our lives. If we are lucky, perhaps the killer will confess or confide in someone who will come forward. Perhaps the dedicated men and women who are working independent of the Boulder police will be successful. Or, perhaps, sadly, this killer will kill again and be brought to justice by a more objective police department. Perhaps public outrage will bring pressure on the police to drop their witch-hunt and go back to square one and try to find the killer. We take some measure of comfort knowing that ultimately, this subhuman creature will come face-to-face with a mighty God, who is the final judge.

*   *   *

August 6, 2000. JonBenét's birthday.

Although John and I tell ourselves that these special days are no more or less difficult than any other day, in reality, the day of JonBenét's birth and the day of her death *are* more difficult. I lie in bed much longer than normal this morning. Perhaps it's the cool gray Michigan sky that is so typical in the immediate aftermath of a passing cold front, even in the summer. Last night we had a soft rain, one where you could smell the moisture in the air. Peaceful really. I had gone to bed last night knowing that today would be more difficult.

We wanted to do something special on JonBenét's birthday. She would have been ten years old. I kept thinking about how I had promised her she could get her ears pierced when she turned ten. We decided to buy some flowers and plant them around the big rock that now marks Lake JonBenét in Charlevoix. Kind friends at Vidosh nursery in Charlevoix arranged to move the five-ton rock we selected as a marker to a special spot near the small lake so it would be in place before her birthday. We picked this rock because it was pinkish in color and flat on top and because it reminded us of how much JonBenét always liked to climb on similar big rocks in the children's playground area of the outdoor Pearl Street Mall in Boulder.

We talked about having a dedication of some sort for the rock but in the end decided to just take along our good friends Chip and Vicki Emery and plant the flowers. Vicki lovingly placed a child-size wrought iron table and two chairs next to the rock—a perfect setting for an angel tea party. It made us feel a bit better. It made me feel closer to JonBenét even though my heart was breaking. My tears silently watered the tender plants as we dug in the dirt. Lake JonBenét is a beautiful spot that will be there for generations to come to remember a sweet child who touched the hearts of people around the world. It made the day special and we felt as if we had honored JonBenét, in a small way.

Happy Birthday, Joni'B. Mommy hopes angels wear pierced earrings in heaven.

34

THE MURDERER

As you've considered JonBenét's murder, perhaps you've wondered if her killer ever walked past your doorstep. What would he look like? Disheveled hair, dark eyes, pockmarked face? Or neatly combed blond hair, blue eyes, and fair complexion? Young or old? How did he act before the murder? How does he act now? Patsy and I know one thing for certain: this deranged assailant of children walks among us, for the moment, undetected by the authorities.

This creature may look perfectly normal on the outside, but on the inside his brain is boiling and in constant turmoil. He may be the quiet neighbor who never said much but always seemed like a nice man. Yet this person is a vicious monster, who by his actions left many clues to his identity, and by his continued actions will identify himself to someone, someday. When that happens, we need that someone to recognize who he is and come forward—hopefully before he kills another innocent child.

The murder of our daughter wasn't his first crime, and it won't be his last. He did not suddenly turn into a monster on the night of December 25 and then return to being a perfectly normal person. His previous crimes and the ones he will commit in the future will help lead us to him.

A rash of "midnight burglaries," as the Boulder police called them, occurred in our part of town in the months just prior to the murder. These burglaries ceased on December 25, 1996. We hope that the police have thoroughly compared all the data from these crimes to the data they have obtained about JonBenét's murder. Could they be related? Possibly.

A man who was working as a house-sitter in the home across the alley from our Boulder house left town shortly after the murder. Was he checked out thoroughly? We don't know. A complete neighborhood canvass was never done.

A young University of Colorado student with blond hair, Susannah Chase, was fatally beaten in the Whittier neighborhood of Boulder on December 21, 1997, almost a year to the day after JonBenét's murder. The morning after Susannah was found, a homeowner called the police department for permission to wash a great deal of blood off the sidewalk in front of his house. Only then did police figure out that Susannah had been assaulted there at Eighteenth and Spruce—where the blood was found—and then dragged to the spot a block away, where her body had been discovered the previous night.

Three weeks later Susannah's close friends were saying that the police had never interviewed them. "I keep reading that statistically (her killer) is someone she knows. Well, you'd think they'd [the Boulder police] be talking to all the other people she knew because it makes sense that they (too) might know the person. They're not," said Jason Breidner, Chase's friend. Susannah's death seemed to have some striking similarities to JonBenét's murder. Sadly, both investigations were overseen by Detective Commander John Eller, and there was poor follow-up. The Boulder police have placed Susannah's investigation on "inactive status" because they have no leads.

Also, in the fall of 1996 Laura Stebe, the lady who kept an eye on our house in Charlevoix when we weren't there, went to the house and found an open, very neatly packed suitcase at the foot of JonBenét's bed. A pair of cowboy boots was sitting beside the suitcase. JonBenét's bed had obviously been slept in. Laura assumed we had given someone permission to use our home after we returned to Colorado. After JonBenét's murder, Laura called this incident to our attention. We had no idea who could have been in our house at that time. Could this intruder be related in some way to JonBenét's murder? Possibly. If someone entered our house and stayed there, why did he pick JonBenét's bed to sleep in? The house had nine beds. More important, who was he? This information was given to the Boulder police, but to our knowledge was never followed up further with Laura. Another suspicious incident in Charlevoix occurred that fall. A man was reported to have observed me in a gas station, and angrily told the attendant that he had "some unfinished business in Colorado."

We've learned that detective work in murder cases is difficult and supremely challenging. It does not happen in the one-hour (minus commercials) murder-mystery format so popular on television. The point is that the killer of JonBenét is not a one-time felon. A criminal of this nature is often responsible for multiple crimes. In Texas recently, a man was convicted of murdering seventeen children over a period of years.

Most people eventually get around to asking us this question: "Who do you think did it?" My response has been the same from the beginning: "We don't know anyone who is capable of being this evil." But after studying all the information that is available to me and listening to experts whose opinions I value (not the so-called TV "experts") and thinking about this every day for the past three years, I believe we are certain of most everything about the killer except his name. We will find that out, as well.

To describe this killer, as I see him, and to theorize about what actually happened to our daughter that night is extremely painful to me. I could not have done this a year ago; it would have been too difficult emotionally. But I do it now because I am committed to finding the killer, and to accomplish that, it is important to talk clinically about the murder.

FIRST, LET'S LOOK AT A DESCRIPTION OF THE KILLER. The murderer is a man. The tremendous blow to JonBenét's head would have required the strength of a man. Further, I believe the killer is a pedophile with a preference for female children. The garrote around JonBenét's neck was most likely part of a sexual fantasy that I have heard referred to as "snuff sex." I'm sorry to learn about these things now and have to put them in this book, but there is evil in the world and we cannot afford to ignore it. Although JonBenét's wrists were tied, her hands were free to move. I'm told this is consistent with sexual bondage situations.

The killer is a psychopath—a person, according to the *American Heritage Dictionary,* with "an antisocial personality disorder, especially one manifested in aggressive, perverted, or criminal behavior." In addition, in contrast to a normal person, his conscience does not operate well, if at all.

He is younger rather than older, and is probably between the ages of twenty-five and thirty-five. He goes to the movies. In fact, he may have seen the movie *Ransom*, which was playing in Boulder shortly before JonBenét's murder. Several of the phrases used in the ransom note came directly from movies, including *Ransom*.

Further, this man is either an ex-con or has been around people who are hardened criminals. He thinks like a criminal. He knew not to bring much with him into the house. He brought the cord and duct tape he used on JonBenét, and then took the remainder with him. As far as we know, he wore gloves. He may be part of a gang or from a foreign country where the use of a garrote would be familiar. The knot making up the garrote was not a simple knot. Whoever tied this complex knot had done it before and knew its purpose well.

After the murder, the killer's strange mannerisms would have been noticeable to those around him. He would have seemed agitated and emotionally upset. He would have taken extreme interest in the case. He watched all the television reports on the murder and read all the newspaper accounts he could find. He talked about the case and espoused his own theories about what happened. In addition, he may have become very religious and reached out for spiritual counsel or assistance in some way.

For some reason known only to the killer and perhaps those closest to him, the number 118 and the letters SBTC had some significance to him. Neither of these were randomly or casually selected by the killer. He may have been jealous of, or angry at, me as well. Maybe I unknowingly crossed him in the business world. Perhaps he hated me because I ran a successful division of Lockheed Martin, a large defense company. Whatever it was, this man may have decided I was a target that could be hit by hurting my child.

Finally, and most important, he had access to a stun gun, and he was in the vicinity of Boulder, Colorado, on December 25, 1996. I'm certain the police have more information in their files that would shed additional light on the killer. The only information I have from the police is what has been given to the media.

Why hasn't this profile already obtained results? From what has been reported in previous chapters, it should be obvious why the investigation of JonBenét's murder has failed so far. In addition, the political posturing as well as the massive media attention and interference created huge problems for the investigation. Public statements from former Colorado Governor Roy Romer in 1998 only added to the chaos and resulted in a complete purging of a number of good people who were quietly, but effectively, trying to find the truth. While we did not have any confidence in the police, we did have faith that the district attorney's investigative team of Smit, Hofstrom, DeMuth, and Ainsworth was objective and committed to finding the killer. However, the media's lynch-mob urgency to hang us seemed to begin building on Romer, and the very public and angry resignation of Steve Thomas from the Boulder police force probably brought matters to a head.

At first we were encouraged to see Romer get involved. We desperately hoped that he would apply the resources of the governor's office to investigate the case and bring the killer to justice. We prayed he would assemble a team of experienced homicide investigators and take the case from the local police. Instead, Romer reacted to the pressure and gave us more attorneys. District Attorney Alex Hunter had no choice but to acquiesce to Romer's demands. As a result, the case was left in the hands of the local police, Hunter's first-string team was banished from the case, and Michael Kane, Mitch Morrissey, and Bruce Levin were brought in. These three attorneys were perhaps great prosecutors, but they had not lived the case for sixteen months like the discarded team.

SECOND, LET'S CONSIDER A SCENARIO OF THE CRIME. What do we believe actually happened the night of December 25, 1996? I believe the killer came into our house while we were at the Whites' for dinner that evening. He could have entered our home in a number of ways. Unfortunately, our old house had many entry and exit points; the first floor alone had six doors leading to the outside and approximately thirty windows.

The killer could have easily watched our house that day, since we lived on a small block bordered by through streets and an alley. It was a very compact, crowded neighborhood. A strange car or strange person would not have drawn any unusual attention. Typically there were always cars parked on the street, and this person could have been in a car near the front of our house for hours without our noticing him. Obviously, if he had been in one of the homes nearby, he could have watched our activities from there.

Somehow the killer knew that we would be gone for a number of hours in the late afternoon and evening on the twenty-fifth. Or perhaps he just knew we were gone and would return later. I believe he entered our house during our absence and was hiding when we returned, possibly in the basement.

Many people have speculated that the killer was familiar with the house. Our home had been open to the public a number of times for various charity events and parties. Around two thousand visitors had streamed through our house during the Christmas 1994 Historic Boulder Homes Tour. It would not have been difficult for the future killer to roam through our place as part of one of those groups, even sneaking downstairs for a look at the basement area or upstairs to find Jon-Benét's room. Our house had been vacant for much of the previous summer when we were in Michigan; a trespasser could have entered the house and literally stayed there for days, and we wouldn't have known it. And the killer had four hours when we were gone during the late afternoon and evening of the twenty-fifth to get a layout of the house if he hadn't done so before then. Or perhaps after we fell asleep he familiarized himself with the house with the aid of a flashlight. A black mag-light type of flashlight was found on the kitchen counter.

On the night of December 25, when we returned home, there was no hint of snow in the air and the driveway, as I remember, was clear. Although the grass had some snow covering, there were bare spots. The grate over the basement window adjoined the stone patio, which almost always was clear, since it got the sun from the south. We know that the basement window was found open on the morning of December 26, and the butler pantry door, which led to the outside, was found unlocked and open. Most likely the killer entered or left by one of these routes. Of course, we don't know exactly what time JonBenét was murdered, but it had to be sometime after we went to sleep around ten o'clock and before we awoke early the next morning around 5:30 A.M.

Experts say that ransom notes are usually what they seem to be; very seldom are they a ploy. The entire setting suggests that the original plan of this man was to kidnap my daughter. In spite of what some of the media have said, I don't believe that the ransom note was coincidental or intended as a decoy. I believe it states the killer's original intentions. The fact that it was written in our home indicates the man was shrewd enough not to have brought the note in with him. If he had been caught, then his purposes would be exposed. He probably had previous experience in this type of break-in and knew exactly what to do. The man cleverly waited in our home until he was sure he hadn't been seen coming in, and then he wrote the note.

As I mentioned earlier, the movie *Ransom* was playing in Boulder around the time of JonBenét's death. The ransom note refers to material that can be found in at least three *Ransom*-type movies and indicates the man was thinking about the possibility of extorting money from us. We were highly visible people, with recent articles about my company's billion-dollar sales figures in the *Boulder Daily Camera*.

The ransom note was written on one of the many note pads we had lying about the house. It was written, I believe, before the killer acted, probably carefully and casually, while we were away at the Whites'. After committing such a horrible act, it is unlikely that anyone would have had the composure to write the note as an afterthought, as the police contend Patsy and I did. Even a hardened serial killer could not do that. He would have been too stimulated by what he had just done. So it had to have been done while we were gone, before the killer moved upstairs to JonBenét's bedroom, or at least before the killing took place. After all, the ransom note was three pages long and the handwriting appears to be in a disguised style, which would have taken much longer to write.

The killer probably crept silently up the rear spiral stairs after we had fallen asleep, and got into JonBenét's bedroom without waking anyone. Quite possibly he silenced her at that time with the stun gun. The coroner referred to the red marks on JonBenét as "abrasions," but in fact the distance between the marks fits the imprint left by a particular brand of stun gun, an Air Taser. This type of weapon is used in two ways: either by firing a probe or by pressing the gun against the skin of the victim and then firing. In either case the victim is instantly shocked with a large electrical voltage (usually thousands of volts but very little current) that can knock a large man into an unconscious state for ten to fifteen minutes. I believe that the stun gun was pressed against JonBenét's skin and fired while she slept.

Now that she was unconscious, the soon-to-be child killer probably tied her wrists together with the cord and moved her quietly to the basement, two floors below. The garrote around JonBenét's neck was not hurriedly put together, nor was it a simple tourniquet. The knots were complex and reflected the sophistication of someone who knew how to use such a garrote. I am told that masochistic-sadists often use this sort of neck device, as it becomes sexually stimulating for them to dance on the edge of the sword. The stick used to twist the garrote apparently was broken off of one of Patsy's paintbrushes, which at the time were in the basement, in a basket right outside the room where I found JonBenét's body. Shreds from the broken brush handle were found in the basket. The action of the stun gun provided the time to set up this bizarre action.

His original intent, I believe, was to kidnap JonBenét. I'd like to ask the police if they ever considered that something could have gone wrong—something that turned a botched kidnapping attempt into a murder. Could an unexpected turn of events have forced this cruel man to change his plans? Did his own lusts push him into unexpected actions that left him feeling he had no alternative but to kill JonBenét? I wonder if JonBenét became conscious again in the basement and recognized her attacker. Did she become so agitated that the man could no longer carry out the kidnapping and ended up killing her? These questions beg for answers.

The coroner's report concluded that JonBenét died from asphyxia due to strangulation, or what could also be described as ligature strangulation. Why the massive blow to the head, then? The police theory has been, as far as I know, that either Patsy or I woke up in the middle of the night, struck JonBenét in a violent rage, and then staged everything else to look like a kidnapping. I've often told friends that if I were trying to stage this, as the police contend, I could have done a much more convincing job.

The police found DNA material underneath JonBenét's fingernails and on her underwear. This DNA did not match anyone in our family. The foreign DNA under her fingernails would indicate to me that she must have awakened at some point and fought her attacker.

A significant piece of evidence that surfaced during the investigation was a neighbor reporting that she heard what she described as a bloodcurdling scream around two in the morning on December 26. The old part of our Boulder house had operated off steam heat from a boiler in the basement. From this boiler room, which was immediately adjacent to the doorway into the concrete-walled room where I found JonBenét's body, a ten- to twelve-inch open ventilation pipe ran through the wall and out the front of the house, aimed roughly in the direction of the neighbor's home. It was very possible to hear a scream from across the street but not three floors up in our bedroom because of the megaphone effect this pipe had on sounds coming from that corner of the basement.

Either from the pain of the attack or waking up while being assaulted, JonBenét must have screamed out of sheer terror. Our neighbor awakened her husband, who said that a short time later he heard the sound of metal scraping against concrete. Could this have been the grate over the basement window? I had discovered a hard Samsonite suitcase standing up against the wall under that window on the morning of the twenty-sixth. Was this suitcase used as a step to get in or out of the window, which was five feet off the floor? Maybe the killer discovered that he couldn't force JonBenét through the window opening, and she could have seen his face during the attack. Possibly the fear of her later identifying him or his inability to shove JonBenét through the window precipitated her death.

While I can only speculate, I think that several things must have occurred between the scream and this man leaving the basement. I don't know that this scenario is true, but it appears to be logical. The massive blow to the head was, I believe, the killer's final act against my daughter. I did not notice any blood on JonBenét when I found her. I am told by medical experts that the massive wound on JonBenét's head—a linear fracture that ran the entire length of the right side of her skull, measuring approximately eight and one-half inches from front to rear—should have resulted in a very large and significant hemorrhage on her brain, which did not occur. In fact, even though the fracture ran down the side of JonBenét's head, the autopsy revealed only a very small amount of blood inside her head. Apparently that condition could only happen if her little heart had stopped beating before the injury occurred. As the coroner noted, she died of strangulation.

That evidence causes me to believe that JonBenét must have been garroted, assaulted, screamed, and finally strangled to death. The head blow was to make sure she was dead. A medical fact that substantiates this chain of events is that JonBenét's eyes were discovered to have petechiae, small pinpoint hemorrhages that occur in strangulation. She would have to be alive for this condition to have developed. Her scream must have frightened the killer into believing that he was about to be discovered, so he pulled the garrote too tight so she wouldn't scream again, and she died.

Perhaps JonBenét's scream is what changed the sexual assault/kidnapping into a murder. Conceivably, this pedophile's bizarre lusts and masochistic tendencies prompted him to attempt one last brutal act. In the ransom note, the killer betrayed a personal preoccupation with death and referred in a number of places to fiendish acts that would mutilate and destroy JonBenét. He may have slammed JonBenét's head against the floor after he strangled her, to make sure she was dead. Such an action would account for the fracture without the usual massive amount of internal bleeding. Because her heart had already stopped, the hemorrhage wouldn't have followed.

As best I can reconstruct it, using the information I have access to, that is what happened the night our daughter was murdered. One of the logjams inside the Boulder Police Department turned out to be their internal disagreement about what must have happened. Detectives Linda Arndt and Steve Thomas had differing theories on how the killing must have occurred. Linda Arndt broke ranks with her fellow officers and spoke publicly on September 13, 1999, on the ABC network show, *Good Morning America.*

Arndt stated her suspicion that I was the killer by describing the moment after I found JonBenét and rushed upstairs carrying her body. She detailed the few seconds that I hysterically laid our child on the living room floor as a time of "silent communication." According to Arndt, at that moment she looked in my eyes and *felt* that I had killed JonBenét.

I wonder if that was the first time Arndt had looked into a distraught father's eyes and told him his daughter was dead? Arndt also maintained that I was suspiciously "cordial" when she first arrived at the house; apparently she had expected me to be hysterical and out of control. Therefore, in her mind I was already looking suspicious. I have no idea what I appeared like, but I know that I was struggling with everything I had to keep my senses sharp. The truth was that on the inside I was anything but cordial. Yet I had to keep focused on the most important task I had ever been handed in life, and that was to get my daughter back safely from a madman. In a similar misstatement, the police report said that I made an unusually calm walk outside to the mailbox, and went through the mail as if nothing were wrong. Consequently, they further concluded that I wasn't acting right.

When I heard of this written report later, I was stunned. First of all, our mail was delivered through a slot in the front door. *There is no outside mailbox.* The mail fell to the floor when pushed through the slot by the postman. More important though, was that I went through the pile of envelopes in hopes that there might be another communication from the killer. Why didn't the police think to do that?

In contrast to Linda Arndt, rookie detective Steve Thomas remained convinced from the very beginning that Patsy was the killer. He had told a friend his conclusion but said that he didn't think it could be proven in such a way that a jury would convict her. The problem illustrated by both Arndt and Thomas is that their statements clearly violate the basic stance a successful detective must take in order to be able to solve complex crimes. The "I'm sure but I can't prove it" mind-set has no place in a criminal investigation, and it reflects the terrible bias and inexperience of the Boulder police. An experienced detective will tell you that an investigation starts at the center of the crime and begins to methodically work its way out, casting a wider and wider net. Veteran homicide detectives would have forced themselves to remain objective for as long as possible; Arndt and Thomas did not. The inability of these two to objectively follow the evidence rather than what they "saw" in our eyes is an important part of what turned JonBenét's case into such a nightmare. I have never held it against them that they didn't have experience, only that they refused help and advice from those who did.

The investigation was severely hampered from the beginning by this type of police faux pas. Yet I believe that it is still possible to find the killer.

THIRD, LET'S LOOK AT THE EVIDENCE THAT WILL LEAD TO THE MURDERER. A killer always leaves evidence at a crime scene—fibers, hair, DNA. JonBenét's killer left evidence behind as well, evidence that will eventually identify him.

In the famous Lindbergh kidnapping case, the police conclusively solved the murder only because they traced the boards used in the makeshift ladder, which was leaned up against the house, back to pieces of the same boards found in the attic of a carpenter, Bruno Hauptmann. This match resulted in Hauptmann's conviction. Ironically, for two years after the kidnapping and murder of Lindbergh's baby boy, many people considered Charles Lindbergh a prime suspect. Fortunately, in the Lindbergh case, the small-town police in New Jersey immediately knew they needed help and called in the FBI and experienced detectives from New York City.

I believe seven pieces of known physical evidence, when combined with other circumstantial evidence, will help determine the identity of JonBenét's killer and bring this case to its conclusion.

1. DNA evidence. Foreign DNA was found under JonBenét's fingernails. Some prosecutors have described this evidence as a "problem." I look at it as a huge clue, and I'm grateful we have it. If JonBenét fought with her killer, she may have given us his DNA, which will ultimately be his downfall. In addition, the DNA from the stain found on JonBenét's underwear cannot be identified. The police have these test results, and we can only hope that they are checking all possible suspects against this genetic fingerprint. Our belief is that this DNA belongs to the killer.

2. The cord and duct tape. The police thoroughly attempted to find more of these two items in our house, without success. Because we think the killer carefully planned what was to be a kidnapping, it is our belief that he brought the cord and duct tape with him, knowing that he couldn't count on finding similar material in our house. After the crime, the police checked through all the ashes in our fireplace in the living room, even removing the bottom of the fireplace and checking the bin beneath it in an effort to make sure that we or someone else hadn't attempted to dispose of any cord or tape in our fireplace. They found nothing.

3. *The pubic hair found on JonBenét's blanket.* We have been led to believe this hair doesn't match anyone in the family or anyone whom we know who may have ever slept on JonBenét's bed. The Boulder police have this evidence, and only they are in a position to do further testing. Obviously, it is a highly significant piece of evidence. If there is DNA in the pubic hair, does it match that found on JonBenét's clothing and under her fingernails?

4. *The ransom note.* Considered earlier and throughout the book, the note was written by the killer and remains an extremely important clue. An adequate amount of handwriting samples from the killer should conclusively tie him to the long and rambling note. With the volume of samples the police have obtained of both Patsy's and my handwriting, they should have been able to definitely identify either of us as the author. They cannot, because we were not the authors. When the right suspect is sampled, the same volume of testing will be part of what sends this creature to the gallows.

5. *The stun gun.* We believe the stun gun was manufactured by Air Taser. This manufacturer requires the purchaser to register his name, and the police should have obtained a list of all the buyers. How many people do you know who own a stun gun? None? It's not a commonly owned device.

6. *The palmprint.* A palmprint was found on the cellar door where I found JonBenét. We know the print did not match Patsy's or my palmprints and remains unidentified, as far as we know. It is still possible that this print could match someone who had a reasonable explanation for being in the basement and means nothing. At the same time, it could be an important clue.

7. *The footprint by JonBenét's body.* In the basement room where I found JonBenét, a funguslike mildew grew on the floors and walls due to the moist climate of the room. This room had no windows and was concrete on four sides and on the ceiling. Next to JonBenét's body the killer,

I believe, left a clear footprint made by the sole of a Hi-Tec hiking shoe, from the area at the heel where the brand name was stamped. The markings are clear and should further help identify the killer.

When the suspect's background, post-murder behavior, and physical evidence are put together, the identity of this monster will be clear to someone who knows him. My prayer is that as someone reads this description, they will return to the night of December 25, 1996, and be forced to admit that a name or a face comes to mind. Some reader will finally realize that he or she has the final pieces of information that will bring this crime to trial. That is how most crimes are solved.

We dearly hope that the police are still actively investigating JonBenét's death. We pray that they will do so with open and objective minds. Ultimately, they must be the ones to find the killer. Certainly, some avenues can still be investigated. We look for the BPD to recontact neighbors in the University Hill area for new information. They could also be comparing lists of people who were in Boulder at that time, to people who were involved in previous crimes, and people who committed suicide after December 26, 1996, as well as people who owned a stun gun. And there is reason for the BPD to look deeper into known sex offenders in Boulder and to follow up on leads that might have been put on the bottom of the pile because of the volume of work to be done.

To avoid an accusation of grandstanding from the media, not much will be said outside of a close circle about our own efforts to find the killer. We will only say that *our goal is to bring the killer to justice.* We will not stop until we have heard the jury say, "Guilty of murder in the first degree." We do take solace in knowing that if justice is not found in this world, the killer *will* eventually stand before the God of the universe, who is a just God.

Patsy and I know that prayer helps. We ask for your prayers to bring the killer forward and reveal the truth of what happened to our daughter that night.

If you think you have any information that could help, please come forward. Or if you know anyone who can make a device like the garrote or the hand ligature (which had a loop on both ends) pictured on the Jameson Web site*, please speak up. Contact us by e-mail at JonBenetTipLine@aol.com, call your local police, or call the Boulder police.

All information will be taken very seriously and will be treated confidentially. I'm convinced this killer will be found by the efforts of the public.

35

PROTECTING YOUR CHILDREN

The tragedy of our Christmas joy being plunged into the most horrible darkness is still too overwhelming for Patsy and me to think about for more than a few moments. How could a day filled with the gift of giving and the wonder of peace on Earth also include the horror of the murder of a child? Innocence died at that time, not only for our precious JonBenét but for many, many others who were deeply scarred by this act of unspeakable violence—our children, our friends, our families, and even the Boulder police.

And yet what happened to Patsy and me is only an extreme form of the spiritual battle that every person in the world must contend with every day of their lives. Fortunately, most people are not plunged into the depths of blackness that the Ramsey family experienced, but the possibility is always waiting at the door. Cheats, liars, thieves, and murderers wait for all of us, standing in the shadows around an innocuous corner. Only the prudent and watchful avoid the attack.

I have read Rabbi Harold S. Kushner's book *When Bad Things Happen to Good People.* My only addendum would be, "Bad things happen to all people." We've learned that almost everyone carries a burden that is painful, making it difficult to wear a smile. When something like this happens, you don't laugh as freely or as heartily as you used to—and you never will.

Perhaps a sociologist could offer many reasons why our family's tragedy caught the attention of the nation with such intensity and longevity. We believe, as all parents believe about their own children, that JonBenét was beautiful, charming, and a delight to both the heart and the eye. The media focused on the "child beauty queen." That was not JonBenét. We were portrayed as people of extraordinary wealth who had the capacity to manipulate the justice system, and this reputation certainly stirred public anger. Our story as told by the media appeared to be another tale of the dark side of Camelot. After these many pages, you now hopefully know that behind the glitter and the tantalizing headlines, we were and are ordinary people who love our children dearly, cherish our family, and want nothing more than to live gentle, peaceful lives. That's what a typical family is like in this country, I believe. As parents we would give our lives in an instant to protect our children. It's a natural instinct. Why would the cops think we would be so perverted as to kill our own child? I worked in a good job for a fine company, and now our tragedy has also destroyed that career as well.

From all this we've learned that assets and material goods are temporary and not of great significance. In fact, they can be great burdens. We are all renters in this life. That is a refreshing and wonderful realization.

Our lives have often been compared to the Lindberghs'. Years before JonBenét's murder, Priscilla White had given Patsy a book by Anne Morrow Lindbergh entitled *A Gift from the Sea,* which was somewhat prophetic. When their infant son was kidnapped and murdered, Charles and Anne Lindbergh experienced the same emptiness and surreal feelings that we have experienced.

Yet a host of people, many of whom we have never met, have supported us. Their kindness is so deeply felt that we can never fully express our appreciation. Letters of support and caring have come in from all over the world. Many of these people felt our struggle simply because they were our fellow human beings. Even though evil stepped out of the shadows and hit us right between the eyes, friends and people whom we didn't even know stepped in to help at various points along the way.

"I'm very sorry for what the media is doing to you," one lady said as she stopped me in the grocery store and shared her feelings. "What a tragedy."

"Thanks," I said. "I appreciate your speaking to me."

At a filling station in Atlanta, one man approached me as we were both pumping gas into our cars. "Excuse me, are you John Ramsey? . . . Your daughter was JonBenét?"

"Yes," I said hesitantly, not knowing what to expect.

"I'm ashamed of what the media has done to you and your family. I just want to apologize for them."

I thanked him and he drove off.

"What an encouragement," I said to Patsy when I got in the car.

Comforting and supportive comments come to us usually when we need them most. I guess that's God's way, isn't it? Throughout these past three years, compassion and caring have come from virtually every group we've encountered, save two: the Boulder police and the media.

Entire congregations are holding us up in prayer. I'm not sure that Patsy and I would have made it without those prayers. Many people are also praying that the killer will be punished. We know that will happen in God's time, not ours.

What have we learned through this ordeal? Surprisingly, we have come beyond this experience, realizing there is much good in the world. In fact, we have been overwhelmed by it. But sadly, we have realized that evil is alive and well, and we can't be naive about it. A number of conclusions cannot be avoided.

FIRST, WE WOULD ENCOURAGE PARENTS TO TAKE SPECIAL NO-TICE OF CERTAIN REALITIES:

1. Realize there are people out there who prey on children, either for sexual pleasure or to satisfy their hate. They can be in any town, anywhere, at any time. Maintain your children's anonymity as best you can and be sure your home is truly a safe haven when you are there, particularly when you sleep, which is a very vulnerable time. A dog can be one of the greatest security systems you can have. (If you don't have a dog, you might consider a "Beware of Dog" sign.) I used to think a home security system was to protect my home when I was away. I never dreamed someone would come into my home while we were there.

2. Be careful whom you allow in your home. Most repairman, plumbers, and cleaning ladies are good, hardworking people. But don't just assume that. If you don't know someone, be wary at first. Check references carefully.

3. Children need to know to be cautious of strangers and not to give out family information over the telephone or the Internet. It is sad that we need to be this way, but we do. The world has good people and evil people, and that is a fact of life. If your child must have a Web page, monitor it carefully. Keep photos, last names, addresses, phone numbers, and any other identifying information off the Internet.

When someone calls your home, teach your child how to respond without admitting you're not there. One approach, which Patsy and her sisters were taught as children, is to say that parents are always "taking a shower" if there's nothing else to explain why they can't come to the phone. One time someone called and asked Patsy's sister Pam, "Is your mom at home?"

"Yes," Pam dutifully and properly responded, "but she's in the shower."

"Is your dad there?" the person asked.

Pam hesitated and then blurted out, "He's in the shower too!"

When the Paughs returned home and heard about this exchange, they weren't bothered by what the caller might have thought. They were thankful that Pam had followed their direction.

4. Take a hard look at your school security. Does the school have a check system so the officials there know who is picking up your children? Make sure there's a code in the office to identify you when you call to request something for your child. When Patsy calls the secretary at Burke's school, she uses a code word to identify herself.

And make it very clear that *no one* is authorized to take your child from the school except you or whom you specify. In all of our difficulties with the police, we learned that if the cops want to interrogate a child without the parents' permission, they sometimes simply go to the school and remove the child. We were amazed that this kind of police power could be imposed on free citizens in a civilized society, and that schools would allow such a thing.

5. Make sure that photos of your family belong to you and are kept in your possession. The Constitution addresses our privacy rights in relation to our government, but our founding fathers didn't anticipate tabloid newspapers and those who almost criminally operate under the umbrella of freedom of speech. If you pay to have your child's picture taken, insist that they are your pictures and not the photographer's. Don't leave negatives behind at the mall or with photographers, even if you have to pay extra. Remember that whoever takes a picture of you or your family has the right to sell or use those pictures as they wish.

6. Protect your special numbers. Don't put social security or driver's license numbers on your checks. And you are not obligated to give your social security number to anyone who asks for it, even if it is to obtain a credit card or bank account. You have no idea what the wrong people might do with this information. Consumer data is bought and sold every day, and some of it is used for nefarious purposes. In this age of instant communication and networked computers, individual privacy is gone. Your life is an open book that can be read by anyone who knows how to manipulate the system.

Shortly after JonBenét's murder, all sorts of our private information was gathered by James J. and Regina Rapp, who owned a business sometimes called Touch Tone Information Acquisition and other times called Dirty Deeds Done Cheap. These parasites obtained confidential information on people—for a price. They devised a scheme called "pretext calling," in which they would lie about their identity to obtain confidential information. For instance, I know that someone called McGuckin Hardware and said he was me. Then he asked for copies of all the credit card charges that Patsy and I had made in the months preceding the murder. Fortunately the McGuckin's people were suspicious, and did not give the caller the data that he could sell to the media, but this call did lead to a media rumor that I had called the store to check on my wife's purchases.

I don't know if this caller was Rapp, but we do know that the Rapps also managed to get personal records and documents, which they reportedly sold to a Palmdale, California, man by the name of Larry Olmstead of "Press Pass Media," a private detective agency whose main clients are tabloid media organizations.

Rapp reported to Larry Olmstead a number of tasks that he had performed to investigate us, including obtaining our personal banking records, our American Express card transactions, as well as information on our son John Andrew's credit purchases. I learned through trial and error that if I charged an airline ticket on my American Express card, the tabloids were always there to greet my arrival. Rapp also acquired both

Patsy's and my cellular phone records and all the ticket records on our commercial airline flights. In addition, he obtained personal information about our friend Jay Elowsky, our housekeeper Linda Hoffmann-Pugh, and the telephone records of our investigative firm, Armistead and Associates. The Rapps had over twelve hundred active customers paying for private information on individuals.

Thankfully, the Jefferson County district attorney discovered the Rapps' illegal activities and charged them with two counts of violating the Colorado Organized Crime Control Act for obtaining information about us and others by misrepresenting themselves to obtain phone records, credit card bills, and bank records. This business had been highly profitable for the Rapps, according to the grand jury indictment. On a typical day the Rapps received in excess of one hundred calls or faxes requesting confidential information. During this period, the business was grossing between four and five thousand dollars a day. They are not the only people out there who make their living doing this. Beware.

7. *Change your locks at least every year and keep a list of who has your house key—and make sure it is a short list.* If you change cleaning ladies, change the locks. You don't know who has made a copy of someone else's key to your house. We thought we had only given a few of our keys to other people, but as we thought about this, we realized there could have been more than twenty keys outside of our hands, which had been given out over a period of five years. We had given keys to contractors who worked on the remodeling of our house, to cleaning ladies, to neighbors, to plumbers and painters. Furthermore, we couldn't be sure who might have copied those keys or who had access to them. Foolish? Yes. Please don't make the same mistake.

8. *Be careful about putting any identification about your family or your views on the windshield or bumper of your car.* For instance, don't put, "I'm pro-life" or "I'm for Bush." You don't know who might pull up behind you and be offended by what is there—and then strike out against you or your children.

Also be cautious about bumper stickers that say "I have an honor student" at such and such a school. If someone starts watching you, he or she will know where your children are during the day.

I questioned the wisdom of one school in our area that put up a big sign congratulating the family of a student whose father owned a local pro-sports team. As a result of that banner in front of the school, anyone who drove by knew that this prominent man's children could be found there any day, Monday through Friday.

SECOND, BASED ON OUR EXPERIENCE, WE ARE EXTREMELY DISTURBED ABOUT HOW DANGEROUS THE AMERICAN JUSTICE SYSTEM IS TODAY. In our opinion, the system is not flawed; it's broken. Police too often act precipitously to make arrests and in some instances they aren't valid. Prosecutors are too willing to rubber-stamp police tactics, and politicians garner votes with a "tough crime" message. An unacceptable number of people in our jails today have been unjustly arrested, prosecuted, and in some cases executed, by a society that congratulates itself on being "civilized." America has more people in prison today per capita than any other industrialized country in the world. Something is very wrong.

In a recent study investigating Chicago's homicide prosecutions dating back to the 1930s, the findings revealed that over three hundred convictions of capital crimes were in fact in error. The study concluded that a number of innocent people were executed. *One is too many.* The emergence of new DNA testing and the submission of updated test results to courts of law have brought the release of over sixty innocent people from prison in the last couple of years.

One Atlanta lawyer we know worked on a case that freed a Georgia man from prison in 1999, after he spent eighteen years in jail for a rape he did not commit. The man refused parole years earlier because a condition of his parole was that he sign a confession. An incident that hits closer to home occurred in Boulder, where a mistrial was declared because a local policeman lied under oath and intentionally misled the prosecutors, attempting to justify the arrest of a man for stabbing three friends.

Do these injustices happen everywhere? Absolutely. Do we hear about most of them? No! Our personal experience has been highly public, but it is only the tip of the iceberg. Right now America is struggling to balance the serious issues of crime and justice. We don't need more police; we need the police we have to be well trained, well paid, and well led. Money should be spent to achieve quality, not quantity. Giving a badge and a gun to an individual who isn't trained or competent to handle that awesome responsibility leads to injustice and abuse. We've met some absolutely outstanding police officers here in Atlanta and Fulton County. We have frequently called on them for help, so our comments are not meant as a sweeping condemnation of all police but rather a caution. There are about eighteen thousand police jurisdictions in this country, and our smaller communities are particularly vulnerable in this area.

You must realize that the justice system, from police to prosecutors, doesn't necessarily exist to protect your rights. Their purpose is to put criminals in jail as fast as they can, and you may end up having to prove you're not one of the bad guys, just as we did. The cops' goal is to arrest someone. The prosecutors' goal is to prosecute. Don't hesitate to seek the best lawyer you can find, but be aware that when you hire an attorney, the police will assume you are guilty. Police officer Steve Thomas said, "Innocent people don't need lawyers." I'd answer, "Ask Richard Jewell, the man who was falsely accused of the Olympic bombing in Atlanta, about that." The police understand the force that good attorneys represent and know they provide a hedge of protection around their clients. That's why they don't want attorneys involved.

Couple an inexperienced and poorly led police force with a flagrantly abusive and irresponsible entertainment media, and the scaffold is built from which innocent people will be hung. The only thing missing is the beer keg and rope. In too many instances, the news organizations in this land have turned what used to be objective reporting into entertainment for profit. The capability of instantaneous communication to create tantalizing "gossip" for millions all over the world has encouraged a mob-rule mentality not unlike that which existed in the West during the late 1800s, when vigilantes bypassed the justice system and hung people from trees.

Although Patsy and I were assumed to be guilty, fortunately we had the financial resources to protect our basic civil rights when the presumption of innocence wasn't extended to us. Even with our resources, it was still extremely hazardous. We believe some prosecutors thought their job was to "get the indictment," and tabloid media published unverified sensational accusations, first for profit and then in a desperate attempt to protect themselves from prosecution by us for libel and slander, which only an indictment of us would stop.

In mid-November 1999 we held one of these tabloids accountable by filing a lawsuit against the *Star* in a federal court in Atlanta for their blaring headline "JonBenét was killed by brother Burke," long after the police had officially and publicly cleared our son. The tabloids had figured out that "Burke sells," so they embarked on a smear campaign against a twelve-year-old child.

On May 25, 1999, the *Star* had run a story with a front-page photograph of JonBenét and Burke and this headline. The article said that Burke was being looked at as the prime suspect. They told how JonBenét had wet her bed on Christmas night and crawled into bed with our son. Then Burke, they said, let loose his pent-up resentment of his sister and killed her. They cited the "fact?" that Burke's Swiss army knife was found next to JonBenét's body, as evidence.

After that, the *Star* ran two other articles, one entitled the "Sad Twisted Life of JonBenét's Brother" on June 1, and the other "What Burke Saw on the Night of JonBenét's Murder" on June 8. Obviously, these articles also subjected our son to public hatred, contempt, and ridicule.

Almost a month later, on June 22, after our attorney had written to the *Star,* the tabloid ran a small retraction, saying oops, our sources were wrong, and admitting that the district attorney's office had unequivocally stated that Burke was not a suspect in the murder. But they never said that the facts about him were untrue.

We as a society may let these tabloid organizations attack our movie stars without retribution, but our children? I hope not.

But it's not just the tabloids who are guilty. Mark Jurkowitz of the *Boston Globe* feels that the shrinking circulation of the tabloids (the *Star*'s numbers, for instance, fell to 1.9 million from almost 2.3 million in two years before 1998) can partly be attributed to the mainstream media—television and newspapers—reporting the same vulgar stories in much the same way. He quotes media analyst and tabloid specialist Chris Ryan as saying, "I see a lot of the same [tabloid] stories anywhere from *Hard Copy* to *Entertainment Tonight* . . . even places like MSNBC and CNN." Ryan specifically cites "the JonBenét Ramsey case . . . I think they are being out-tabloided by the mainstream media."

In fact, JonBenét's murder dominated the stories on broadcast news in October 1999, according to Lisa de Moraes in her article "Earthquake! CB's 'Black Rock' Withstands the Big One." Moraes cites NewsTV Reports, which tracks every story aired on broadcast TV news programs: "There were 19 segments on the subject on the broadcast prime-time news-magazines." NewsTV defines a newsmagazine to include *Extra* and *Inside Edition* as well as ABC's *20/20*, CBS's *48 Hours*, *60 Minutes* and *60 Minutes II*, and NBC's *Dateline*.

According to NewsTV, at the end of October 1999, our daughter's death "has generated so many stories since . . . January 1997—259 and counting—that she now stood second only to Princess Di, whose death racked up 355 reports." And JonBenét stories "also topped the morning news programs, which collectively logged 55 segments in October, beating the World Series' 44 segments and the Matthew Shepard murder case with 29 segments." Truly the media have exploited the tragic story of our daughter's murder.

THIRD, WE WORRY ABOUT OUR SOCIETY. Maybe it's because Patsy and I are getting older (I'm fifty-six), and older people tend to think the younger generation is in bad shape. What's wrong, I feel, is that my generation is not providing wise leadership for our country, as it should. Wherever Patsy and I look, we find signs of this. As we follow the national political scene, the evidence is inescapable. People seek leaders who look like sports heroes or movie stars. Rather than elevating wisdom, we elect people who make a good appearance on television. When "a good face" becomes the best commodity for an elected official, trouble is not far behind. The government ends up being run by polls and negotiable morals. The next step is a feel-good society, concerned only with the means rather than the ends.

Out of thin air, Governor Bill Owens of Colorado, a first-term governor elected by an extremely narrow margin, suddenly made statements on television implying our guilt in JonBenét's death. At a press conference on October 27, 1999, as he was announcing that he would not appoint a special prosecutor, Governor Owens said, "If I could speak to John and Patsy Ramsey, I'd tell them to quit hiding behind their attorneys, quit hiding behind their PR firm, come back to Colorado and work with us to find the killers in this case, no matter where that trail may lead."

The governor went on to say, "There is a lot of evidence that points in a certain direction."

When Owens was asked if he was implicating us by this statement, he answered, "No comment," a reply that is notorious for confirming the question.

Several times Governor Owens referred to JonBenét's "killers." He then said his use of the plural was deliberate. Few people missed the insinuation that he was implicating the parents.

Were we hiding behind our attorneys? I think we've documented clearly that we did not. Were we deliberately avoiding Colorado? The truth is that *we* had asked to meet with Governor Owens for a number of days prior to that media appearance, and we had offered to meet with his advisory committee.

Why make such a vicious attack? From our perspective, the man's motivations were for his own personal political gain. Barely voted in as governor, he must be looking toward the next election. And we were not the only people to wonder about his motives. Reporter Kevin Flynn said in the *Denver Rocky Mountain News*, "Whether intentional or not, Owens's criticism of John and Patsy Ramsey's behavior in the investigation tapped into public frustration over the conduct of the case and won him some popularity points. It also got him some 'face time' on such programs as NBC's *Today Show*, helping to fashion a national image for a governor often seen as stiff and impersonal."

F. Lee Bailey made the suggestion that the state of Colorado ought to put up a couple of million dollars as a reward if Governor Owens really wanted to help find JonBenét's killer.

All we ever asked of Owens was to put competent investigators on the case. Not more attorneys.

Even though Owens is the only politician we know of who seemed to use our personal tragedy to garner votes, it is another example of what's wrong in America today.

Patsy and I often talk about what we can or should try to do to affect the morass the country has slipped into. We decided we could either leave or stay and try to make a difference. Americans must promote wise leadership if we are going to endure, whether it is the chief of police in Boulder or the president of the United States. No one knows how much time we have to correct these problems, but often time is shorter than we think.

FOURTH, WE DO HAVE A MESSAGE FOR THE KILLER. Patsy and I and our families want you to know that *we will be after you until we find you.* The pursuit will not stop. Every morning when you wake up, you will know that this may be your last day of freedom. Beware. The person who looks at you strangely, or who seems to be following you, could be your captor. Eventually you will be identified. Trust us. It will happen.

In mid-December 1999, Lou Smit came to Atlanta to help his niece move back to Colorado. The last time we had seen Detective Smit in Colorado, he told us that he wanted to visit JonBenét's grave someday, and now this trip was the right time. He called about going to Marietta, and I was glad to take him.

As we drove the freeway north to St. James Episcopal Cemetery, we talked about how things had been going with Patsy and me, and I wanted to hear Lou's thoughts. Of course, he couldn't talk about any of what had occurred with the grand jury, so we didn't have any detailed discussion of the case. But we were able to share our hopes for the future. Lou made the same offer to us that he had made to the police and the district attorney several months earlier. He would work *with us* but not *for us.* While Lou wouldn't talk in specifics, he made it clear that he intended to continue working to find the truth about JonBenét's death.

"John," Lou said, "one of the most important things you can do is to figure out some way to help get the Boulder police to move beyond you and Patsy and look down a different path."

"Definitely," I agreed.

"After all, the police are the people who will have to solve this case for us to get a prosecution.

"Justice does not take sides," Lou said with his customary deliberate, firm tone. "Both the police and I have the same goal. It's just that the police have taken a different path to get to the objective."

I turned off the freeway and drove toward the cemetery. We both became silent, but I kept thinking about Lou's wise observation. He was right. Even though the police had looked hard at Patsy and me, they had to because we were in the house. Now they need to cast a wider net to find the killer.

Days come and go when Patsy and I still wonder what life is about. During the painful moments, we are tempted to conclude that the terrible journey of the last several years has turned our struggle into a hopeless future. Ups and downs are muted. *Is life nothing more than a gigantic steamroller that will eventually flatten all of us out on the ground?* we wonder. At such moments, Patsy and I must get back in touch with the message that has picked us up, dusted us off, and given our lives meaning. We have discovered the truth and the peace that is to be found in Jesus Christ and him alone. He promised he would be with us when we needed him—and he was, and he is.

Why do we share this? As Mother Teresa said, "I have discovered a great treasure, and it is limitless. There is enough for me and you, too, if you want."

EPILOGUE

The best place for us to think about the future and meaning of the days ahead has always been at St. James Cemetery, where JonBenét and Beth are buried. On Sundays only the sound of the freight train whistle in the distance and the clang of bells from nearby churches, like St. James Episcopal Church, a block away, break the silence. The old Episcopal cemetery is just twenty minutes from our home, and we can easily drive north up the I-75 freeway to get there—except, of course, during the infamous Atlanta afternoon rush hours.

Not far from the freeway exit, we go a few blocks and then turn left across the traffic. The drive along the magnolia-lined street always prepares us to enter the old and hallowed cemetery, which has been there since 1849. More than seven generations of families are buried here. The Civil War was recent news when the first person was laid to rest in this spot. Some of the older graves are those of infants. In those days, protecting a child from fatal disease was a parent's biggest challenge.

Just to the east of St. James Cemetery is Marietta High School, and the school kids often walk down the cracked street past the cemetery on their way home, laughing, shouting, and cavorting with each other, seemingly insulated from the sadness that lies across the street. To the north of the cemetery is a small fire station where the firemen sit out front and look over the weathered gray headstones, shaded by old oaks.

Patsy and I and Beth's mother, Cindy, have done some gardening around our part of the cemetery. We planted azaleas, camellias, boxwoods, and English ivy that have now grown enough to provide an eternally green and bright border next to the fence at the south side of our plot. Southerners keep cemeteries in immaculate condition with extra granite borders, statuary, flowers, and decorations; you can always tell someone's been working there recently.

Beautiful angel ornaments, which look like special Christmas decorations, now hang on the old dogwood tree that stretches its arms over the two graves of our daughters. The angels sway in the breeze and remind me of the ornaments that adorned JonBenét's Christmas tree in her bedroom. The first collection of these angels came from our friends in Boulder after the one-year remembrance service. Later, as other visitors came, more ornaments appeared. People from across this country have left behind notes, cards, and poems that touched us deeply. We know that each twinkling angel represents a person, a family, and, in many cases, a child who has been touched by JonBenét. The little figurines sway in the wind and seem to be saying, "we remember" . . . "we care" . . . "we still hope" . . . "we love you." Most important, they seem to be watching over the girls, whose graves are side by side.

On JonBenét's headstone, after much thought, we inscribed these words that fit her so well:

JONBENÉT PATRICIA RAMSEY
AUGUST 6, 1990
DECEMBER 25, 1996
Love, Purity, and Joy
A Gift to her family and the world,
Home in the peace of God

I specifically decided to show her date of death as December 25, which raised new allegations from many media people, and probably fueled the suspicion of the police.

Of course, we don't know exactly when JonBenét died; the killer had said in the ransom note, "I will call tomorrow," and her small body was cool and rigid when I found her. I selected December 25 because I didn't want the world to ever forget what it did to our daughter on the day of joy and peace, Christmas Day. I want people fifty years from now, a hundred years from now, to look at that marker and say, "The world went mad on that Christmas Day, and someone brutally murdered a child during the peace of Christmas night."

Maybe then the visitors will want to try to make a difference in their generation.

A little stone bench under the dogwood affords a peaceful place to listen to the quiet breeze blowing through the tree overhead and the nearby Georgia pine trees. We sit . . . and think . . . and listen . . . and talk to Beth and JonBenét.

Only a parent who has lost a child can truly understand the pain that will forever be in our hearts. Children are supposed to bury their parents, not the other way around. I have buried both my parents. I know the difference. While the intense pain of loss may diminish with time, the child will be missed with the same intensity that he or she was missed on the first day.

Birds occasionally fly in and out of the old dogwood tree and seem to be checking on us as we try to make sense out of the journey that we so thoughtlessly call life. Quiet seclusion quickly settles around us, walling the world out and beckoning us closer to the bridge separating life and death. The remoteness of our little cemetery always pulls us near to that last sacred divide and helps us remember what is permanent and what is temporary.

So, today, where do we go from here?

Our acquaintance with Lou Smit introduced us to a philosophy he developed thirty years ago as a young homicide detective. At that time he reached into the future in an almost prophetic way and described where I'm beginning to think Patsy and I must go next in our journey. At the time Detective Smit wrote this "guiding philosophy," he was describing how he felt at three in the morning, looking down at a lifeless corpse for the first time. Lou wondered, *Who is he? How was he killed? Who did it? Why?* So many questions, so few answers. Lou started making sketches, recording information on physical description, blood, wounds, clothing.

Lou's attention was drawn to the victim's shoes. Something about the soles, the heels, the leather, caused the young detective to consider the thoughts that this person may have had on that last day. Obviously, he had no idea that this would be the last day he would ever put on those shoes. "Shoes, shoes, the dead man's shoes, who will stand in the dead man's shoes?" Lou wrote. "The detective stands in the dead man's shoes to protect 'his' interests against those of anyone else in the world."

JonBenét's death has forced Patsy and me to stand in a similar place and think about our daughter's shoes. Her shoes used to tiptoe and tap-dance and skip and point to the sky when she stood on her head. Now they are silent. Things that were important to us before seem unimportant. We need to make a difference in the world for JonBenét, since she can't do that now without our help. We believe her legacy should center around the protection of children in our society.

America should be known as a country that cares about its children above all else. Yet today in the United States, a child is eight times more likely to be murdered than in any other industrialized country. We want this country's pedophiles and child murderers to know that their horrible deeds will not be ignored or forgotten by a busy world. Our task will be to walk in the victims' shoes until the perpetrators are captured and properly punished.

Our goal is to encourage our society to come down with its full might in the pursuit of murderers of children. Track them down, prosecute them, and send a warning to all: America protects her children. Harm them, and the full might of the most powerful country on earth will find you and hold you accountable.

We hope to start an organization called SHOES as an outreach of the JonBenét Ramsey Children's Foundation, which will advocate legislation, offer resources and rewards, and establish computer databases—all focused as effective tools to both prevent violent crimes against children and to assist in the capture of child murderers.

We will use computerized tools to track pedophiles and sex offenders and also use experienced, retired detectives and top experts as resources to aid, and in some cases challenge, local police departments. We will put funds in place to offer significant rewards for information, when appropriate, to apprehend child killers.

SHOES will advocate legislation to elevate the murder of a child under the age of thirteen to a federal offense. After all, a bank robbery is a federal offense, and by law our nation treats this as a most serious crime. Do we as a country care more about our money than our children?

Patsy and I would have been spared some of our agony if we could have immediately received help from a team skilled in pursuing child killers on the morning of December 26, 1996. Local police deal with everything from cats caught in a tree to bicycle thefts to serial homicides. In many cases the officers cannot develop the long-term knowledge needed to effectively respond to a child murder.

After years of working on hundreds of homicides, Detective Lou Smit's bottom line is simple and clear. We must work for the victim, always placing the case first, systematically following the evidence wherever it leads. The detective's ego or feelings cannot be placed in front of his or her real job: representing the victim. We can learn to put ourselves in the position of walking in someone else's shoes and, by doing so, bring the case a step closer to a successful conclusion.

Detective Smit concluded his philosophy by describing an ultimate, final dimension to what it might mean to help murder victims. He wrote:

> When the case is finished: You may experience a great deal of satisfaction; you may be thanked by the victim's family and loved one; I would also like to think that someday, as we travel through eternity, we will meet that victim, who will say, "Well done, friend, well done."

We trust that someday in that ultimate realm, JonBenét will come running toward us with arms open wide and shout, "Welcome home, Dad and Mom, well done."

While we wait for that day, Patsy and I want to do everything in our power to make sure that no one else has to walk in our shoes.

APPENDIX A

A CHRONICLE OF COOPERATION

- Boulder police officers, including detectives, questioned John and Patsy Ramsey throughout the day December 26.

- Police interviewed and questioned John and Patsy on December 27 and John again on December 28. BPD detectives were with John and Patsy numerous times during the period December 26–29 (when the Ramseys left to go to Atlanta for the funeral).

- Police interrogated Burke on December 26 (tape recorded, without either parent present and without parental consent) and again with a police-approved psychologist on January 8 (videotaped). Burke was again interviewed in May of 1998 for three days.

- Police were with the Ramseys twenty-four hours a day from 6:00 A.M. December 26 through about 2:00 P.M. Sunday, December 29. The police officers were usually within a few feet of John and Patsy, and could hear their conversations. In addition, Victims Assistance workers from the Boulder Police Department and the County Sheriff's office were also there off and on.

- Handwriting samples were given by John (December 26, 28, and January 5); Patsy (December 28, January 4, February 28, April 12, and May 20); and Burke (December 28).

- After the Ramseys returned from JonBenét's funeral, their attorneys offered to make them available for a joint interview on January 18, 1997, at 10:00 A.M. The police declined this offer and stated in writing that such an interview would not "be helpful" because "the time for interviewing John and Patsy as witnesses who could provide critical information that would be helpful in the initial stages of our investigation has passed."

- The police countered with an offer that the Ramseys come to the police station at 6:00 P.M. on a Friday night and subject themselves to an open-ended interrogation. That suggestion was rejected, in part because of the written statement above.

- Patsy and John gave hair and blood samples, as well as fingerprints, immediately when the police requested them; so did all other members of the family. In February 1997 both Patsy and John voluntarily gave pubic hair samples.

- Very early in the investigation, the Ramseys offered to let the police search both of their houses, John's office, their cars, and his airplane hangar without a search warrant.

- On Friday, April 11, 1997, John and Patsy Ramsey, with their attorneys, met with Peter Hofstrom of the DA's office and Tom Wickman of the Boulder Police Department. This meeting was held at Mr. Hofstrom's and Detective Wickman's request. An apology was given for the way the family had been treated. The Ramseys were asked to give additional interviews and continue their previous cooperation. John accepted their apology and agreed to move forward. No conditions were placed on the manner in which the interviews would be conducted.

- On Saturday, April 12, 1997, the Ramseys also agreed to let authorities search their house again without a warrant; agreed to destructive testing of walls located at their home; agreed to identify Patsy Ramsey's prior writings; and agreed to make themselves available for separate interviews on Wednesday, April 23, 1997, beginning at 9:30 A.M. The Ramseys agreed to answer any questions put to them. On April 22, the Boulder police canceled the scheduled interviews.

- The Ramseys agreed to be interrogated by the Boulder police and district attorney's office on April 30, 1997. Those interviews lasted two hours (for John) and six hours (for Patsy).

- The Ramseys were also interrogated by the district attorney's office for three full days each in June 1998. No additional interviews were requested.

- During the course of the investigation, the Ramseys signed over one hundred releases for information requested by the police, ranging from medical records to credit card records and even videotape rental records. The Ramseys provided all evidence and information requested by the police.

- Burke Ramsey, John Andrew Ramsey, and Melinda Ramsey Long all were subpoenaed and testified before the grand jury.

- John and Patsy offered to testify before the grand jury, but they were never subpoenaed. The Ramseys asked to meet with the governor and his advisory council. The request went unanswered.

APPENDIX B

PARADE ENTRY FORM

In his book *JonBenét: Inside the Murder Investigation*, Steve Thomas concludes that Patsy wrote the ransom letter. He cites Donald Foster's claim that Patsy changed the way she wrote the letter *a* after JonBenét's murder. According to Foster, before the murder, Patsy consistently used a manuscript, not a cursive, *a*. As you can see from the following sample, dated December 6, 1996, many of Patsy's *a*'s are cursive.

Entry Form

1996 Lights of December Parade
Friday, December 6, 1996
Downtown Boulder

Theme: City Lights
Staging: 5:30 p.m.   Parade: 7:00 p.m.
Entry Deadline: November 25, 1996

Mail entry to: Lights of December Parade, c/o DBI, 1491 Walnut #303, Boulder, CO 80302, 449-3774.

Keep this portion for your records.

Name of Organization America's Tiny Royale Miss, JonBenét Ram

Contact Person Patsy Ramsey — assist with Pam Archuletta, Exec. Dir.

Address 755 15th St. Boulder or Boulder County United Way.

Phone (day) 442-1378 (fax) (evening)

Please check one:

☐ Commercial entry—Please enclose $100 entry fee with application.

☒ Non-profit organization

Please check your category (check more than one, if applicable):

☐ Color Guard   ☐ Marching Unit/Drill Team   ☐ Marching Band
☐ Motorized Unit   ☐ Horse Drawn   ☐ Antique Vehicle
☐ Costume Entry   ☐ Bicycle/Human Powered-vehicle   ☒ Other Convertible Car

PLEASE, NO LIVE SANTAS!

Please describe your entry. Include dates and make of vehicles, number of people, complete name of business and any other information that would be helpful to the announcers and event staff:

Six year old JonBenét Ramsey was crowned America's Tiny Royal Miss last July. She is a kindergarten student at High Peaks Elementary School in Boulder.

Pam Archuletta is exec. director of the Boulder County United Way.

Please note that the parade start is one half hour earlier this year at 7:00 p.m. Questions, call Downtown Boulder Inc. at 449-3774.

PERMISSIONS

We'd like to thank the following organizations for permission to reprint materials from their newspapers or broadcast material:

INTERNET EXCERPTS
Jameson's Web site: *Remember the Child,* <http://www.jameson245.com>
Used with the permission of Susan I. Bennett.

TELEVISION EXCERPTS
CNN, Used with the permission of CNN.
    "Interview with Parents of Slain Beauty Queen," *Early Prime,* January 1, 1997.
    "Death of Two Princesses," *Larry King Live,* September 2, 1997.

ABC, Used with the permission of ABC News.
    Vincent Bugliosi, interview with Elizabeth Vargas on *20/20,* September 27, 1998.
    Linda Arndt, interview on *Good Morning America,* September 13, 1999.
    Dr. Francesco Beuf, interview with Diane Sawyer on *Prime Time Live,* September 10, 1997.

NBC, Used with the permission of NBC News.
    John Douglas, interview with Chris Hansen on *Dateline,* January 28, 1997.

NEWSPAPER EXCERPTS

Boulder Daily Camera: Used with the permission of the *Boulder Daily Camera.*

    Christopher Anderson, "Fleet White Claims Bias in Ramsey Case," 25 August 1998.

    Everette Davis, "Unchecked News Is Worse Than No News at All," 8 February 1998.

    Kristin Hussey, "Tabloid in a Frenzy Over Case: *Globe* editor a TV star in wake of photo task," 19 January 1997.

    Alli Krupski, "Ramseys Send DA Scathing Letter," 24 April 1997.

    Alli Krupski, "Officials List Conditions for Ramsey Interviews," 25 April 1997.

    Alli Krupski, "Ramsey Case Detective Seeks Florida Chief Post," 4 June 1997.

    Alli Krupski, "DA Nixed Search of Office, Hangar, Sources Say: Request Made Just After JonBenét Killing," 4 September 1997.

    Matt Sebastian, "New Grand Jury Is Seated," 23 April 1998.

    Nadia White, "Chase Friends Frustrated by Investigation," 15 January 1998.

Denver Post: Used with the permission of the *Denver Post.*

    Series with Janet McReynolds, 25–27 March 1997.

    Peter G. Chronis, "Writing Analysis a Delicate Art," 12 February 1997.

    Chuck Green, "Ramsey Case at a Standstill," 18 January 1998.

Denver Rocky Mountain News: Used with the permission of the *Denver Rocky Mountain News.*

    Charlie Brennan, "Ramsey Case a Tragedy of Errors," 8 June 1997.

    "Governor Wins Favor with Harsh Words," 27 October 1999.

Traverse City Record Eagle: Used with the permission of the *Traverse City Record Eagle.*

    "Charlevoix Under Seige," 9 November 1997.

OTHER

"I Am the Bread of Life" by Suzanne Toolan [b. 1927]; adaptation of John 6.

Marlene Early letter: Used with the permission of Marlene Early.

Margaret Harrington letter: Used with the permission of Margaret Harrington.

"Helping a Homicide Survivor Heal," Alan D. Wolfelt, Ph.D., Director, Center for Loss & Life Transition, 3735 Bow Rd., Ft. Collins, CO 80526, Phone: (970) 226-6050.

"The Shooting Star" by Susan Merriman. Used with the permission of Susan Merriman.

Quinn Haisley story: Used with permission of Charles Haisley.

Lou Smit resignation letter: Used with the permission of Andrew L. Smit.

Witthoeft letter: Used with the permission of A.J. Witthoeft.